EBORACVM

The Village

Graham Clews

*We at Trafford believe that it is the responsibility of us all, as both individuals
and corporations, to make choices that are environmentally and socially sound.
You, in turn, are supporting this responsible conduct each time you purchase a
Trafford book, or make use of our publishing services. To find out how you are
helping, please visit www.trafford.com/responsiblepublishing.html*

*Our mission is to efficiently provide the world's finest, most comprehensive
book publishing service, enabling every author to experience success.
To find out how to publish your book, your way, and have it available
worldwide, visit us online at www.trafford.com/10510*

 www.trafford.com

North America & international
toll-free: 1 888 232 4444 (USA & Canada)
phone: 250 383 6864 ♦ fax: 250 383 6804 ♦ email: info@trafford.com

The United Kingdom & Europe
phone: +44 (0)1865 722 113 ♦ local rate: 0845 230 9601
facsimile: +44 (0)1865 722 868 ♦ email: info.uk@trafford.com

10 9 8 7 6 5 4

To Marie, who gamely plodded over hill and dale (literally),
helping explore nearly every Roman ruin in Northern England.

Eboracvm, The Village

Contents

    I   The Roman Legions,
                Late First Century A.D.

    II   Glossary

    III   Place names

    IV   Commentary and trivia

Notes

Certain words or place names have been typed in italics;
please refer to
Appendix II or III, respectively, for modern definitions

See the Appendix IV, page 452, for the use of the
Roman numeral: VIIII

Prologue

The Rabalia River, Lower Germania, A.D. 70

A charnel stink hung like damp fog over a hundred sputtering funeral pyres, scudding across the carnage-clogged battlefield, in a haze of drifting smoke. Dark figures flitted through the gloom, stripping the dead of what was worthwhile and setting what remained on carts for burning. The sharp odour of blood lingered despite the rain, and the stench of bloated guts and burnt flesh tugged hard at the nostrils.

The three cloaked riders rode in line, their skittish horses held on a tight rein. The stocky brown animals, black manes heavy with moisture, picked their way through the littered field in the dim light of yet another waterlogged autumn dawn. Iron rang on stone as the lead horse found the road, its muscled legs breaking free of the clinging mud, in a slow trot. When it settled to an even gait, its rider beckoned over one shoulder without bothering to turn.

The dark figure behind whipped his horse forward, and all three pressed on through the slashing rain in a silent triangle, the third rider trailing discreetly behind. When the piles of dead had thinned to no more than a haphazard scattering of bodies at the edge of the battlefield, the leader sighed and threw back the cowl that covered his face. His eyes remained half closed, squinting at the drizzle-shrouded ruin of a bridge a half mile farther down the road.

"It's been a long time, young Trebo," he muttered, again not bothering to turn.

"Yes, sir," Gaius Sabinius Trebonius replied, glancing carefully sideways.

The face he saw, pale beneath the rivulets of rain, was middle aged and hard. The mouth was drawn tight above a square soldier's jaw thrust stubbornly forward against the weather. The man's expression might have suggested anger or, just as easily, stoic impatience. Gaius's own features felt taut, and probably looked just as hard. How else would they appear, under an endless torrent of bone-chilling rain, and months of treacherous campaigning?

Gaius returned his gaze to the mud-splattered road. Almost a decade had passed since he had last spoken to the general, and Cerialis looked no better or worse than might be expected. He had put on weight. The cheeks carried more flesh, and were beginning to jowl. Oddly enough, it was the long, thin, patrician nose that showed the most startling change. It had been broken, more than once by the look of it, for it was shorter and flatter. It gave him the look of a gladiator. As did his neck, muscled like a bull's. Gaius wondered if the hair remained thick under the plumed parade helmet. It had been black and curly a decade ago at Lindum, much like his own was now. Perversely, he hoped the ornate helmet covered nothing more than a balding dome.

"So what do you see, young Trebo?" the general murmured, again blinking into the rain. "Yourself in ten years? It has been ten, hasn't it?"

"About that, sir. When the Iceni woman—" Gaius broke off in embarrassment and chose another tack. "The province of Britannia. Lindum."

"Aaah! The Iceni woman! Trebonius, you have the tact of a warthog." The general snorted, and finally turned his head. "You find it difficult to speak her name?" When Gaius said nothing, Cerialis's mouth broke into a cold, humourless grin. "I don't, and have far more reason to forget. Boudicca! The fey bitch whipped my arse halfway across the province. Yours too, I might add. We're both lucky to be alive. Not many who were there can say that, hey?"

Gaius nodded but still said nothing, for there was nothing to be said. The failure was a thing of the past; a battle lost, and nothing more—no point scratching at old wounds. He shook his head. It had not been a battle; it had been a rout. A disaster. A calamity that happened a lifetime ago. Though in truth, the memory often seemed as fresh as yesterday.

He'd been a tribune in the Ninth Hispana Legion, a youth barely in his twenties. Two thousand men had been lost, yet not all were dead when the general abandoned the field, fleeing with the regiment's small contingent of cavalry. Gaius flushed, despite the cold. There had been no choice, of course; the miserably small force had been overwhelmed. Strung out in column of march, there had been no warning. Yet there should have been. And whose fault was that?

General Quintus Petilius Cerialis!

Gaius sighed. Shit ran downhill, as the saying went among the rank and file. Yet when it first fell, it landed on top; but none ever seemed to stick to the general. Cerialis had remained virtually untouched. The man had luck. More important, he had connections.

"By the way, congratulations."

The general's praise caught Gaius by surprise. "Sir?"

"Two silver spears, and a gold standard. Not bad, at your age. Not bad at all."

"The wrong place at the right time," Gaius murmured, at first flattered and making light of decorations earned over a decade of campaigning. Then, as his mind turned the words over, he realized the general had made inquiries. Such an interest could spell good fortune or, more likely, nothing but plain trouble.

"No such thing as the wrong place, Trebonius," Cerialis snapped, his eyes again on the bridge. "Destiny is forged by ourselves and the gods. Don't make light of it."

Gaius didn't argue, instead simply muttering agreement. A good dose of influence didn't hurt either, he thought cynically, and the general had been amply favoured. Then he smiled to himself. Perhaps the old man was right. Influence in itself was good fortune, and where else did good fortune come from, but the gods? Cerialis had been blessed with more luck than a grey-haired gladiator. In battle, the man's bumbling had more than once almost snatched defeat from the jaws of victory. Yet each time he had been rescued by the luck of the gods, likely the same gods who had given him Emperor Vespasian's daughter as wife. Gaius frowned as something clicked in his memory. Perhaps fortune did not always smile. The woman had died last year.

As if reading the direction of Gaius's thoughts, Cerialis chuckled. "Of course, I might point out that who you know counts a peck more than a poor man's prayer. A senator here, a consul there, and of course the occasional emperor doesn't hurt, either." He turned in his saddle and grinned at Gaius, a glint in his black eyes. "There can be advantage in knowing the right people, young Trebo."

Gaius couldn't stop the look of dismay that crossed his features. The vague comment was rife with inference, most of it likely reeking trouble. He glanced cautiously at Cerialis, and the general roared with laughter.

"Don't worry, young Trebo, I'm not asking you to hoist your *pteruges*. What I have in mind is of mutual advantage." The general pulled on the reins, slowing his horse to a walk, and removed his helmet. Gaius was disappointed to see a thick mop of curly, iron-grey hair. Hiding the helmet under his cloak, Cerialis nodded toward the bridge. "We're almost there."

Gaius stared hard down the rain-misted road. A pair of centurions had spotted the riders, and were forming the sodden soldiers into ranks on either side. At least two hundred crowded the end of a bridge that only two days ago had spanned the swollen Nabalia. It was now a ruin. Gaius's own men of the Second Adiutrix had ripped the jagged gap in its centre. It had been done in order to arrange a truce with Julius Civilis, former governor of Lower Germania, and now another failed, would-be emperor of Rome. Civilis's army, largely local Batavi, had been beaten brutally back, retreating to the far side of the river. The man was willing to discuss terms, but only across the safety of a gaping hole in the bridge deck.

Gaius smiled, for the sight of the bridge answered questions that had plagued his mind since the dark hours of the morning. Why had the general asked for him by name? How had the old man even known he was with Second Adiutrix? The answer was simple. Someone would have mentioned the name of the officer who destroyed the bridge. He could imagine Cerialis snapping his stubby fingers, trying to place where he'd heard it. There would have been a smile of satisfaction when the memory came.

That still left the reason for the general's interest. Gaius thought he might have the answer to that, too. Soldiers loved the familiar; and the name of Gaius Trebonius would have been familiar. It was the way of the army: both men had served in the same unit; both had fought side by side when the Iceni woman slaughtered their commands; both had survived almost certain death. Such events forged a bond, one that held as tight as if they'd been whelped from the same litter. It also acted as a talisman, a sort of good luck charm, and Cerialis had certainly been lucky the last time they served together. Gaius nodded his satisfaction as he watched the centurions jostle the soldiers into a semblance of order.

Cerialis settled back in the saddle, his body swaying gently with the plodding gait of his horse. "This will be over today, Trebo. Are you wondering what happens next?"

"The thought had crossed my mind, sir."

"I imagine," the general said dryly. "You're probably looking at another three year stint on the frontier. You came up here with the Second, did you not?"

Gaius nodded. The legion had been formed the prior year at the port of Ravenna, drawing its ranks primarily from the fleet. The desperate need for soldiers had been created by the ambition of too many men like Civilis, each grasping for the purple. Gaius had been passing through the port returning from leave, and found himself suddenly tasked to the new legion. The general's next words, however, told him the question held more than a passing interest.

"Before that you were attached to the Fifth Macedonica."

"Yes, sir. In Judaea."

"Where you earned the gold crown." Cerialis grunted his satisfaction as Gaius nodded again. "Well, there's no telling how long the Second will remain in Lower Germania, Trebo, but I can assure you that wherever it goes, it's not going to be as hot as Judaea."

"I don't know, sir." Gaius smiled. "It can get very hot up here. Even in midwinter."

"Different types of heat, huh?" the general said, and chuckled. "Personally, I prefer the warmth of Rome. I look forward to a pleasant winter in the sun, fighting off the married tarts rushing to bed a hero. I'm willing to lose a battle or two on that front, I suppose. After that, the old bastard is going to send me safely out of the way. Back to Britannia to slaughter barbarians."

"The western tribes, or the Brigantes?" Gaius asked; there was no need to ask who the "old bastard" was. "Another campaign?"

"Yes, yes, and probably." Cerialis did not seem to relish the idea. "Vespasian wants me to be the next governor. Three years, I suppose. Might take your regiment with me. The Second."

"Oh?" Gaius kept his voice neutral, but the phrase "your regiment" almost stopped his heart.

The legate of the Second was ill. The man had suffered terrible belly pains since coming north, the flesh melting from his body like ice in the desert sun. Now the campaign was closing, the poor man was returning to Rome, though few thought much of his chances of getting there. The command would be open, something Gaius had never dared hope for. Not the way things stood in Rome; not with his family's dismal choice of politics.

His mind flew over the possibility. He was the right age for such a command, certainly, but there was his background. Poor circumstance had forced him to spend the past decade with the legions. A "correct" path for someone of his birth would have sent him in other directions: minor political aspirations, an administrative post in the provinces perhaps, certainly a better marriage than the one he had made, and then back to a stint commanding a legion. Instead necessity had driven him back to the army, following his initial service as a young tribune.

Cerialis ignored the implied question as a sharp command rang out from one of the centurions. The men lining the road clattered raggedly to attention, the long cold of a wet night drowning any enthusiasm. The three men rode silently between the dark ranks, the general offering the merest nod in reply to the salutes.

The dull clop of hooves echoed loud on the wooden deck as the animals plodded onto the bridge, where they stopped short of the gap torn in the centre. Gaius looked down at the swirling current with satisfaction. A good man riding an exceptionally good horse might clear the span at a fast gallop. The same man on foot might just as well try leaping the river itself. The milky-brown soup of the swollen Nabalia oozed below the jagged breach in a torrent that would swallow, without trace, the man who failed. The distance between the two torn ends had been measured with that intention.

Civilis had as yet assembled no troops on the other side of the bridge. A few curious Batavi cavalry lingered on the far bank of the river, sitting their horses in silent watch. A decanus was on the bridge keeping one eye out for any movement; the other was on a dozen men setting the final touches to a tent module erected precariously close to the gap. Two soldiers broke away and took the reins of the horses. The decanus followed, tossing a salute as the three riders dismounted.

"Announce who's here to the world, son," Cerialis muttered, and nodded toward the Batavi riders. A pair of them wheeled their horses and galloped away.

"Sorry, sir," the decanus flushed a deep red, defying the icy rain on his cheeks.

"Think, lad, always think," Cerialis muttered, and turned to the third rider. "Take a quick look, primus."

"Sir!" Titus Aurelius Urbicus, primus pilus of the Second Adiutrix, nodded curtly and moved off with the decanus.

The half-module of leather tenting had been erected on the bridge deck, with the open side three paces back from the gap. Several chairs sat in line under its dripping canopy, the centre seat a large, carved oak throne covered in dark red leather. Before it sat a low table, laden with food and large pitchers of wine.

"Appearance, Trebo, appearance." Cerialis chuckled as he walked to the very edge of the ragged gap and stared down at the bloated river. "Awe your enemy. Maintain the advantage."

"Yes, sir," Gaius mumbled dutifully, his mind still whirling with the possibilities of Cerialis's earlier words.

The general's focus swung back again. "Brigantia. Not a bad place, were it not for the people, the food, and the weather."

Gaius decided that was a joke, and laughed. Then he coughed to keep the excitement out of his voice. "My regiment? Where would the Second be posted, sir? Should you take it with you."

"The Second?" Cerialis shrugged, as if the legion was of little importance. "If I do take them, it will be to Lindum. To replace our old regiment. The Ninth. It will be going north."

Gaius tried to remember what lay beyond the fortress at Lindum, and drew a blank. "I thought Lindum *was* the north."

"It is now, I suppose, but not for long." Cerialis snorted as if disgusted. "The Brigantes are pissing on the pact we made. This is the third time, and Vespasian's had enough."

"The Brigantes." Gaius racked his brain, trying to remember anything of the past that might impress the general. "Aren't they led by a woman?"

"They were. Cartimandua," Cerialis's eyes grew vacant as he stared down at the current, smiling as if lost in memory. Then he shook his head as if to clear it, but the smile remained. "Quite the woman. A good head, a pretty face, and the body of Venus. You know, Trebo, those barbarian women have a damned healthy attitude toward their men. And Catey was no exception." The smile broadened, then he saw fit to add, "Or so I heard. The woman doesn't particularly like Rome, Gaius, but she's practical. *She* keeps the peace. Venutius is the hothead who breaks it. He is, or was, her husband. Trouble is, most of the chieftains are moving into his camp now, not hers. Typical of the stupid bastards."

"So what happened to the woman, sir?" Gaius asked, intrigued by the general's undertone, the Second momentarily forgotten.

"You find barbarian women interesting, do you, Trebo?" Cerialis leered, then laughed. "She took up with her husband's right-hand man. Doesn't surprise me. Catey was a fine, lusty woman. Well rid of the old one."

"Er, how old is she, sir?" Gaius ventured.

"Don't clutter your mind with prurient thoughts." Cerialis sounded thoroughly amused. "The woman's old. Maybe even older than I am. She's probably turned into a wrinkled crone, these last ten years. Native women seem to do that."

"The shield bearer apparently doesn't think so," Gaius suggested, but his mind had returned to the vacant command. "So the Second Adiutrix might be stationed at Lindum."

"And the Ninth will move north, tasked with ensuring that Venutius keeps the peace. Or beating him into it, if he does not. The regiment's first tasking is to site a fortress in Brigantia."

Cerialis paused and turned to stare at the open-ended tent module. The primus was under its shelter, instructing the decanus. Several soldiers fussed over the table, and two others were spacing the chairs. Cerialis cupped his chin in one hand as he eyed the arrangement. It struck Gaius that the general was seeing it from the same angle as Civilis, several hours from now.

"Primus!" Cerialis barked.

"Sir?"

"I think a dozen of our tallest men, in a single rank behind the chairs. And three or four more on either side." Cerialis nodded as if pleased with the idea. "See if you can find a few planks for those behind to stand on. Make them look taller."

"Sir."

"And fill the area between the tent and the bridge rails with troops. Full battle order, in three ranks."

"What about a troop of mounted cavalry straddling the ramp onto the bridge?"

"Good idea. Make it two, and see they're cleaned up and fresh."

Gaius tried to envisage the effect. The general was striving for pomp, strength, and most important, a show of confidence. It was too bad the weather was so damned cold and miserable. "The only thing missing is a blazing fire," he joked when the general turned away, apparently satisfied.

"Shit! You trying to burn the rest of the bridge down?" Cerialis growled, seemingly taking the remark at face value.

"Er, no sir." Gaius flushed. When nothing more was said, he added, "So we're establishing a fortress, sir?"

"Yes; have you ever built one before?"

The question was unexpected, and all Gaius could muster was a vague, "Sir?"

"A fortress, dammit," Cerialis said testily. "You know what a fortress is, don't you? Ramparts, gates, palisades, that kind of shit. Soldiers live inside. Thousands of them. You're supposed to be an engineer, aren't you? Have you ever built one?"

"N-not a full-sized fortress," Gaius stammered, hopes plummeting as he grasped where the questions were leading. "I've overseen the construction of forts, watch towers, armed camps, and more roads than I've probably marched, but never a full-sized fortress. Never been attached to a legion that's been tasked with it."

"Well, you are now," Cerialis grunted, suddenly impatient—or, Gaius wondered, shocked at the idea, was he suddenly edgy? "At the beginning of the new year, you'll be back with the Ninth."

"Sounds interesting, sir," Gaius said, his tone noncommittal as his mind skidded lower down the slope of possibilities.

Cerialis said nothing more for a moment, biting on his lip as if hesitant. Then he grunted, and turned to face Gaius, looking directly into his eyes. "Brigantia has turned into a swamp of intrigue, Trebo. *Agrippina* herself might have been sucked under by it." The general began ticking facts off on his fingers. "Venutius is conspiring with the northern tribes—the Carvetii, maybe even the Selgovae. He's building an army on bribes and promises, and he's getting money from somewhere. Some of it may even be from Vellocatus, his old shield bearer. He's a chief in his own right, perhaps even a minor king, and not poor. It's possible he's playing both sides. Regardless, the traders say Venutius seems to have more coin than is good for a barbarian."

"You trust the traders, sir?"

"As far as the tip of my sword," Cerialis growled, and spat sideways into the river. "They have their uses, but I'm not a fool; there's not one that won't barter his daughter for a price. But what they say fits well with what we hear from the barbarian queen."

"Carta …?"

"Cartimandua. Catey. She favours Rome, but only because it makes sense. Satisfying her taste in luxuries doesn't hurt, either. Petronius, the Ninth's legate, takes care of that, and listens to her whining. But I've no doubt she has him in the palm of her hand." The thought made Cerialis shake his head. "Knowing Catey, I'd make a shrewd guess as to what part is in that hand, too."

"The woman's that wanton?" Gaius asked, incredulous.

The general grinned. "No, not really. The comment is probably half regret."

"Petronius, sir—how long has he been in command?"

"A year now, and he'll likely go the other two." Cerialis's eyes narrowed, as if gauging Gaius. "Nice fellow. He's been sitting on his backside, though, and needs a little prodding. I hope to be there in the spring, but there's trouble in the west too, and that is going to—"

"You want me to prod a legate, sir?" Gaius blurted, appalled at the idea.

"Not at all," Cerialis said smoothly, and turned to face the tent module where the primus stood, hands on hips, eyeing the results. "I need someone who is keen. Sharp. Someone who will set an example for Petronius. Someone I know, to keep an eye on him. A man who can help lead from one step behind. A man I can trust." The general glanced sideways, one eyebrow raised, as if expecting a response.

"I have enjoyed the complete trust of every commander I served," Gaius said stiffly.

"Which is the way it should be, Trebo, the way it should be. But for myself, I trust a man far more when he also wants something from me." Cerialis's eyes swung back to the leather tent, and his chin thrust upward as he gazed blankly at the neat array of seats. "Which is doubly true when I want something from him, too."

Gaius felt a bead of moisture trickle down his back that was not rain. When he spoke, his voice was unsteady. "Sir?"

"Don't go looking for vipers in the bedsheets, tribune; there are none." Cerialis paused and turned to face the river, his voice falling to almost a whisper. "Dammit, Trebo, I don't want to finish another campaign accused of shitting in my own nest. Petronius is a career man, not a real soldier, and his primus pilus is inexperienced. Weak. I need reassurance. I need a real soldier on the ground in Brigantia. A soldier's soldier. Not just one who can build a lousy fortress. I want someone there who's got talent, as well as luck. You've got plenty of both."

The words stunned him. He hadn't thought he'd been particularly blessed with either, and certainly not over-endowed with luck. He glanced warily toward the tent module, but it was out of earshot. He coughed nervously as Cerialis continued.

"I can replace the primus." The general nodded toward the tent module. "You'll take Titus with you. But Petronius must stay." Cerialis sniffed and ran a hand across the end of his nose. "Funnily enough, I like the man. Decent sort. Perhaps his only problem is lack of good people."

Gaius, on the downward drift of disappointment, simply shrugged. "I'll do my best, sir."

"Good, good. That's all a man can ask!" Cerialis slapped him heartily on the shoulder, his voice suddenly light. "It's a good posting, one that certainly won't do your career any harm. I'll keep an eye on you."

Which could mean anything, Gaius thought bitterly as the general turned his attention to the tent module. To make sure he'd understood, though, he asked, "And that's all, then?"

Cerialis hesitated, as if pondering the question. "No, nothing else, really. Just keep an eye open. Let me know what's happening." He shook his head, paused, then snapped his fingers as if remembering. "Oh yes, there is one thing you might look out for."

"Sir?" Gaius asked, sure the main thrust of the conversation was coming.

"You're probably aware that my wife died."

"Yes; my condolences, sir."

"Yes, thank you, Trebo." Cerialis waved one hand, dismissing the sympathy. "We had a good marriage, you know—or as good as a soldier can ever have—but it left me childless. Without a son. Of course, I adjusted and said nothing, but now she's gone, there is no need."

"And now you want to father a child?" Gaius asked, astonished at the direction of the talk.

"No, dammit." The general whirled impatiently to face him. "There is reason to believe I already have one. In Brigantia. It's not that important, but if you hear anything while you're there, let me know."

"Of course." Gaius felt his cheeks flush, and fumbled for something to say. How long had it been since the Iceni woman? A decade? "How old is he, sir? Nine? Ten?"

Cerialis snorted with laughter. "Double that. This did not happen when I was legate of the Ninth, Trebo. It was when I was a raw tribune serving the Twentieth. If the boy exists, I'd like to see how it sits with his birthright. If he even has one. The mother's supposedly Cartimandua."

"C-Catey?" Gaius found himself again caught off guard.

"She was young, then, and lusty." Cerialis could not repress a smile. "And as to the lad's birthright, there's likely a kingdom there when his mother dies. Rome values that. And along with it, a ransom in barbarian trinkets. There's a gold torque that's rumoured to weigh more than Caesar's sword, and it's ten times as precious."

"So I would ...?" Gaius asked nervously, letting the words hang.

"If the lad exists and seems likely to follow his mother's path, he'll be a good friend to Rome. If not, then what is his is also mine by law, and the *procurator* be damned." Cerialis licked his lips. "I'll sort it out later with Vespasian."

"So he's with his mother, then?"

"Could be. Could be with Venutius, too, I suppose."

"So it happened when she was married to ..." Gaius stopped, his mind boggling; when nothing more seemed forthcoming, he gulped and not too subtly said, "So that's what you want *me* to do!"

Cerialis uttered an audible sigh, as if relieved the business was finally in the open. He hurried on as if anxious to put an end to the talk. "At the moment, the Ninth has nobody of senatorial rank other than the legate. The lack leaves you effectively the second officer in command, not drawn from the ranks. I'll see that it stays that way. Petronius is lazy and lax, which will give you all the freedom you need to enjoy the posting."

"I have enjoyed every posting I've been assigned to, sir." Gaius was again stiff, finding nothing but disadvantage in being Cerialis's eyes in northern Britannia.

"This posting, Trebo—" Cerialis coughed, as if embarrassed to raise the subject "—this posting will set your career back on the course it should have held, were it not for the odour attached to the name 'Sabinius.' A sad turn of events, a fall from rank due entirely to your late father. And your brother. You are how old now, Trebo? Thirty? Thirty-one?"

"Thirty-two, sir."

"When I was your age, I was finishing my tour of duty as legate. With your talent," Cerialis tapped the front of Gaius's cloak, which hid the decorations on his breastplate, "such rank is still possible."

Gaius flushed. "Perhaps, sir."

"I would say it is. Do we clearly understand each other?"

"Clearly, sir."

Cerialis nodded, his face devoid of expression, and with no further word beckoned the primus pilus. Titus had been fidgeting with the chairs, tactfully awaiting the summons. He marched up to the general, hobnailed boots slamming against the wooden deck as he snapped to attention.

"Everything to your satisfaction, sir?"

"More or less, primus," Cerialis muttered, his eyes scanning the neat, court-like array of chairs and the heavily laden tables. "One final detail, perhaps. Throw a layer of mud and stone on top of the wood. I want a large fire burning when Civilis arrives. The bastard will be soaking wet and surly. When he sees me toasting my feet like Nero at an orgy, it'll set his piss to boiling."

Gaius rolled his eyes, his lips twisting wryly on hearing the order. "Typical!" he muttered silently.

Chapter 3

Dawn came fast, and with it a foul headache and a bursting bladder that forced Cethen Lamh-fada from his warm bed earlier than was decent. For a while he tried to stay the inevitable, tossing about the rope mattress in bloated torment. Elena finally put an end to his misery.

"Get up and piss, oaf, or neither of us will have peace," she muttered in a thick voice, then sniffed loudly and wailed, "Did someone let the hogs loose? It stinks in here."

She rolled over and buried her head beneath the covers, leaving Cethen to curse and crawl from his bed. He swung his bare feet onto the icy floor with a painful groan, and sat gazing numbly about the lodge. Vague memories flooded his mind, like cold water seeping across a dirt floor. The room was packed with people. More than a score lay sprawled about the hut where they had either bedded down or fallen in a drunken stupor. The reek of vomit filled his nose, piercing the ripe odour of dank clothing, unwashed bodies, wet boots, cold ashes, and beery farts.

"Shit!" Cethen cursed and shook his head, which was a mistake. He groaned again, then peered bleary eyed in search of the night bucket. It was nowhere to be found. Perhaps it was just as well, for the place already stank worse than a pig sty. He fumbled for the cloak that had served as a blanket, and staggered to his feet. The need for relief was urgent, and a quick search for his boots proved fruitless. They should have been beside the bed, which was where he always left them, but another glance revealed only one, soaked and limp under the weight of an upturned beer jug.

A second curse fell from his lips and his eyes wandered over several pairs of boots scattered near the dead ashes. None of them were his, but one pair seemed a likely size; he slipped them on. They were ice cold with the night's dampness, but at least they weren't soaked in stale beer. That thought was enough for a final curse, then Cethen lurched to his feet and tottered outside.

The early morning brilliance made his eyeballs hurt, but it also prompted a broad smile. The sky, dark and heavy for months, was cloudless. The air was sharp, but the sun warmed his face and the change of weather was welcome. The small stone lodge and the surrounding clutter of huts had felt like an island in a sea of snow and slushy mud. If the bright skies lasted, the village might finally rid itself of winter and welcome the warm green of spring.

Feeling better for the thought, Cethen shuffled to an open pit dug close by the stake fence that circled the tiny village. He balanced on the edge, opened his cloak, and sighed at the pleasure of relief.

"A deaf man with his nose plugged couldn't sleep in there," a voice complained.

Cethen turned to find Elena standing with her arms folded across her chest, and a grim, determined look on her face. He groaned, not because of the dull throb that pounded in his head, but because of The Look. Fifteen years married to the woman had taught him to be wary of it. Elena said nothing more, but stood with her cloak belted tight around her waist and her head cocked to one side. After a moment she calmly began combing with her fingers at the tangle in her hair.

The ache in his head throbbed harder. "Not here." Cethen nodded meaningfully toward the lodge and, without waiting for a reply, started down to the river. If there was enough on his wife's mind, he reasoned, she would follow. If she didn't, then so much the better—but he knew she would. The distance to the dock was about two hundred paces, and she caught up before he was halfway there. Cethen limped along the mucky path, determined not to speak the first word.

Such minor matters of pride were of no concern to Elena. "So what are you going to do?"

"About what?" Cethen was deliberately obtuse.

"You know damned well about what," Elena growled, and gestured back to the lodge. "That idiot in there!"

"He's not an idiot, he's my king!" Cethen said stiffly. "I do as he tells me."

"You all do. That's what sticks in my gut. Look what it did for you last time." Elena gestured angrily toward his leg. "You were lucky. Your da wasn't."

Cethen flinched, his father's death still an open sore. He spun on one heel, letting anger fill his features as he shook a finger and struggled for the right words.

Elena spoke before they were found, her tone softer. "I don't want the same thing happening to you as happened to your da, Cethen. And neither do the children."

Cethen glared, one part of his mind reluctant to accept the truth of her words, the other annoyed at the challenge. Lost for words, he finally turned and stalked off down the slope. The sun still sparkled off the melting snow and glittered across the rippled surface of the river, but it no longer lifted his spirits. He had awakened in a foul, aching mood, and now nothing was going to pry it from him. Certainly not his wife.

They said no more until they reached the dock, a crude, planked structure lashed to the top of thick log pilings, and set against the shallow curve in the riverbank. Cethen grunted as he stepped onto the rough deck and limped over to the edge.

"You have a queen as well as a king," Elena persisted as she followed. The pair stood side by side, she almost as tall as her husband, both staring down at their reflection in the muddy water.

"Queen? Queen of what?" Cethen snorted in contempt. "When Venutius left her, that was the end of it. The woman has no more right to rule than a mule."

"She was the one who left him."

"He left her. She took up with that weasel Vellocatus."

"Just as I said. She left him."

"He left her first because the treacherous bitch handed Caradoc

over to the Romans. Everyone knows that," Cethen said contemptuously, and turned to face his wife. "She's in the pay of Rome, Elena. For
that alone she deserves no loyalty."

"She simply made peace with the Romans. Cartimandua is practical. If you are forced to deal with a pack of wolves, you make the best
bargain you can," Elena said, then added self-righteously, "And she
took up with Vellocatus long before that. So there, it was she who left
him."

"Ha!"

"If you decide to follow Venutius, Cethen, I'm not going," Elena
said, her eyes narrowed, as if testing him. "And the children aren't going, either. Damn him! Why couldn't the old bugger just keep going
north and leave us alone?"

"The children will go," Cethen growled. "Dammit, even Vellocatus
is following Venutius now."

"A moment ago Vellocatus was a weasel," Elena crowed. "Now
you want to do what he's doing. Just because he arrived yesterday with
Venutius doesn't mean he's a changed man."

"Well, he's here, and that's good enough for me," Cethen snapped.
"He's following his king. So there to you, as well! That's another man
who's left her."

"Following someone blindly makes a man a sheep, not a weasel."

"Following his king means he's come to his senses." Cethen
whirled on his wife, his hands outstretched in impatience. "And why
not? He was once Venutius's friend. For the love of Dagda, he was the
man's shield bearer. The Romans are going to war again. He remembered where his true loyalty lies. I'm a warrior too. I understand that."

"It's not the Romans who are going to war again. It's that idiot up
there, stinking up my home," Elena sniffed, and started back to the village. "If you want to believe Vellocatus has had a change of heart, that's
fine by me. Just don't ask me to trust it and follow."

Cethen called out to Elena's back as she stepped up onto the bank,
"Why wouldn't I believe he's had a change of heart?"

Elena ignored the question and continued up the muddy path.
Cethen watched for a moment, then cursed and slumped down on the
edge of the dock, feet dangling above the dark water. His mind was as

muddled as the ache inside his head. Why was life always so difficult? Why was there always more than one path to choose? And worse yet, why was someone always pushing him to make a choice?

Perhaps Elena was right in some small way, he reflected as he watched the *Abus'* dark water flow below his feet; but dammit, the woman did not understand the way of the world. Loyalty! Above all, a man had to have loyalty, and loyalty was a sword honed on both sides of the blade. He had given his to Venutius. If he breached his side of the pact, how could he expect any in return? The throbbing inside his head grew. Cethen grudgingly agreed with his wife on one point: why hadn't the old bugger just kept going north, and left them alone?

Venutius had arrived late the previous day, with a dozen warriors and a bard. No druid this time, just a bard. There was always a bard, for someone had to spread honey on the king's words. While Venutius spoke of Roman treachery and angrily called for warriors who would fight, the bard sang softly of battles won and glories past.

Ah, but the man had been glorious, hadn't he?

Cethen smiled at the memory, despite his aching head and his nagging doubts. The bard had been exceptional: a man named Eoghan, from the mountains far to the southwest. He had a fine, beautiful voice that plucked at the ache in a man's heart. The words had turned the night mellow and Cethen's *kin*, the Eburi, had been stirred. Few as they were, to a man each was eager to follow his king. Just as the old bugger intended!

And Vellocatus had been there too, which was a surprise. Venutius had displayed his old shield bearer as if the man were a war trophy. His wife's lover, yet! Cethen shook his head at the very idea. Even so, the king's visit had been a triumph. The Eburi village was one of the last on the old man's long trek before returning north. Venutius had swept the southern limits of his simmering kingdom, calling on the *tuaths* to send warriors. Warriors who were loyal to the old ways. Warriors who lusted for battle. Warriors who would fight, the old man cried. And he spoke of a thousand recruits camped half a day to the west, eagerly awaiting his return so they could start north. Or so he claimed.

"And where is Cethen in this?" Venutius had asked.

The question had at first set a chill in the lodge, but as the evening warmed to the soft glow of the fire, the bard sang the old songs and told the old tales: of warriors and gods; and of heroes, and undying love. The messages were warm and stirring, each cloaked in a smoky haze of beer, wine, and mead; and all of it consumed in great quantity, Elena had whispered more than once, with every drop supplied by Cethen Lamh-fada!

Cethen grunted his annoyance. The words Venutius spoke might have been smooth, but they did ring true. Besides, what other choice was there? Could Elena not see that? The throbbing in Cethen's temples threatened to explode.

"So, you going north, then?"

The question came from nowhere and made Cethen's heart leap. Horrified, he looked skyward for the source, then down at the murky waters. The voice repeated the question, this time clearly echoing from below. Cethen peered between his feet, relieved to see old Skolan pushing his coracle from under the dock.

"You could murder a man with his own thoughts, hiding down there like a river rat," Cethen muttered.

"Wasn't hiding. Was pulling the nets."

"And listening to the talk of your betters."

"I was here first," the old man said stubbornly, pulling at the tangled mesh in the bottom of his small craft.

"Catch anything?" Cethen's curiosity got the better of his mood.

"A couple of dace, a few perch, and an eel." Skolan pointed to a bucket, but his own curiosity was still hanging. "I suppose no answer means you're going. By yourself."

"Oh, she'll change her mind."

"Wouldn't be so sure."

Cethen bridled at the comment, especially from one of the kin with no status, no *honour price*. "She'll do as I tell her, and there's an end to it."

Skolan merely grinned through his tangled beard. "Then I'm sure it's settled."

Cethen climbed to his feet, annoyed that even the most menial of the kin were conspiring against him. The pounding returned full force and he stood on the edge of the dock, swaying slightly, and glared down at Skolan crouched in his coracle. The ache had grown; it seemed to be throbbing outside his head, as well as within. Puzzled, he cocked an ear and listened. A dull, thudding noise filled the air, a perfect match for the blood throbbing through his skull.

"Do you hear anything?" Cethen asked warily, afraid his mind was being taken.

"Aye." Skolan calmly moved the small boat over to a ladder lashed to one of the pilings. "It's a drumbeat."

"A what?"

"A drumbeat. Somebody pounding on a drum. Likely on a boat."

"I know what a drumbeat is," Cethen said irritably and stared downriver, but there was nothing to be seen. "It must be a trader. We haven't seen a trader in months."

Skolan gasped under the weight of the fish splashing inside the bucket, and heaved himself onto the dock. There was a tight, smug smile on his face that failed to cover his nervousness as he squinted along the broad reach of water downstream. "The beer still has your head, Cethen," the old man muttered. "Traders don't beat time like that. That there's got to be a Roman boat."

"Roman soldiers?" Cethen tried to focus downriver to the first bend, which was the better part of a mile away, but still saw nothing. "They must know Venutius is here."

"Aye, mebbe." The old man paused, savouring the taste of bad news. "Of course, one drum could be keeping time for ten of 'em."

"What do you mean?" Cethen felt as if his wits had vanished.

Skolan explained. "You can't expect ten ships to pound their drums all at the same time, can you? It would addle those boats what's close by." The old man pondered his words. "Though I suppose it might not, 'cause the drum is on the boat itself, and so only thems what's on it would mebbe hear and ..."

Skolan was talking to himself. Cethen had bolted from the dock, haring up the snow-covered slope with barely the trace of a limp. The brightly coloured cloak streamed from his shoulders, and his feet sprayed slush and muck in every direction. He cleared the stake fence like a deer and burst into the lodge gasping for breath.

"Up, up, you lazy turds," he roared. "Romans are coming."

Elena gaped as her husband discarded his cloak, stumbled over a half-dozen groaning bodies, and rummaged through a mound of loose clothing piled alongside the bed.

"My sword," Cethen roared as he pushed the jumbled heap aside and whirled on his wife. "Dammit, woman. Where's my sword? I left it right here!"

"Don't snap at me. It's probably where you put it."

"Shit." Cethen returned to rummaging through the pile. "The damned kids. Why can't they leave—ah-hah!"

He plucked the sword from the bottom of the heap, smiling grimly as he hefted its weight in his right hand. The weapon was a broad, flat piece of iron with a plain hilt. Cethen eased it in the scabbard to make sure it slid free, then slammed it firmly back in place. The headache had miraculously vanished, but he shook his head to be certain. His grim smile broadened.

"Cethen!"

He turned to find Venutius lying beside the ashes of the fire, propped on one elbow. The soft wolf hide cover had slipped to his waist, baring a surprisingly skinny, milk-white torso crisscrossed with a livid pucker of scars. He gazed balefully at Cethen, his eyes red and rheumy, brows raised in question. "How many?"

"Didn't wait to see. They're warships, though. The beat is too fast and loud for a trader."

"So they're not trying to surprise us, are they." Venutius yawned and sat up, his eyes falling over Cethen's nakedness. "You figure on scaring them off, then?"

Cethen glanced down at his mud-splattered body and the filthy boots. He shook his head in disgust, laid the sword on the bed, and began picking through the pile of clothing.

"I'd keep hold of that blade, if I were you," a voice crowed from across the lodge. "It's by far the prouder weapon."

The quip came from Vellocatus, and it drew a chuckle. The shield bearer's voice came from inside a tunic that was halfway over his head. The garment was splotched dark with dampness, and probably reeked of beer. Cethen shivered, as did Vellocatus as it slid past his shoulders. Others about the lodge were hastily dressing, shouting angrily as they searched for clothing carelessly shed the night before, when the ice cold building had been warm, and the mood even warmer. Only Venutius appeared calm.

The door crashed open on its leather hinges. Cethen's two oldest children burst in, each yelling as they added their discovery to the confusion.

"Da, Da, there's a ship coming."

"Just the one, girl?" Venutius stretched his legs under warm pelts.

Coira, the taller of the twins, seemed pleased to be singled out. "Yes, sir. It's got a big mast. And a lot of oars."

"There's only one row of oars," her brother Rhun said scornfully, as if downplaying the news because it was now his sister's.

Venutius lumbered to his feet and fumbled for his tunic. "If it's just the one, and a wee one at that, then there's not much to worry over, is there? Not if we're careful. Dermat!" he called to a small, hard-faced man with a black beard streaked with grey, and a body as thick and solid as an oak trunk. "There's little time left for us to leave. Keep the horses herded close in by the trees, as if they belong here."

Dermat nodded, but hesitated. "Why don't we just ride?"

Venutius sighed. Cethen didn't know if it was because that was exactly what the old man wanted to do, or if it was to show Dermat he was being thick. Whatever the reason, Cethen knew that if Venutius's men were seen to be leaving in a hurry, it would likely mean trouble for him and the kin. He waited anxiously for the answer.

"If we run, Dermat, everyone in the village is up to his arse in shit, because the Romans will want to know what's going on," Venutius explained, jerking a thumb toward the river and the thump of the ship's drum throbbing across the field. "Just make sure our people stay hidden. We're only a dozen; we could almost blend in."

Dermat nodded and turned to go, but Venutius stayed him for one more order. "Make sure the horses remain ready, though." He turned and shrugged helplessly at Cethen. "After all, if the bastards do look like they're searching for me, we'll have to run anyway."

Cethen nodded agreement, but was careful not to look in Elena's direction.

Venutius slid into his tunic, muttering that a king was too damned important to be killed by a chance encounter with a boatload of Roman turds. He cinched his belt and peered about the hard-packed floor, then glared accusingly at the others stumbling about the room. "Has anyone seen my boots?"

The deck was an anthill of activity as the small ship shot past the final bend in the river and bore down on the village. The dull throb of the drum climbed, and three dozen sweating sailors heaved against the oars, straining to keep up with the beat. A harried centurion bawled orders in the boat's waist, and four decani, each in turn, screamed at their eight-man squads to form up on the narrow deck. In silent contrast, a small detachment of archers, gathered by the offside railing, strung their bows as casually as if at practice.

Gaius Sabinius Trebonius stood close by the stern with three other officers, all staring upstream as the craft leapt forward, slicing through the murky current of the Abus. Early morning sunlight glittered on the river's swirling surface, and a fresh breeze blew crossways from the south. The crisp, clean air was invigorating, and Gaius smiled. The day had dawned golden, the gods were happy, and all sat well with Rome.

"I like to impress the barbarians," Tertius Aquila, captain of the galley, muttered the words softly, one eye on the riverbank as the boat sped toward the dock. The other remained warily on the soldiers milling about the deck of his ship.

"Not much to impress." Publius Quintus Flavinus, a slight, pimply faced young man barely out of his teens, curled his lip at the rude clutter of huts in the distance.

There were no more than a half-dozen, set well back on a rise beyond a rough planked dock built into the north bank of the river. Gaius pursed his lips and said nothing. The largest hovel, a low stone structure with a conical roof of weather-blackened reeds, would be the chief's. The rest were nothing more than a slum of poorly built shacks and pens, hemmed in by a low stake fence more suitable for keeping animals in than enemies out. The place looked deserted. No smoke rose from the buildings despite the morning chill, though on the south bank, a grey plume of smoke drifted lazily from a log building, one of several that stood at the end of a narrow pasture spotted with melting snow.

"It doesn't matter who they are, Publius, grabbing their respect is what counts," Gaius finally growled. "Rule one with the barbarian: gain his respect!"

"I dare say, but there's a lot to be said for fear." Publius was the youngest and newest tribune in the Ninth Hispana, and he spoke the words confidently. His features twisted in a broad smirk as two riders crashed from the cover of the forest, thrashing their horses across the slush-covered field toward the village. "I imagine fear is what's goading those two."

"Fear is a good starter," Tertius said absently, then roared for the pace to be raised a further beat, a seemingly pointless order because the oarsmen looked to be already at their limit. The steersman edged the boat closer to the riverbank, gliding past the mouth of a smaller river that had appeared on the right, almost hidden by a low, swampy island and a jungle of willows.

"They're a little late with their warning, but—whoa-hah!" Gaius chuckled as the lead horse lost its footing. Its rider tumbled forward in a spray of mud and snow, and slid to a halt at the feet of a tall barbarian who had emerged from behind the crude stockade.

"I'd say we're about ready, Gaius." Titus Urbicus, the new primus pilus of the Ninth Hispana, eyed the small contingent of soldiers formed on the deck: four eight-man squads, each soldier stiffly at attention, and all facing the shore side of the ship. A centurion stalked through the lines checking gear and weapons, muttering under his breath as he tugged and pulled at the bindings. Winter dress was the standing order, each man wearing leggings, lined boots, and a thick woolen shirt under a leather tunic that protected his skin from the iron bands of his *lorica*.

Gaius turned his gaze to the belly of the ship, then back to the village. "Good enough, Titus." He pointed toward the dock. "Form them up in two ranks on the riverbank, but stay close to the landing until we see what's there. Have Tertius arm the crew once they're done, and hold them ready."

31

Titus stared over the bow and coughed. "Er, the captain is going straight in, then?"

Gaius bit his lip, suddenly realizing the concern. Tertius seemed intent on rowing up to the dock, rather than upstream where he could turn and drift gently down to the wooden landing. "The captain knows what he's doing," Gaius murmured, but nonetheless glanced sideways at the ship's master. Tertius had moved over to the rail, his eyes shifting quickly between the river and the dock, as if gauging the vessel's course and speed against the current.

"Quite a pace," Gaius observed, forcing the doubt from his voice.

Tertius grinned. "As I said, I like to impress the barbarians. Does them good to see a bit of Roman skill and efficiency. Look at them up there. Gaping!"

The tall barbarian had been joined by a score or more villagers. They clustered about the gate of the stockade, watching intently as the ship closed on the dock. Gaius edged over to the rail and stood behind Tertius, skeptically watching the wooden landing draw rapidly near.

"Steady, steady," the captain called to the man on the sweep. "Closer to the shore—just a touch …that's it. Steaaaady! That's good. *Ship oars!*"

The order rang loud along the deck, and should anyone within a half-mile not have heard, other voices repeated it twice more. The oars were dragged noisily inboard, and the drumbeat abruptly ceased. An eerie silence fell over the vessel, broken only by the creak of rigging and the whispering ripple of water.

"In a shade, just a touch," Tertius drawled as the small ship lined up with the edge of the dock. "Straighten out—that's good, hold it there. Hold it!"

The ship slid smoothly toward the lip of the wooden pier. For a moment Gaius thought the current would hold them short. That meant the oars would have to be ignominiously run out and a second attempt made, all of which would take place in front of a crowd of jeering barbarians. Then, just as suddenly, he realized the vessel was travelling too fast.

Tertius seemed to realize it too, and cursed as two sailors leapt onto the dock, each dropping the loop of a mooring line over the top of a log piling. Two other crewmen remained on deck, gripping the other end of the lines, which were wrapped around mooring cleats.

"Give them slack, dammit, give them slack!" Tertius screamed.

The aft sailor was not quick enough. The poor man tried to snake the rope free, but it was bound on the cleat. The ship groaned and shuddered with the sudden tension, and the stern swung hard against the side of the dock. The downstream piling groaned under the enormous pressure and heaved slowly up from the riverbed, raising with it a long stretch of plank decking.

Gaius watched in disbelief as the bog-stinking pile rose under his nose, so close he could reach out and touch its slimy surface. "Shit," he muttered to the pilus. "There goes the fucking dock."

For a moment it appeared as if the entire landing would be torn away, but the river finally caught the boat in its grip and eased the creaking vessel back. The bow, trapped in the relentless current, drifted slowly outward.

"Tighten that rope, dammit, tighten that rope!" Tertius screamed at the hapless sailor who had just managed to free the forward line mere moments before.

Two other crewmen rushed forward and, with burning hands, checked the drift. The small ship finally held at a forty-five degree angle to the dock. The ooze-coated piling gurgled slowly back into the mud and the plank decking, for the most part, settled once more into place.

"Have you impressed them enough, Tertius?" Gaius snarled.

The captain, his face a mottled pomegranate, stalked angrily toward the bow. The primus pilus, his face equally livid, glared down into the belly of the ship. The smart ranks of soldiers were a shambles of arms, legs, and weapons scattered along the length of the deck.

"That's the first time I've seen that bitch smile since she came on board," Publius muttered, nodding toward the bow.

A tall, heavyset woman rose smoothly to her feet, amusement scribed on her plain features. She wore a bright wool tunic and a pair of bleached doeskin britches. A short Roman sword hung from her waist, and an oval shield rested casually over one shoulder. In spite of her size, the woman moved with the grace of cat. She walked silently across the deck and stood by the rail, where she waited calmly for the gangplank to be run out. She glanced disdainfully at the fallen soldiers, and yawned.

"Niamh." Gaius beckoned. "Come here."

"Never was anyone more inaptly named," the primus muttered under his breath as the woman shrugged herself away from the ship's rail.

"How so?" Publius asked.

"It means beauty. The Parisi have a sense of humour."

Niamh's bovine features showed no expression as she ambled to a halt in front of Gaius. The Parisi interpreter stood half a head taller, and the tribune was not a short man. She emphasized her height by standing fully erect, though her voice was nothing more than a lazy grunt: "Huh?"

"You will remain on my left when we approach these people," Gaius instructed. "I want my sword hand free. Understood?"

Niamh nodded.

"The primus pilus understands a good deal of the language," Gaius lied, in a weak attempt to ensure the translation was accurate. "I want you to listen for what is *not* obvious."

Again the Parisi woman nodded, and Gaius returned his attention to the village. It seemed the entire population had gathered at the edge of the wood-staked compound, where they stood staring down at the small ship. Two figures, a man and a woman, stood out from the rest.

"Who is that?" Gaius demanded.

Niamh seemed to decide he meant the man. "Cethen something or other. Minor chief. Belongs to the tuath of Maeldav Mael. Maeldav lives at *Isurium*."

"Isn't that where we're supposed to meet up with the Tungri auxiliaries?" Gaius asked, as much to Titus as the Parisi woman.

"If they're there yet," Titus said. "Is it another pile of sticks and mud like this?"

Niamh shook her head. "It's a much larger village. More like a small town. A decent day's walk upriver."

"And this particular mud pile—does it have a name?"

"Not that I know of. *Ebur*, perhaps? The people are the Eburi."

"Ebor?" Publius's interest suddenly picked up. "There are wild boar here?" He turned to Gaius with an eager grin. "Perhaps we'll find sport."

Niamh's face didn't change, though a glint flashed across her dark eyes. "These people are not Roman. Ebur means yew trees. The place of the yew trees."

The ship's hull shuddered as the sailors finally snugged the bow against the dock, and the rumble of wood on wood announced the running out of the gangplank. The centurion started his men off the vessel and up onto the riverbank, forming them in ranks facing the village.

"They're coming to us." The primus nodded toward the low stockade.

A dozen or more Eburi, all adults, tramped down the slush-covered track toward the dock, the man and woman in the lead. The three officers quickly donned helmets, threw scarlet cloaks over one shoulder, and clattered off the ship. Niamh followed dumbly behind, assuming her station to Gaius's left as he took up position in front of the infantry. The villagers continued silently down the slope.

"I wonder if the bastard got his limp fighting us," Publius murmured, noting that the tall man favoured one leg.

"I'd like to think so," Gaius replied in the same low tone, easing his cloak to one side to clear the hilt of his sword.

"Look at them," the primus scoffed. "There are at least a dozen, and not a single one in step with another."

"Amazing people, aren't they?" Publius giggled. "I wonder how they do it?"

"Natural talent." The primus sniggered.

Gaius growled them both into silence.

❦

There was only one Roman boat, and Cethen grudgingly admitted that it was almost a thing of beauty as it thrust its way upstream. His hand tightened on the hilt of his sword, and he shifted the oval shield forward on his shoulder. Elena moved quietly alongside, her own shield slung on her left arm and a spear clutched tightly in her right hand. Behind both, the kin gathered to watch the Roman ship as it sliced prettily through the current like a fresh sharpened plough.

The drumbeat grew louder and faster, but another, heavier sound drowned the dull throb. Cethen turned to see two riders lashing their horses across the snow-covered pasture that lay on the downstream side of the village. Both animals were soaked from fording the Fosse, the smaller river that bordered the village to the northeast. The lead rider was pushing his mount far too fast, and only at the last moment did he pull savagely back on the reins. The animal's head jerked sideways, and it slithered back on its haunches, forelegs splayed in the slop. The poor beast's eyes rolled in terror as it tried to regain its footing, in vain—rider and horse pitched sideways in a spray of filthy slush, sliding to a halt not three paces from where Cethen stood.

"In a hurry, Cian?" Cethen murmured, a wary eye on the horse as it struggled to its feet. Someone ran forward to grab the reins, while others cursed and wiped at the slop spattered on their clothes and skin.

"Romans!" Cethen's brother rose to his knees dripping ooze, and gestured vaguely back the way he'd come. "Soldiers are coming."

Cethen misunderstood. He spun around in alarm and looked to the woods, thinking that perhaps a second force was skulking through the trees. "Where?" he cried. "Where, dammit!"

The second rider, a large, solid man, pulled his horse in and calmly answered, "On the boat." He nodded a greeting to Elena. "There's a ship. A Roman warship, from the looks of it."

"I can see that, Balor!"

Cethen adopted the same casual manner as Venutius moments before, and sighed as if his patience was being tested. In truth, he felt relief at the explanation. Even so, he gestured scornfully to the Roman ship. As his son Rhun had pointed out, there was only one bank of oars.

"And there's just the one ship," Elena murmured, the trace of a smile on her lips.

Cian clambered to his feet, his eyes turning wildly to the river as he tried to wipe the mud from his clothes.

"You and Balor are a sorry pair," Cethen said, and carefully moved back with a look of distaste. "If the Romans were going to attack, they wouldn't pound out a warning, would they?"

Balor looked sheepish, but Cian was not to be put off. "They're pulling in. Look, the deck's packed with soldiers."

"How many do you count?" Venutius elbowed his way through

the small crowd of villagers, careful to remain out of sight.

"Er, let me see." Cethen frowned and mentally parcelled the Romans into groups of five, a task that quickly grew confusing. "Maybe sixty. And the rowers, another forty or sixty. Though there's some on the deck with bows that aren't really soldiers. I don't know, what do you think? A hundred? Hundred and fifty?"

"Close enough," Venutius muttered, as if numbers did not sit well on the sharp side of his blade, either.

"There's about thirty lined up in ranks." Elena didn't keep the scorn out of her voice. "Plus eight archers. A dozen soldiers gathering gear, plus the officers. With the crew, I'd guess less than a hundred. Oh, and there's a woman at the front. At least I think it's a woman. I wonder what she's doing there?"

Cethen sniffed. "That's what I said. About a hundred."

Cian was still not satisfied. "If they're lined up like that, they're getting ready to fight. There's too many to stop them. We should run."

"No, they're not getting ready to fight. Your brother's right," Venutius said softly. "Look, the archers haven't notched their arrows. In fact, they've shouldered their bows."

The vessel edged closer to the shore, skimming smartly toward the dock. The cadence increased as the captain pushed for more speed to counter the current. A sharp command echoed faintly from the river, and the oars lifted inboard with a low, grating rumble, each dripping bright sparkles of water. The boat drifted quickly up to the dock, and those gathered shared a sharp intake of breath. It was moving far too fast.

Two men leapt onto the landing, each tossing a rope around the huge pilings that supported the wooden platform. The stern line jerked tight and a loud, creaking groan rolled up the slope as the ship's forward drift was violently checked. The craft lurched sideways, the stern thudding hard against the dock. The downstream pile heaved upward from the riverbed with a slick, sucking sound that was audible even at the village.

"Shit," Cethen muttered to Elena in disbelief. "There goes the fucking dock."

The villagers watched in silence as the wooden landing rose and threatened to shatter. For a moment its destruction hung in the balance, then the ship's stern settled alongside the dock, and the groaning structure sank slowly back into place. The vessel's prow slid ponderously into the current, where it was stopped short by the bow line tied to the upstream pile. There it remained, while a stream of curses drifted faintly up the slope.

Cian could not resist. With a grin that showed pearl white through the mud smeared on his face, he tossed his head back and yelled, "Hiyaaaa! Where'd you find the fishing boat?"

"Don't push it, boy," Venutius growled, and slapped him across the back of the head.

"Did you see what they did?" Cian crowed, ignoring the blow and pointing to the ship.

"Aye, and the last thing I want is to piss on their pride." Venutius glanced at his muddy hand in disgust, and wiped it on the back of Cian's tunic. "Cethen!"

"What?"

"I don't want them prying around here, either."

Cethen glanced over his shoulder in surprise. "Neither do I."

"Then slide your arse down there and see what they want. Although I think I know."

Both Cethen and Elena turned in surprise. "You do?"

"See that gear those men are unloading? Those things with the wooden legs, and them big rolls of cord?"

"Yes."

"That's what they use when they mark off where they want to build."

The tall barbarian ambled down the slope and halted in front of Gaius, the man's wife slipping silently alongside. Their faces were sullen and defiant. The rest of the villagers bunched up behind and stood fidgeting, as if uneasy at the closeness of foreign troops.

Gaius narrowed his eyes in amusement as he watched the Brigante chieftain struggle to hold his features as expressionless as his own. It was a hopeless cause. The Briton's pale blue eyes were as transparent as water. Nonetheless, he thought as his gaze flitted over the man's tall figure, the barbarian was an impressive brute. They were about the same age, the other man perhaps a few years older; it was hard to tell. He was well proportioned and lithely muscled, though thickening about the belly. He wore the huge, ridiculous moustaches most of them affected, but for some odd reason, on this one they seemed to add to his stature. His long arms and long legs offered a reach that would be deadly if properly trained, yet his languid stance was not that of a fighter. The lazy, blond-lashed eyes suggested more than a hint of idleness.

The woman was another matter, though. Gaius allowed his eyes to meet hers, and deliberately smirked at the venom he saw there. Set that look in the eyes of her mate, he thought, and you would have a warrior. No, a gladiator. On the other hand, leave it where it was, and you had a damned fine woman begging to be tamed, with long hair the colour of honey, and deep hazel eyes that glittered green with contempt.

Gaius reluctantly forced his gaze back to the Briton. The man's eyes had shifted briefly to the solid ranks of Roman infantry, and he swallowed—hard. The brute was obviously bright enough to know what harm those men were capable of doing. Like Publius, he wondered how the fellow had earned his limp.

Feigning amusement, Gaius finally broke the silence that was quickly becoming a test of who would speak first. He spoke to Niamh, without moving his gaze. "Ask his name, tell him who I am, and inform him that it is our intention to remain here for most of the day. We will not harm him or his people, unless there is trouble." Gaius paused, then added, "Ask the name of the woman, as well."

An exchange of words followed, the Parisi's voice surprising soft as she spoke the Eburi dialect. At one point the barbarian woman smiled without humour, glanced at Gaius, then turned and spat upon the ground. Niamh had apparently done as instructed.

"He says his name is Cethen," Niamh said. "He wants to know what you plan to build here, and when."

The question took Gaius by surprise, then he realized the man must have observed the unloading of the survey equipment. It served as a subtle reminder that there was often a tendency to overestimate

the ignorance of the barbarian. "Tell this Cethen that nothing will necessarily be built here. We are simply looking at the site. We are looking
at many others."

Again the exchange, and Cethen's expression turned bitter as he
spoke.

"He says there are no others to compare," Niamh translated, "and
that you must know that. He wants to know what your intention is
with his people."

"Intention?" The thought had not occurred to Gaius. If they behaved, the barbarians could stay or leave, depending on their whim.
That was not his responsibility. Some form of settlement usually remained, often right alongside whatever structure that Rome built.
In this instance, if the site proved suitable, the full-sized fortress that
Cerialis had ordered for the Ninth legion. Whether or not this particular rabble stayed would depend on their behaviour, and the pleasure of
the legion's legate. Regardless, it was no concern of his. It was a problem for the *procurator*.

"What he means is, do you intend to push them off the place?"
Niamh explained. "He may be hinting at some sort of compensation."

"Arrogant bastard," Publius muttered.

Gaius tightened his lips at Niamh's translation. He was about to
berate the man for his insolence when he noticed a small, dark-haired
barbarian had clenched his jaw at Publius's insult. Satisfaction welled up
inside Gaius, and he watched carefully as he gave the next instruction.

"Tell him that if we do build here, which as yet isn't certain, he will
likely be allowed the privilege of retaining land close by. But only if he
behaves, and acknowledges Rome."

All eyes except those of the dark-haired man swung toward
Niamh, hanging on the translation. Gaius took a chance and pointed
his finger before she could speak.

"You! You tell your master that. You can also tell him that work
and prosperity follow wherever we build. As to the matter of compensation, that in itself is more than enough."

A murmur of confusion passed among Cethen's people and the
dark-haired man glanced about as if cornered. Then he shrugged helplessly to the others as if in apology, and provided the translation. *And*

that, Tertius, is how you impress the barbarian, Gaius thought smugly.

As the man spoke, Niamh whispered, "He is not of the tribe. The mountains to the southwest would be my guess."

Gaius nodded his understanding, watching in amusement as new words were exchanged between the dark-haired man and his master. The barbarian woman joined in, and all three moved several paces to one side, as if arguing. Cethen waved his free arm angrily as he spoke. The smaller man finally returned, leaving the other two behind to glare at the three Roman officers.

"He prefers that all things remain as they are—the village, his people, and the spirits of the ancestors who dwell here. He asks if there is anything he can offer to make you go away."

Gaius shook his head, as his ear picked up the difference in the small man's accent. It had a lilting, almost musical tone to it. "There is nothing," he replied. "We will be gone before the day is over, and may never return. Now tell me, what intrigue draws you from your mountains?"

The comment was meant to throw the man's poise, but it seemed expected. "I'm a poet." The man threw his arms outward, palms raised. "Eoghan, the bard. A man of song. It is how I live. Men such as I are keepers of our people's spirit, and of our past. We travel far."

Gaius stared doubtfully, reminding himself that Hercules himself probably had a ready excuse for his presence in the underworld. The man's story seemed fair enough, though, and he knew such travellers were common. Anyway, what did it matter? His tasking was to assess the site, not discipline the barbarians who lived there. Besides, he was feeling quite pleased with himself for baring the man's duplicity.

"Does your master have anything more to say?" he asked.

Eoghan turned to Cethen, read the expressions he found there, and answered. "No. I don't believe he has."

"Good," Gaius snapped. "Neither do I."

With that he turned to Titus, nodded a curt, wordless instruction to carry on, and made his way back to the dock. Halfway there it occurred to him that the Brigante woman's name had not been given; or at least, Niamh had not offered it. Regardless, it wasn't a matter of concern.

Chapter JJ

Cethen stormed into the lodge, Elena close on his heels. He sent the shield skittering across the floor with a savage backhand, followed in short order by his helmet, sword, and belt. The cloak was next: ripped off, balled up, and hurled onto the bed. He glared down at the night pot, which was magically back by the door where it belonged, and drew one foot back to kick. Elena screeched in his ear, and he sensibly changed his mind. Instead, he kicked peevishly at the dried rushes strewn about the floor, and when that didn't satisfy his fury, he kicked at the air itself.

He whirled indignantly on those inside the hut, seeking moral support. The place was packed with far more people than when he had left, and those who had followed him to the river were now crowding in behind. Not a single one appeared to share his rage. In fact, nobody seemed to give a faerie's fart.

"Arrogant Roman shit!" Cethen roared in voice that threatened to shake the thatch.

Venutius squatted by the low table, contentedly chewing on whatever it was he had found in Cethen's larder. Like his men, he appeared more interested in filling his mouth. Cethen glared about the lodge. Every man and his hound were helping themselves to his dwindling winter food stocks. As for the others behind him, each seemed to have started eating on passing through his door. The veins on his temple began to throb.

"It is one thing to feed the damned king," Cethen hissed to Cian, who stood beside him gnawing at the core of a dried-up apple. "It is another to slop his whole kingdom *and* my kin!"

His brother airily waved a hand still sticky with crumbs of honeyed bread. He responded in a mumble, his mouth stuffed with the shrivelled fruit. Another glare about the lodge revealed that Cian was not the only one munching on the precious apples. Last year's crop had been sparse, and he knew Elena was down to the dregs. Now every last set of teeth appeared to be crunching the damned things, including his mud-coated, face-stuffing, cocky little rooster of a brother.

"Stop stuffing your gob, and say what's on your tiny mind, turd," Cethen snapped.

Cian finished the mouthful with infuriating slowness. "I said, calm down. You'll hurt yourself."

Cethen could not trust himself to reply. His brother chose to ignore his scowl.

"Remember Urchar?" Cian continued self-righteously. "The smith? He got hisself angry like that, and fell over dead. We don't want that to happen, do we?"

Cethen glanced at Elena in disbelief, as if to confirm what he'd just heard. She stared back with a face of stone and continued banging her pots on the kitchen table. He whirled on Cian, set to grab him by the scruff of his neck, but Venutius called his name.

The old man was grinning from ear to ear, which only prodded Cethen's rage. "Cian's right, you know." Venutius bit into a chunk of honey cake. "Same thing happened to a man I once knew. Coran the Surly. Same age, I'd say. His face turned as purple as an angry prick. Just like yours. Then he dropped dead! *Phut!*" He snapped his fingers in the same airy manner as Cian, and popped another piece of honeyed cake into his mouth.

Cethen remembered that the honey crop hadn't been a huge success either, and the cake he saw disappearing had been set aside for him by Elena, only yesterday. How did the old bastard find it? His chest felt fit to burst.

"What would you really, truly, like to do right now?" Venutius stared at Cethen, one eyebrow raised as he casually sucked his fingers, one at a time, to rid them of the last of the sticky crumbs. He grinned wolfishly, and added, "Not to me, Cethen. To the Romans."

Cethen grunted. "To them? I'd like to take a hundred warriors and push the bastards back into the Abus. Then stand on the shore and watch them drown."

"Do you think a hundred would do it?"

"At the moment, ten who feel as I do would be more than enough!"

Venutius shook his head as if in despair and leaned back against the wall. He spoke directly to Eoghan. "Did you learn anything from them that would be of use?"

The poet paused long enough to clear his mouth of a large slice from the same cake. "It is as you say. They plan to build here, though the Roman insists they're only looking. It's a lie, of course. He's clever, though. Somehow he knew I understood his tongue. It was like magic. He pointed straight at me and spoke to me."

Venutius snorted. "Fool. You probably stood there mouthing the words in Gael, as he spoke them in Latin. How long are they to remain here?"

"They will leave before the day is over."

"Damn." Venutius looked thoughtful. "If they finish early, there may not be time."

"Time for what?" Cethen glanced about the small lodge. With the exception of those who had followed him to the dock, everyone looked smug. Cian licked his chops like a well fed wolf, and the twins, his own children, were bursting with whatever it was they knew.

"I dispatched Vellocatus to bring up the others," Venutius said carelessly. "However, it will be well into the afternoon before they arrive."

Pottery clattered in the cooking area, followed by a loud crash. Everyone turned to look at Elena. She shoved the pots and jars back into place with an expression that would have forced a rabid dog to think twice before it bit. Perhaps not everyone was pleased, Cethen decided.

"How many did you say you had out there?" he asked.

"I spoke of over a thousand."

"You sent for a thousand warriors?" Cethen exclaimed.

Venutius looked pained. "Not all the people who join us are warriors, Cethen. We gather men from many different places. Some bring their women and children. Somewhat more than half the number we have in camp are warriors. Or at least, men and women willing to fight."

"So what, then—five, six hundred?" Cethen asked, then winced at the absurd conclusion.

"I sent for half of them, upward of three hundred," Venutius continued patiently. "I need the rest to guard the camp. Once we have dealt with the, er …what did you call him? Arrogant Roman bastard? We will fall back and continue north. This time tomorrow, we will be well away from here."

Cethen felt his anger drain as he realized what was being said. He glanced quickly toward Elena, just as another piece of pottery crashed to the floor.

"And what do the Eburi do?" she demanded. "Remain here, and wait for the Romans to return and take their revenge?"

Venutius affected surprise. "Of course not, my dear. You and your family will come north with us. With your people. You'll be better off there, anyway. The stronghold at Stannick is greater than any that even the Romans are capable of—"

"That's—that's pig piss!" Elena almost shook with anger. "Just because some strutting, arrogant, horse-haired, tin-clad lump of Roman shit picks his way up your nose," she shouted, "you move my family, destroy my home, and get my husband killed!"

"Woman, we kill the Romans wherever we can," Venutius snarled, and turned back to Cethen with an expression that clearly told him to get a tighter rein on his woman. "Here's how we do it. When Vellocatus arrives, half his force will use the cover of the forest to circle behind the village. They will wait there, in hiding. Vellocatus himself will lead the other half—"

"Vellocatus is going to split his force?" Cian, his belly full, was never slow to voice an opinion.

Venutius scowled, but otherwise ignored the comment. "As I started to say, Vellocatus will lead the other half of his force down to the river and begin the attack. That force will burst from the trees, run along the riverbank, and secure the ship. The infantry and any others on shore will be cut off from their boat, thus splitting *their* force!" He sniffed scornfully at Cian. "And then, when the fight begins and the Romans already on shore rush to help those on the boat, our warriors in the forest will attack from behind. At that time, we here in the village will come out and join them."

Venutius leaned back against the wall and stared at the rapt faces, as if daring them to object. One by one they nodded, most of them looking pleased with a plan that was already in motion. Cethen risked a glance at Elena, relieved to find her attention was, for the moment, focused on the floor and the broken pottery.

Above anything else in life, Gaius Trebonius was a soldier; but he was also an engineer. A very good and a very competent engineer. The prospect of constructing a full-sized fortress brought a welcome renewal of interest in an otherwise sagging career. Such a structure would not only be a challenge, it would be a monument. Though built of wood, it would be a monument erected by Gaius Sabinius Trebonius. When he was long dead, men of the Ninth Hispana would remember that. And perhaps, at some time, a permanent marker would tell as much.

It was with such thoughts that Gaius paced the site with ice cold feet, his boots sodden with the melting snow. Not that he cared, for as the barbarian chieftain had pointed out, there was no better place to build.

The large and the smaller river formed a great Y, offering a defensive barrier on all sides except the northwest. The ground rose to form a low, dry ridge between the two rivers; not much perhaps, but more than enough on which to build a fortress. The barbarians had obviously set their village on the same ridge out of necessity, for the traders spoke of rare, but occasional flooding, a fact borne out by driftwood lodged in the fields on either side of the river. It was a minor nuisance, though, and to be expected; and if expected, it might be used to advantage. The same traders also said the tidewater ran all the way from the coast to the village, making the site useful as a port. There was also an abundance of trees for building, all of which would require clearing anyway. And there was a final plus: the strategic fork in the river was in the very underbelly of Brigantia.

Gaius's mood improved as the day wore on, and the survey confirmed all that his practised eye had first seen. The Eburi village was indeed ideal. The untidy cluster of hovels would have to go, of course, and it seemed the villagers realized that. They had remained inside all day, probably sulking and seething, which only made his job that much easier. By late afternoon, he had gathered all the information he needed from the site.

"The man has his hut set right about where the *Porta Praetoria* will sit," the primus observed as the survey detail began moving its equipment back to the ship. The sun was on its downward drift toward the horizon, and the shadows of the forest were quickly growing cold. The three officers stood at the very edge of the pasture, where Gaius judged the northeast wall of the fortress would eventually stand.

"We can move the ramparts back fifty paces, so he's not disturbed," Publius quipped, and all three chuckled.

"It's a fairly level site," Titus offered.

"Given what we're usually faced with, it's almost perfect." Gaius gazed across the open patch of farmland to where the rivers met. "It falls off down there by the willows, but all in all, it's damned near perfect. I'm going to recommend it, gentlemen. Get used to the place."

"Which means that we're done here for now, then?" Publius asked.

Gaius nodded. Most of the soldiers had fallen back to the ship, and the few left on the field were tramping slowly toward the river. A mass of cold, grey cloud crowded the sky, blowing slowly in from the east.

"I'll go hurry the men, Gaius, or they'll stand there with their fingers up their arse until long after sunset," Titus muttered, and strode off toward the dock.

Publius glanced hesitantly between the two.

"Go ahead," Gaius suggested. "I want a last look to fix it firm in my mind."

He turned away as the young tribune trotted after the pilus, and walked over to the trunk of an ancient tree that lay rotting on the ground at the edge of the forest. He scrambled on top and stood gazing down toward the river, his mind wandering over the site's possibilities.

The barbarians had built a ford a few paces upstream, but it was already impassable under the heavy spring runoff. Only the gods knew what it was like the rest of the year. A bridge would be an early priority. An ideal spot to build it would be where the Eburi had placed the dock. The wooded hill on the far side of the river would take a straight road, despite its steepness. Its path would surely be the beginning of a higher, dryer route south, rather than the ferry crossing at *Petuaria*, a good way downriver near the coast.

A faint shout caught his attention, and his eyes fell on Titus, standing on the riverbank. The survey crew had stowed its gear on the ship, and the centurion in charge was calling in the last of his infantry. Gaius waved, almost reluctant to leave. Indeed, there was only one more pressing duty that required attention. He turned his back to the field, raised his tunic, unlaced his britches, and with a great sigh relieved himself. His mind again fixed on the unbuilt fortress, as he gazed blankly into the blur of the forest.

After several long, soothing moments, he grew vaguely aware of a dim shape, off in the distance—a shape at odds with the stark, dark outline of the leafless trees. Something was odd; something did not quite blend.

With a start, his mind snapped to the present and his heart skipped. A barbarian warrior stood frozen in mid-step not fifty paces away, half hidden by the deepening shadows. Gaius's mind registered first the man's shield, held tipped to one side, then a spear, carried low as if marching, and finally the barbarian himself. He was plainly hoping to remain unnoticed. For a moment neither moved, but eye contact quickly destroyed all pretence. The Briton offered a disarming grin and shrugged, as if caught with his hand in someone's purse.

"You might well smile, you bastard," Gaius whispered to himself, and slowly reached down to draw his sword.

He filled his lungs to shout a warning to Titus, but a second statue-like figure formed in the gloom of the forest as if by magic, off to the first man's right. Gaius blinked and focused. He saw yet another figure beyond. And another ...and—

"Oh, shit!" he mumbled. He spun around, leapt from the log, and raced toward the dock, screaming the alarm at the top of his voice. The forest erupted in a snapping, crackling clamour of breaking branches and shrieking howls. Gaius's feet dug frantically into the slushy pasture, his senses blanked by the sheer terror of panic; but as he raced madly across the field, sword waving uselessly, the soldier inside gradually assumed control: *Never panic! Panic kills!*

His mind began to reason. He had a good head start, and as long he kept his mind clear, the odds might still be in his favour. All he had to do was reach his own troops ahead of the barbarians, and his hopes surged at the sight of the infantry, now forming a ragged line on the riverbank. Behind, pushing the soldiers on, were the familiar faces of Publius and Titus. The thought flashed through Gaius's mind that perhaps he should turn and fight, but just as quickly he discarded the idea as foolish. There could be a score or more warriors behind him!

Hardly had his fears ebbed, than the straggling line of soldiers halted, as if suddenly uncertain. Gaius's belly turned to ice. Something thudded close on his heels, and he heard another dull thud off to his left. From the corner of his eye, he glimpsed a spear strike the frozen ground, then slither across the snow. Then Titus's booming voice roared an order that was too far away to make out, and the small squad of soldiers began falling back to the ship.

"Shit!" Gaius again cried in despair, and then again. "Shit!"

Thirty or forty Britons had emerged from the hovels, led by the lanky Eburi chieftain. The small force was spreading out, blocking his line of retreat. Gaius's thoughts ran the gamut from panic, to resignation, and finally to desperation, as his legs pounded on through the slush of their own accord. Perhaps if he met the barbarian line at its weakest point …if he could find it. He was not dead yet … If he cut hard with his sword where they least expected …A Roman was worth ten barbarians in a fight, everyone knew that. It was a fact. Perhaps …

Gaius feverishly began bargaining with the gods: if they would help just this once, just one more time, he would build an altar, a shrine, a dedication; an expensive monument, one large enough to assure his devotion. It was a promise, a heartfelt promise, given freely and gladly, if they would only, please, get him safely through this one tiny battle with as little damage as possible …

Gaius breathlessly finished his plea, hefted his sword—and tripped. He sprawled in the slush, the weapon slithering through the melting snow as if it were alive. Half crawling, half running, he scrambled forward and grabbed at the hilt with both hands. Only then, as he tried to regain his feet, did Gaius realize one hand had been clutching his britches. Now it was too late. The damned things had slithered downward, and he again pitched forward. He was on all fours, cursing the gods for the ingrates they were, as the first of the barbarians caught up.

The lead warrior thrust his spear at Gaius's lower back just as he tumbled forward. The point slid under the bottom of his armour, and snaked its way upward until it thumped against the inside of the shoulder plates. The shaft snapped as the man rushed past, vainly trying to pull the weapon free. Gaius tumbled head over heels, a burning pain searing the length of his spine.

"This is it!" Venutius cried as yelps drifted through the door of the lodge.

The men pushed their way outside, each yelling his courage and determined to be the first to prove it. Cethen led the way, leaping over the low stockade only to halt short in dismay. There was no sign of Vellocatus and his band of warriors. The king's shield bearer should have been running along the riverbank with his men, intent on taking the ship. The Romans were instead deployed in line, as if preparing to advance on the village.

"Sheep shit," Cethen muttered, and wondered who had been yelping.

The wild screams of the Eburi fell to nothing as they watched the Roman infantry shuffling forward. Almost at once, however, the double ranks halted as if confused and stood staring toward the forest. The sharp yip of distant war cries grew louder.

"Look at that!" Venutius shouted, a broad smile splitting his face.

Cethen turned. The Roman officer—he never had given his name—was running across the field like a frightened deer ahead of the hounds. His left hand held his britches in a death grip, while his right hand clutched a sword that pumped up and down with every stride. Wet snow sprayed each time his feet struck the ground. Behind him, the forest spewed forth scores and scores of screaming warriors.

"Stop him!" Cian cried, and led the charge to block Gaius's path.

The small band of Eburi yelled and crowed as the distance narrowed, though more than one glanced nervously back at the ranks of soldiers. The Roman infantry seemed to have opted for discretion, or the likelihood they were too far away to help. Whatever the reason, they were falling back on the ship. The "arrogant bastard" had been sacrificed, Cethen realized.

A moment later the bastard tripped and sprawled in a spray of wet snow.

"Come on, man, get up!" A voice yelled derisively as the Roman tried to regain his footing, first crawling, then stumbling, until he finally grasped the hilt of his sword. A great whoop rose from the Britons as he staggered to his feet and his britches drooped. They roared with laughter as he once again crashed forward.

"They got him!" a second voice screeched as the horde overwhelmed the fallen figure, savaging him as they ran past.

"No, no, the bugger's still going," Cian cried, watching the contest as if it were a bear baiting.

Unbelievably, the Roman staggered to his feet, sword flailing as Venutius's warriors raced by, their eyes fixed on the main body of soldiers edging back onto the dock. One man took a swing with his axe, sending the Roman officer's sword flying as he tried to parry. Another took a backhanded swipe with a heavy, iron blade that smashed into his chest armour and sent him tumbling backward. He rolled over, narrowly avoiding a vicious spear thrust that, for a moment, looked likely to spit him. Then a small, chubby warrior came panting up a good ten yards behind the others, just as the Roman was once more trying to stagger to his feet.

"Look out!" Cian cried, then glanced sheepishly around, as if expecting reproof. But everyone was caught up in the one-sided contest.

The final blow came as the Roman struggled to his knees, one hand in the cold slush as he tried to regain his feet. The Briton's sword swung in a high arc and crashed down on the plumed helmet, slicing through the crested guard on top. The weapon jammed tight in the metal and the small warrior, panting with effort, tried to wrench it loose. The battered helmet jerked free with sickening twist. Whooping with glee, the chubby warrior pried it off the blade, set it on the point of his sword, and ran onward holding the trophy aloft. The Roman, blood pouring from the top of his skull, slumped forward and lay still.

A cheer rose from the Eburi, but there was no time for celebration. The first warriors were drawing near, slowing down as they came upon Venutius; but the king would have none of it. "Keep moving, dammit, there's your enemy," he roared, and pointed to the dock with his sword. "Don't give them time to get to the boat."

"Come on, let's go," Cethen called, and with Cian one step behind, he started to the river. He glimpsed Elena in the corner of his eye as she sprinted from the compound. Turning on the run, he screamed at her, "Stay there, woman. The children!"

She grinned savagely, gestured rudely with her spear, and ignored him. Cethen cursed and turned back to the river. The bank and the dock swarmed with the ship's crew. The two ranks of infantry were falling steadily back as the sailors worked frantically to free the vessel from its mooring. The officers ran back and forth, pushing men into place, screaming at the crew to come forward and bolster the line.

Cethen roared in triumph as he recognized the Romans' dilemma. If the soldiers broke to board the boat, they would be swarmed. Only a steady, disciplined retreat across the dock could prevent the fight shifting to the vessel's deck. Astonishingly, the small Roman force showed no hint of panic, nor did it even seem to hurry.

The first of Venutius's men were almost on them when an order rang out from one of the officers. A shower of spears arched through the air, falling among the lead warriors. The short, wooden shafts were mounted with slender iron necks topped by small, sharp points. Most found only shields, but the thin metal penetrated, bent, and stuck fast.

Cian leaped ahead of his brother as Venutius's men slammed into the Roman line, not with a crash, but with a ragged, rippling splatter.

Those following flung themselves in behind, but the Romans stubbornly defended the dock as the crew scrambled to clear the ship. The grim ranks held fast, each man thumping forward with his heavy shield, and stabbing with his sword. Shield bosses smashed against teeth as the short, deadly blades shot back and forth, each soldier protecting himself, and the man alongside.

Cethen felt the onset of panic. Romans and Britons were falling, but by far the most were Venutius's people, peeling away or dropping in the slop as a flashing iron blade found its mark. The Romans were heavily outnumbered, yet their ranks were firm, hardly wavering. He glanced nervously to his left, where a new threat had arisen: the small squad of archers were shooting from the deck of the ship, their arrows picking off men at random.

Cethen's frustration grew to a red fog, and he slashed wildly as one of Venutius's own people, blood gushing from his throat, tumbled to the ground at his feet. The blow was fruitless, he knew that, even as it bit into the Roman's shield and stuck. A short, bloodied blade shot out, and he was nearly gutted by the man to the soldier's left. Venutius took that blow with his own weapon, but instead of using brute force, twisted his sword and thrust up under the soldier's chin. The man fell back in a gurgling spray of blood, and the old man pushed his way into the opening, a half dozen others squeezing behind.

When Cethen tried to follow, though, the gap had already closed. Cursing, he slashed down on the same shield, joining a handful of warriors on either side trying in vain to force their way through and follow their king. The small, venomous blades struck back. The man to his left lurched away clutching his belly, and the one on his right simply dropped where he stood. Cethen stumbled backward as a sword slid off the leather of his belt, and he tumbled over a figure crouched low behind. It was Elena, thrusting wildly under the Roman shield wall with her spear.

"What are you doing?" Cethen cried. "Get back!"

"I'm using my brain," she shouted, but glanced upward as a low wail rose from the ragged line of Britons. Word of Venutius's disappearance had spread like fire.

"They got the old bugger." Cethen gestured with his shield toward the Roman line, and an arrow thudded into its heavy wood surface. Rolling backward, he pulled at Elena's belt, forcing her further from the fight. A few of Venutius's warriors had also fallen away from the line; and while not fleeing, they seemed unsure of what to do next. Oddly, so did some of the Romans. One or two looked over to the decani for guidance, as if uncertain whether to advance, or continue the retreat to the ship.

It was then that Vellocatus's men finally struck.

Cethen grew dimly aware of voices roaring off to his right. Those of Venutius's men still fighting could sense, rather than see, the enemy crumble. To a man, they pushed forward with renewed vigour. The small wooden dock suddenly seethed with a brawl of crashing, slashing warriors. Cethen and Elena clambered to their feet and for the moment stood on the riverbank, watching in awe.

The advantage of Roman discipline had vanished in an instant. Screaming a series of orders that no one could obey, the officers were reeling back to the ship, the infantry stumbling along as best they could. Venutius's warriors plunged down onto the dock, swinging and hacking even as they jumped. Cethen grimaced as he saw his brother, screaming triumph, swing his sword in a wide circle. The blade bit deep into the neck of a decanus, angling in below the man's skewed helmet. The Roman fell, blood spewing over the battered plates of his *lorica*.

"The ship," Cethen roared and lunged forward. "We can take the ship."

Elena grabbed the back of his tunic. "Don't be a fool. It's a death trap. What would you do with the damned thing, anyway?"

"Let go, woman," Cethen shouted, and jerked free.

"Forget the stupid boat. Help those on the dock," Elena cried as she followed. "Besides, it's too late."

Someone had slashed the mooring lines. The sleek vessel drifted slowly out into the river, the severed ropes trailing in the water. Three or four oars slid raggedly from the hull, as an order rang out above the dying clash of battle. The long blades dipped haphazardly at the current, slowly pulling the ship into the mainstream of the Abus.

Roaring his courage, Cethen leapt onto the dock, but found little left to do. A few Romans remained, trapped on the small platform, but each faced more than a dozen warriors, whose blood was up. The small vessel did not dare close in to help. Cethen turned to watch it drift farther away, dismayed at the carnage on board. Elena had been right. Those men rash enough to jump on board were helplessly cut off. Several leapt into the river, but those who stayed were doomed. One by one they were cut down, the bodies tossed into the Abus behind those able to swim to shore .

The exception was a solitary warrior crouched in the vessel's bow, snarling like a cornered wolf. The Romans seemed in no hurry to finish the fight. Perhaps it was the warrior's age, for he didn't seem particularly dangerous. It was Venutius.

The Parisi woman stood close by at the bow rail, as if the fight were none of her concern. She had taken no part, but even so, she blocked the old man's retreat. Several soldiers edged forward, triumph on their faces as they moved down on the cornered king. On the dock, the shouting and screaming faded as, one by one, the jubilant Britons realized what was happening

Venutius wavered, his sword shifting in his hand as he leaned low, as if preparing to fight. Then, as the first of the Romans lunged, he chose the cold waters of the Abus instead. He flung his sword in the man's face, followed with his shield, and vaulted over the railing. Both legs were clear of the side when the Parisi woman's arm shot out and grabbed the neck of his tunic. He tumbled ingloriously back onto the deck, feet flailing the air. The soldiers moved forward to put an end to it, but the woman drew her sword and waved them off.

Elena, beside Cethen, muttered, "The bitch knows who he is!"

The Roman primus pushed his way forward as if ready to upbraid the woman, but she muttered something and pointed toward the dock with her sword. The man's eyes followed the point of the blade, and he quickly moved to the side of the ship.

"For certain she knows," Cethen agreed, and cursed.

"It would seem so." Vellocatus joined them, his expression uncertain.

"You know," Elena said quietly, "it's not us they're staring at."

One by one those on the shore turned their eyes toward the village, and gaped in astonishment. The Roman officer lurched down the slope, staggering like a battered drunk. Blood streamed from a gash that had peeled his scalp from ear to ear, and his left hand clutched his chest, where a great dent had been beaten into the breastplate. His britches sagged, held up only by the broken spear shaft jammed under his armour. The elusive sword, dripping mud and melting snow, was once more clutched in his right hand.

He was about fifty paces from the nearest Briton when he halted, as if suddenly aware that something was dreadfully wrong. For a moment his body swayed as if about to topple, then he slowly fell to a crouch, head swinging from side to side like that of a baited bear. His eyes, two huge orbs in a thick plaster of mud, narrowed as if he realized someone blocked his path. His left arm rose upward as if ready to ward off a blow, and the short stabbing sword came to the ready position. Slowly, he resumed his weaving trudge down the slope.

As one, the Britons drew slowly back, leaving a pathway clear down to the landing. Cethen, Elena, and several others stood at the end, watching in amazement as the Roman hobbled cautiously into the gap, his weapon at the ready.

"He's our trade goods for Venutius," Elena whispered.

"Not if they know who he is," Cethen countered, immediately regretting his slow wit.

Elena huffed her annoyance. "And we'll not find out if they do, unless we try."

"I know, I know," he growled, then looked toward the staggering Roman and roared, "Nobody harm him."

Vellocatus echoed the words, but the order was unnecessary. Not one of those watching seemed ready to put an end to the Roman's tottering march. Every last warrior stared in fascination as the man reeled forward, each wondering how long he could last. Suddenly, from somewhere in the crowd, a voice rang out. It was Cian's.

"He's the *Crodha*."

"Hi-yeah, the valiant!"

"Hey Roman," another yelled. "Go to it, boy-o, go. Yip, yip, yip, yip, yeaaaaah!"

Others joined in, and the cry was quickly taken up on all sides. The Roman plodded on with a dazed, muddled expression on his face, eyes squinting through the layer of muck. The cheering continued until he reached the dock, where he edged carefully onto the wooden planks, turning from side to side as if trying to make sense of it all. His progress brought him to the edge, where he stood looking first to the ship, then to the shore. The noise gradually died.

A voice hailed them from the ship. It was the Parisi woman. "A trade. Your man for ours."

Vellocatus moved to reply, but Elena stepped forward. "I'll make the old bastard sweat," she whispered, as much to herself as anyone else. Before anyone could speak, she cried out, "The old man and what else?"

A gasp rippled along the dock, which Elena ignored. The woman translated the words to the primus, who appeared angry and argued with her. The second officer strode forward, and a heated discussion followed. It ended with the primus tight-lipped, and the other officer digging deep into his tunic as he spoke to the Parisi.

"The old man and a gold coin," the Parisi called, the officer holding it up as she spoke.

Cethen opened his mouth to accept, but once more Elena shouted first. "Make it five and we will trade."

Again there was a rush of breath. Only the sound of the oars filled the silence, dipping in and out of the water as its captain kept the ship balanced with the current. The officer thrust his hand once more into his tunic, and examined what he found there.

"He's an old man and near useless. You're getting a bargain," Elena shouted, giggling almost hysterically as Cethen squeezed her arm hard enough to hurt.

"Three gold coins and three—no, four silver," came the reply as the primus stalked toward the rear of the ship.

"Agreed," Cethen shouted quickly, before his wife could reply.

"Give the coins to the old man," Elena cried, and looked impishly up at her husband. "I think we've emptied the Roman's purse."

The coins were passed, and the boat gradually wheeled against the current until the bow pointed toward the dock. The officer gestured with his hand for the crowd to move, and the Parisi called for them all to stand away from the dock.

"Your people too," Cethen replied, as Vellocatus ordered the reluctant Britons up onto the riverbank.

Soon only he and Elena remained on the landing, standing alongside the swaying Roman, who stared at the ship through eyes of glass. The bow cut slowly toward the dock, the officer and the Parisi woman standing one on each side of their captive. But as they drew near, Venutius dropped suddenly to his knees, wriggled free of the woman's grip, and lunged forward. This time, he cleared the rail before the Parisi could move. There was a loud splash, followed by dead silence.

Cethen's temper flared. What was the old fool doing? A trade had been brokered! It was taking place as promised! It was going to plan. Why had the old bugger changed it? He strode quickly to the edge of the dock to see if Venutius was sinking or swimming, but the move took him close by his prisoner, and his intention was misunderstood. The Roman clumsily raised his sword, took one step backward, and disappeared over the side of the dock. A second loud splash was followed by silence.

It didn't last. The boat's oars dug into the water, ragged and disordered, as orders rang out on either side. Cethen peered down at the dark waters. Only a small trail of bubbles marked the spot where the Roman had disappeared.

"Shit," he muttered quietly, then glanced toward the ship. Several archers were swinging their bows, all of them toward him. "Oh shit!" Cethen cried again and frantically shook his head, one palm raised as a signal for the archers to stop.

He tossed his heavy shield aside, then the sword and helmet, and jumped into the river. The icy water grabbed him like a winter's grave. He raised his arms to sink lower into the murky water, but instead tangled with the Roman, who was struggling upward, desperate for air. They both began to sink, then Cethen grasped the Roman by the top of his breastplate, and kicked his way desperately back to the surface. The current had pushed them downriver, but the slimy curve of the dock's corner post slid close by his shoulder. He reached out and wrapped one arm around it, hooking the other under the Roman's shoulder.

"Cethen, grab the rope."

Spluttering, he looked up to find a dozen faces peering over the edge of the dock. One of them was Cian, the remnant of a mooring loop in his hand. Cethen shook his head, and looked instead to the boat. It had begun drifting again, but the two officers and the woman remained in the bow. "Throw a line," Cethen yelled.

At first they didn't understand, then the Parisi woman spoke, and an order was quickly relayed. One of the crew ran forward. A coil of rope unfurled neatly in the air, falling just upstream from the piling. Cethen let go of the post and clutched the line before it could float past, intending to tie it about the Roman's chest. His friends could tow him back to the boat, dead or alive, Cethen supposed; it no longer mattered. He had done what he could.

Instead, the rope grew taut, as someone hauled on it the moment the damned thing was in hand! Cethen's mind panicked. If he let go, the Roman would certainly drown, and perversely, he found he didn't want that. There was no reason, he just didn't want it to happen. Perhaps the gutsy bastard had earned the right to live, at least for now; besides, a trade had been made. He, Cethen Lamh-fada, had agreed to hand the man over. He had given his word.

Yet would the Romans have honoured such a bargain? Of course not! Cethen shivered, and sighed. He was tempted to let go, but there were those archers …Unable to decide, cursing his own foolishness, and not even knowing if his captive was alive, he instead hung on.

The ship's prow loomed high above Cethen's head. He heard a splash. Someone else was in the water, but whoever it was simply looped another rope about the Roman's chest, somehow raising him to secure the knot. Cethen found himself suddenly face to face with his half-drowned captive, their noses almost touching. The Roman's dark eyes were glazed, but for a moment they focused and he mumbled something. Then those on the ship hauled on the line, and his body rose eerily upward, the water running red as it dripped down the man's face and across his battered armour. The sword was still clutched firmly in his right hand.

Cethen kicked away from the boat, swimming warily backward. If he was going to receive an arrow or a spear, then the bastards could look him in the eye as they aimed it. But as the distance grew between him and the wall of impassive faces lining the ship's rail, his numbed mind reasoned there was a warrior's code of honour, even among the Romans. Somewhere onboard a voice shouted and he flinched, but it was meant for the crew, not the soldiers. One bank of oars began to back paddle, forcing the boat into a wide, steady turn.

"You! Cethen!" The Roman primus appeared, hands resting on the rail. He nodded his head in silent recognition, then shouted to be heard above the din aboard the ship. "Why?"

Later, Cethen thought of all sorts of things he could have said. Some of them were witty, some nonchalant, and others would have put the man in his place. But at the time all he could think of was how bone-chilling cold the water was, and that he wasn't sure how far away lay the safety of the riverbank. So he rolled over, and started swimming.

"Where's Venutius?" Cethen demanded as a score of willing hands pulled him from the water, a good fifty paces downriver.

"He's on his way to the village, Da, see?" Rhun gestured toward a group of men milling about the gateway to the compound.

"What a story to tell, Cethen." Cian slapped his brother on the back. "I'll trade for the old man and what else? I think he was ready to choke you."

Elena pushed past him. "Come on, idiot. Survive the battle, and die of a fever. Let's get you inside." She grasped her husband by the arm and pulled him along the pathway back to the lodge, her own cloak wrapped about his shoulders. Cethen didn't resist.

"Why did you jump in and save him, Da?" Coira asked the question, walking ahead of them, backward, so she would miss nothing. She wore a puzzled expression.

"B-because s-someone pushed me off the d-damned dock," Cethen stuttered. The day still retained a trace of its mildness, but as they made their way up the slope, his feet felt like chunks of frozen mutton, and he shivered uncontrollably. He glanced back toward the river. The dead were scattered on the dock and about the snow speckled field, dark shapes that already looked like grave mounds. Cethen shuddered and decided his own needs came first: a dry refuge with a warm fire.

"Come on, Da," Coira persisted.

"Why did you, Cethen?" asked the slow voice of Balor, who was holding onto Cethen's side, should he stumble. He sounded even more baffled than the twin.

"Because he had no choice, oaf," Cian interjected. "He'd agreed to the trade."

"Because he's a man, and short on good sense," Elena countered from behind, where she followed with her husband's sword and shield.

"Then what about Venutius and *his* word?" Balor persisted. "He broke free and jumped."

"I would g-guess he didn't trust the Romans," Cethen said. "But then, who does? He probably thought there was less chance of t-treachery if he was a free man. Anyway, he didn't agree to make the trade. I did."

Elena snorted. Cethen let it pass. His wife's mood wasn't something he wanted to explore at that moment. Her blood had flowed hot during the fight, as she screamed and hacked alongside the rest of them. Now it was over, he guessed her mind was already plunging ahead to the turmoil that would now fall on their home.

The next question came from Rhun, and they all laughed. "Da, what are you going to do with the gold coins the Roman gave?"

The warmth greeted them like a blanket as they entered the lodge. The building was packed. A fire blazed in the centre of the dirt floor and a cauldron of hot water steamed above it. Some of those hurt in the fight had walked back and sat, impassive for the most part, as their wounds were washed and stitched. Venutius perched cross-legged on the bed, naked but for a fur shawl about his shoulders. Much to Cethen's annoyance, the man had found something else to chew on, and was washing it down with a flagon of hot mead. Eating and drinking were all the old bugger and his men seemed to do.

"So, my life is not worth that of a Roman?" Venutius growled, glaring owlishly at Cethen.

"It's worth much more, sir. Th-that's why Elena asked for the extra c-coin to even the balance," Cethen said, his teeth chattering.

Venutius puzzled the logic for a moment, then roared with laughter. He picked something off the bed and was about to toss it to Cethen, then changed his mind and threw it to Elena.

"The way you count, I could almost believe your reasoning. Here, woman."

"That's all?" she complained, looking down at one of the gold coins. "The bargain was worth at least twice as much as I got."

This time everyone laughed except Balor, who stood puzzled as he tried to balance the logic of the sums.

"So are you coming with us?" Venutius asked. He looked up at Cethen and Elena with eyebrows raised in amusement, his lips pursed like a child who knew his transgressions would not be punished.

Chapter III

Publius began stripping the uniform from Gaius's body the moment the sailors set his limp form facedown on the deck. A chill wind whipped across the ship's railing, made colder by the gathering clouds and the deepening shadows of evening. His fingers grew numb as they fumbled at the leather ties of the chest armour, and he cursed the weather, the barbarians, the gods, and the stubborn fastenings now drawn tight by the frigid water. A shadow loomed over his shoulder, and a knife thudded into the deck alongside his knee.

"Cut it."

A pile of dry cloaks followed, landing alongside with a soft *whump*. Publius nodded without looking up and, after slicing with the blade, soon pulled the body armour free. The broken spear shaft clattered to the deck, and he threw it to one side after the battered armour. The soft leather under-tunic was next, as wet and greasy as fresh caught eel, and just as hard to work with. Titus knelt down beside him, added his own curses, and began slicing at Gaius's britches, which were half off anyway.

"He's turning blue," the primus muttered, and glanced at the pile of cloaks. "We'll be needing all of those. Nobody's going to claim the damned things anyway."

"Right, and thanks," Publius muttered, flinching as he slid the tunic over Gaius's head, a handsbreadth of scalp peeling back from the skull.

"That's going to sting," Titus muttered. He pulled the britches free. "And what do you mean, thanks? For what?"

"Those." Publius nodded to the pile of cloaks. He started unlacing the linen undershirt, and since the knife was now a hindrance, flicked it into the planking of the deck. "And for that."

"You're a brave man, tribune." Titus smiled grimly. "I wouldn't dare throw a blade into Tertius's precious deck. Ship captains are touchy about that sort of thing."

"But you—"

"I didn't toss it there. It was the woman." Titus glanced toward the bow, where Niamh stood at the ship's rail, staring impassively toward the Eburi village.

"I'm surprised she'd even lift a …" Publius began, but found he was talking to himself. The primus was on his feet, staring over the ship's prow, annoyance written on his face.

"Where in this bog-buggered land is the man going?" Titus muttered, then roared, "Captain!"

The soft thump of the drum started up, and Tertius emerged from the lower deck. His tunic was covered in blood, and he looked grim. "I lost a good half-dozen of my crew," he shouted.

"I bleed for them," Titus snapped. He gestured about the deck. Several soldiers, one the chief surveyor, lay lifeless alongside the aft rail. A dozen more huddled close by the mast, cursing and groaning as their wounds were staunched by other members of their squad. Dark, glistening patches of blood stained a deck littered with helmets, weapons, and broken equipment. "But they're not my problem at the moment," Titus grated. "Where is this damned river scow going? It's pointed the wrong way!"

Tertius looked baffled. "Isurium; where else?"

"That was before I lost half my men to a horde of raving barbarians," Titus shouted. "We need to get back to Petuaria. This man needs competent help. And so do others." He gestured at Gaius's corpselike body, now stripped of the linen undershirt. An ugly wound gouged by the spearhead sliced raggedly up the left side of his spine. A good slice of his scalp had fallen forward, baring the blood-smeared, ivory dome of the skull. From his shoulders to his feet, his skin was alabaster tinged with blue.

"We're supposed to meet up with the Tungri, and one of the Ninth's cohorts," Tertius said.

"I'm not willing to take a chance on that."

"There's a bunch of supplies to deliver," Tertius persisted. "And dispatches."

"Er, Isurium is closer, primus," Publius ventured nervously.

Titus hesitated, his eyes on Gaius as Publius rolled him onto a bed of cloaks like a slab of cold meat, and piled a half-dozen more on top. He bit his lip, then shook his head. "The Tungri might have been up there for a week, lad, or they might not get there for another. The camp at Petuaria has a hospital. And a surgeon. We go there." He glared at Tertius, one hand moving unconsciously to the hilt of his sword. "And there will be no halts, and we row fast. If that's alright with you, captain!"

"I'm only the man in charge of this scow," Tertius muttered, and with a shrug turned on his heel. "I'll send Niamh over to help."

"What do we want with a barbarian translator?" Publius asked.

Tertius looked back over his shoulder, a hard, humourless grin on his face. "She's the best man I have on board with a needle and thread."

"Shit," Publius muttered.

Titus merely nodded agreement. "Some hot wine, spiced, wouldn't hurt the insides, either, captain."

"His or yours?"

When Titus growled, Tertius hurried away, muttering that he would see what he could do.

Gaius was drifting in and out of consciousness as the ship slid alongside the dock at Petuaria the following day. He lay on his belly beneath the bloodstained stack of cloaks, half drunk and reeking of cheap wine. His face was a mottled rainbow of colour, mostly a dark purple that extended down to below his eyes. A neat web of black stitches crossed the top of his shaved head, as if the skull had been split in two and carefully spliced together again. A second row of stitching, long, jag-

65

ged and hidden below the thick layer of cloaks, snaked along his back, puckering the flesh like a freshly trussed joint of raw beef.

"Not much more I can do for him, except keep things clean," the surgeon muttered after Gaius was stretchered into the hospital—a rough, wooden building that still held the odour of fresh cut lumber. His eyes took in the stitches as the orderly daubed a goose fat mixture along the jagged lines of the wound. "Whose work is that? I could use him here."

"*He* is not one of ours," Titus said, grimacing as Gaius twitched. "And besides, he's a she."

"Is our man going to live?" Publius asked.

"Seen worse," the surgeon replied, noncommittal. "Fever's more likely a problem. Depends how he heals."

"He-he'll live," Gaius muttered weakly, his eyes flickering. "You b-bastards can stop talking as if I'm not here."

Titus chuckled and wandered over to the doorway while the orderlies transferred Gaius to a cot. He stepped onto the porch and stared down the road leading south from the headquarters building. There was little to be seen other than the muddy street, and the mast tops of a half-dozen ships, poking above the peeled logs of the southern wall.

Petuaria lay in Parisi territory, on the north shore of the broad Abus estuary, thirty miles inland from the sea. It served as both a deep sea port and a landing stage for goods and personnel ferried across from the south. The tiny port bustled, but mainly with its own construction. A set of ramparts surrounded the heart of the camp, topped by wooden palisades and the usual corner towers. Some sections of the enclosure were scattered with tents, but much of the interior was taken up by neat rows of freshly planked buildings, many with cheery columns of smoke blowing from the chimneys.

"Anybody important come in?" Titus asked. A trireme had arrived at the dock sometime after they had begun their journey along the Abus, just four days ago.

"The normal plague of gold-grabbers and backstabbers," the surgeon muttered. "I think the new *procurator* was one of them. Came in yesterday."

"And trouble always follows on *his* heels," Titus murmured.

"It might already be on its way," Publius said from the other side of the hospital, which faced the headquarters building.

A dark, curly haired man, about the same age as Publius and dressed in a spotless tunic and leggings, picked his way across the street. He was hip-hopping from side to side, vainly trying to avoid the puddles. A wide leather pouch dangled from one hand, and an orange clay jug was clutched firmly in the other. He leapt onto the wooden footpath that ranged down each side of the street, and glanced down at his sandals. They were caked with mud. With a snort of disgust, he looked up at Titus and offered a broad smile that revealed a perfect set of teeth.

"Was a Gaius Sabinius Trebonius brought in here?" he asked cheerfully.

"Who wants to know?"

"Me, primus, me," the young man said, his eyes taking in the rank on Titus's uniform. "Julius Fortinus. I come bearing words of wisdom from the great man himself. Can Trebo make it to the temple of tablets," he gestured across the street to the headquarters building, "or do I attend him here?"

"You'll see him here, unless you want to carry him over," Titus muttered, and gestured with his thumb. "He's the one facedown, with the beady black backbone."

"I thought that might be the way of it. How badly is he hurt?"

"Bad enough," Titus said, then added gruffly, "He'll make it if there's no infection."

Julius nodded, smiled again, and held up the jug. "Then this should help the cure."

"Or kill him."

The young man whistled low as he walked inside the building and circled Gaius's cot, then finally crouched down so the two of them were eye to eye. He raised the jug in a silent question. Gaius stared for a moment, then he gingerly shook his head and belched.

Julius twitched his nose in disgust, and waved his hand to clear the air. "I see you've been taking your medicine."

"I don't need another arsehole, " Gaius croaked, in no mood for humour. "Who are you, and what do you want?

Julius was not to be put off. "From the look of things, you came damned close to getting one. My name's Julius Fortinus. With the Twentieth."

"That answers the first question."

"Yes; well, Uncle sent me," Julius said, and looked up long enough to wave the two orderlies near the cot out of earshot. "The meat stitcher too, if you please," he added.

The surgeon raised his eyebrows, but moved off to attend the other wounded being offloaded from the ship.

Julius settled cross-legged on the floor, unsealed the jug, and took a deep swig. "It's late enough in the day, I suppose."

"Uncle who?"

"Petilius."

"Shit, just what I need." Gaius twitched and groaned, as much from annoyance as the pain. "Tell him his damned fortress might take a while."

"If you say so. Just as long as it's ready for all the nice soldiers by the end of summer. Got a site picked yet?"

Gaius tried to nod his head, but it didn't seem to want to obey. "Since you ask, yes, I have. I'll ask Tertius to take you there. Tomorrow, perhaps?"

Julius frowned as if considering the offer. "Mmm, perhaps not. Too busy." His voice dropped to a whisper. "Is there anything else you've got to tell him?"

"I just got here!"

"Just curious. Didn't really expect anything yet." Julius grinned, a disarming gesture that only made Gaius grunt in annoyance.

"Well, that's what you've got. Nothing!" Gaius muttered. "What did he tell you, anyway?"

"Pretty well everything," Julius replied, leaving the answer deliberately vague. "I was hoping to get here before you went upriver."

"You didn't miss anything."

"Oh, I probably did. It's supposed to be a secret for the moment, but Carta-what's-her-name is travelling with the Tungris. The ones you obviously didn't meet up with, because they are at Isurium, and you—"

"And I am here." Gaius frowned. "Cerialis is your uncle? Does that mean Vespasian is your …?"

"Grandfather?" Julius shrugged. "No. Wrong side of the family, unfortunately. Though on reflection, it's probably the safer side."

"And you came all the way here to tell me a barbarian queen is at Isurium? Why?"

"It's all part of a plan—her plan—to put herself back on the throne. Third time lucky, I guess." The grin appeared again.

"No." Gaius yawned. "What I meant is, why did Cerialis send you all the way here to tell me about Cartimandua? Doesn't make sense."

"He didn't. I think Mother—his sister, that is—told him to keep me out of trouble while I was getting the 'young tribune' stage of my life over and done with." Julius tried unsuccessfully to look disgusted about that. "Uncle sent me on a tour of the province so I could see everything for myself—to get me out of the way, I think. With a suitable escort, of course. I regret to tell you this, but you are only one item on a long list of instructions."

"That's nice." Gaius closed his eyes, grimacing as pain lanced down his back. The wine might not be a bad idea after all. "Was that it?"

"No, there's this," Julius said and stood to loop the leather pouch on a peg above the cot. "I suspect most of what's inside deals with what I've told you, but I wouldn't know that. There are a couple of words from your wife, though."

"That's wonderful." Gaius yawned again.

"Yeah. A new legate's been appointed for the Second Adiutrix. He should be here early summer, soon after the regiment arrives from Germania."

"That's also nice," Gaius sighed, and when there was no reply, he raised his eyes. "So?"

"So your wife's coming out to the province early this summer, travelling under his escort."

"Whaat? Arrrgh!" Gaius tried to jerk himself upright, but stopped short as a terrible pain again lanced down his back. "Shit! Shit, shit, shit!"

Julius backed away from the cot with a huge grin on his face, in no doubt about whether the cursing was due to the pain, or the fact that Gaius's wife was on her way to Britannia. "Uncle warned me you might say that."

Chapter IV

Elena was still fuming when Venutius left the lodge at daybreak the following morning. She stood in the doorway next to Cethen, glaring as the last of the king's warriors vanished into the woods. Her gaze shifted to the tiny village, where the kin moved sullenly among the huts, gathering what could be taken. Her eyes glinted with anger when they fell on the twins, bickering back and forth as they strapped the household bedding on one of the horses. She turned away.

"They'll burn the place, you know," she said, staring about the low, stone-walled room with its stripped bed frames, the strangely empty cooking area, and the cold grey ashes in the fire pit. It was home, and yet it already had a ransacked look. "Such a waste."

"They were going to destroy it anyway," Cethen muttered, tightening his belt buckle before heaving the battered shield onto his shoulder.

"We don't know that."

"They were going to build here, Elena. That means the entire village would be gone. This way, there may still be a chance they won't. We may have scared them off."

"Scared them off? Hah!" His wife's words were scornful. "We killed what, twenty, thirty Romans? You think that's going to frighten them? All we did was poke a stick in a nest of wasps. Cethen, if you're going to fight, you do it at a time and place that makes sense, when

71

you can rid the land of all of them! What's the point in trying to kill a few soldiers who come ahead of thousands? It's like kicking a bull in the balls!"

Cethen's voice rose in annoyance. "It has to start somewhere."

"What exactly has to start?" Elena persisted. "Instead or wandering north with our arses freezing, we should be holding a council to decide what's best. Dammit, that's what we agreed to do the night the old bugger got here, wasn't it? Sure, some of the younger ones would have gone north to fight. A few, maybe. Most would have stayed, though—I'm certain. Especially when they sobered up. Instead, that cunning old bastard gave us no choice. And you let him!"

"That's unfair," Cethen protested. "He's our king. And like you said, I had no choice."

"I'm not certain he's my king—and you didn't so much as say a word to stop it."

"I didn't know he'd sent for his men, did I? I was too busy freezing *my* balls off in the damned river."

"Saving Romans!"

"You just finished saying you didn't want them killed!" Cethen cried, and threw up his arms in frustration.

The bickering might have gone on, but Cethen stalked out of the lodge in search of his brother. Perhaps *he* might be more amiable company. It took some time to locate him, but he found him down by the Fosse, watering his horse. Cian, too, had decided that his wife was probably best left alone.

The Eburi caught up with Venutius late that afternoon at a small farmstead that lay a few miles south of Isurium, on the opposite side of the Abus. The ragtag force had followed lesser trails that wound their way a safe distance from the river, and were now scattered about a large, snow-dotted pasture carved out of the forest. Cethen decided the old man had not been exaggerating their numbers. There had to be a thousand or more gathered in the clearing, young and old, men and women, plus a good number of cattle, horses, and hounds.

The old king had spread the word that there would be no fires, and everyone should be ready to move after nightfall. He intended to creep past Isurium in the darkness, using the side trails that linked the farmsteads east of the small town. It was a good enough idea, Cethen thought, his confidence reinforced by the belief that Venutius knew what he was doing. So he sent Balor to see that Elena was coping with the three children, for he still wasn't up to finding out himself, and set out with Cian to find out what was happening.

The solitary farmstead stood at the far edge of the clearing, half hidden in the shelter of the forest. A wisp of smoke drifted lazily up from the roof. The pair found Venutius lounging inside with others of his tuath, comfortable and cross-legged by a large, blazing fire. Only Vellocatus looked up as they entered, offering the same mocking smile with which he had greeted them two days before. It was a veiled look, almost defensive, as if challenging anyone to question why he was there.

"You people are stopping early, aren't you?" Cethen asked, unconsciously using the word "you" rather than "we." As the day had worn on, plodding wearily northward along the slushy trail, he'd felt more and more divorced from Venutius's army of recruits.

"It seems the Romans have moved in on Isurium," Vellocatus explained. "We daren't move farther in daylight, so we'll *probably* start out as soon as it's dark."

Cethen shrugged, threw his cloak on the dirt floor, and sat down. Cian followed suit. They each grabbed a handful of bread and hard-rinded cheese that someone had spread on a cloth, close by the fire. It was probably his own anyway, he thought moodily as he filled his mouth. The two brothers eased their boots off with sighs of relief and placed them close to the flames. They soon reeked with the fetid odour of dank duck down, but no more so than a dozen others already set there.

"So why 'probably'?" Cethen asked quietly.

"Some of the chiefs think we should attack, " Vellocatus replied.

"And Venutius?" Cian asked, his bare feet steaming with warmth as he stretched his legs toward the flames.

"He's wavering. He wants to get these people to Stannick and keep the buildup going. In truth, the fortress there isn't as far along as he would like. On the sharper edge of the blade, he hates to miss a chance."

"Do tell," Cian remarked dryly.

"Cethen! What do you think? You know this area."

Venutius called the question from across the fire and Cethen, his thoughts devoted more than anything to getting warmth into his icy feet, looked up in surprise. He countered with a question of his own, vaguely hoping it fit with the discussion. "How many Romans are there?"

"That's the problem, we don't know," Venutius replied, his tone impatient. "That's why we were discussing a scouting party, to find out exactly what's there. You'll go, of course."

It was a statement, not a question, and Cethen cursed under his breath, even as he heard himself say, "Of course. When do we leave?"

"As soon as it's dark. Vellocatus, you'll want to go too, I suppose."

Again, it was a statement, not a question. The only response was a lean, wolfish grin that Venutius took as assent, nodding his satisfaction. Vellocatus glanced sideways, and Cethen found a warm trace of kinship. The mocking eyes revealed the same lukewarm enthusiasm that he felt.

"Er ...um, sir?"

All eyes turned to Cian, who had raised his hand to draw attention. "I'd like to go too."

As the long shadows of evening turned to night, the air grew colder. The order against fires seemed less important, and the warm smoke curling from the farmstead roof had not gone unnoticed. A score or more fires blazed cheerily about the clearing, and a low haze of grey smoke hung in the air, along with the crisp aroma of roasting meat. Cethen sat on a log beside the fire that warmed the Eburi kin, pondering how to break the word to Elena that, for the moment, the family would continue on to Stannick by itself. Matters had been cool enough since he had returned from the hut; they would now either grow cooler, or quickly flare.

"You heard that the women and children are moving on after dark?" he began, tugging at the long tendrils of his moustache.

"You told me," she said, and looked at him sharply, as if recognizing his tone. "You also said that most of the warriors were staying behind. To guard the women and children as they pass Isurium."

"Mmm."

"To protect poor, defenseless souls like me, if I recall," she added dryly, when Cethen gave no further response.

"Mmm," Cethen mumbled again, and wondered why, when a man had something to tell a woman that she wouldn't like, he stepped around it as if it were a sleeping bear—even when he had the right of it!

Elena stood up and began pushing the pots and the leftovers into a large pack strapped to one of the horses. Cethen rose too and began pacing. As usual, she solved the problem for him.

"So what does that oaf have you doing, that you don't want to tell me?"

"Oaf? Who?"

Elena's glare could have ripped the horns off a charging bull. Cethen decided there was no further gain in dithering—as if there ever had been. "Oh, Venutius," he said, as if finally understanding the question. "Nothing much, really. As I said, we're sending the women and children ahead. Keeping those at the rear who can fight and protect them. We don't know how many Romans are at Isurium. Venutius is just being careful."

"That's certainly a change for the better. Yesterday he didn't give a pile of pig shit about careful, especially when it came to us. And you still haven't answered my question."

"Oh," Cethen again feigned surprise. "Well, there's supposed to be a small party going across the river. To see what strength the Romans have." He waited for the expected tirade, but none seemed forthcoming. Instead, Rhun and Coira tugged at his clothing.

"Can we come too, Da?"

Much to their annoyance, their father bent over and held them both in a long, close bear hug. "You two stay here and look after your little brother. And your mam. I'll catch up with all of you before morning."

"Mam will look after me," Tuis sniffed indignantly from beside the warm coals. "They're too young."

"Always the boy." Cethen smiled and ruffled the lad's dark, tangled hair.

Elena took advantage of her son's comment. "Your mam may have to do that, my lad," she said, and glared at her husband for a moment, then sighed hopelessly. "Oh, Cethen, be careful."

She pushed the twins gently aside, and pulled his face down to meet hers. They stood, locked in embrace, while the children growled their embarrassment and looked elsewhere. When she pushed him away, her eyes were moist. "And don't get lost. Now bugger off, your friends are coming."

Vellocatus had ridden up with two others trailing close behind, the man called Dermat and another he named as Ebric. The pair nodded silently, and quietly sat their small horses, each eyeing Cethen with much the same caution as he eyed them. Ebric, like his companion, was small and hard-muscled. The two might have been brothers, about the same middling age as Vellocatus, with hair greying at the temples. But that didn't soften the aura of menace that clung to either one, each armed with sword and dagger, and riding a horse bare of its saddle.

"By the curly hairs of Dagda," Elena muttered, as she saw Cian approaching. "He's going too? Now I am worried."

Cethen's brother rode the same animal he'd almost ruined the day before, and was fully armed with shield, spear, helmet, and sword. Cethen swung up onto his own horse, his best animal, an ageing gelding called Flint. He growled at Cian, "If you're coming, shut up. Don't speak unless spoken to. And get rid of the extra iron. It's noisy. We're hiding, not leading a parade." He kneed Flint ahead without waiting for a reply, following the other three as they disappeared into the darkening forest.

They would have to cross the Abus, and a guide had been found to lead them to a place where the riverbank ran low. The small, cowled figure stood on the path, half hidden in the shadows of the trees, and they followed the spirit-like shape along a winding trail better suited to deer than horses. The forest itself was as dark as jet and Cethen soon felt hopelessly lost, but the guide soon led them to another clearing, a small field fenced for pasture. A quarter moon broke through the thin blanket of clouds, offering light enough to see the black outline of the river. The riders dismounted and walked their horses to the bank, where they stood eyeing the cold, forbidding current.

"Freeze your balls off, huh?" Cian whispered cheerily, and Cethen growled.

Dermat and Ebric wordlessly removed their cloaks, placing them carefully on the ground where the long grass had outpaced the snow. They removed their boots, weapons, and everything else they wore, tossing it all onto their cloak to make a bundle. The two brothers did the same, and soon they were all naked and shivering, tottering on the makeshift packs in a vain attempt to at least keep their feet warm.

Vellocatus spent an interminable length of time speaking to the guide, who from time to time pointed to the moon, the river, and the opposite bank. He finally seemed satisfied, and began to disrobe. Their silent escort turned to go, but not before standing insolently in front of the four naked warriors, inspecting them slowly, one at a time.

"See something you like, fellow?" Ebric growled and moved forward, his voice full of menace.

Dermat laid a restraining hand on his shoulder and the dark figure threw back its cowl, revealing the amused features of a young girl, barely into her teens. Cethen instinctively dropped his hands, acutely aware that his shrunken manhood was seeking refuge behind his belly button.

"Seen much better in the hog barn—fellow!" the girl jeered, and quickly fled back along the trail, giggling as she vanished into the night.

"Women!" Ebric grumbled, setting the bundle atop his horse before swinging onto its back.

Cethen did the same, glad of the warm feel of the animal's back, then, as the others moved forward, he dug his heels into its belly. The small horses moved nervously to the edge of the river and, one after another, stepped reluctantly into the icy current. The water rose quickly to chest level. Each man held his bundle high with one hand, and clung to the animal's mane with the other. The short swim seemed to take forever, but finally they lurched onto the far bank, teeth chattering, and shivering like wind-blown aspen. Quickly dismounting, each of them raced to pull on the dry clothes that had magically taken on a warmth of their own.

Still trembling from the cold, but not ready to climb back onto wet horses, they followed Vellocatus along a trail that ran alongside the river. Each man led his horse in an eerie, plodding silence, until the track opened onto yet another small meadow. The stale, ashy odour of old smoke filled the air as they crunched across the field of crisping snow. The dim shape of a hut appeared, nestled gloomily in the dark cover of the forest.

"A man sneaking about attracts nothing but attention," Vellocatus murmured, and moved boldly toward the hovel.

"What else would he do if he's spying?" Ebric demanded.

"He might walk about as if he lives here, and has nothing to hide," Vellocatus replied. "We do, after all, belong here. Though I think to-night, we might do better as hewers of wood. I don't feel like climbing on a freezing wet horse."

The hut was surrounded by a cluster of small sheds and the stink of hogs. As they drew near, the hounds began baying the alarm, the loud growls quickly turning to howls. Vellocatus ignored the yapping animals as they plunged out to greet him, and pulled his horse over to a lean-to that protected a large stack of firewood. He motioned Ebric to the hut, but the door opened before he could get there.

A squat, brawny, balding man glared at them. He was naked, except for a cloth wrapped around his groin that looked filthy even in the darkness. He gripped a long cudgel in one fist. "What you want?" he demanded.

"To fairly gain some of your woodpile," Vellocatus said. "Also your silence."

"Huh?"

"We're going to buy some wood, and you keep yer gob shut," Dermat growled.

The man frowned and considered the statement. "How much?" he finally asked.

Vellocatus turned to the others. "How much coin do you have?" he hissed.

A chorus of protests arose. Nobody admitted to having any.

"Cethen, you got the gold coin from Venutius. Give him that," Dermat said.

"For a pile of wood? That's madness. Anyway, Elena has it. Honest."

"Women," Ebric muttered.

"Shut up, and dig deep," Vellocatus snarled. "I don't want to leave ill will behind us when we go from here. Not unless I have to. I prefer to let the Romans do that."

Everyone reluctantly searched through the pouches hanging from their belts. The result, or at least the admitted result, was one small silver coin, and a half dozen of alloyed lead, all Roman. The foreign currency was in common use because of its value with the traders, who preferred it to the mixture of iron bars and trinkets often used by the Britons. To someone like the burly pig farmer it was hard to value, though, and he stared dubiously at the handful of coins, biting his lip. The silver one was no longer among them.

"The coins are worth far more than a few bundles of wood," Vellocatus snarled, moving forward to tower over the man. "I suggest you take it."

The man made up his mind and reached for the money, but instead found a clenched hand.

"And rope. To secure the loads."

A grimy finger pointed reluctantly to the larger of the sheds.

"And a word as to what is happening up here. The Romans, for example."

The pig farmer shrugged. "They've been here five or six days. They're building a camp where they dug the field out when they marched through here ten years ago. Up by where the river curves. This time, they plan on staying."

"And what makes you think that?"

"'Cause they brought an army of wagons with them. And they brought the bitch queen, too."

Vellocatus started as if stung by a wasp. "She's here?"

"I seen her come. With the Romans." He raised the cudgel and pointed off into the darkness. "They rode right past, on't main road."

"How many Romans?"

"Thousands of them." The man gestured clumsily with his free arm. "Like ants on honey. As I said, they're building summat. I think it's one of them ...er ..." He struggled for the word.

"A fort?"

The man beamed, and when Vellocatus made to open his palm he twitched, but the hand closed again as a final question occurred. "The bitch queen, as you so quaintly call her. Do you know where she stays?"

"In Maeldav's house. The big one of stone. Where else?" The man seemed surprised.

Satisfied, Vellocatus finally unclenched his fist and the coins disappeared as if by magic, as did the pig farmer himself. The door slammed shut, and the five were left with nothing more to look at than the moist clouds of breath blowing from their mouths.

Loading the firewood did not take long. The small train of animals moved off into the darkness, and were soon on the well-used trail that led to Isurium. Cethen and Vellocatus took the lead. The five horses, roped together and loaded with wood, hung their heads and plodded behind as if shamed. Cian, appearing equally disgruntled, walked alongside the rear animal to goad it on. Dermat and Ebric melted into the night with orders to keep pace in the darkness.

Vellocatus trudged along as if preoccupied, and Cethen sensed it had to do with the word that his wife, the so called "bitch queen," was close by. He knew that the woman, as was her right, had divorced Venutius, and taken up with the man who now walked beside him. But Vellocatus, in turn, had left her, to return to his former king. Or at least he had until a few moments ago, and Cethen grew uneasy with the thoughts that were forming in his mind.

"So, on what terms did you leave her?" he finally ventured.

"Huh?"

Cethen knew he had been heard, but repeated the question. Vellocatus chuckled quietly before he spoke. "I told her I was going hunting."

Cethen laughed too. "Really?"

"Uh-huh."

"How long ago was that?"

"Oh, about a month or two ago. Probably three, now. Maybe more."

Cethen let it hang for a moment, then said, "I suppose if we could find a dead deer somewhere …?"

Vellocatus laughed and his brooding mood seemed to break, though for a while neither spoke. They plodded along the trail side by side, feet crunching on the freezing mud. Cethen hobbled slightly, his limp a vague inconvenience, not hurting, but the flesh in his thigh was twisted enough to turn each step awkward. He was curious about Cartimandua, as were all in the kin, and he wanted to hear more. After a while, his patience was rewarded. As if speaking to himself, Vellocatus began telling of her choppy marriage to the ageing king.

The match had been doomed from the start, he said, a matter of political convenience. It was not the love match the Brigantes loved to hear of in their songs. It was a contract, meant to bind the people: he from the rolling reaches of the north, she from the wooded lowlands of the south where Rome, in many ways, was now the closest neighbour.

In one manner the pair had been matched, Vellocatus suggested, though Venutius was a good ten or fifteen years older. They were both stubborn and forceful, but there it ended. His nature was bold, and impulsive to the point of recklessness. Hers was controlled, a finely balanced web of deviousness—or diplomacy, as she liked to call it. They had first lived together at Stannick, at a time when the fortress was strengthened following the Roman crossing from Gaul. It was her dealings, her compromises with those same Romans, that had jammed in the old king's throat. Vellocatus added, with a low chuckle, that two stubborn tempers hadn't helped.

"It really made his piss boil when they rode through here as if they owned the place. He fought back several times, little fights here and there, like picking at a sore until it bleeds. But she always managed to keep the 'pax,' as the Romans called it." Vellocatus shook his head as he remembered. "The first time they put her back on the throne, Venutius came back. But it didn't last long. The thing with Caradoc was what finally cut the rope that bound them."

"That's what they say," Cethen said carefully, surprised at the candour. Then he gleefully remembered Elena's words. "Was that before you and she ...you know ..."

"Not exactly." Vellocatus chuckled again, as he confessed. "He was always gone, and he certainly wasn't leading a gelding's life himself. Catey's a robust woman."

"But he did leave her?" Cethen asked, feeling a trace of satisfaction.

"Well, she was the one who left Stannick, which is where he was. I went with her. But she had to leave, because there was no way she could stay. So who left who? And what does it matter? She took some of his kin south with her, as hostages. Venutius was out hunting." Vellocatus laughed at the ironic parallel to his own excuse.

"I see," Cethen said, mulling over the words. There was the other thing, though, and that truly bothered him. There would be no better time to find out. "What made you stay? Later. When she—you know, the Caradoc thing."

"You mean how could I stay loyal to the woman I was ploughing, when she turned in the hero who'd fought the Romans? And after he almost won!"

"Well ..."

Vellocatus mused over the question, then, as if ignoring it altogether, said, "She was kin to Caradoc, you know."

"Uh-huh," Cethen replied noncommittally. He hadn't known that.

"Did you know he's still alive?"

Cethen was startled. "He is?"

"Oh, yes. And all his family. They live somewhere close to Rome. A pensioned trophy to the city's glory. A living monument to the prowess of Claudius, though the drooling fart's long since dead. Don't you find that strange? That he was allowed to live?"

"Shit, I didn't know he did live. I thought he was, well ..."

"Think about it, Cethen. He comes to his kinfolk for help. She turns him in, and he lives. After littering the countryside with Roman dead. How many others has that happened to?"

Vellocatus sliced a hand across his throat in answer to his own question.

Cethen pondered the words for a good while before he finally spoke. "And you and her?"

"Me? I was in lust with Catey long before the Caradoc thing. So, when she let Venutius know he was divorced for good, one thing followed another, though not necessarily in that order."

"That doesn't bother Venutius today?"

"Why should it? As I said, his marriage was an agreement."

"But you were his shield bearer. His friend."

"And I still am," Vellocatus said cheerfully. "I didn't betray him. At least, not any more than he did her. And we go back a long time, Catey and I. Were it not for the pact, it might have been me she married. I owed a loyalty to her, long before I owed him."

"Then why are you returning?" Cethen asked boldly.

"Because this time the Romans are invading Brigantia in full force, and for good. No tribesman can stand idly by while that happens. But there's another reason, too. This time, I think we might win."

"Oh?"

"Look, before this, we never learned to fight like the Romans. Or build. That's all I'll say on the matter. When we reach Stannick, you'll see."

Cethen pondered the comment as they plodded along the widening trail. The black trees that hemmed them in had begun to thin, and through the dim, snow-lit gloom, he glimpsed several small farmsteads. From time to time yapping dogs announced their passing, a restless chorus taken up by hounds farther along the trail. There was no such thing as complete surprise in Brigantia, but the yapping was a two-edged sword. It also warned those who wandered the night of what lay ahead.

Cethen was curious about what Elena's queen was really like and chanced the question, since Vellocatus seemed willing to talk.

"She can be a bitch sometimes," Vellocatus replied, again with a chuckle, "but she can also be …" His voice faded, swallowed by the pounding of hooves, many of them, rapidly approaching from behind. "Keep your head bowed," he called back to Cian and, without waiting for a reply, led the small string of animals off to the side of the trail.

A column of Roman cavalry loomed out of the dark, splattering past at a slow canter. Dark, silent, self-absorbed men, armed with great oval shields and long spears, all clad in chain armour, helmets, and cloaks. They thundered on, perhaps close to three score in all, ignoring the still, bent forms of the three woodcutters. Close to their base, with the promise of a hot meal and a good drink, the troopers were plainly impatient.

The damp thud of the hooves quickly faded into the night and, other than a clinging film of mud and slush, the three might never have known the troop had passed by. They moved quietly back onto the trail, still tense, but silently congratulating themselves that the danger was past. For a while, they plodded on in silence.

"So what is she like?" Cian finally called from beside the last horse, no longer able to contain himself.

Vellocatus turned, surprised their conversation had carried that far. He looked annoyed. "As I said, she can be a bit of a bitch sometimes, but that's no concern of yours. If you're ever unfortunate enough to meet the woman, then you can ..."

His voice again faded as the rhythmic thud of more hooves drifted from behind, though not the same, heavy pounding as before. Once more the three moved to the side of the trail, heads held low. This time the Romans passed at a slow, laboured trot, and there were only four. The last animal was lame in the rear quarter, its rider paired up behind one of the other troopers.

At first it appeared that they would carry on, but the man riding double muttered something, and the others reined in and turned about. They halted, the horses panting a steaming mist, and stared silently at the small pack train, and the dark, hooded figures of the three Britons. The injured animal, glad of the chance to rest, lifted its hoof gingerly from the mud, shook its head, and whinnied.

Its owner slid to the ground, stamped his feet, and walked over to Vellocatus and Cethen. Other than a quick glance in their direction, he barely looked. The horses held his interest. He called to the others in a dialect Cethen could not understand, and the three Romans kneed their mounts forward for a closer look. The two Britons nervously moved back, hemmed in against the wood-laden animals.

Vellocatus bobbed his head and, speaking a deliberately broken

84

Latin, told the riders they were woodcutters from Isurium, and mumbled excuses for their lateness. The man's eyes ignored him, slowly surveying the horse from tail to head, falling finally on the bridle. It was a fancy piece, made of ornate, carved leather, inlaid with brass. It did not belong on a pack animal. Cethen gulped at the foolishness that had caused them to leave it there, but Vellocatus was ready with the answer. The animal belonged to Cartimandua herself, he said, as the Roman leaned over to feel the leatherwork. The man's other hand moved to rest on the hilt of his sword.

Vellocatus switched to his own tongue, with no change in the wheedling tone he had used with the Romans. "I think we're in trouble. When I move, take the one on the left. Unhorse him."

"My sword—" Cethen muttered.

"Use your knife, there's no time," Vellocatus growled softly, but even as he spoke, two of the riders reined their horses backward, suspicion on their faces.

Vellocatus moved briefly away from the trooper fondling the bridle, then whirled, his right hand thumping sharply up under the man's chin. The Roman uttered a gurgling scream and crumpled, the faint outline of a knife blade glittering briefly in the darkness. Stunned, Cethen didn't move; things were happening too fast.

Vellocatus dropped to his knees and lunged up between the nearest two horses, causing both to shy and throwing their riders off balance. He leapt forward and grasped them by the loose chain tunics they wore, pulling both to the ground.

"The other one. Get the other one, dammit!" he cried.

The fourth rider was already jerking savagely on the reins. The horse pranced nervously sideways. The man's sword slid out, shining dully in the moonlight, and his mouth opened in an angry cry. Cethen glanced down at his knife, which looked like a toothpick in his big hands, and turned to run behind the packed horse in search of his sword. The trooper kicked his heels, and the animal plunged forward. Cian chose the moment to strike.

Cethen had forgotten his brother, and the fourth rider had missed him completely. Running forward and leaping into the air, Cian grabbed the Roman around the waist. One hand clasped a dagger and it plunged downward, ripping into the Roman's thigh, more by accident than intent. The man howled and twisted sharply in the saddle, causing Cian to slip forward across the bleeding leg. The trooper brought the hilt of his sword down, catching Cian squarely behind the ear. With a grunt of pain, he slid down the side of the prancing horse and fell unconscious onto the muddy trail.

"Stupid ass!" Cethen cried, his voice full of anguish as he fumbled vainly for the sword.

The trooper regained control of his horse, and once more hefted his sword. The look on his face turned to triumph, as he again raised his heels. This time Cethen fought the urge to turn and run, and crouched low, the small dagger feeling useless in his hand. The Roman thumped both feet downward, and the horse lunged forward. The man's legs promptly flew in the air, and he somersaulted backward over the animal's hindquarters. The sword arced off into the night.

The horse fled blindly past Cethen, revealing Ebric standing in the trail, the hem of the rider's cloak gripped firmly in both hands. The Roman lay winded at his feet, which perhaps was just as well, for Ebric looked to be in no fit condition to do anything, he was laughing so hard.

"Did you ever see the like?" he finally crowed. "Who was more surprised? You or him?"

Cethen, his mind catching up with his heartbeat, merely scowled. Then he remembered what else was going on and turned to help Vellocatus, but Dermat was already there. Two bodies lay in the snow alongside the trail while the third, the Roman who had first walked over to look at the horses, writhed on the ground, a black stream pulsing from under his chin. Dermat leaned over and casually slit the man's throat.

The blood was up in all of them and took a while to settle. Cian groaned his way to semiconsciousness and dragged himself over to sit on one of the dead Romans. He leaned forward moaning, his head cradled in both hands as the others made sure that each knew exactly what Vellocatus had done.

The deed was a glorious one, one that could be told again and again. Three at once, for Dermat graciously admitted that his presence hadn't really been necessary, which Vellocatus denied, stating that without it, things would surely have been in the balance. No one but Cethen had seen Ebric's hand in the sudden charge by the fourth cavalryman, so he gladly spoke of it, making sure to draw out the hilarious conclusion. Ebric stood with his head bent to one side in modest pride, grinning, yet still hanging firmly to the hem of the fallen trooper's cloak. Nobody saw fit to comment on Cethen's ineptness, and he certainly did not.

The fourth trooper was on his knees, struggling for breath. He was plastered with mud, and blood seeped freely from the wound in his thigh. His head hung forward as if in resignation; the man plainly expected the worst. Vellocatus walked over and, using the flat of his bloody blade, lifted the fellow's chin. The trooper wasn't much more than a youth, his face soft and unlined, his long moustache thin and silky.

"You are Roman auxiliary. Where are you from?" This time Vellocatus's Latin was deliberate and precise.

The man looked defiant, yet unsure. The knife twisted enough that the blade dug in. "You will kill me anyway," the trooper mumbled, glancing involuntarily at the bodies of his companions.

"Perhaps. Perhaps not. Where are you from?"

Both men spoke slowly and Cethen found himself able to follow parts of it, for more than a few words of bastardized Latin had been gained from the traders.

The Roman shrugged as if deciding there was always hope, and his information was probably no great secret anyway. "Tungri. From across the sea."

Vellocatus nodded as if he knew where the Tungri came from. "How many?"

The man at first did not answer. Vellocatus applied more pressure to the blade, forcing his head backward. The long, bare throat showed pale and vulnerable in the darkness.

"Six troops. You saw two of them."

"What else is up there?" Vellocatus nodded toward Isurium.

"A cohort. From the Ninth legion."

"Full strength?"

The man made to nod, but flinched as his chin met the blade. "Almost," he whispered hoarsely. "Really."

Vellocatus frowned as his mind absorbed the information, before translating it to numbers for the others. "There's up to a hundred and eighty cavalry, and about four hundred and fifty infantry from the legion itself. That confirms the pig farmer's bit about building. That's probably why they've brought her with them. They do mean to stay."

No one asked who "her" was. Vellocatus had another question, though, one that had also picked at Cethen's curiosity. "Why did you attack us?" he asked. "The bridle?"

The Tungri appeared puzzled. "You attacked us."

"Because you were going to do it first." Vellocatus withdrew the knife.

The man shook his head, protesting, "We were not!"

"Then why did you stop? Why did you crowd in on us like that?"

"We were looking at your horses." His eyes shifted to one of the bodies on the ground. "Him there. Crom. The one riding double. His animal was lame. Your animals looked to be good ones. He thought the—the troop's—horse buyer?"

Vellocatus nodded his understanding as the man struggled with the words.

"That he might buy the horses. We are short, and—" The Tungri's eyes momentarily lost their fear as he understood what had taken place, and he shook his head. "Balls!"

The revelation started them all talking at once. Each found it amusing except Cian, who clutched his temples as he sat on the dead man's chest, groaning. Nobody was upset that a mistake had been made. The riders were their enemy, and were now dead; the mistake simply added to the telling of the tale. And most important, they had the information they'd been sent to get: five or six hundred Romans were at Isurium, far too many to attack.

Ebric and Dermat prepared to return to Venutius. Cian, still cradling his head, didn't seem to care where he went. It was the sensible thing to do, Cethen thought, for they had the information they needed. In addition, they'd gained four good horses as loot, presuming the lame one could be treated, and whatever could be plundered from the Tungri themselves. And above all, there was a glorious story to be told.

But Vellocatus had his mind set elsewhere. "Dermat, Ebric, hide these bodies, then return to Venutius." He nodded toward the Tungri kneeling at his feet. "Take him with you. There's information in his head that might be of use. If he gives trouble, kill him; if he doesn't die on you first."

He glanced down at Cian. "And you?" The response was a pitiful groan, and Vellocatus's teeth shone white in the gloom as he looked to Dermat. "Take this one too. Don't let him bring up the rear, though. You might lose him, and never know it." He then turned to Cethen. "I don't think I'm going back with them. Not for a day or two, anyway. One horse loaded with firewood should do as well as five, I think—or should we make it two?"

The question was a challenge, one made in front of both Ebric and Dermat, and Cethen cursed the unfairness of it. Despite the darkness, he could almost see the mocking leer in Vellocatus's eyes as he waited for an answer—or was it simply the tone of his voice? Whatever it was, he had no choice. Oh, there was the curiosity about the so-called bitch queen, but dammit, he wasn't that inquisitive.

"We'd better change the bridles for halters this time," he heard himself mutter, then he gestured toward the captive. "It also wouldn't hurt if we knew more about where we're going."

The trail climbed as the Tungri said it would, leading inland from where the river changed course and curved west. The forest grew sparse as the land rose, and when they abandoned the cover of the trees altogether, it was to see the warm glow of fires in the darkness ahead. Without hesitation, Vellocatus made his way toward them. He insisted on speaking normally as they trudged at the head of the two plodding animals. It was the natural thing to do, he reasoned, and Cethen nervously complied, though forever after he would never remember a word of what was said.

When they drew close to the camp, he could see that the Romans had not only built the dirt ramparts of their fort, timber palisades also had been placed along the top. Cethen thought it was incredible, for they could only have been there a matter of days. Vellocatus observed that the Roman stronghold was set farther back from the river than others he'd seen elsewhere. He suggested it might be because the village, a market centre and large by Brigante standards, was already sited there. If the Tungri had spoken the truth, the fair-sized stone lodge that stood close by the entrance to the camp belonged to Maeldav.

Cethen had no desire to meet up with the chieftain to whom he owed allegiance. It wasn't for any particular reason other than he simply detested the man—a fat, overbearing lout who had bred two sons, each promising to follow in his father's fat, overbearing footsteps. Yet there was satisfaction to be found in the fact that Cartimandua had taken over his lodge. It probably meant Maeldav had been displaced, and forced to settle for lesser quarters.

They were nearing the dark outline of the stone lodge when, for the third time that night, they heard the pounding hooves. Cethen felt his heart sink. They were so close. "There's no place to hide," he said, louder than intended.

"Just keep going," Vellocatus hissed. "Pull over to the side, as far as you can."

They counted eight riders, several dragging extra mounts behind. Most were auxiliary troopers, but two wore the plated armour of the legions. They rode to the gate of the fort, where they were briefly challenged before disappearing inside.

"The Tungri lied," Cethen growled. "He didn't tell us they had legion cavalry here."

"Nor do they," Vellocatus said.

"So what are they, then—the faerie?"

"Cethen, look and learn. Those men are probably running messages." Vellocatus spoke like a tired druid instructing a novice. "The legions don't have any great amount of cavalry; they rely on auxiliaries such as the Tungri. They keep only enough riders for their own needs—dispatches, escorts, and the like."

Cethen looked at him suspiciously. "How do you know so much about the Romans?"

"So you have doubts about me, too, do you?" Vellocatus stopped and faced him, his expression serious. "Think what you will, but know your enemy, Cethen Lamh-fada. He certainly knows you. It has forever been our weakness not to know him, and thus not learn."

Cethen felt chastened, but not completely. They'd skirmished with the Romans before, sometimes successfully, sometimes not. His limp came from one of the latter encounters. "And that brings success?" he asked doubtfully.

Vellocatus snorted, and resumed his steady plodding. "No, but as sure as Lug himself has three faces to greet each day, it decreases the chance of failure."

In the short time it took to reach the compound that surrounded Maeldav's lodge, Cethen listened and grew a little wiser in the ways of the legions. The one claim he refused to accept, though, was what Vellocatus cynically described as the Romans' greatest advantage in battle: the warlike temperament of the Britons themselves.

They were challenged at the entrance to Maldaev's compound, a double gate cut to the height of a tall man. One side was open, guarded by a half squad of Roman regulars. The decanus demanded they identify themselves; but a young, bearded man, lounging with several others around an open fire close inside the walls, climbed languidly to his feet and called for attention.

"That's Criff," Vellocatus whispered to Cethen, as the decanus turned. "Among other things, he plays the role of Catey's bard."

"I know this man," the man said, and sauntered over to the gate.

"Hey, Criff, " Vellocatus roared. "I need to unload this wood."

"Where have you been, you useless tits?" Criff called back, glaring at Vellocatus. "Get in here. You'll be lucky if she doesn't have your backs bruised."

Satisfied, the decanus stepped aside. Vellocatus and Cethen led the packed horses through the gateway and followed Criff to the rear of the lodge. Once out of sight, Vellocatus and Criff clasped each other in a bear hug.

The older man mussed the younger's hair. "I'll be lucky if it's only my back that gets bruised," he suggested wryly, nodding toward the lodge.

"You'll be lucky if your oysters aren't nailed to the doorpost." Criff grinned.

Cethen stared about the moonlit compound as the two men talked, surprised at its size. The shuffle of hooves and the muffled munching of hay was that of a good many animals, somewhere further back in the darkness of their pens. And at least half a dozen outbuildings showed dark against the skyline. Another, smaller fire burned at the rear of the stockade.

A young lad appeared from nowhere, and took the horses. "Stack the wood, and see they're fed," Criff ordered, then gestured to the lodge with a grin. "Let's go in the back door. Spies don't use the front."

Vellocatus shoved the young man playfully on the shoulder, and he pretended to stagger toward an open door in the lodge's rear wall through which beckoned a soft, orange glow. They pushed past a boy carrying slops and trudged into a warm kitchen area, where two women were clearing the remains of the evening meal. They both looked up and smiled.

"You're back," said the older of the two, a plump, mousey-haired woman, obviously pleased to see Vellocatus.

He patted his chest, as if surprised. "So I am!"

"Fool. Are you hungry?"

He feigned innocence. "Hungry? For what?"

The woman laughed. "If it's not for food, then it's not me you're wanting." She inclined her head toward a door that led deeper into the building.

"Anyone with her?"

"The last time I looked, it was just her and her women. And Criff. But I see he's with you now."

"What's going on out there?" Vellocatus nodded in the general direction of the Roman camp.

The woman shrugged. "Still building, I suppose. A young Roman officer and two of his men were here earlier, but they left—as soon as they could. In fact, I think they retreated." She laughed again, her expression amused as she waited to see what Vellocatus was going to do.

"Then lets face the dragon queen together." Vellocatus rolled his eyes upward as he turned to Cethen and, grabbing his sleeve, pulled him toward the inner door.

But he paused before pushing it open, then turned and retraced his steps, a huge grin on his face. He lifted a pair of gutted hares from a wooden peg, where they hung ripening against the coolness of the stone wall. "Not exactly a deer, but they'll do," he said, with a chuckle.

All three quietly entered the living area, a large, open-beamed room lit by a dozen red-clay oil lamps. A woman of middle years sat quietly on a padded leather stool near the centre. Two others fussed on either side, one bathing her feet and the second combing her hair. A fourth woman stood piling freshly washed clothing on a low, richly carved side table. Criff walked past them all, quietly humming a funeral dirge, his lips curved in amusement. The bard dropped down next to the fire, and picked up a harp that lay close by the hearth. He seemed to make a point of keeping his head down as he tuned it.

"Hello, dear heart." Vellocatus almost sang the words, holding the hares up high by their ears. Cethen saw that he wore his usual mocking smile, and wondered if he even knew it was there. "I'm home from the hunt."

The woman hesitated but a moment, then grabbed the comb from her maid and flung it hard. It was a silver piece, studded with coloured glass, and looked heavy enough to be lethal. Vellocatus ducked. It flew past his head, and crashed somewhere inside the kitchen.

Criff stirred, his fingers sliding pleasantly across the strings. "Welcome home, Vell. Welcome home."

"Thanks, Criff," Vellocatus said, then to nobody in particular, "Er, this is Cethen. Of the Eburi. From farther downriver. He's—well, I suppose he's a fellow hunter."

"Then he's a damned poor one," Cartimandua snapped, staring at Cethen, her eyes icily appraising him. "The clod can't even catch a rabbit."

Cethen switched his gazed uncomfortably to the rafters. Cartimandua waved the woman away from her feet, and slipped a pair of red leather sandals over her painted toes. She rose from the chair and padded like a cat over to Vellocatus, stopping a half pace away. She stared up at him with lips pursed, her expression as brittle as flint. Her husband slowly wilted under her gaze, and he wet his lips as if to speak; but her hand shot out like a striking adder and grabbed his scrotum. With gritted teeth, she squeezed—hard.

Cethen winced as Vellocatus gasped and doubled forward, but Cartimandua held firm to his shoulder with her free arm. The tearful grunt seemed to satisfy, though, for she smiled, and just as quickly released her grip. Slowly raising the same hand, she lifted his chin until they once more stared into each other's eyes. His were moist; hers were twinkling.

"I missed you, louse," she whispered, and kissed him.

Her mood shifted. She spun about and walked to a side table that held four goblets and a tall, fluted jug of wine. Each piece was of a pale, misty green glass and Cethen was awed, for he'd never seen such fragile pieces. While she poured the ruby liquid, he glanced furtively about the large room and saw the presence of Rome everywhere. For a moment he wondered if the wealth of goods belonged to Maeldav, then remembered the man preferred to count his coin rather than spend it. His eyes returned to Cartimandua.

She handed one of the goblets to Vellocatus, who took it with one hand while gently soothing the pain in his crotch with the other. As if in afterthought, she nodded permission to Cethen to pour one for himself, then ignored him.

"So how is my first husband?" she demanded of Vellocatus. "Still fighting a lost cause?"

"How would I know? I was hunting."

Her laugh was derisive. "Of course you were. And I was out slaughtering Romans. Where is the madman? He must be close, if you've chosen to visit me. Or are you back to stay?"

"For a little while."

"How little is little?"

She turned and sat on one of several lounges that bordered the stone walls, raising her legs so they stretched luxuriously along its length. She wore a long, emerald robe that she coyly draped to cover her legs, and even her toes. Cethen decided that, for her age, the woman looked damned good. A few years older and she might well have been his mother, yet her figure rivalled that of Elena, and her black, silky hair, while turning grey, glistened like that of a young woman.

"A day or two. Perhaps three?" Vellocatus shrugged. "Perhaps tomorrow morning, if you prefer."

Cethen vaguely wondered if that mocking, knowing smile was his appeal.

"Or maybe tonight," Cartimandua mused, then with a sigh turned to the bard, idly plucking his harp by the fire. "Criff, why don't you and our other fearless hunter find something to do? Go and amuse the Romans, perhaps."

Cethen blinked. Dismissed! Just like that. Yet when he thought on it, he was relieved rather than annoyed. The woman was overpowering.

Criff simply grinned, as if expecting the casual ejection. Rising lithely from the warmth of the fire, he strolled into the kitchen. Cethen followed. On reflection, he would have been quite content to sit by the fire, unnoticed, for as long as it took; but then, he supposed, what did it matter? The quick glass of wine had settled on his belly, and he was suddenly hungry. A meaty lamb bone vanished from its hook as they passed through the back door.

Instead of taking Cethen somewhere to wait, or at least back to his horse so he could leave, Criff sauntered casually toward the fort and its newly built ramparts. Cethen's gorge rose in panic. Romans were everywhere! Yet they didn't seem to bother Criff, for he went straight inside the stronghold as if he lived there.

There was no gate to pass through, just a gap in the huge earthen berm; though the foundation was staked out, and lengths of timber stacked close by. The earthworks had been built as tall as a man, and a wall of wooden stakes had been pounded into the top for as far as he could see. There were eight guards on duty at the dark opening, all in plated armour and carrying weapons. Surely these men could hear his heart pounding, Cethen thought, but Criff merely nodded to them as he walked through.

Inside, Cethen stared in amazement. How had so much been done in less than a week? Row upon row of tents filled the camp, and a wooden building had already been built in the centre. The rich, heavy odour of horses hung in the air, drifting pleasantly from the tethering lines set to one side of the fort. The animals seemed content, their heads bobbing up and down as they pulled at the fodder, their hooves shifting quietly as they settled for the night. The fort was bathed in the glow of a hundred flickering torches, evenly spaced along a dozen squared off paths that gave access to both the tents and the central building of

the unfinished fort. Rough planks had been laid over the mud and, as the two walked along the wood surface, Cethen found they gave a pleasant spring to his step.

Criff headed straight for the centre of the camp, to the rough-sawn building. An area had been left open in front where several fires blazed. As they neared, Cethen saw that each was surrounded by what seemed to be hundreds of Roman troops. His blood turned as cold as his feet, and his belly sank toward his groin.

"What are you doing?" he demanded of Criff.

"I'm obeying orders," came the reply, and there was laughter in his tone. "We're going to amuse the Romans."

"We?" Cethen almost choked.

"Well, if you lack the talent, then I suppose it's me."

Criff said no more. He made his way to the largest group, which proved to be the same troop of Tungri that had passed them on the trail. Though he knew they could not possibly recognize him, Cethen instinctively lowered his eyes as he shuffled past, trying hard to control the limp. The troopers were eating, and the bard received a chorus of muffled, mouth-stuffed greetings. A place was quickly found for the both of them, close by the warmth of the fire, and a pair of tar-caulked leather mugs filled with a heavy, tepid beer appeared as if by magic. The bard was plainly known and accepted and so, by association it seemed, was his companion.

Several mugs of beer and a dozen songs later, Cethen's mellowing mind had turned full circle. He might have been back with the kin at the Eburi village. The Tungri called on Criff as soon as he sat down. The bard readily obliged, plucking at the harp as he sang in a rich, deep baritone. The tales were light, and mostly bawdy. The low, sombre tone brought a dark humour to the songs, and Criff's features matched the antics of the words. The music rolled softly across the flames and into the darkness beyond the fire's glow. Criff encouraged the troopers to sing the choruses, and the strong, deep ring of a hundred male voices soon echoed through the night.

Like any good bard, Criff had picked up on the lore and music of his audience over the past few days; and like any good bard, he used it to tease and play on their feelings. The Tungri seemed to expect nothing less, finding pleasure or solace in every mood evoked. Small groups of Roman infantry clustered in the shadows at the edge of the circle's glow, some joining in, if only to hum. Cethen didn't know if such gatherings took place every night, and if so, how long they might last. The way this one was going, it might last until morning. Warmed by the music and the beer, he could not have cared less.

A single trooper edged his way into the circle of men, and beckoned to several others who sat close by the heat of the flames. They clambered reluctantly to their feet and followed the man to the far edge of the fire's glow, where they stood huddled together, talking. The singing quickly died as all heads turned, waiting. Criff whispered that the trooper's name was Noricus, the officer who commanded the cavalry detail. Cethen cringed as hard voices barked an abrupt string of orders. On all sides of the fire warmed, mellowed troopers climbed stiffly to their feet, grumbling as they made their way toward the horse lines.

Cethen was sure he knew the cause, and the warm glow vanished like a wisp of stale smoke. He had dismissed the four missing riders from his thoughts, but their own kind were plainly not of the same mind. Nighttime or not, they were going searching for them. A couple of decent trackers would no doubt trail Dermat and the others back to the river. They might not see the blood on the road, not at first, but if they had half an eye, they would see signs of the struggle that had taken place.

If the Tungri had really good trackers, Cethen reasoned, then before morning they could be following his own trail right back to the fort. He shook his head. Surely not. Any tracks that he and Vellocatus had left would surely be obliterated by the Tungri when they rode out. Or would they? His mind was getting befuddled.

He turned to Criff. "I have to leave. So does Vellocatus."

The easy smile never left Criff's face, and he continued idly strumming the harp. His quiet words matched the lilting notes that fell from the instrument, and anyone passing might have thought he was singing. "Give it more time, friend. Everyone's le-eaving. The night's getting la-ate. It will settle down. For this is a ca-amp, boy. Not an inn full of drunks. So panic not, friend. Just give it more time."

And time seemed to take forever. When the two finally left the stifling, walled-in enclosure, Cethen could smell his own sweat—or perhaps it was his fear. Armed soldiers now walked the parapets, and more had been posted at the entrance. Even the guard at the lodge had been increased, but with Criff leading the way, they passed inside without challenge.

Cethen quickly retrieved his sword from the woodpile where Criff had hidden it. He felt slightly better with the familiar weight in his hand, though he knew it was worthless under the circumstances. When he entered the lodge to find Vellocatus, Criff held back using the excuse of fetching the horses. With no other choice, Cethen fumbled through the kitchen by himself and entered the main room. It was now lit by a single oil lamp, and at first there appeared to be no sign of life. Then, as he stood motionless in the semidarkness, his ears caught the steady gasp of heavy breathing coming from one of the curtained side rooms.

"Oh, for the love of Dagda!" Cethen groaned in despair, and fell to his knees.

The breathing suddenly stopped, replaced by a low, protracted moan that quickly became a rush of hog like grunts, ending in a sharp, muffled scream. For what seemed an eternity, Cethen waited patiently for the panting to stop. When little more than mild gasps drifted from behind the curtain, he called Vellocatus's name. There was no reply. He waited a moment, then tried again.

"Bugger off."

"We have to leave," Cethen replied hoarsely.

This time a female voice answered. "Are you deaf? He said bugger off—turd!"

"The Tungri troopers went out again! We've got to go."

"Ahhh, shit," the male voice grumbled, and voices whispered angrily behind the curtain. A moment later Vellocatus appeared, stark naked and not looking happy.

"What did you expect them to do?" he growled. "They're in hostile country, and four of their men are missing."

Cethen fumbled for an excuse as he climbed to his feet, one that didn't give the appearance of saving his own hide. "But the information we have—it has to get to Venutius."

Vellocatus frowned, as if he'd missed something. "Isn't that why we sent Dermat and Ebric back?" An angry whisper drifted through the curtain. Vellocatus glanced over his shoulder and murmured something soothing.

Cethen's insides boiled with frustration. "The Tungri will probably track them," he hissed. "Remember, there are women and children in that column."

Vellocatus gave a long, heavy sigh that spoke of a different kind of frustration. He pondered the dilemma for a moment, and finally shrugged. "Then go warn them," he said, and slipped behind the curtain again.

Cethen stared dumbly at the dark folds as they settled back into place. For a moment he considered pushing through to press home his argument, then remembered who else was on the other side. He threw his arms out in disgust, forgetting he held the sword, and felt it strike something that crashed to the floor. It was a good time to leave. Cursing, he bumped his way out through the dark kitchen and into the night. Criff stood waiting, grinning, and with only one horse bridled and ready to go.

"Thanks," Cethen muttered, taking Flint's reins and glancing angrily at the stake wall. He wondered if it would be as easy to ride out, as it had been to ride in.

As if reading his thoughts, Criff gestured toward the back of the compound. He then produced a shield of a design Cethen had not seen before, along with a single spear. "It will be of help," he said.

"Against so many?" Cethen said miserably.

Criff patiently tapped the pattern on the front of the shield. "It's one of those used by her retainers. It will help you get away from here, if you are stopped."

Feeling foolish, Cethen swung up onto the horse and took the shield from the bard. He settled it on his arm, and clasped the spear behind it. Criff led him out of a small gate that was set, almost invisibly, into the rear wall of the compound.

"Thanks," Cethen said, staring down into the bard's pale, upturned face. He inclined his head toward the lodge. "Do you think he's going to stay here?"

"No, he'll catch up with you," Criff replied, and shrugged. "If not tomorrow, then the next day. Or the one after that. And by the way, don't thank me. It serves me as well as it serves you."

"How so?" Cethen asked, intrigued.

"One day, in the right company, it will be a tale to be told. With a few lies added, if need be." Criff grinned as he slapped the animal's rump, calling into the darkness as the beast leapt forward. "It all adds to the stuff that stories are made of."

Flint quickly found the track that led down to the ford. There were no challenges. The horse splashed across the water at a careful trot, but once on the other side it settled into a slow, easy lope, much like the gait of the Tungri cavalry earlier that night. Cethen let the animal have its head for a while, but it wasn't a pace to be kept while riding a dim cart track cut through the trees. He reined in to a brisk walk, content to listen to the steady, reassuring thump of hooves on the damp earth.

Eventually, it struck him that the Tungri might already have back-tracked and found the bodies. Already, they could be following Ebric and Dermat's trail back across the river, and north. Even now, they might be closing in behind. Nervous, Cethen dug his heels in once more, and Flint, after a whinny of protest, broke into a canter.

Chapter V

The captain docked his ship at the Eburi landing with considerably less flourish than Tertius's effort earlier in the year. The craft slid alongside the sturdy new dock by drifting downriver with the current, after turning a good hundred paces upstream. The snow had vanished in the months following the disastrous attack, and the small fields about the village were filled with the lush green of mature spring pasture. A half-dozen other ships, all traders and transports, nestled against the curve of the riverbank, gangplanks out and davits busy. Stacks of lumber, crates of hardware, sacks of grain, amphorae, kegs, and a hundred other supply needs of a full legion were piled along the shore.

Gaius walked carefully across the gangplank, scowling as he glanced down at the muddy water of the Abus. It was the same spot where he'd almost lost his life, and he paused in midstride; but there was little use in brooding over the matter, and he quickly moved on, deftly dodging the sailors and the cargo-crowded dock. He stepped onto the riverbank, no longer having to clamber upward to gain solid footing. He stopped beside a pile of sacks stuffed with barley, and stood gazing up the slope to where the Eburi village had once stood.

Small piles of rubble were still being cleared from the site, and wisps of smoke drifted from the charred remains of the crude buildings. Work crews were setting debris on carts, hauling it away as fill for the dirt ramparts. Gaius smiled. The site already had the familiar, comfortable feel of military occupation. Just beyond the ugly hills of trash, row upon row of leather tents were pitched in neat lines, all within the area staked off for the fortress walls. Almost two thousand men were in camp, and more were on their way. Most were working on the earthen embankment that formed the base of the defenses.

A large, modular command post had been erected in the centre of the sea of tents, with two similar, smaller structures on either side. Gaius started forward, his personal slave, Metellus, trailing behind. As he picked his way through the labouring soldiers, his gaze drifted involuntarily north, in an attempt to trace his flight from the barbarians. It was impossible. The forest itself had been pushed back, leaving a field of sawn-off stumps, and even those were being moved by teams of sweating horses. The large, rotten log where he'd first seen the startled Briton had simply disappeared. He smiled ruefully at the memory, realizing what Titus and the others had seen as they stood by the dock. They had reminded him often enough.

The headquarters tent was not crowded. A few clerks fussed behind a row of collapsible tables in its front module, all either busy or pretending to be. No other staff were around. The curtains that screened the rear module were drawn back, and it appeared empty.

Gaius had half expected to find Cerialis there, but one of the clerks confirmed that he was still at Petuaria, along with the Ninth's legate, Petronius Veranius. Both, he was told, were expected at any time. And as to his own quarters, no one had informed the clerks where they might be. The second modular, perhaps—the one next door, to the right? The primus and some of the tribunes had stowed their gear in there. Perhaps he might like …

Typical, Gaius thought, and walked out into the fresh breeze that blew cool from across the river. Everything organized; nothing organized! Grumbling to himself, he looked about for any sign of Titus, but the primus was nowhere to be seen. The squaring of the site was finished, though, something the old veteran would have attended to himself, and the work on the ramparts would soon be completed. The primus was probably somewhere on the north side of the site, where most of the men seemed to be working.

He turned and ordered Metellus back to the boat for the balance of his gear, and settled on the second modular as his new home—at least for the present. Then something else caught his eye down by the river. A smaller vessel was closing in on the dock, arriving from upstream. Which seemed highly unusual, he thought, until he remembered the detachment at Isurium.

The boat's captain, or the crew, or perhaps both, did not have the skill of a Roman ship master. Which might not say much, he thought, chuckling at the memory of Tertius, and his first visit. This particular craft wallowed in the current, just short of the dock. An angry, high-pitched female voice rang across the water, clearly screaming orders. The ship's prow swung slowly inward, closing clumsily on the mooring. Intrigued, Gaius found his feet retracing their way toward the dock.

A sailor leapt off the bow and snagged a line around one of the pilings. The vessel swung with the flow of the river and settled against the wooden platform with a deep thud. A tall, dark-haired woman stalked off the deck, barely allowing time for the gangplank to settle. She strode impatiently across the dock, onto the riverbank, and up the path toward the camp. A young tribune in full dress uniform trailed behind, followed by a gaggle of Britons and a small contingent of infantry. Bemused, Gaius leaned against the side of an empty freight wagon and settled down to watch.

No sooner had the woman started up the slope than she stopped and whirled angrily around. Those behind bunched up like a flock of sheep. She shouted, hands waving, and most scuttled back again, probably because they were empty handed, Gaius decided. Then just as suddenly, she resumed her long stride up the dirt path.

At first Gaius thought the woman would pass by, but she stopped abruptly, as if something odd had caught her attention. She glanced sideways, slowly eyeing him up and down, as if assessing the value of a slave. Her eyes swept over his uniform, narrowed as they fell on his rank insignia, then moved up to the top of his skull where the yellow, green, and purple of his bruises gleamed through the dark bristle of his scalp. Her features settled in amusement. "You're lucky. They struck you in the only place that won't do a Roman permanent damage." In case Gaius had missed the point, she added, "Your skull."

He stared back, both irritated and drawn by the cool, imperious features. There were tiny lines of age etched about her eyes and mouth, and her hair, once raven, was streaked with grey; unlike many Roman women, though, she made no attempt to hide it. But it was her eyes that held him. They were a dark, greyish blue, and seemed to pierce his thoughts. They had the sharp focus of intelligence and, despite her abrasiveness, a glint of something that could only be humour.

He nodded, and decided to respond in kind. "It did catch my attention, at the time."

"You were gawping," she accused.

Again he nodded, and shrugged. "True."

She seemed amused. "And what do you see, Roman?"

Gaius decided the simple truth would serve best and, without thinking of the other side of his words, replied, "You must have been very beautiful when you were young."

The woman's eyes widened in surprise, and for a moment she seemed completely nonplussed. The backhandedness of the compliment suddenly struck him, and he squeezed his eyes shut at the gaffe. Then her lips twisted into a grim smile. She spoke one word and began to laugh.

"Turd!"

Some of the straggling flock had caught up. Gaius recognized the soldier in dress uniform as Julius Fortinus, and tried to keep a straight face. He nodded a greeting, and the young officer simply rolled his eyes upward, as if appealing to the gods.

"Where is Petilius?" the woman demanded.

Gaius bit his lip at the familiarity, and wondered how he should reply. He had no doubt who she was. "I have no idea," he said carefully.

"He was supposed to be here today."

"At any time, I heard."

"Then take me to the senior officer. Is the legate here?"

"No, he's not."

"Then take me to whoever else is—" she broke off, looked down at her feet as if gathering patience, then looked up again. "I suppose that's you?"

Gaius decided to extemporize, dragging out the details in order to irritate. The impulse was irresistible. "Well, our rank structure is a little difficult to understand, unless you really know how it works. The primus pilus is here, but he's from the ranks. He's actually very senior, the top centurion of the first cohort. Probably exerts more influence than I do, particularly with the troops. Doesn't hesitate to use it, either, I might add. But you asked for an officer, which I suppose means you want someone of at least *equestrian* rank, or better. There's the *senatorial* lad, Publius, but like most young tribunes he's a bit raw. Still in training. So, if you really want—"

"Shiiiiit!"

"—want the senior officer, a real officer, then I suppose yes, that's probably me. For the moment." He offered an impudent smile and bowed stiffly at the waist, which sent a jagged pain lancing along his spine. The pose seemed to strike the correct note, though, for she threw her hand in the air as if in surrender. The pain seemed worth the effort.

"And you are?"

"Gaius. Gaius Sabinius Trebonius. Senior tribune, commander of the first cohort, and chief engineering officer of the Ninth Hispana. And you are?"

Her eyes flashed, but not with malice. "You know damned well who I am. And with all those ridiculous titles, if you don't, then you effing well should. Now show me where I'm staying."

Cartimandua resumed her progress into the camp and Gaius fell in alongside, suddenly aware of his sore ribs as he hurried to match her pace. The flock dutifully followed.

"We have nothing set aside. I'll see what the governor—"

"Of course there is nothing set aside. Why should there be? No one knew I was coming."

"Then perhaps we might be—"

"A tent of my own would be nice. A large one. Well lit, and warm. I like it to be warm." She turned and looked pointedly at Gaius, her eyes glinting. "We older people like the warmth, you know. It's very important to us, turd. Perhaps that's what I should name you: turd."

Gaius bowed his head. "Whatever company you prefer to keep, ma'am."

Cartimandua acknowledged the sally with a smile, and looked ahead. "I think I'll take that one. The large one at the centre. I might be able to fit all my people inside." She pointed to the headquarters tent which, with its modular construction, could have slept a couple of hundred men if they were cold and tired enough.

"Uh, that's the command centre," Gaius demurred. "It's already in use. We should be able to find a spare module or two we can put together, though."

She ignored the comment. "So who tried to carve your brains out, turd?"

Gaius found himself suddenly annoyed as the slur was repeated, and appeared ready to stick. That was the last thing he needed. The reply fell from his lips before he could stop it. "Why don't we make a pact? You don't call me turd, and I won't call you bitch." He immediately regretted the outburst, but her response surprised him.

"You'll have to do better than that. I freely admit I'm a bitch. Does that mean you admit you're a turd?"

They had passed through the gap in the newly built rampart, and onto the wide, grassy path that would one day become the *Porta Praetoria*. It struck Gaius that the two of them were, in a manner, probably the first to walk formally through the gate and march down the main road to where the permanent headquarters building would be built. They even appeared to be leading a small parade.

"I can be at times," Gaius admitted, "but never when dealing with women."

"Not even your wife?" Her face expressed surprise.

"Well, with most women." He grinned, then tried to correct his blunder. "I truly meant my earlier remark as a compliment. After all, by inference, it indicates you still have some attraction." He almost added "even now," but managed to rein in his babbling. Yet again, it was too late.

"You are digging a deeper pit for yourself, Roman. *Still* have *some* attraction? You could be discussing a worn out harlot. You are talking to a queen. Bold and shameless compliments are the form. Lying about such matters is a requisite. Try it sometime. Turd!"

Gaius decided to move the topic to safer ground. "It was your husband."

"What?"

"You asked who tried to carve my brains out. It was a raiding party led by your husband. Right here, last winter. Over there, actually." He gestured vaguely ahead, to the east of the headquarters tent.

"Vellocatus? He was here?"

Her voice was surprised and demanding, and Gaius stared at her, perplexed. "Who is Vellocatus?"

"My husband, and may his nether parts grow warts, the egg-sucking weasel. I believe you mean the other one, though. Venutius. I knew there had been a fight. He was the one involved?"

"Oh yes, he was," Gaius said ruefully, remembering how close they had been to capturing the man. "At the time, we didn't know. The neighbouring Parisi certainly informed us later."

"And the old bastard would have made sure they did." She seemed to find humour in the news.

"So how many husbands do you have?" he asked, smiling.

"Only one at a time." She glanced sideways with a wicked leer on her face, one eyebrow raised. "At the moment, the position appears temporarily vacant."

It was Gaius's turn to look nonplussed, and she roared with laughter.

"Don't worry, I'm not looking. The last one will come slavering back at some point in time, I'm sure. But even if I was looking, you can rest assured that it wouldn't be a Roman. As a make-do I suppose they are adequate, but they do tend to be a little stiff when it comes to romance. In their attitude, I mean. Which reminds me, when Petilius arrives, do let me know."

They had arrived at the headquarters module. Too dumfounded at the openness of her comment to say more, Gaius stood gaping by the entrance as Cartimandua swept inside and took command. She had her baggage dumped on the ground, and sent most of her people back to the ship for more. Those who remained seemed to fill the huge tent, all of them busy with some sort of task, Roman and Briton alike. In despair, Gaius went outside, only to find the tribune, Julius, standing with his arms folded, as if wondering what to do next.

"Good trip downriver?" Gaius asked cheerily, unable to resist picking at the young man.

"I don't know what you're so swollen up about," the tribune answered moodily. "You've got to tell Uncle she's taken over his command post."

Gaius spent the rest of the day wandering the site, catching up on the work done in the few days since the troops had arrived. Try as he might, he found it difficult to find fault. The four ramparts were perfectly aligned, their length in accord with the "off the shelf" dimensions of a full-sized fortress. The main gate was exactly where he would have placed it, about a hundred paces back from the riverbank, where the slope began to level out. It was above any likelihood of flooding, offered distance enough for an army to march in between, yet was close enough to protect the docks from the palisades.

And not too far inside was where the Briton's hovel had stood, he guessed, remembering the primus's rough estimate when assessing the site. Now, it was nothing more than a pile of rubble, and he supposed there was some satisfaction to be gained in that. Gaius stood chatting with Titus, both watching the progress on the huge earthworks. At least a thousand men toiled with picks and shovels, reinforcing the packed dirt with heavy tree limbs and logs.

A small, darkly bearded man appeared, coming from the direction of the headquarters tent. He ambled through the lines of sweating soldiers with an aimless, bow-legged gait. He halted before Gaius, and stared up at his bruised scalp. Apparently satisfied by what he saw, he spoke in barely understandable Latin. "You would be named Gaius?"

He received a disdainful nod, and continued.. "You are to be at her tent. For the evening meal. She expects you at sunset."

Titus chuckled. "It appears you have a command performance. At *her* tent."

"That's all?" Gaius asked, irritated at the order implicit in the invitation.

The man stared at the ground, his brow furrowed, as if carefully reviewing his instructions. "Yes, there is more," he said at last, looking pleased with his memory. "You are permitted to bring two other officers with you."

"Fine," Gaius snapped, and turned to Titus as if the Briton no longer existed. Permitted! The word rankled. The man simply shrugged and ambled away.

"Want to dine with royalty this evening?" he asked testily.

Titus chuckled. "I don't have a problem with it. You can guarantee the food will be better than we'll find in the mess. And probably the company, too."

The primus's prediction proved to be true, but Gaius was strangely irked by the evening. He had asked Publius along as the woman's third guest, and the three arrived at the command tent at the specified time; the sun was setting gently beyond the Abus, a fiery, glowing orb that glittered crimson over the long stretch of river. The beauty of it was lost on Gaius. He was in a contrary mood, and determined to remain that way.

The first thing he noticed was that the clerks had not removed all the equipment when they were ejected. Two portable tables, the legs sawn short, now sat toward the rear of the first module, each standing no taller than a man's knee. Gaius was unreasonably irritated at the offhand manner in which the army's property had been altered.

Tight bundles of fresh hay had been placed end on to the tables, hidden under colourful lengths of cloth. The forage added a sweet, heavy scent that offset the smell of the module's long-tanned leather. Gaius decided it reminded him of a stable. Someone had set large pillows at the end of each bundle, turning them into dining couches, which was the Roman way rather than that of the barbarian. They looked crude, he thought, and not nearly as effective. A third table stood off to one side: collapsible, wood, Hispana VIIII, property of. It functioned as a side cabinet from which food and drink could be served. That one, at least, had escaped mutilation.

The dark walls of the tent reflected the flickering glow of small

Graham Clews

clay oil lamps. The mouth-watering aroma of spices and seared meat drifted in from the second module. This, too, irritated him, for it appeared that the clerks' living quarters had been wantonly appropriated as a kitchen. And to further annoy, the woman wasn't there to greet them! The three stood chatting by the makeshift serving counter, sipping a red wine—which was excellent—and waiting, and waiting ...

Cartimandua finally made her entrance without apology, as if about to descend the great marble steps of the *Senaculum*. Gaius shook his head, realizing his irritation was growing beyond reason, but he again grew nettled at the affectations of his companions. Publius was actually fawning over the woman!

Certainly she had taken care with her dress, for she wore a long, low-cut gown of red, yellow, and blue squares, all of them, in some clever manner, spaced within each other. The blended pattern seemed to subdue the otherwise loud colours. A broad leather belt interwoven with heavy gold wire cinched the garment at her waist, its buckle studded with chunks of ruby-coloured glass. They had to be glass, Gaius decided critically, for they were surely too large to be real gems. He grudgingly admitted that the belt highlighted a ripe, provocative body, and could see why Cerialis, who was more of an age with her, might show interest.

She was affable enough, waving them to the makeshift couches, then lying down with a feline grace as she stretched along her own. And the meal, as Titus promised, was excellent. Yet later, looking back, Gaius decided the entire evening had been vexing—if not downright annoying. He was particularly galled with Titus, and the manner in which the woman played the man as if she were a cat and he a mouse.

There was one moment after dinner, though, when the talk turned almost ugly, and the primus was the cause. By then, all four were relaxing and sipping a sweet wine, idly picking at the preserved fruits and pastries spread abundantly on the hacked-up table. The incident followed a question involving Gaius's injuries, a subject that, though irritating, was innocent enough in itself.

"You said my first husband was here when you were wounded, Gaius. What happened?"

The thought crossed his mind that she knew exactly what had

110

happened, but before he could respond, Titus made a comment that took him unaware.

"In fact, lady, I believe both your husbands were here."

"Really?" She expressed surprise, as did Gaius, but his own was at least genuine.

"One of the failings of your people," Titus mumbled, removing a date pit from his mouth, "is that a deed well done is too good to hold secret. It must be told, and told again."

"It is both a joy and a vice with which our people must live," Cartimandua acknowledged cautiously.

"It is, alas, a trait that might also compromise a lady."

"Compromise?" The grey-blue eyes narrowed.

"For example—" The primus shifted on his elbow so that his eyes met hers. "For example, if a man stole into a lady's bedroom in the middle of the night, under the very noses of his enemy, and later that night, left to arrange the slaughter of a company of that same enemy's cavalry, then surely such a tale would have to be told. Over and over again, I would guess."

Cartimandua's features flushed and turned hard, as if she was fighting an impulse to throw the man out. Even Gaius felt vaguely uncomfortable. On the one side of the blade, Titus appeared to be accusing the woman of treason against Rome. On the other, there was a time and place for everything, and she had just been blatantly challenged, perhaps insulted, at her own table. Even if it was a Roman table, in a Roman tent.

"Are you telling me my husband *stole* into his own bed?" Cartimandua sounded not the least cowed. "Something I didn't know was possible—then left to slaughter your unfortunate auxiliaries?" Her tone was angry, and the words fell like ice.

Titus shook his head as if appalled, but nonetheless took time to finish the mouthful of almond pastry. "Of course not. *I* wouldn't say such a thing." He shook his head again, then added, "But there are others who seem to be doing so. And they speak not of your husband."

The silence that followed was overpowering, so much so that Titus seemed to find himself compelled to break it. "As I said, it is not I who speaks of treason and infidelities. It is what I hear."

"Then you hear far too much," Cartimandua growled, then angrily called, "Criff!"

Gaius turned to see a young man push aside the tent flaps that screened the makeshift kitchen. He wore a full beard and long brown hair, and his face seemed vaguely familiar. He clutched a small harp under one arm, and his mouth was still full of leftovers from the meal. He wiped a sleeve across his lips, clearly surprised at the early call.

"Tell our Roman *friends*," Cartimandua ordered, disgust written on her face, "the name of the man who left my lodge the night the cavalry troop was attacked, further up river. The one you showed the road to, after he was told he was not wanted there."

Criff looked confused, as if he unsure of what reply she expected.

"The truth, man, the truth. Who was it?" she snapped.

"Er, Cethen." He spoke the name almost as a question, looking uncertainly at the faces of the three officers, then back to his queen. "Cethen Lamh-fada. The Eburi."

Gaius frowned, for the name sounded familiar, but Cartimandua spoke again. "And what did he do that night?"

"He stopped by your lodge, briefly, my lady," Criff answered with more confidence. "He was not wanted at your lodge, so the two of us went to the fort to amuse the Romans. It was still being built then. We remained until after the Tungri patrols departed. They were in a hurry. Cethen departed soon after. The night had yet to reach its waning." He raised his eyebrows, silently querying the aptness of his response.

Cartimandua inclined her head slightly, smiling grimly. "There you go, gentlemen, and with no words placed in his mouth," she said, staring coolly around the low table, then added words that Gaius saw only as a caution for her bard. "So Cethen Lamh-fada, an Eburi of Maeldav's tuath, stops by to see his chieftain, and finds him gone. He stays for a while, then leaves. *After* several Tungri patrols departed. What happened to one of those patrols is common knowledge, but it was certainly none of my affair. If it was subsequently slaughtered, do not look to me as the cause! And I can also tell you this, damn you: the man Criff speaks of was not my husband. Nor did he 'steal' into my bed!"

Both Titus and Gaius spoke at the same time, neither giving ground and apologizing.

"Which way did he go?" Gaius began. "Was he travelling alone—"

"Cethen!" Titus said, snapping his fingers. "The Eburi—not the one who jumped in the water after Gaius?"

Criff nodded and Cartimandua, who for a moment appeared ready to climb to her feet and leave, quickly picked up on the primus' question. "Jumped in the water after Gaius? What's that all about? It sounds intriguing."

The name suddenly connected, and Gaius himself was at first intrigued to learn it was the same man. Then he listened in disgust as Cartimandua skilfully drew from Titus the story of his flight across the barbarians' field. Publius eagerly filled in any detail the primus overlooked. The part about the britches was particularly humiliating, especially when she turned a coy, head-shaking glance of amusement his way. She was mocking him! By the time the pair were finished, the woman was actually flirting with Titus, and worse, he was lapping it up like a debagged dog sniffing a bitch.

Titus and Publius both left in a warm, alcoholic haze, and Gaius walked with them in brooding silence. For some reason the primus, not the barbarian woman, dug at his craw—his fawning attention, when he should have been asking her questions. Just before they left the tent, Gaius had again tried to turn matters to the night at Isurium, and the ambush of the Tungri cavalry. He asked a question to which he truly wanted the answer and, in its asking, also wanted to remind the primus of the woman's likely duplicity.

"So where is your husband?"

Cartimandua turned to face him with a crooked smile that again seemed to mock, as if she found the question amusing—or was it her answer? "He's gone hunting."

Chapter VI

"We'll go back. One day we will go back," Cethen promised.

Elena ignored him, as she had done all morning, except as the unwilling target for her complaints—which were many. The latest was the huge iron cooking pot, the one that had hung over the fire and could boil enough water for a complete bath. Which then led to another complaint: not only had the pot been left behind, forever, so had the smaller copper tub that always stood near the fire. Both had been obtained at great expense from the traders, and each one, especially the tub, had been prized possessions, admired—and sometimes used—by others of the kin. And forever, she reminded her husband, was a long time. A long, long time.

"We hid them when we left," Cethen insisted, "because they were too large to carry. We'll get them back after the Romans lea—are beaten."

"Will you stop that!"

'Huh?" He looked at his wife, surprised at the passion in her voice.

"Oh Cethen," she wailed, gesturing around the inside of the small, mean hut. "Look! Just look at it."

"What?" He held his palms out as if bewildered, though he knew full well what she meant.

Elena sat down on one of the short, upended pine logs that served as seats, and slumped back against the mud-chinked wall. Lifting the knife she'd been using to separate dark, stringy strips of meat from a rack of beef ribs, she flung it at one of the other logs scattered about the hut. It lodged in the bark-covered wood with a satisfying thud, and held fast.

"This, this—shack! We could place it ten times inside our old lodge. And—"

"That's not true," Cethen protested. "The lodge wasn't that big. You couldn't place it much more than two or…" Elena's glare withered him into silence.

"And we had our own space, separate from the children. And proper furnishings. And—and—and all the other things …" Her voice faded, the tone growing wistful. "A river is a blessing to live by, Cethen, and we had two rivers. The Abus will have cleared by now, you know. It sparkles blue at this time of year. The grass along the bank will be tall and green, and the willows! Do you remember the willows, down where the rivers join? We spent a lot of time there when—"

She sat upright, suddenly angry again. "Aaah shit, what's the use! Here—here there's nothing but a miserable, muddy stream running through a lousy place so full of people it's an anthill. And the stream's not even that; it's a beck that'll dry up before summer's over. You wait and see."

Elena lapsed into a long, painful silence that Cethen didn't care to break.

"I wonder if Caradoc promised his wife they would all return, when *he* went north to fight the damned Romans," she mused.

"West," Cethen muttered.

"West, south, north, what's the difference?" Elena said, then felt compelled to add, "It was actually northwest."

Angry silence threatened again, so Cethen spoke. "He's living in Rome, you know. With his family. I meant to tell you."

"Caradoc is?" Her brows rose in interest. "I thought they killed him."

"No. Vellocatus told me. He says the bitch queen bargained for his life before she gave him up."

"Well, that doesn't exactly make her a bitch, then, does it?"

115

"Well, everyone calls her the—"

"And furthermore, if all the gods in creation abandoned us and moved to the heart of Rome itself, I still wouldn't want to go there. I simply want to go back home!"

"I told you, one day we'll go back, I promise," he cried.

Elena rolled her eyes and, with a groan of the oppressed, pushed herself to her feet. Plucking the knife from the log, she went back to hacking at the beef. Cethen decided it would be prudent to wander outside in search of other things to do.

Elena did have cause for complaint, Cethen reluctantly acknowledged, sitting moodily on the top rail of the small pen built for the horses. If only she would give it time. The Romans could not remain there forever. There were tens upon tens of thousands of people that Venutius was calling to his cause, for the tribes farther north were also growing nervous. The old man had been talking to their hill cousins, the Carvetii, who lived for the most part in the wilds of Cumbria. And there were others, even farther beyond. No, Elena was wrong—but he also understood how this place was dragging at her. Especially after life at the village.

He gazed miserably about the sea of huts and animal pens surrounding their small home, and then at the long, earthen embankments that enclosed it all. He felt a dull, indefinable ache inside. Stannick wouldn't have been a bad place to live, Cethen thought, had it not been teeming with people.

The great, rambling enclosure was crowded and cluttered, and cursed with the ever-present stink of humanity. Though after a while you did get used to it ...sort of. The fortress town filled a low depression that had probably once been lush and green—two such depressions really, now that the ramparts had been enlarged to take in more land to the south. Yet this type of living wasn't the way of the people. The Brigantes didn't herd together as if they were a great, stinking, milling flock of sheep penned behind walls. Granted, living with the kin back at the village, a person could feel penned in at times, but inside these walls it was—well, Elena had called it an anthill. She was right. And dammit, she was right about the river, too.

The Abus had a life of its own. The gods lived there, keeping the river alive, along with every creature that dwelt along its winding path. The rivers and the gods took care of the kin in both good times and bad, and there had been mainly good times there. Which meant the gods had been pleased.

It was odd that Elena remembered the willows with such fondness, though. As far as he could recall, he was always having to coax her down there. Cethen smiled at the thought. The first time had been just before Beltane …how many years ago?

Beltane! That was another thing to gnaw on. The festival was drawing near, but at Stannick, even the celebration of spring lacked the keen excitement it had conjured back home. At the village, the children had started gathering wood to build the huge bonfires weeks and weeks before the day they were finally lit. At Stannick, the druids organized work parties of slaves. Well ahead of time, two large, neat stacks of logs stood outside the walls, ready for the frightened livestock to be driven between. The great mounds were not the haphazard bonfires gathered by the youngsters who, until they were lit, saw them as hill forts to be defended, or dens in which they could play and dream.

And the day itself. At home there had always been bustling, chattering, gossiping crowds of women organizing the food and drink, planning the games, singing the songs, and ready with an ear for the stories. There would be no such chance at Stannick to tease and dally, nip at the food, pinch a buttock, or tweak a breast.

Instead, the day had been set out by the men of Venutius's tuath, under the fussy direction of the druids. It was all so organized it made you sick. Prayers would be offered, and sacrifices made. There seemed to be no joy in it at all, just orders. It was something a person might have expected from the Romans: you will be on the plain west of the wall when the sun peaks; you will bring cattle to the holding pens before midday of the day before; you will take one keg of ale to the hill fort by early evening; you will not enter the …

"Your woman being an old sow as well?" Cian heaved himself onto the railing, hooked his feet onto the second rung to keep his balance, and delivered a hearty slap to his brother's back. Cethen almost fell from his perch.

"Nuada not too happy?" Cethen asked, almost resentful at the company. He had been quite content in his brooding solitude.

"No more than Elena, I imagine. We should put the two together. They'd find joy in their misery."

"Not necessarily. Sometimes people like to be left alone," Cethen said, but the hint missed its target. Cian's mind was elsewhere.

"I was at the great hall again today," he said, letting the comment dangle.

"Mingling with the mighty?" Cethen muttered, ignoring the unspoken demand to be asked why.

Cian laughed, determined not to be nettled. "Elena's really been squeezing your balls. Has she got you doing the cooking yet?"

Cethen reluctantly grinned, and shoved his brother sideways. Cian almost fell backward into the pen, but his feet held the lower rail, and he pulled himself upright with his stomach muscles. "Not bad, huh? A belly like an iron pot—not like others I know," he crowed, then when Cethen didn't respond, added, "So you don't want to ask what's happening?"

"Me, ask? About what? Whose arse you were kissing at the *big* hall?"

Cian grinned. "Nice of you to say so, but no, I wasn't kissing arse. It seems, however, that my big brother has been noticed. As soon as Beltane is over and everyone sobers up, Venutius is having a council. At the *big* hall. And my *big* brother will go, for I hear there are *big* things the old fart wants you to do."

"Oh?"

"Yes," Cian replied, then fell infuriatingly silent.

"Alright, arse-nuzzler, tell me what's happening," Cethen growled. "And, why me?"

His brother feigned surprise. "So you do want to know. I thought you were too busy being miserable."

Cethen growled, "Just get—"

"I'm getting there, I'm getting there. Whoa, but someone's got a sore tooth today," Cian sniffed. "It would seem you've fallen prey to your own success."

"What success?"

"Well, looking at it from the old man's point of view, you've had quite a bit."

"Hah!"

"Think about it. He comes to the village, and you help him lead an attack on the Romans. The fact that your young brother was right there alongside seems to escape his memory, but there you go. It's all a matter of who you are, isn't it? Anyway, you then jump off the dock to save the Roman, which, while stupid, lets him know you've got balls, and you're a man of your word. Then comes the 'test.' He sends you off spying with Vellocatus, though again, he seems to forget I was there and almost got killed saving your life. By the way, I think Vellocatus was being tested there, too. But that doesn't matter. Sooooo …then what happens?"

Cethen's mind flashed back, painfully recalling his initial funk at the killing of the three Tungri, and the nervous turmoil that racked his belly inside the fort. He said nothing, simply shrugged. It was too shameful.

"I'll tell you, brother," Cian continued eagerly. "While Vellocatus stayed for the best part of a week at Isurium ploughing his wife— which left everyone wondering about his loyalty, by the way, especially Venutius, whose wife she used to be—what did you do next?"

"I came back," Cethen mumbled.

"That's right." Cian punched Cethen on the shoulder. "But before that, Ebric and what's-his-name returned with me strung over the back of my horse, one lousy prisoner, and, unknown to everyone, a hundred raging Romans on their tail. And what happens? My *big* brother rides in like a prowling wolf. He's been *inside* the Roman fort, knows exactly who's living there, *and* warns about the cavalry sneaking up our backsides. Which allows Venutius to set up an ambush! Cethen, everyone in the old man's tuath talks about it. And about you."

Cethen grunted his surprise, but not without a certain amount of pleasure. Nonetheless, what had really occurred compelled him to be modest. "They'd have slaughtered the Tungri anyway. We had way more men than they did."

"Ah, but what damage would they have done first? Especially to the stragglers. And they would probably have broke off and run."

"Maybe," Cethen said, then another thought struck him. "Ebric and Dermat came back with nothing more than a Tungri prisoner?"

"And a lame horse."

Cethen roared with laughter. "You buggers had three other Tungri horses with you when you left, good ones, and loot enough from the owners to keep all of us happy. What happened?"

Cian looked puzzled. "Truth be known, I don't recollect much after the Romans stopped. Perhaps we should have a talk with Dermat and Ebric."

"Aye, maybe," Cethen said, just a shade reluctant to place a claim for loot that he hadn't done much to collect. "Tell me, have you any idea what Venutius wants of me?"

Cian shook his head. "They say he's puffed up about ambushing the Tungri, and wants to try something bigger."

With a sinking feeling, Cethen wondered what Venutius had in mind. An odd sense of loss swept over him, mixed with a sudden empathy for Elena, and her aching need to return to the peace and quiet of their village. Just to sit on the edge of the dock, looking out over the smooth, rippling surface of the river …

"What are you and Elena doing, the night of Beltane?" Cian asked, the silence shifting his mind to other matters.

Cethen was about to say that he hadn't really thought about it, but that wasn't true. He had, and at some length. He heaved his shoulders as if indifferent. "I don't know. Go see the cattle brought in. Then join the feasting, I suppose. But the way things are, we'll probably end up back here telling stories to the children and ignoring each other."

Beltane was not the disappointment Cethen expected. It was more ordered than their own haphazard celebrations with the kin, but that was not all for the bad. The main part of the ceremony, which took place the day before Beltane itself, was carried out under the skilled hands of the druids. There were six of them under the charge of Trencoss, who was the oldest. It was an impressive number. They'd rarely seen a druid at all in the village of late, and then only if one was passing through.

The mere size of the herds brought in for purification was a sight to behold. Thousands of restless, lowing cattle had been gathered on the slopes surrounding the fortress. The druids, Trencoss foremost among them, white robed and magnificently bearded, were no more than dim shapes, lost in the rolling, billowing clouds of smoke that blew sideways from the blazing bonfires on a stiff easterly breeze. They stood on two enormous mounds piled close by the flames, hands high in supplication, and chanting as the cattle stampeded between the two great pyres. The herd itself was a living sea of heaving backs and tossing horns. The animals, terrified by the smoke and the crackling roar of the burning logs, jostled and bellowed as they thundered through with eyes rolling, only to dash into the calm, open fields beyond, completely bewildered.

More bulls than Cethen could count were then sacrificed. Smaller fires were lit and, under a sunlit, windswept sky, the celebration of Beltane began. Perhaps the feasting was too organized, but then it had to be, with so many to feed. Perhaps there were too many people—countless thousands were there that day—but such a number did serve to create a fair-like air. There was almost too much to take in, a hundred celebrations happening at once, both inside and outside the fortress; but it was lively and friendly, and there was much to see and do.

Late that night, when everything had been said that could be said, and everything had been done that could be done, Elena and Cethen grudgingly decided that if Beltane was no longer the way it used to be, then at least it was still worthwhile. When they went to bed, for the first time since they'd left the village, their lovemaking was open and honest.

On the second night of Beltane, Cian found himself once more in the company of Venutius's own people. Of the two brothers, it was he who loved to be at the hub of the tribal wheel, close to the axle on which events turned. Cethen, the head of the kin, was content to let things be, patiently waiting for the rim of the same wheel to roll its way around to where he sat.

121

It was late, and the drinking had shifted to the home of a man Cian had never met, a huge brute called Luga. He lived in the oldest part of the fortifications, beyond the high stone walls where Venutius dwelt with his closest kin. Luga's home was not a bad place. In fact, Cian found it luxurious compared to the slipshod huts in the south compound where he and Cethen lived. It was a smaller version of Maeldav's lodge, with stone walls, a solid, turf-covered roof, and a floor freshly strewn with straw.

The place was full, and had a warm, beery fog of goodwill about it. Cian sprawled with his back against the stone wall, well away from the fire, which had dimmed to nothing more than a pile of glowing embers. He clutched a mug of ale in one hand and, as happens at Beltane, a pair of soft, willing shoulders in the other. The young woman snuggled alongside was a plump, pleasant, warm-hearted companion, full of the warm, hazy glow of spring. Despite the differences in dialect, the two found no difficulty understanding each other, cooing in voices that were soft and low, and with eyes locked even in the dim light.

Cian was oblivious to the uncomfortable looks cast his way by others in the hut, until someone kicked him hard on the leg. "Look where you're going," he muttered, not particularly annoyed, for his attention and his free hand were focused on the girl's soft, ripe breast.

"What do you think you're doing?" a deep voice demanded.

The room fell silent. Cian blinked glassily upward. A large, hairy mountain of a man, clad in a fur vest, glared down at him. The question seemed to demand an answer. "S-since you ask, I'm feeling—er …" Cian looked at the girl, his face a puzzle. "Hey, luvvie," he slurred, "what's your name?"

"Her name is Aefe. And she's my wife," the mountain snarled.

Cian didn't remove his hand. He blinked up at the man with a bleary smile. "As I was s-starting to say, I'm feeling Aefe's tit. What's your name?"

The man's eyes glittered fire. "Luga!"

It meant nothing to Cian. He belched contentedly. "Well, let me tell you, Luga, you have a lovely wife."

With a strangled cry, Luga lurched forward, not for the man deserving his wrath, but for Aefe. He grasped her wrist and tried to pull her to her feet Had Cian been sensible, that might have been the end of it. Instead, he held onto the other wrist, and the woman was caught between.

"Do you want to go with this great, stinking lout, or would you rather stay with me?" Cian slurred, grunting with the effort of holding onto Aefe's arm.

"I live here, fool," she squeaked.

Cian held on as he pondered the words, then finally shook his head as if the thought was too much. "I repeat my queshton. Do you want to—*ayeeeh!*"

Luga released his wife's wrist and grabbed the front of Cian's tunic, jerking him to his feet like a sack of oats. "One more word, you little shit, and I'll rip your head off!" he roared into Cian's face.

His face was no more than a handsbreadth away, and Cian flung his head back as if the sour fumes of Luga's beery breath had blown it there. But he quickly flung it forward again, and his forehead smashed into the bridge of the big man's nose. Luga howled and fell backward onto his rump, both hands covering his face. Blood oozed through his fingers onto his matted beard. Cian slid quietly to the ground and remained there, senseless as a sack of beans. Aefe took the opportunity to slide quietly out the door.

Luga finally struggled to his feet, clearly intent on making good his threat to remove Cian's head, a practice not uncommon among the tuath. Several others grabbed him, though, and held him back, muttering that it would not be right until Cian recovered his senses. Grumbling, Luga reluctantly allowed them to calm him down, and accepted another mug in place of the one that lay shattered on the floor. He slumped by the dying fire and wiped at the blood with the back of his sleeve. Soon the whole incident seemed forgotten.

Again, that might have been the end of it, but some time later Cian stirred, and stared blearily around the hut. His eyes focused on Luga, hunched by the fire, quietly sipping his ale. It penetrated his foggy brain that this was the man who had, in some vague manner, offended him. Fumbling for the nearest weapon, a half-empty wine jug, he lurched to his feet and stumbled toward the fire.

"Hey, swineherd, stand up," he yelled.

Luga stared owlishly at the tottering figure and started to his feet, but before he was fully erect, Cian smashed the jug down on his skull. Luga groaned, sank to the dirt floor, and stayed there. Half a dozen of the big man's friends promptly grabbed Cian and, raining their fists down on him, hauled him from the hut, all the way to the south gate of the old fort. There they threw him down the escarpment, a dozen booted feet helping him on his way. Then, and only then, did Cian stagger to his feet and weave his way home to Nuada.

Chapter VII

Governor Petilius Cerialis arrived at the camp the day follow-
ing Cartimandua's descent on his new fortifications. Along with him
came the legate of the Ninth Hispana, Petronius Veranius Secundus,
and three more of the nine cohorts assigned to build the fortress. The
final cohort, which happened to be the Seventh, would quickly follow, bringing with it all that remained of the Ninth's equipment and
supplies. The regiment's old barracks at Lindum were concurrently
being garrisoned by the Second Adiutrix, freshly arrived from Lower
Germania.

Everybody in the camp was quick to note that the barbarian queen
retained her quarters. The governor and the legate took up residence
in the second largest modular, the one closest to that taken over by
Cartimandua. The third largest, which Gaius thought the officers had
neatly appropriated by depositing their kit, became the headquarters
building. It was also noted, not without snide comment, that construction began at once on a permanent headquarters building and a commander's residence.

A fourth modular tent was found, by far the smallest and the last
available, and quickly erected. It became the new home of the remaining officers. Much bitching and griping accompanied the living arrangements, most of it directed at Cartimandua, which was simply the
way of the army. It probably hadn't changed since Alexander, Gaius

decided. Nor had commanding generals, for Cerialis called an orders group the day after his arrival. It was scheduled for daybreak.

The governor always made a point of being the first to arrive. Titus explained as much to Gaius, when he rousted him early from his bed. It was a deliberate ploy by Cerialis, designed to leave everyone else with a guilty sense of keeping him waiting. Word must have got around, though, for the two arrived while it was still almost dark, and the tent was almost full.

"Caution, gentlemen, caution and preparation!"

The governor started to speak as the two senior officers slid into the tent and sank onto the rear most bench. He paused and frowned, which served only to draw attention to their lateness. When the pair finally settled down, flushed and feeling like rankers late for parade, he continued.

"This campaign will be conducted with those two premises ever in mind. Caution and preparation. We start here with this base, and ensure it is well equipped and well supplied. Then, and only then, do we move into the field. One step at a time. Our supply lines will be kept open and secure. As we move north, permanent fortified camps will be built at intervals of a day's march. We will not blink unless we know what the barbarian is doing. We will not fight without choosing the time and place."

Cerialis stared hard at the rows of stolid faces. Totally deadpan, he added, "Last time I was in this province, I got my arse whipped by a woman. That will not happen again!"

Gaius, the only other man present who had been there at the time, allowed himself a taut smile. The others, Titus included, seemed unsure how to take the admission.

"There is no need to look startled, gentlemen," Cerialis rasped, as an awkward silence filled the tent. "Shit will fly, and when it does, it sticks. You can't ignore the stink. Let what happened be a lesson to us all. Our strength is our discipline and our preparation. The enemy's weakness is the lack of either. However, we must never forget that there are hundreds of thousands of the bastards out there. If they surprise us, then our efforts are for naught."

The governor paused for his words to sink in, then brusquely turned to another matter. "Now," he said, his expression suddenly amused, "many of you are probably wondering about the woman. Cartimandua."

The tent, already quiet, seemed to transcend silence itself. The legate Petronius, seated close by the governor, was unable to prevent his eyes from wandering sideways, as if confirming what his ears had heard.

At the very back of the module, close by the open flap, Titus risked a whisper to Gaius. "He'll start on the Germania campaign next."

Gaius wordlessly nodded his understanding. Only by the breadth of a hair had Cerialis snatched his army from the jaws of defeat, which everyone in the legions considered only fair, for he had carelessly led it there to begin with.

The governor appeared sensitive to the mood in the room, for his face twitched with the barest trace of a smile. "The *woman*," he said, leaning heavily on the word, "was brought here, gentlemen, on the thin hope that she might rally some of the barbarians to her cause. It appears the strategy is not likely to be effective. The chief at Isurium, always a staunch base of support for her, appears to have opted to lead his tuath north. She has come here to …to …" He peered about the inside of the tent as if puzzled. "What do we call this misbegotten place, anyway? Has a name been fixed to it?"

"I think the barbarians called it Eburi or something," one of the centurions ventured. "That's how the men refer to it, only they shorten it. Ebur."

"I don't think we know what the barbarians actually called the place itself," the young tribune, Julius Fortinus, interjected. "Eburi was the name of the people who lived here."

"Who gives a damn," Cerialis muttered. "*Ebor* it is. E-b-o-r. Primus, make a note of it. Now, where was I?"

"Actually, I think it's pronounced Eb-ur, sir. E-b-u-r," Julius persisted. The moment after he opened his mouth, Cerialis made him wish he had kept it shut.

"That's Ebor, tribune!" Cerialis glowered at him. " E-b-o-r. Can you remember that?"

Julius nodded sheepishly and the governor continued. "Ah, yes …the woman. She finds it preferable to remain here at Ebor—that's E-b-o-r, if anyone hasn't got it yet—rather than return to her own tuath in the hills at *Camulodunum*. She still hopes to regain the support of her barbarians after we defeat them. Personally, I think she has as much hope as a vestal virgin in a whore house."

Cerialis remained at the fortress for only two days, then departed south to return to his other three legions. Petronius Veranius was immensely relieved to see the governor go. Not because there was any animosity, he confided to Gaius, but because it was much like riding your own horse with someone sitting behind, holding the reins.

The normal regimen of the legion quickly slipped into place, a routine beginning at dawn when the legate carried out his own orders groups. These were held in the front module of the headquarters tent, as the senior officers ate a small, first meal of the day. The food was set to one side of the entrance, and as each man arrived, he took what he wanted, then sat according to his rank.

It was at one such meeting, several weeks after the governor's departure, that Petronius slumped down with a sour look on his face and tossed a dispatch onto the table in front of him. "It would seem, gentlemen, that we are a victim of our own success."

He grabbed a slice of bread and irritably spread honey on top, then peered about the table, looking for something to go with it. He settled on a mixture of boiled lentils and chestnuts, which he ladled into a bowl, and took a handful of dried figs for good measure. An orderly filled a mug with a hot, herbal brew to wash it down, a concoction the legate insisted upon drinking at the start of each day. It was boiled from a mixture of dried roots imported from his home in Hispania; he claimed it kept his innards clear and his bowels open. The mixture looked like tanning fluid, and the odour was little better.

Gaius dutifully asked the expected question. "How's that, sir?"

Petronius jerked his chin toward the message. "It's from Governor Cerialis. I suspect it's in response to my last progress report. He's satisfied, as well he should be, but so much so that he's decided to start pushing north of Isurium with another outpost."

"That's a change of mind," Titus said. "If I recall, his orders were: supply lines open, and one step at a time."

"Another fort a day's march north would be defensible, I suppose." The legate scratched his chin, picking at a scab where his orderly had been careless shaving. "The palisades are complete at Isurium. The gates are all in. There'll be lots of time later in the year to work on the buildings inside. It is, after all, still officially spring. For a week or so, anyway."

Gaius marvelled at the adaptability of commanding officers. A moment ago this one had been annoyed at the order, but at the first hint of criticism, he defended it as if it were his own. "Is that all he's telling us to do, sir?" he asked.

"I suppose he's worried about the man Venutius." Petronius paused long enough to stare owlishly at Publius. "The one you paid them to take back, remember? The governor feels the time is ripe for a fort to be built a day's march north of Isurium. Give the barbarians something to think about, I suppose. In a way, it is the natural next step, since the defenses at Isurium are more or less complete."

"That could place us less than a day's march from Stannick itself," Gaius said.

"I imagine that's the intent. Show them we can do it. This Venutius fellow has surely been strengthening his fortifications there. They must be nearing completion, though we've had damned little intelligence on it. I imagine the governor has it in mind to knock it down."

"I suppose a fort beyond Isurium would give us a base of attack," Titus murmured, also scratching his chin as if figuring the logistics of constructing a stronghold forty miles north of Ebor: a cobweb of supply lines winding through a countryside full of marsh and forest, all within close reach of the enemy.

"Where is the governor at the moment, sir?"

The question came from Marcus Aurelius, a grey-haired, grizzled ex-ranker who held the post of praefectus castrorum. Marcus commanded those forces remaining in camp when the legion took to the field. Like most old soldiers, he was a cynic, especially where the whims of senior officers were concerned. Most around the table smiled, knowing the reason for his question.

"It was dispatched from the Twentieth. *Agricola's* regiment," Petronius replied, glancing sardonically at Marcus as he emphasized the name. "Does that *specifically* answer your question?"

"Very specific, sir. Thank you."

Smiles broadened at the confirmation of the praefectus's suspicions. Gnaius Julius Agricola, commander of the Twentieth, was not known for any lack of boldness. Gaius could almost see the two generals, heads together as the younger planted the seed: *"Move fast, sir. In strength. Build a fort right under their damned noses. That should bring them out!"*

"A day's march north of Isurium, then." Petronius glanced down the table. "Care to comment, Salvius?"

The praefectus of the Tungri cavalry regiment choked in surprise, and quickly swallowed the mouthful of spelt porridge he'd just shovelled in. Salvius Modestinus rarely attended the morning orders groups, for duty usually found him elsewhere.

"Er, yes sir. Yes. I think there is a likely site around there. Not a bad one. Yes, I suppose it would be about a day's march from Isurium. Eventually. Once a straight road's been built. Flat ground, lots of trees. Marshy in places, though. The river curves west there. And there's a settlement. Have to be moved, of course. Yes, a good spot, I'd say." Salvius swallowed again and cleared his throat, frowning in thought. "Er, there's a useable ford. The river itself is not deep. And it's right on the line of march north. Yes. Good position for a fort."

"Do you know exactly how far that would be from Stannick?"

Salvius shrugged. "Haven't actually seen the man's fortress myself. Too many barbarians. It's supposed to be—well, from where that settlement is, less than a day's march. That's just a guess. Again, based on a good straight road. Which there isn't. Yet."

A long pause followed his words, unbroken by Petronius as he kept his gaze steady upon his cavalry commander.

"I ...er, I suppose we had better scout it, then, sir. Get more solid information," Salvius spluttered, finally taking the hint.

"I want you started tomorrow. The governor says he'll be here again in about a week. He'll want to know the progress being made on *his* new fort," Petronius murmured, as if unconsciously distancing himself from the project. "Marcus, get started on the logistics. Titus, you had better go with Salvius, and assess the site. Or find one that's better."

"And the ground itself? As far as construction?" Gaius asked.

"You'll volunteer for that, I suppose," Petronius said, and turned to Titus with the trace of a smile on his lips. "This time, primus, if the senior tribune has to take a piss, keep a close eye on him."

Gaius inspected progress on the commanding officer's residence later the same day. If the governor was due back in a week, it would be prudent to have a roof over his head. His quarters at Ebor would not be topped by neat rows of red tile, however, or walled with chiselled sandstone; it would be a rough-sawn wooden building, caulked, and thickly plastered on the inside. Rough-built or not, the design was standard: a spacious rectangular building centred on a large, atrium. One day it might be built of stone, should the fortress prove permanent. In the meantime, Gaius decided, it was damned luxurious by local standards.

He was speaking to the centurion in charge of the project when he saw, standing next to him, the same bow-legged Briton who had delivered the summons to Cartimandua's tent. He ignored the man until he was finished, but the lingering presence was distracting. The Briton didn't seem to mind. He was engrossed in the soldiers hammering on the rafters above, and shook his head, as if amazed that Roman warriors did such work.

"Well?" Gaius demanded, after the centurion had nodded his understanding and departed.

"Oh!" The Briton, his mind still on the construction, seemed startled. "She says you are to come with me. To her tent." With the same annoying assumption that his queen's order would be obeyed, the man turned and ambled off. Gaius wavered, cursed, then sighed and followed.

The first module of Cartimandua's quarters was empty, except for a menial who was down on his knees, trying to blow life into the grey ashes of a charcoal brazier. The place had the clinging, tasteless odour of stale food. The apron of cloth that concealed the second module was open, and a voice sounded from inside.

"Come in. See what I found."

Gaius peered into the dim interior, unsure what to expect. Cartimandua sat cross-legged on the floor, talking to someone whose back was to the entrance. The figure seemed vaguely familiar. As he entered, it turned cautiously to look.

"Marc!" Gaius cried.

"Father."

Cartimandua appeared bemused. "I found the lad down by the dock when I was out walking. You might say I rescued him."

"What are you doing here, boy?" Gaius asked.

Marcus climbed to his feet, unwilling to look Gaius in the eye. "I wanted to come."

"Why?"

"I don't know." The boy seemed miserable. "I suppose I was getting ...bored."

"Well, you can go right back. This is no place for a youngster. We're in hostile territory," Gaius said sternly.

"Father, it's a construction site. And I'm fifteen. You even have women here." He gestured to Cartimandua, and to her female attendants, fussing at the rear of the tent.

"I believe your father rates me as one of the hostiles, my dear," Cartimandua said, and smiled.

"Oh, I didn't—"

"It's nothing you should worry about, my boy." She turned to Gaius with a smirk. "I would guess the boy has run off to join the army. Fine looking young man. Of course, ours are already blooded at that age. Though we do keep them on a bit of a leash, I suppose."

"Well, this one is going back to Lindum." Gaius tried to control his anger as a dozen questions ran through his mind. "Dammit, how did you get transport? Does your mother know you're gone? She'll be frantic. Tell me she at least knows you're gone."

Marcus's expression grew sullen, and he seemed angry in turn. "She knows I'm gone. She agreed I could come and see you, stay as long as I want. The legate himself arranged transport and a pass."

"Oh." Gaius stared at his son, perplexed. What could possibly be the boy's motive? Or his mother's, for that matter. "Is there any trouble?"

Marc seemed to consider the question, then shrugged. "You know I'll pass through the army sooner or later. I wanted to see what it was like. In the field. And I wanted to get away." His voice trailed away. He waited.

"I'm leaving tomorrow, Marc," Gaius said, glancing quickly toward Cartimandua, unwilling to say anything more in her presence.

"Your father will be gone for four or five days, Marcus," Cartimandua said, and smiled demurely at Gaius. "He's going north to site a fort, while some of the others push on to see what they can find up around Stannick. Do you know about Stannick?"

Marc didn't answer; he was staring at his father's face. Gaius realized he was gaping at the barbarian woman in disbelief, and snapped his jaw shut.

"You may have to return to Lindum while your father is away, but I'll tell you all about Stannick before you go. Or at least, the way it used to be. Unless, of course," she looked brightly at Gaius, "you wish him to remain here with me. He won't be a pest. I adore his accent. "

Gaius closed his eyes and shook his head, "How did you …?"

"How did I what?"

"Never mind. We'll talk later," he snapped, and glowered at Marc. "You'll come with me. I have the very place for you. Octavius. Octavius Frugius's squad. If you're going to stay for a while, that's where it will be. If you want a taste of the army, he'll give it." He glanced at Cartimandua. "You would *adore* the man. And his accent. Now come on."

He motioned Marc through the entrance, and gave a curt nod to Cartimandua, intent on following. But before he could turn and leave, she held a hand up to stay him.

"A moment."

Gaius did not bother to hide his annoyance at the delay.

"The lad has other reasons for coming," she said. "I think it's wise not to push too hard on his shield. Perhaps then you might find out what they are."

Gaius clenched his jaw as he digested the words. "What did he tell you?"

"Nothing. We talked about what it is like here, and I promised to teach him our tongue. Nothing more. The boy seemed please. Its just that I sense something is bothering the lad."

Gaius turned as if to go, but she was not finished.

"One other thing."

He glared back. The woman was intruding to the point of unpleasantness. "What?" he demanded.

"Did you notice," she said, with a smile that dripped both vinegar and honey, "that not once did I call you a turd? Even though you thoroughly deserved it."

Chapter VIII

Several days after Beltane, Venutius called his chieftains to the great hall for a gathering that would later be known, not unkindly, as the council of deceit. It began shortly after midday, a strategy that allowed those invited to first recover from any effects of the night before. Early afternoon also made it more likely that they would not start up again, until at least the meeting was over.

The great hall stood in the oldest part of the stronghold, below the old hill fort site that dominated the stone-walled enclosure. It was a wooden-roofed building, with the fresh, tart smell of raw timber hanging in the rafters. The structure was not more than ten years old, and the interior still unfinished. There were doors on all four sides that permitted ready access, yet they were carefully spaced to allow those forced to remain outside opportunity to listen.

Only three doors had been opened, for Venutius's throne sat at one end of the building on a low dais before the fourth door, which remained barred. Great and lesser chiefs sat on the rush- and hide-strewn floor in a great horseshoe close about the dais. Warriors of lesser standing took their places farther back, and those who could not crowd inside remained by the open doors.

Cethen found a place three rows away from the dais, at the centre of the horseshoe. Nobody challenged his right to sit there. He really had no idea where he ranked, and suspected most of the others didn't either. Venutius's people were gathered from all over Brigantia, some even from beyond. Most were strangers to each other. Offence appeared to be taken only when someone of known acquaintance, but lesser standing, sat closer to the king. Since Cethen was hardly acquainted with anyone, nobody appeared ready to take issue.

As he glanced about the sea of faces, he saw many women. One in particular caught his eye, in the forefront, sat close by the dais. She seemed bored, with her head hunched forward, arms folded, and her long, slender legs tucked under her chin. She took no notice of the bustle and chatter. In fact, she appeared to be asleep, though he couldn't be certain, for her dark chestnut hair had fallen forward, concealing her features.

Cethen eyed the still figure, curious to know who she was, why she was seated so close to the king's throne, and what she looked like beneath the rich, glossy mane—not necessarily in that order. Others were also intrigued, for many glances fell her way, and more than one man nudged his neighbour and asked if he knew what she was doing there. No one seemed to have an answer.

The babble of conversation died away as the door behind the dais was thrown open. Three men entered. Venutius wore an ermine-fringed cloak over the armoured trappings of his office. The great, ancient torque of Brigantia was about his throat. A dragon's head snarled from either end of the heavy, solid gold rope, each with a set of dark, ruby eyes that flashed as if in anger.

The druids claimed that the Goddess Brigantia herself wrought the golden circlet more than a thousand years before, and had given it to the people with her own hand. As long as it was worn by the true ruler, the Brigantes remained free. Cethen had seen it only once before, on the eve of the battle where his father died. On that occasion, it had graced the throat of Cartimandua. He wondered how it came to be around the neck of Venutius. It could only have found its way there by theft—or perhaps by divine intervention, he mused, depending on which side of the fire you sat. He shook his head, wondering if he was growing as distrustful as his wife.

Dermat and Vellocatus flanked the old man, the queen's husband standing on the right. Cethen was surprised to see Dermat there, stand-

136

ing in such a place of honour. He had not realized the man held significant rank within the tribe, for there had been no sign on the raid. Even now, as he stood silently beside his master, the man's small stature and dark-bearded features gave little hint of anything more than a warrior: the quiet, stolid warrior who had wordlessly packed wood, in response to a curt order from Vellocatus.

Venutius began the council by having the chiefs stand and state their names, and the place of their tuath or kin. The chestnut-haired woman spoke first, seemingly indifferent to her surroundings. When she tossed back her hair to reveal her face, Cethen at first decided it was not a disappointment. Her nose was straight yet womanly, her full lips held the deep crimson tint of berries, and her eyes flashed pale emerald. Yet when the woman's gaze swept disdainfully about the hall, they were as flat and cold as green ice.

She said her name was Morallta, there to represent the Carvetii. She was also there, Cethen realized with unusual insight, to determine if Venutius's cause was worthwhile. Which was undoubtedly why she had been given a place of honour close by the dais. Or had she simply sat there? Cethen shook his head, and decided he was doing too much thinking.

The Carvetii presence sent a murmur through the crowd, which continued even as others stood and spoke their names. When Cethen's turn eventually came, he was surprised to hear a whisper run through the assembly, along with loud shouts of approval. He felt his face flush and he resumed his seat, his mind so jumbled he missed the words of those chiefs who had yet to say their names. Which weren't many, as it turned out, for as far as the ranking went, Cethen found himself well down the line.

The council began, and for a while Venutius let the words take their own course. There was always a good deal of bickering at such meetings, as each chieftain made sure that everyone else knew he was not only present, but had something to say.

The discussion began on the safe ground of the Beltane celebrations, and several stories were told before the topic turned to the skirmish at the Eburi village. It was dissected with as much fuss and bother as a druid exploring the guts of a dead chicken. The tale of the Roman's britches was prominent, though the story of the coins was tactfully toned down. Cethen was not surprised that the futile battle itself received little discussion, because it had almost failed. When the subject again turned, this time to the trek north, the ambush of the Tungri cavalry was talked about at great length, for it had been an outstanding success.

It was midafternoon before Venutius, who for the most part sat quietly on his throne cradling a mug of mead, decided it was time to address the reason for the council. He placed his drink on the broad arm of the throne and rose, leaving the heavy, fur-lined robe draped across the seat. The talk died as if by magic, for it had already begun to drag. Venutius had wisely allowed enough to be said that almost everyone was now ready to listen.

"I am not going to speak any longer of the slaughter of Tungri tribesmen ambushed in the middle of the night, glorious as it was," Venutius began, scowling about the hall. "I want to speak of a fight that took place where the Eburi lived. That one was not near so glorious. In fact, it was damned near a disaster."

Several who had been there looked indignant, while those who had not, which was most of them, nodded and cried their agreement.

"The gods toss matters of chance into every battle," the king continued, his loud voice emphasizing his displeasure. "It is how they amuse themselves. But hear this, and hear it well! A Roman soldier taking a piss on a log is no damned excuse for failing such a trial! Oh yes, it made pig piss of our plans, certainly! But there were two hundred warriors who charged out of the woods to fight less than fifty. We had them outnumbered ten to one! They should have been ours!"

Venutius glared about the sea of faces, many showing annoyance, and the chiefs began to mutter among themselves. Cethen, though, had been there. And in fairness to Venutius, he found nothing wrong with the words—including the old king's working of his numbers.

"So what happened?" Venutius cried angrily. Nobody said a word, but when the grumbling grew louder, he pressed on. "Tell me! What happened? Why did we almost get our arses sliced off and rammed down our throats? Because *that* is what almost happened!"

His voice fell, and his tone grew sarcastic. "It was only when another two hundred arrived and took the Romans in the flank, that they finally foundered. Which is shit. Absolute shit. We should have had them long before that." Shouts of anger echoed through the hall, but nobody responded to the question. Venutius waited until the muttering had died away. "No one wants to say why, do they. Do they?" He stood with his shoulders back and hands on his hips, glaring about the vast room. "I thought not!"

He leaned suddenly forward, his voice thundering, finger pointing. "Because you don't fucking-well know why! Do you? Any of you! And until you do know, and learn from it, we'll never beat the bastards. Ever!"

Venutius took a step backward and snapped his fingers over one shoulder. His old shield bearer stepped forward to stand at his side. "Tell them. One word. Tell them. You know the Romans as well as any of us."

Vellocatus's mocking gaze seemed to fall on everyone as he stared about the hall. Cethen decided the bucket had already been filled, for the answer came ready enough: "Discipline!" he roared, then again. "Discipline!"

"That—is—correct!" Venutius roared, stepping forward again. "It is the one thing they have that we don't! There they stood, outnumbered and backs to the river. Two ranks of shields, two ranks of spears, two ranks of warriors—and more discipline among those few men than in my entire army! They didn't flinch, they didn't panic, and—more important—they stood together. As one. We didn't get past them until we caught them in the flank—and only then, by surprise! Which—" he paused, waving his finger for effect "—which is the only reason we took the Tungri cavalry. By surprise!"

He gave a great sigh, as if he despaired of the lot of them, then threw up his hands and turned once more to Vellocatus. "Tell them," he said, and returned to the throne, where he sat down and stared moodily into his flagon of mead.

The hall grew unusually silent. Vellocatus moved to the front of the dais, his manner decidedly less explosive than that of his king. "So we only achieve victory when we have surprise. Does anyone disagree?" He waited, hands held out before him as if coaxing a reply, then continued before any might give one. "Who here would like to see us do that—take them by surprise? For example, at the village of the Eburi, where the Roman vermin have yet to complete their fortress?" Vellocatus spread his arms wide and high, and let the words sink in.

The response was astonishment, then slowly, gradually, a low roar of approval began to build, rising up until it echoed through the hall and beyond. Vellocatus glanced at Venutius with a great, lopsided grin as they both waited for the din to subside. The old man had a wisp of a smile on his face, but buried it in his mug.

"The king will, of course, need the support of all who are here to do that," Vellocatus continued, his voice growing louder. "Such an attack will require many men. The army Venutius leads must number more than ten thousand. The attack must be a surprise." The stir of excitement grew, and he raised his voice to a shout. "Such an attack will take place in the dark, when they cannot see. We must strike before they know we arc there. We must destroy them!"

"We will send them running back into the sea!" Venutius cried, and stepped forward with the beer flagon raised high as a great roar filled the hall.

The council broke up with a general feeling of goodwill, and a great deal of noise. The great hall had barely begun to clear when a shout echoed from the far side of the room, followed by a clamour, and scuffling. Something fell over with a crash, and a voice yelled out above all others, "You stupid lump of pig shit!"

Cethen cringed. The voice could only belong to Cian. More scuffling followed as he pushed his way toward the shouting. A milling crowd of warriors plugged one of the open doorways, all shouting and whooping and elbowing for a better look. A large ring had formed, men standing with arms linked to hold the circle, while others behind hopped up and down to catch a glimpse.

Half knowing what he'd find, Cethen pushed his way roughly to the centre. Two men were in the ring, each crouched low, knife in hand, one circling the other. The smaller was Cian. The other was a great, bearded hulk of a man who moved like a bear. Though twice his brother's size, it took only a moment to see that he also moved half as fast—so the odds were not as uneven as size made them appear. In fact, they were probably in favour of Cian. Or so Cethen hoped.

The assessment was of no consequence. Before the two could come to blows, Venutius himself broke the circle, face mottled with rage. Both fighters stood back, sullenly looking anywhere but at the king. Vellocatus stepped forward and, moving quickly, deftly removed the weapons.

"What the fuck is going on!" Venutius demanded, glaring at the two.

As Cethen might have expected, Cian answered first, his voice a shrill protest. "It's a feud. It began during Beltane when this man," he pointed, "Luga, kicked me. For no reason."

Luga scowled, but kept his head low. "I had a reason," he mumbled. "He was lying with my wife."

Venutius raised his eyebrows, but before he could say a word, Cian's indignant voice again rose in protest. "That's a lie. A filthy lie. I only lay beside her. I wasn't ploughing her."

"I didn't say you were ploughing her. I said you were lying with her, and you were." Luga raised his eyes, but seemed to find the next words difficult, and lowered them again. "You were—you were playing with her tits. I take offence at that."

Several men snickered, and even Venutius had to stifle a smile, but Cian was incensed. "It was Beltane, you ignorant clod! She's a woman of Brigantia. She can do what she damned well likes. And she wasn't objecting." He turned in appeal to the circle of onlookers, as if Luga had stabbed him in the back. His glance caught Cethen's glare, and he shrugged.

Luga pondered his reply at length, then brushed back his tangled mop of hair and pointed to a large goose egg that still showed round and angry, high on his forehead. "He broke a wine jug on my head. That offence has yet to be settled."

"You knocked me unconscious first, you rock-headed oaf." Cian sounded less certain on that point, but he pointed to a fading bruise stretched across the top of his own forehead.

It was Luga's turn to look indignant. He, too, looked to his king as if bladed from the rear. Venutius covered his face with both hands, held them there for moment as he shook his head, then looked up with a sigh. He glanced wearily from one antagonist to the other.

"Is there any way you two can settle your differences peacefully?"

Neither answered. Cethen couldn't remember a better time for his brother to open his big, fat gob and say something, but for once he kept it shut. He tried to will the words into Cian's mouth, but it was useless.

Venutius shook his head again and, although he already knew the answer, turned to Cian first. "Can you bring yourself to apologize for the wrong this man feels you have done him?"

Cian thought this over for a moment, then said, "Yes."

Cethen, totally surprised, sighed in relief. Around him, the excitement of the crowd dropped like a falling arrow, as it sensed the fight slipping away. But Cian didn't disappoint.

"But since he offended me first, then he must apologize first," he added. Cethen felt the crowd's rush of expectation.

Venutius asked Luga the same question. The big man again lowered his head, giving more thought to the question than Cian had, but he had the trapped look of a cornered fox. Slowly, he shook his massive head. "I can, but he must apologize to me first."

Venutius sighed in resignation. "So be it. Settle your differences fairly, in front of others, and with whatever weapons you can agree upon. But you'll do it outside. I don't want your fool's blood all over my hall."

Both men nodded, grim-faced at the finality of the order. The matter was no longer the hot, flaming issue it had been moments ago, when tempers flared. Luga did not look happy, but Cian, true to his character, put his best front on it, and stood with his chest thrown out like a rooster. Cethen turned his head slightly to catch Vellocatus's eye, and raised his eyebrows in question. He was rewarded with a slight nod.

"When, sir?" Vellocatus asked.

"Huh?"

"*When* sir?" he repeated, emphasizing the word. "When should such a settlement take place?"

Venutius studied his shield bearer's bemused expression, and read the message there. He turned back to Cian and Luga. "I do, however, refuse to see my warriors die uselessly," he said. "The time and place will be set when we return from battle. In the meantime, Dermat …? Dermat!" He glanced impatiently about the hall until he found the equally grim features of the stocky chieftain. "Dermat, see that these two are placed at the very front of our attack. They can fight among themselves to see who's first over the walls. If they're still alive after that, *then* they can kill each other."

The hall cleared slowly. Small groups of tribesmen clustered outside the hall, eager to argue over what had really been said at the meeting. Cethen tried to catch up with his brother, but Cian seemed to have made himself scarce. After a brief search, he decided there would be time enough later to give him a slice off his temper. Which was probably wise, for it would have cooled by then. Cethen noticed that Venutius and Dermat had also left quickly. As had the tall, auburn-haired Carveti woman. Vellocatus had not, though, and was pushing through the crowd toward him.

"Come with me," he murmured quietly as he strode past.

Cethen followed him into the sunshine, and up the gentle slope that led toward the north wall. They hadn't gone far when Vellocatus ducked into the low doorway of a rectangular stone hut. Inside it was dark, but a skivvy was bent over, touching a lit taper to a row of oil lamps set along a shelf on the back wall. As the room grew brighter, Cethen saw that Venutius stood talking to two others in the room. They all turned as he entered with Vellocatus. Cethen did not recognize the other man who stood there, but the third figure was the Carveti woman. Cethen smiled and bobbed his head in greeting, and received a cold, expressionless stare in return.

"Cethen, you've actually been inside the stronghold," Venutius said without preamble. "Tell us what you found."

"Er, the s-stronghold?" he stuttered, his mind shifting to the Roman fortress being built at his village. The one that was supposed to be attacked before it was completed. The one that had once been his home!

The skivvy snuffed the flame between a finger and thumb, as he turned from lighting the lamps. He walked to the door and tossed the smoking taper outside, his words a low growl as he passed by Cethen. "The one at Isurium, clod."

Startled, he looked down into the skivvy's face. It was Dermat.

"Oh, I see," Cethen said, composing himself before looking at the expectant faces. "Well, it's the usual kind of thing, I suppose," he began, unconsciously sounding as if he had explored the insides of a dozen Roman forts. "The dirt is stacked as tall as a man on all four sides. It's dug from in front, so there's a ditch there about five paces wide. And so is the dirt for the wall. About five paces wide."

"A wooden wall on top, I suppose?" Vellocatus prompted.

"That's right. I'd guess it's about this high." Cethen held his hand at chest level. "They were putting a walkway behind it when I was there. They'd only just begun building a few days before. It's amazing how fast they—"

"What about gates?" the man beside Venutius interrupted; he was a fleshy, dark haired man with a fat, bull-like neck. "And the towers—what about the towers?"

"There will be four of them—gates, that is. I don't know how many towers. None of them were built yet, though I would think they are now." He paused, considering what else to say. "There were hardly any buildings inside, but there were hundreds of tents. I would imagine more have been put up by now, though. Buildings, I mean. As I started to say, it's amazing how fast they get things up."

"They're not the only ones, huh?" Dermat chuckled, and thumped Vellocatus on the shoulder. The Carveti woman snorted in disgust.

Cethen found himself tongue-tied and felt he should be telling more, then he remembered the smell of the animals. "They had all their horses inside, tethered along the wall to the north. And both the gates and the walls were well guarded."

"How many men?" the woman asked.

"Numbers? The rider we took said there were a couple hundred cavalry." Cethen frowned, and remembered the ambush that had followed his departure. "I don't know what they have left now."

The remark drew a chuckle, but Venutius silenced it. "There are

der, and the honour bestowed on Uncle Cian. Coira finally voiced both their thoughts. "Isn't that like getting rewarded for doing something he shouldn't have done, picking a fight with what's-his-name?"

"Luga," Rhun volunteered. "He didn't pick a fight. Luga kicked him."

'I know it doesn't sound right, rabbit," Cethen agreed, and tousled Coira's hair, unwilling to diminish Cian's glory, "but Venutius is a king. He can do what he wants."

"Ha! A reward!" Elena's voice was full of disdain. "At least one of them will be killed, probably both."

Cethen shrugged. "One of them will be killed anyway, if the fools don't find some way out of their quarrel. And I'm sure it will be Luga."

"And I'm sure it will make a big difference to Nuada and the children if Cian dies on the end of a Roman spear, rather than getting his head split in half by Luga."

All three looked shocked, and spoke at the same time. "Of course it will!"

"Course it will," Tuis echoed, wiping his chubby cheeks free of pike, and looking about for approval of his fishbone stockade.

Elena threw her hands up in despair, but reluctantly ceded the right of it. "Perhaps it will, but he'll be just as dead."

Later, as Elena cleared the meal, Cethen took his sword from where it hung under the pine rafters. He sat down on the edge of the bed and began slowly oiling and honing the blade. Rhun decided it would be a good time to do the same to his own small dagger. Coira scowled her displeasure as her mother made her help clean up the room.

"Are you in the forefront as well?" Elena asked, setting a clay platter down with more force than necessary.

"I don't know where I'll be, though Vellocatus did say Venutius will probably want me for something or other." He paused, recalling that perhaps he should have remained at the hall. "Our kin don't number that many, so I suppose we'll be part of Maeldav's band. Though I don't remember seeing him there today."

"That's because he's dead."

"Really?" Because Maeldav had been such a hard man, Cethen asked, "Was he slain?"

"No, though there were probably enough in line to do it, including his sons," Elena said. "Essa told me when she brought the water in this morning. It happened a day or two ago. Fever and bloat. The druids were there, but couldn't help. He finally vomited and died."

Essa, the house skivvy, looked up as she heard her name mentioned, and Cethen asked her, "Did you hear who might be elected in his place?"

She shook her head, and Cethen returned to honing the blade. Essa's silent answer set his mind walking slowly across a field of possibilities, and his brows knitted with concentration. From the corner of one eye, he noticed Elena surreptitiously watching him, her lips tight with amusement. It wasn't the first time that he wondered if the woman could read his mind! He deliberately grated the whetstone against the iron, and tried to ignore her.

Was there a possibility that his newfound esteem might merit such rank within the tuath? Maeldav had left two sons, both of them no better than the old man himself. One would want the title. Or both, for that matter, which meant they would probably fight each other if they couldn't agree. Yet they would still have to be elected, and Venutius would have thoughts on that. Which in turn raised other possibilities. Was there one that he might hope on? The Eburi had lived in a small village, though, and their kin was equally small in number. Who even knew of them? Yet perhaps not. Many now knew of Cethen Lamh-fada.

On the other edge of that blade, there was no village anymore, so that sort of left him.....

The whetstone suddenly fell still, as another thought struck Cethen. Isurium was in Roman hands now. So where did that leave the chieftain of Maeldav's tuath, anyway? No better than the chieftain of the Eburi, that was where! So, if Maeldav was gone....

It was all too much to think on, Cethen finally decided, and Venutius was likely going to make the decisions anyway. He shook his head, and went back to honing the blade. Elena's look of amusement broke into a broad smile, but it was one of affection. It didn't remain that way for long.

"Da, can I go? When you find out what you're going to do?"

Cethen glanced up to see Rhun standing before him with the sharpened dagger, looking both eager and unsure.

"Don't be daft," Coira said. "Look at you!"

Rhun scowled at his sister, but for once didn't return the taunt. He simply stood before his father, an imploring expression on his face.

"Son, both you and I know that you're far too—too young to wield a sword in battle," Cethen began gently, then fell silent as he considered the boy's years, rather than his size. He'd deliberately used the word "young," for the lad was conscious of his small stature—something his sister didn't let him forget, twin or not. It had been the same for Cethen at that age. His own growth hadn't spurted until he was about fourteen, or as his da had put it, *"The boy grew like a stiff pecker, once his balls dropped."*

He glanced back and forth between the twins, realizing his son was starting to catch up to his taller sister. The boy was almost fourteen. The lad had been given his first blade, as he had himself, when hardly able to walk. And the youngster had to see the battlefield sooner or later. The way things were at present, it was probably best done sooner. Though it would be best done from a distance. That was always the way. Introduce them to it gradually—if possible.

Rhun's face had fallen at the words, and Cethen smiled. "However," he said, careful not to look at Elena, "I know you can sit a horse as if you were tied to its back. So, if—and only if—there is something I see for you to do, you might be able to ride with us. You might be of use as a messenger."

Cethen couldn't help glancing at Elena, but he quickly returned his attention to the sword. The expression on her face reminded him of another thing his da had said: *in truth, son, it's harder to wean the mother than the child.*

The matter was not yet over. Coira pouted. "I have the same age as Rhun, and I'm taller. And I can ride as good as he can. I should go, too."

"No." Both Elena and Cethen were in accord on that one.

"Your mam needs you," Cethen said, "and many are remaining behind. In fact, most will be staying. Grown warriors, and lots of them. It wouldn't do if we won a battle and there was no place to come back to, would it?"

"And it wouldn't do if you lost it, either," Elena muttered.

"Da, that's not fair," Coira protested, ignoring her mother's gibe.

Cethen stood and walked over to his daughter, patting her gently on the cheek as he put an end to her protests. "That's probably very true, my little sparrow hawk. But then, neither is life."

Chapter VIIII

Gaius had no chance to speak to his son before leaving with the patrol the following morning. It was a large force for the task assigned: two full troops of cavalry numbering sixty in total, plus a third troop that was being posted to Isurium. They crossed the Abus just north of the Ebor fortress, where a mixed detail of soldiers and slaves were building up the old ford.

Isurium was an easy ride, and they found themselves at the fort not long after noon. Gaius studied the small stronghold as they drew near, and felt a kindred pride. The newly peeled stakes of the palisade ran neatly along the top of the ramparts, glistening almost white in the bright sunlight. The gates were open wide in welcome, and a guard detail stood at attention under the newly built towers. The squared, orderly defences spoke of permanence, as did the fresh-sawn buildings that greeted them inside.

The patrol left before dawn the next morning, riding along the west side of yet another river that meandered north. Salvius threw out a screen of scouts as the force moved deeper into the forest-covered countryside. The land felt close and uncomfortable, and the trail was far from straight. It ran in and out of heavy woods, following the wandering contours of whatever hard ground the first travellers had found. Recent rain had dampened the track, which in many places was as dark as night below the canopy of heavily leafed trees. Thick tangles of undergrowth ate into either side, where an army of thousands might be hidden a mere twenty paces away.

Yet where the thick cover of the forest fell away, it opened onto the small, rich fields of scattered farmsteads, or just as often, the lush green of watery clearings that fell away to the east. The crops were already high in the rich soil and starting to head, and the marshy meadows were thick with grass and reeds.

When the sun neared its zenith, the horses were watered and a rest made at the head of a large, natural meadow. A small beck snaked along the centre, bubbling its way through tall, swaying spears of marsh grass in search of the river to the east. The clearing was a long, open lea the shape of a dog's hind leg, and the river itself was hidden in the distance beyond a screen of trees. A small farmstead lay halfway along the pasture, tucked in the crook of the leg. The owner and his family had needlessly fled at the troops' approach.

Salvius announced the likely site of the fort around midafternoon, a small village, much like that of the Eburi. It lay sprawled along the edge of a riverbank, well away from the nearest trees. The dogs had little time to yap their warning before the patrol cleared the cover of the woods. Yet the cluster of huts was well placed. The trail that led north, after closely following the river all day, now crossed it where the flow coursed briefly from the west. Gaius saw that a small ford had been built, though the depth and current seemed of no consequence to a man on horseback. The settlement showed little sign of life.

The troopers dismounted, horses and men alike drinking from the clear water of the river. The decurios quickly set pickets along the several trails that led away from the village. Several children, along with a few older women, stood outside the hovels, staring sullenly as the foreign soldiers moved through their tiny settlement at will.

"Something must be going on," Titus muttered, gesturing toward the cluster of huts. "There's not a prime male in sight."

"Or female, for that matter," Gaius added.

"It wasn't a sudden departure," Salvius suggested. "It's too open here. If they're not inside the huts, then they're off somewhere. They couldn't have heard us and be gone that fast."

Gaius nodded first toward the pens, and then to where a few children tended those animals out on pasture. "Only two horses, and one's nothing but dog meat. And the oxen show no sign of use. Venutius must be in the field again."

"Or gathering his people," Titus added.

"How long do you plan to remain here?" Salvius asked, glancing warily about the quiet, sunlit fields, where nothing could be heard but the droning hum of insects.

"Not long enough to make these dullards wonder why we're here," Gaius replied, also glancing about, but with different motive. "Titus, I like the looks of this place. We might ride up- and downstream a little, see if there's a better site. If not, pace off this area. Sample the ground itself, perhaps, but that should do it for now."

"Let's have Salvius's men turn the place on its head while we're here, then," Titus suggested. "They'll think it's nothing more than a search for weapons. I'm also curious whether there's anyone hiding inside the huts. Should we clear them out?"

"Burn them?" Salvius asked.

"No, we're not here on reprisals," Gaius said. "Though if you find anything out of order, by all means, go ahead."

Titus and Gaius mounted and turned their animals downstream, moving along the low riverbank at a slow walk.

"Good, level land. It will require some clearing and drainage, but there's an excellent field of view."

"But ...?" Titus smiled, as if sensing a lack of enthusiasm.

"But!" Gaius growled. "It seems a bit premature."

"We pushed forts into the hills of western Britannia, and in worse country than this. It worked well for us there."

"True," Gaius said, "but they weren't built a half-day's ride from fifty thousand hostiles. Or more."

"That's why you and I are out here. We only think that's the figure."

This time Gaius smiled. "The fifty thousand, or the half-day?"

"Either or," Titus replied. "Since we are here anyway, do you want to go along and find out?"

The question caught Gaius by surprise. "What?"

"Salvius is sending a dozen men to scout this so-called impregnable fortress. There was nothing in Petronius's orders to say that we shouldn't be two of them."

The land had grown low and soggy, and the small river had turned its wandering course southward. "I'd say there's no point going any farther," Gaius muttered, and swung his horse about. "Let's check further upstream from the village before we decide."

"On what?" Titus grinned. "The site of the fort, or riding with the scouts?"

"Either or." Gaius laughed, but for the moment made no commitment. The truth was, he'd had other matters on his mind. Since they'd left the fortress at Ebor the day before, his thoughts, when they hadn't dwelt on screaming barbarians erupting from the forest, were on his own family. Specifically, on the words of Cartimandua, when he'd left her tent with Marc in tow. What had she meant when she said something was bothering the boy? The lad's problems were there in the open, weren't they? Surely! He'd left home because he was bored! He wanted to be where his father was. He wanted to experience the army. It was something he might have done himself at that age. Surely the woman was gnawing at a meatless bone. Even so, the comment had stuck. The sooner he returned and sorted matters out, the better.

And now Titus wanted him to extend the patrol, to go scouting around Stannick. With the lamest of excuses, that might have been heard from a raw recruit: "There was nothing in Petronius's orders to say that we shouldn't be two of them!" There was nothing in them to say that they should, either!

Two senior officers! It was madness. When he heard about it, the legate would be wearing the purple on his face, not on the borders of his tunic. And the primus knew it. The trouble was, Titus was a brave, restless man and, like others of his breed, assumed all his peers were forged from the same bar of iron. It was not that Gaius didn't consider himself brave, though he thought the word much overused; it was that he didn't consider himself foolhardy, either. Not by a good, long margin! Though Stannick was probably only a half-day away. And they were mounted on animals that were far superior to the barbarians' …

"Fine," he finally heard himself say as they neared the village. "We'll go take a look."

One of the hovels was in flames, and Salvius's men moved noisily through the others. A score or more villagers stood off to one side with their familiar, sullen expressions, silently watching the troopers tear through their homes. A male corpse lay headless before the burning hut with a sword, half covered in dirt, not more than an arm's length from its hand. A woman knelt alongside side, keening back and forth as she cradled the severed head in her lap. Two young children, both girls, stood helplessly behind, sobbing and clinging tightly to each other.

"The idiot spat in my face," Salvius said indignantly, pulling his horse alongside Gaius. "Found him hiding under the bed. That must be his nag, out in the pen. My guess is he didn't have time to reach it, before we got here."

"Then we'll get it for him," Titus grunted. "Send one of your men. Though what we'll do with the sorry beast, I don't know. Kill it if you can't use it. In fact, kill both animals."

"What do you say?" Salvius said, his hand sweeping the cluster of huts. "Burn the lot?"

Gaius glanced about the mean, shabby settlement. "No point, really. If we build here, these people might prove useful. If we burn them out, they'll probably move north and join Venutius. I prefer to keep 'em where we can see them."

"The woman? The two brats? She was hiding him. They'll fetch a price."

Titus looked exasperated. "We can't take them with us, Salvius. We're going the other way."

Gaius stared hard at the woman wailing over the headless corpse. "Leave them be," he finally muttered, then turned his horse upstream.

The patrol continued north at a slower pace, for the animals needed to remain fresh. The land rolled upward into higher country, though not nearly as high as the dark range of hills that followed them, far off to the west. Camp that night was in the haven of yet another natural meadow, found after following a small brook almost a mile off the trail.

Rations were eaten cold, and washed down with icy water taken from the stream.

The night proved long and uncomfortable. Without the heat of a crackling campfire, the rustle and creak of the forest echoed tenfold in the tar-black night. Most of the men, Roman and Tungri alike, held a firm belief that the darkness belonged to the other world. The goddess of Dawn, whatever each man chose to name her, took a good deal longer to appear than usual.

Another cold meal broke their fast. Salvius chose to remain with Titus, Gaius, and the scouts. He picked ten troopers, and sent the rest back to Isurium with orders to return by the same path taken on the way out. It was against the rules, but the risk was calculated. The Britons had long since given up any hope of ambushing a returning patrol, for it never came back along the original trail taken. It was important to let the enemy know that this patrol had returned, though, to cloak the fact that some remained in the area.

They followed the brook back along its course, moving directly west. The land climbed quickly, and the going was slow and heavy. The small column wound back and forth in a vain attempt to avoid the thick tangle of undergrowth, yet stay clear of the growing number of open fields and meadows. Several wide, well used trails were encountered that appeared to wander in the right direction, but riding them only increased the risk of discovery.

By late morning, however, excess caution seemed less important than finding some sign, any sign, of the fortress. A few of the well-used trails were finally followed, but each either disappeared or, more often, ended with barking dogs. When midday arrived, it came with a foul mood, and a growing sense of frustration. Salvius came across yet another wide, well-used track that followed the edge of yet another long meadow. They stared at it from the cover of the forest, and decided it was time to call a halt.

The long pasture was man-made, and sloped gently upward to a tree-capped ridge. The trail, which appeared more heavily used than any other they had seen, cut across the open grassland before turning north, where it disappeared beyond the ridge. They had seen a dozen such fields that morning.

Titus broke the silence, shifting in his saddle as they gazed through the thin screen of trees. "Gentlemen, I think we might give it a little while longer, then we either go home, or ask directions."

"Perhaps midafternoon, primus," Salvius said, as if feeling responsible for the fruitless wandering.

"Perhaps the gods are sending help to the needy." The Tungri decurio edged his horse close to the edge of the trees, and whispered the words over his shoulder.

"Do you think we have time to wait for the gods?" Salvius asked sarcastically.

The Tungri grinned through his thick moustaches. "They may have already provided."

He gestured farther back along the track, just as the faint creak of turning wheels drifted through the trees. A voice followed, a single voice. Its owner sounded as if he was talking to himself, for there was no response. Salvius raised his arms skyward with a smile on his face, and acknowledged the gift.

"I was being flippant about asking directions," Titus said with a grin.

An oxcart came into view, and a stooped, grey-bearded man who walked alongside the yoked team with a whip. He appeared to be muttering at the two great beasts hauling the wagon, then Gaius saw a passenger, a towheaded boy about three or four years old, perched on top of the meagre cargo. The lad was too intent on digging in his ear and inspecting the results to pay attention to the old man's words. The cart, while not large, sat heavy on the wheels, causing them to squeal and groan.

Titus swept his arm in a gesture that encompassed the huge pasture, and raised his eyebrows in question. The decurio looked carefully about, then turned and shook his head. No one else was in sight. With no further signal, both men urged their horses forward into the open. Salvius held up four fingers, and waved to the nearest troopers to follow. The rest hung back.

The cart had started to angle away up the rise, but the Briton seemed to sense the Romans as soon as the first horse left the shelter of the trees. He whirled about, in the same motion drawing a long sword from the bed of the cart. A second, smaller blade appeared as if by magic in his other hand. But as six more horsemen emerged one by one from the dark forest, the man's weapons slowly drooped until they were pointed at the ground.

Titus pointed his own blade at the boy, and when he was sure the message was understood, gestured. With the despair of defeat on his face, the man released his grip and the sword and the dagger thudded onto the dirt. The youngster began to wail.

They drove the oxcart deep into the shelter of the trees, where everyone dismounted. The cause of the groaning wheels was soon discovered. The sniffling young boy sat on a load of long iron bars, each of a size to be forged into a wide-bladed sword.

"This man doesn't need a seer to tell his future," Titus muttered, throwing the cover aside.

"Salvius, would you find out where the damned fortress is?" Gaius said. "We'll deal with the iron later."

The praefectus nodded. He spoke the Briton's language fluently, and asked the question himself.

"The fortress of Venutius. How far is it from here?"

The old Briton, who from the start had adopted a stony, resigned silence, was staring vacantly into the forest. The question seemed to catch him by surprise. He glanced briefly at Salvius with a puzzled expression, then as if realizing he had shown a response where none should have been forthcoming, he resumed his indifference.

"Where? Where is it? How many men are there?"

This time he shouted the questions, but they might have been hurled at a rock. Salvius drew his dagger and held the point hard against the man's throat, forcing his head backward as the weapon drew blood. Then just as quickly, he pulled it back. The young boy's sobs turned to a wail.

"I should know better," Salvius said, looking toward Titus and Gaius. "This fellow already considers himself dead. He's just as likely to thrust the knife at his own throat as heed the threat. There are other ways." He pointed to the boy atop the cart. Long, wet streaks coursed down his grimy cheeks. When he saw Salvius look his way his lips quivered, and he wiped both eyes on his sleeves: two deep, frightened orbs of sapphire blue.

"Your son?" The knife waved casually toward the youngster. The Briton's jaw tightened and he glanced from the cavalry commander to the boy, weighing the question carefully. He seemed to decide it was worthy of answer.

"My grandson."

"Ah, even better." Again the knife waved carelessly in the boy's direction, this time the flat of the blade coming to rest on the lad's thigh. "And if we spared his life, would you answer my questions? For at this moment, for our own safety, it is forfeit."

The man's expression turned bitter and he raised one hand, palm down, in a gesture that clearly asked for a moment to think. His face echoed the struggle of indecision, and finally he asked, "If his life is forfeit for your safety, why would that change if I answer your questions?"

Salvius's reply was quick. "We will take him with us."

Again he raised a hand, but only for a moment. "Your questions are, where is the fortress, and how many men does Venutius have there. Is that all?"

Salvius thought that over, then nodded.

"Do you have children of your own?" the Briton asked.

The question was unexpected. Salvius answered almost automatically, "Yes; two."

"Name them."

Salvius suddenly began to feel uneasy. "Julius and Simplicia."

The Briton turned to the Tungri. "Is that true?"

The decurio probably had no idea one way or the other, but decided it was likely true, for he nodded.

Apparently satisfied, the Briton turned back. "I will answer your questions. But first you will pledge, in the name of your gods, the lives of your children against your promise to keep my grandson safe." He shrugged. "If you will not do that, then your word is of no use, and we will both die anyway."

There was a long pause during which Salvius bowed his head and said, "Shit," while the decurio struggled to suppress a grin.

The Briton saw fit to add, "The boy's name is Ethrin."

The cavalry commander sighed and lifted his head as if to ask something of Titus, then changed his mind and returned his attention to the stooped figure. The old man gazed at his grandson, unmoving, his jaw clenched. More haggling took place, then everyone watched in amazement as the praefectus grasped his own sword with both hands, held it before him, and repeated word for word those spoken by the doomed man. The name Ethrin figured prominently.

The ritual over, the questions were repeated. The man answered slowly, which seemed to cause more haggling. Then Salvius raised his voice in anger, and swore in Latin. When the interrogation finally ended, the praefectus turned to the others with a wry expression on his face.

"The man says he cannot be sure how many men Venutius has under arms at the moment, but he says the number spoken about the camp is between twenty and thirty thousand. They are not all actually in the fortress, but most are, and most of the rest are nearby. There are others beyond this number who will also come at his call, some very fast. However, the old man hasn't a number on these. And there are recruits arriving every week. He also says that when Venutius has enough men to gain a chance of beating us, the tribes to the north will join him."

"In other words, once he's got what he needs, they'll send more." Titus snorted. "Sounds like the damned pharisees."

"Did he tell you where the fortress is located?" Gaius asked impatiently.

Salvius didn't answer right away, but stared at the ground with an amused look on his face. Then he lifted his head and pointed through the undergrowth to the far side of the lea. "You see where the track goes through the trees on top of the rise?"

Both men nodded.

"Well, when it breaks out of the forest on the north side, you can see it below."

Like Salvius, all of them were at first angry, but each one could see the black humour of it. As always, it was the way the gods played. The old man had to be given credit, though, the crafty bastard. The Briton had resumed his indifferent stance, only his eyes had now grown moist as he gazed fondly at his grandson.

"The barbarian, sir?" The decurio gestured toward the droop-shouldered man.

"Get rid of him," Titus replied, "but watch him carefully."

"He won't run; there's the grandchild," Gaius said confidently, adding almost as an afterthought, "I suppose there's no need for the child to see it. Take him off somewhere."

The Briton seemed to understand what was being said, for he reached up and plucked the child from the deck of the wagon. No one moved to stop him. He wiped the tears from the boy's eyes with his sleeve, and for good measure wiped the lad's nose too, for it was needed. Then he stared hard into the boy's face as if the image might be taken to the otherworld, hugged him close to his chest, kissed him on the cheek, and handed him to a startled Salvius. He glared into the cavalryman's eyes with the intensity of a curse, then nodded to himself as if finally satisfied.

Several of the other troopers whipped the oxen deeper into the woods, with orders to release the cart, mark its location well, then set the animals free. The iron was valuable and, if possible, would be retrieved later.

"The brat looks good on you," Titus gibed, breaking the silence that followed. "What are you going to do with it?"

"I don't know; leave him where his people can find him, I suppose."

"We can't leave him until we abandon this place. If you don't want to hang onto him, we may have to send him on the same journey as his grandfather."

The decurio moved closer, and growled something to Salvius in his own dialect.

"Yes, I know," Salvius replied, "but I didn't say I was going to adopt him, either."

"What are you talking about?" Gaius asked.

"In order to get the information, I pledged to keep the boy safe. My Tungri friend seems to think there's some permanence to it."

"What did you pledge for your oath?"

"Something I don't want to risk breaking. Something I daren't break. But now I think on the pledge he had me repeat, there could be more to it. Perhaps I did adopt him. It's as confusing as a damned oracle."

Titus snorted at the cavalry commander's ill-ease, and nodded to the dark forest. "Well, it's too late to clarify the matter, isn't it? You'll have to decide where it rests."

Stannick proved to be exactly where the dead Briton said they would find it: on the other side of the next ridge. The stronghold embraced an area large enough to hold an entire city, but there the resemblance ended. It was of a haphazard design, if indeed there had been any design at all, for the place seemed to be built in three sections. What appeared to be the oldest lay to the north. It was the smallest part of the fortress, walled with stone and packed with buildings, some crude and some well built.

Another, ramparted wall, also topped with stone, enclosed what appeared to be the second of the older defenses. The third and southernmost area was by far the largest, and still being built. Its huge perimeter was marked by long dirt ramparts, capped by stone in some areas, and with a simple wooden parapet in others. In a few places, it was little better than what might be thrown up to defend a marching camp.

Hidden in a dense thicket at the edge of the woods that topped the ridge, Gaius and Titus peered down on the massive settlement in silent amazement. Stannick sprawled across a great, shallow valley. A long, gentle slope fell away below them, rising slightly where it met the first rampart. Hundreds of men milled about on horseback in front of the defenses, while at least a thousand more moved on foot in long, uneven, multicoloured ranks. Metal glinted, everyone seemed to be shouting, and the thin clatter of clashing weapons drifted over the sunlit pasture. It took a moment to understand.

"Would you believe it? They're actually training together," Gaius muttered after watching the back and forth flow of fighting, and seeing no one fall.

"Makes you want to go down and show them how to get it right," Titus said. "Look at those ranks. I've seen camels' backs that were straighter."

"True," Gaius muttered, but he wasn't sure. "Maybe that's why they're practising."

They both watched for awhile, criticizing, then turned their attention to the stronghold itself.

"It must be a mile or more across," Gaius breathed, looking to where a long stone wall crested the ridge to the north.

Titus shifted beside him. "That doesn't make it invincible," he countered, unimpressed. "See the shorter part with the stake palisade? It's not much more than a fence. You'd hardly need scaling ladders to storm the damn thing. And once we get inside with a torch, that whole mess will go up faster than a tart's tunic."

The "mess" was a huge, haphazard sprawl of huts, pens, granaries, and sheds, strewn about the south compound as if tossed there. It looked as though the area had then been quickly enclosed by the long rampart, thrown up along a line that was probably once intended to contain horses and cattle. It now appeared to be nothing more than an enclosure to protect Venutius's growing army, thought Gaius. Certainly little attention had been paid to order; the crude, hastily built structures seemed to have been set down wherever an open space could be found. The two older parts of the stronghold had been laid out with greater care; Gaius could see a loose pattern in the dirt streets and the order of the buildings there.

"They would probably fall back behind the stone walls as their main defense," he said, pointing to the far edge of the huge complex. "They'd need lots of warning, though, or they'd just plug up around the gates." He gazed at the flow of movement inside the walls. The entire area crawled with people. "They're like flies on shit," he murmured. "Should we try to count them, or settle for the barbarian's estimate?"

Titus chuckled at the impossibility. "I'll settle for the barbarian's estimate. The poor bastard couldn't have been far off."

The two men lay still, each chiselling the image into his memory, and seeking answers to his own questions. How great was the distance from where they lay, and where was the nearest cover? What were the weakest points of defense? What lay beyond the northern wall that was hidden from their field of vision—perhaps that might be looked at later. How tall were the stone walls of the older defenses? How strong? What would be needed to smash through them?

They stayed no longer than necessary, then slid quietly back into the trees. Now two of Salvius's troopers stood patiently waiting with the horses, where before there had been only one.

"Anything wrong?" Titus asked, glancing quickly across the thicket of trees.

"No sir," the trooper said with a smile. "That's what the praefectus sent *me* up here for—to find out if anything was wrong."

"Then we'll ride down together and tell him there isn't," Titus said, checking the cinch on his saddle.

"Is it as large as they say, sir?" the trooper asked.

"It's probably larger," Titus said, then grinned. "Don't worry. Size isn't everything, soldier. It's talent that counts. And talent is what we specialize in. Do you want to have a look?"

"At what, sir?" The trooper grinned back.

"Piss on your boots," Titus chuckled, and gestured toward the gorse thicket. "The fortress! Go see what you might one day die for. But be quick about it, and quiet, as well."

"You can go too," Gaius said when he saw the second man's look of disappointment.

The pair moved quietly off through the trees, leaving the two officers holding onto the horses. Titus removed a leather wineskin from his saddle and poured a thin stream of the diluted red liquid into his mouth. He handed it Gaius. "So how far do you think we've travelled from where Cerialis wants his new fort built?"

Gaius took a long draught, wiped his chin, and returned the wineskin. "Between yesterday and this morning, we've done well over a day. I'd guess if we'd known where we were going, though, we'd have travelled for less than half that time. We'll ride toward the sun on the way back; that will give us some…."

The sound of feet crashing through the undergrowth stopped him. The two troopers charged wildly toward them, their arms high to ward off the low brush, all care and caution abandoned.

"They're coming. A hundred, at least—on horseback," the first man shouted.

"Shit. I said be careful, didn't I?" Titus roared, fumbling with the reins of the horses. The animals shied, sensing panic, but he kept a firm grip.

"They were halfway up the rise when we got there, sir," the trooper protested. "It wasn't us."

The distant thud of hooves and the sharp, short yelp of riders filtered through woods. The four men swung nimbly into their saddles and slammed their heels into the horses' bellies. The animals took off like rabbits, leaping over deadfalls and weaving through the trees. The Britons crashed into the forest behind, whooping and yelling as if running a stag.

The four of them quickly broke out of the forest and into the bright meadow. There was no sign of Salvius and the others, which was as it should be. The primus, who had cut the trail first, savagely pulled his mount to a halt and pointed to the man closest to him. "Trooper, you come with me," he ordered, and glanced at Gaius. "It's better we split. It doubles our chances, if we go back by separate ways. I suggest you join with Salvius later, if you can. If not, try to get home."

Titus was off before he'd finished speaking, wheeling his horse to the southwest with the trooper close behind, each racing toward the distant cover of the trees. Gaius and the second trooper needed no further urging. Leaning low over the necks of their own animals, they lashed them ruthlessly along the track taken earlier.

As they charged down on the spot where the old Briton had been taken with his oxcart, Salvius emerged from the forest, the boy settled on his lap behind the pommel. The praefectus stopped and blinked, his eyes quickly taking in the panicked flight of the two riders. Then, using instincts honed by more patrols than he cared to remember, he promptly edged back into the cover of the forest. Gaius had been about to yell a warning; instead he muttered, "Arsehole!" and thundered past.

The two riders quickly neared the end of the long meadow, where the trail turned and once more disappeared into the darkness of the forest. Gaius risked a glance over one shoulder, and saw the first of Venutius's cavalry erupt from the trees. There was no doubt which of the two pairs of horsemen they had seen, and would follow accordingly.

But the situation wasn't hopeless, he decided, for their own horses were fairly fresh, and hadn't been run. Those of the barbarians had likely been fighting mock battles all morning. Plus he rode his own mount, Rufus, a large chestnut with an equally large heart. The Roman horses were faster, larger, and stronger than the Britons', and each took the trail as sure-footed as a fox.

Even so, Gaius called on the gods for help, and remembered, in guilty panic, that he still owed them for his last promises. But then, that hadn't turned out well at all, had it? He recalled that he'd slipped and fallen the moment he'd finished his pledges—had that been their answer to his prayers? He was still alive, dammit, wasn't he? Gaius fervently began renewing his vows.

The two animals pounded recklessly along a damp trail that seemed to go on forever, winding through the silent forest, up and down mud-bottomed gullies, across soggy, swarded meadows, and finally into another long, open stretch of pasture. A cluster of huts stood at the centre, and those who lived there stood gaping as the two Roman horsemen thundered by.

The track forked in several directions at the end of the long field, and Gaius glanced up to see where the sun sat, intent on taking the trail that led south. A blanket of cloud now hid the yellow orb, and he cursed the gods, just as quickly apologized, and once more began pleading for help.

The rightmost track seemed to hold most promise. As he headed toward the dark opening in the forest, he again risked a glance backward, and was relieved to see that none of the enemy had entered the clearing. The Britons were falling behind, and would waste even more time figuring out which path had been taken. He thanked the gods, promised them double the pledge made at Ebor, and once more turned his attention to the rough trail as Rufus lunged into the trees.

Gaius blinked, adjusting his eyes to the gloom under the forest's leafy canopy. They opened to a baffling vision that briefly, ever so briefly, became crystal clear. A white-haired old man stood in the middle of the track, his mouth wide with fear, and both his long, thin arms raised helplessly before him. One hand clutched the halter rope of the sorriest looking nag Gaius had ever seen. The creature's head hung low and to one side, as if the poor beast was flinching. An enormous pile of fodder was bundled high on its ancient back.

The hay burst open in a cloud as the two animals collided, and the old hack was bowled to the ground as if struck by lightning. Gaius flew forward through a bramble thicket, and struck the ground on the other side with a sickening thud. The trooper's mount veered nimbly sideways, and took off into the trees; its rider continued down the trail, rolling and bouncing on the grassy ruts, until finally thudding to a halt. He blinked, gathered his wits, then jerked spasmodically as if he trying to roll over and gain his feet; but he couldn't seem to move—not even a finger.

Moments later, the Britons thundered through the same black opening, a crowd of cheering villagers pointing to the correct path. Three dozen must have charged into the darkness of the forest before someone finally managed to crawl out and halt any who still followed.

Chapter X

"You should have seen it," Cian cried, shaking his head and clucking at the shame of it. "There must have been fifty piled up on the trail. Horses screaming. Men screaming. Broken bones. And for some reason, everything was covered with little bits of hay."

"Was anyone killed?" Elena asked as she sat down beside her husband and poured herself a mug of the same thin ale that the two men sipped.

"Two. Three, if you include the Roman. All from broken necks. Only, oddly enough, the Roman's head seems to have got broken right off!"

The two brothers laughed, and Elena snorted. "He might have been more use alive. You could have worked him on the walls, or found out what he knows. Or both, I suppose."

"Not with a broken neck, we couldn't," Cian said. "We did him a favour. At first I thought maybe Luga might have been killed, which would have saved me the trouble later. That huge, ugly horse of his was fast enough to be near the front of the pack. But when I rode into the forest to sort things out, the dumb ox was standing right in the middle of it all. Not a scratch. It was as if the gods had placed a charm on him."

"You better hope it's not still there when you fight him," Elena said, "unless you find the good sense to change your mind."

"The man offended him," Cethen protested.

"The way I heard it, if anyone was offended, it was Nuada."

"Anyway," Cian spoke hastily, "one of the Carvetii that came with that red-haired vixen had his back broke. I think he'll die too. And at least two others will never walk right again."

"You said you were chasing two Romans," Cethen said. "Did the other one get away?"

"No, Venutius has him."

"Why is his head still attached, if the other one's isn't?"

"Yeah, I was coming to that," Cian said, and slapped the table excitedly. "It was for two reasons. The first was, nobody found him right away, otherwise I'm sure he'd have lost it, because everyone's piss was still boiling. But he'd been thrown through a bush, and it was only when we were gathering up the horses that we found him. There was a bitch of an argument, because the head-hackers wanted his for their doorposts. That's all those stupid hill-climbers can think about. Anyway, Dermat—you remember Dermat? He put a stop to it, because he recognized the man. It was your Roman!" He again slapped his hand on the table, looking gleefully at Cethen's puzzled face.

"My Roman?"

"The one you pulled out of the river."

"He's still alive, then!" Elena sniffed, as if sorry to hear it.

"That may be open to question," Cian said. "Last time I looked, he was off with the faerie. Maybe they'll keep him."

"I wonder what Venutius will do with him," Cethen mused, surprised that he wanted to know. "That's if the faerie don't want him."

Two druids arrived shortly before the evening meal was to be eaten. It was their usual part of that day to come calling—the timing ensured a meal, for no one would refuse to share with them, yet it also offered opportunity for escape, should the food appear less than appetizing.

Vellocatus came with them to show the way. He told Cethen he was growing bored. The last he'd heard, Catey had gone downriver to the new Roman camp, which meant he could no longer vanish for a visit. Not that he intended to, he insisted, for the last time had been by chance, but it was one less opportunity to relieve the tedium. Elena, listening as she went to find something for them all to drink, simply grunted.

The frail, white-bearded druid named Trencoss sniffed at the rich, savoury aroma that filled the hut. As if searching for confirmation, he glanced to where Essa toasted a rack of groat cakes on the fire, each sizzling with butter, fat-hen, and the bacon she'd stuffed inside. For good measure, a crisp leg of spring lamb roasted alongside. With a sigh of contentment, the old man eased his skinny rump onto one of the hides placed around the low counter of boards that served as a table.

The second druid, a pale, thin, clean-shaven youth with dark, oily hair tied back in a pony's tail, sat disdainfully down beside him. The two seemed a contrast in everything, including their clothing. Trencoss wore a clean, white robe, while the younger druid's was a tattered brown that looked grimy even in the dim light of the hut.

"This is Sorcha," Trencoss said, and gestured to his companion, who didn't bother to acknowledge the courtesy.

They both reached for the jug of ale that Elena placed on the table, and poured a good measure without leave or thanks. The old man wasted no time in getting down to the matters at hand. He was clearly hungry; drool glistened on the white hair at both corners of his mouth.

"Did you know that our people retrieved the 'fish' you pulled from the river when the Romans came to your village?" he asked.

"Yes, of course," Cethen said, looking pleased that for once his information was one step ahead of someone else's. He seemed to remember his manners, and gestured for Vellocatus to sit down. "I heard he was senseless. Is he now in the land of the living?"

"Yes, though I would guess his head still pounds like a drum. He moves as if it were an eggshell." The old druid smiled. "An egg that appears already once cracked."

"He's lucky it's still attached to his neck," Elena said, leaning over Essa's shoulder to look at the browning groat cakes, wondering if there were enough. If not, the children might perhaps go over to Nuada's, and she could feed them. There would be food enough there. Cian was likely in the old part of the fortress by now anyway, for the lot of them would be reliving the day's chase. By midnight, it would have turned into a triumph.

"Of course." Trencoss looked shocked. "It is not for us to remove it."

"It's not?" both Cethen and Elena asked in surprise.

"Of course not," Sorcha spoke as if addressing the simpleminded. "The man is in the care of the gods. It is obvious." His cold stare held them both for a moment, then he seemed to decide that perhaps it wasn't obvious, at least not to these two churls, and explained with exaggerated patience, "The man should have died at your village. He did not. They say he was struck at least three times that day. Each blow should have killed him. Yet the gods allowed him to live. He should have drowned, yet he was saved. Why, we don't yet know. And now? He should have died in his fall from the horse, yet the gods delivered him up to us. Perhaps it was even Brigantia herself. We must wait, and find out why. If there is one thing that is certain, we cannot kill him."

Vellocatus leaned back in his chair, the old amused expression twitching at his face. "It makes you think, doesn't it? We receive a gift from the gods, and it's a Roman! Stretches the mind."

"So if he's not to be killed, what are you going to do with him?" Elena asked, as an inkling of the druid's mission teased the back of her mind.

Trencoss pulled at the long, white tangle of beard before he spoke. "It is sometimes difficult to determine why the gods do what they do, or what it is they want. They act in strange ways. But we do know the Roman owes his life to you."

"I couldn't agree more," Elena said, now firmly ahead of the druid's words.

"We feel that the gods, Brigantia herself perhaps, has in some manner woven the man's life pattern with that of your husband's. They have returned him here. But for what? And to who?"

"Really?" Cethen seemed to find the thought intriguing, but Elena spoke before he could ask further.

"What did he come here with?"

"What do you mean?" Trencoss asked.

"Well, he didn't arrive naked and on foot, did he? What was found with him?"

Sorcha saw the drift of her question, and in this he seemed to be two paces ahead of the old druid. He answered with a sneer, "His weapons, his armour, and his horse. And a battered helmet."

"The man doesn't do too well by his helmets, does he?" Cethen chuckled, looking about the low table as if trying to lighten the mood, which had suddenly turned tense. "That's two he's ruined. I wonder what they cost?"

"You expect us to hold the Roman for you, isn't that so?" Elena persisted. "I'd guess that's the reason you are here. If the gods have given him to our care, then his goods are part of the bargain. I'll warrant he had a purse, too. We'll decide what to do with them."

Remembering everything that had been abandoned in their flight from the village, Elena felt pleased. Perhaps the gods, in their wisdom, were now repaying at least part of what the Romans had taken from them. And if it wasn't the gods repaying the debt, then the Roman himself could. If it cost Venutius his booty, so much the better. The old bugger owed them.

Cethen suddenly spoke up, his mind seemingly one pace ahead of his wife's, not a common event. "What sort of a horse was the Roman riding?" he asked. Sorcha snorted in disgust, but Trencoss smiled quietly to himself, as if amused.

"A big chestnut with a white blaze on his face," Vellocatus interrupted, laughing as if amused by Elena's obstinacy. "Alas, it's been gelded. Which is something Venutius is likely to do to you, when you take that animal from his stables."

The Roman was brought to his new home the following afternoon, as if leading a rabble army. He sat in the saddle of the great chestnut horse, staring stonily ahead. The animal's reins were held firmly by Vellocatus, who rode alongside, grinning and waving to the crowd. A half-dozen warriors followed on foot, there to protect the Roman; but the people were in a cheerful mood. The man had not been taken in a battle heavy with losses, nor had there been an ignominious defeat. A foreign prisoner was a welcome sight, a pleasant change in the humdrum routine of the huge camp.

The small procession had soon gathered a long, disorderly tail of the curious as it passed through the three compounds. When it finally arrived at Cethen's small, ramshackle lodge, hundreds and hundreds milled about, wanting nothing more than to see what would happen.

"Look at that beast," Cethen breathed to Elena, his eyes on the sleek horse. "Why would he cut an animal like that?"

"Because there are probably a thousand others where it came from," she replied, then her voice softened. "He is beautiful, isn't he."

The Roman slid unsteadily from the horse, and when he staggered, Vellocatus helped him keep his feet. The morning had been spent in the questioning hands of Venutius and the druids, and he was still unsteady. The chestnut skittered nervously to one side, its head high, nostrils flared, and the great brown eyes rolling at the closeness of the crowd.

"Where do you want him?" Vellocatus asked.

Cethen grinned. "The Roman or the horse?"

"Both, I suppose, though I know which one will be the least trouble." He nodded toward the gelding. "I was talking about the horse."

"In that pen—the nearest." Cethen pointed to an enclosure where several smaller animals stood, each with its head pushed over the top rail, eyeing the new arrival.

"Can I take him, Da?"

The twins jumped up and down for attention, both wanting to be the first to have the animal's care. Vellocatus resolved the issue by handing a rein to each. The gesture didn't please either, but the pair moved away together, towing the chestnut behind.

"And the Roman?"

"He'll be spending most of his time in there, as soon as it's finished. Which it will be before this evening." Cethen nodded toward a small, windowless shed being built close by the lodge. The framework was in place, and the wall, so far, stood at chest height. When completed, the structure would permit a man to lie down in comfort, but not much more.

Vellocatus eyed it critically, but didn't opine. "And until then?"

"Let's take him inside and decide. If nothing else, we can ask him how he's been since we last saw him."

The door to the tiny lodge was open, and everyone who considered themselves kin tried to follow inside. The hut soon became a crush. The Roman remained aloof, staring upward at the peeled pole rafters. He still wore his chest armour. His eyes widened in surprise when one of the other warriors dumped a large, blanket-covered bundle on the table, and the rest of his equipment spilled out. He clearly hadn't expected to see it again.

"Even the damned helmet," Elena said, as someone picked the damaged headgear up and passed it around. A large dent flattened the left side of the crown. "I didn't think we'd see the horse, let alone his belongings."

"The druids are working themselves into a state on this one." Vellocatus seemed amused. "They're finding more signs in the Roman's capture than warts on a toad. Which is the same as saying *they* don't want to bugger up what they think the gods are telling them. So if they've sent the Roman back to Cethen Lamh-fada, then all that came with him should go to Cethen Lamh-fada. Future problems included."

"What do they expect me to do with him?" Cethen asked, suddenly eyeing the Roman with doubt written on his face.

"Work him, I suppose, and keep him under guard," Vellocatus said, and shrugged. "There are gangs working the walls. Put him there. He'll look less offensive without the armour—dress him in something else. Mind you, right now he doesn't look as if he could cut the throat of a newborn lamb."

The Roman's face and arms were covered with welts and scratches from his flight through the brambles, and a great, purple bump rose above the faded bruises on his forehead. A jagged scar showed livid through his short growth of hair, testament to his last encounter with Cethen's kin. Despite his proud aloofness, his shoulders were slumped. He looked tired.

"We'll have the armour off first, then," Cethen said. "Tell him to take it off, or we'll do it for him."

Vellocatus spoke, and without a word the man held out his bound wrists. The rope was cut, and for a while he stood rubbing the feeling back into his hands. Then, at a grunt from Cethen, the fastenings on the moulded breastplate were undone. The two pieces of armour thudded to the dirt floor, to be quickly retrieved and passed about by a score of curious hands.

Vellocatus murmured another instruction, and the supple leather over-tunic followed, carefully pulled over the battered head.

"Let me feel," Elena said, drawn by the fineness of it.

Vellocatus passed it to her, and she held it in both hands, testing the softness of the blood-red leather. She buried her face in the smooth folds, breathing in the warm, heavy odour. It was of a better quality than she'd seen before. Her mind turned over the possibilities, weighing the amount of material to be had from it.

Her gaze drifted back to the Roman, clad only in boots and a linen under-tunic that fell to just above his knees. His lower jaw moved to one side as if amused, yet his features showed scorn. Without a word, he pulled the garment over his head. He bundled the grubby white cloth into a tight ball, and tossed it to her. She caught it instinctively, and added it to the armful of crimson leather.

Several of those watching laughed at the gesture, others growled at the arrogance, but most simply stared. The man stood only in a set of drawers, tied at the waist, which barely covered his groin. In the dimness of the hut, the fabric glowed white in stark contrast with his skin and the black hair that matted his chest and belly. Elena's eyes, with a will of their own, swept quickly up and down the almost naked body, focusing involuntarily on the snowy material, and the outline of his maleness.

Catching herself, she jerked her eyes upward to meet his, and she felt her face heat. The Roman smiled sardonically, shook his head slowly as if despairing of her, and tugged at the string about his waist. With a swift movement he stepped out of the snowy garment, bundled it, and threw that to her as well. A whoop went up around the room as he stood naked, hands on his hips, staring at Elena. She glared back, for once speechless.

Gaius grunted his disgust, then turned as if suddenly aware of the press of alien faces. It was as if he were on display, an animal pacing its cage before being tossed into the arena. He let his contempt show on his face as his gut burned with the bile of his rage. He wanted to strike out, hit them, show the awesome power that lay behind him and his people. Then, just as quickly, it faded. They were buffoons, all of them, as ignorant as a pack of their slobbering dogs. In fact, they looked exactly like a pack of dogs, drooling, jostling each other, pushing, waiting eagerly to see which way the prey would leap. Well, they wouldn't be disappointed.

He dropped to a crouch and let one arm dangle, scratching himself with the other, as if infested with lice. Thrusting his lower jaw angrily forward, he began hopping up and down, chattering like an ape.

The gesture was completely lost.

Gaius's days quickly settled into routine. Two warriors huddled outside his small prison every night, wrapped in warm, woolen cloaks, and armed with long cudgels. A huge razorback hound, one that had announced Gaius's arrival at the Eburi village earlier that spring, kept them both company. Of the three, the huge animal was by far the more vigilant. On the few occasions Gaius tested the walls of his cell, the beast was instantly on the other side, sniffing and growling, often startling the guards as much as the prisoner.

At the first gleam of daylight, a young girl Gaius came to know as Coira brought food and water from the lodge, and the two sleepy warriors unbarred the door. The single shackle that secured one of Gaius's arms to the side of the shed was released, and the guards brought him outside. There was irony in the fact that the device itself had once belonged to Rome.

Once he was fed and his night pot emptied, he was led off to the walls and given over to the charge of a surly, hulking ox of a man called Con. From then until evening he toiled, with only one real break for the midday meal, which was generally dry bread and a tasteless stew. He dug ditches and piled dirt alongside countless other men. Most were slaves, but many were tribesmen who had fallen foul of Brigante raiders. A few were captive auxiliaries, and more than a few were simply men of Brigantia, who had the bad luck to have been born low, and with no *honour price*.

The work itself was unhurried, carried out at a steady, endless, throbbing measure that at first twisted and tortured muscles that Gaius hadn't known existed. The dull giant Con and his underlings bothered no one as long they laboured well, but those who rested for more than a few moments were bullied back with thin, supple willow switches.

The daylight seemed interminable, for the summer solstice was nearing. Each evening, it was late when he returned, dead on his feet, and feeling as if a walk, even to the edge of the fortress, was beyond his ability. The warrior escort opened the door to Cethen's lodge to make sure someone was inside, then Gaius was pushed roughly through. The leavings from the evening meal always awaited him, piled cold on a platter at the table.

The dull, mindless, bone-tiring routine had, like so many things of late, gotten off to a very bad start. At the end of his first day of labour, Cethen's woman had spoken only one word, her face expressionless as she pointed to the leftovers. "Eat."

Gaius had stepped uncertainly into the hut, squinting about the dim interior. She sat on the end of the cot working on his leather tunic, which was now in three pieces. There was no sign of Cethen. The three children played with a small puppy, which pulled fiercely at the end of a piece of kindling. They stopped their teasing and stared wordlessly as Gaius crossed to the table. He was too tired to be hungry, but the soldier in him knew enough to take food when it was to be had. So he eased his stiff muscles down onto the skins piled by the low table, and ate.

The woman muttered something, and the girl Coira went to a large, earthen crock set low in the ground, and ladled some liquid into a mug. She set it cautiously on the table, then squatted across from Gaius and continued to stare. He nodded his thanks, and stared back.

He found the girl quite appealing, and her curiosity not unwelcome. Perhaps it was because she appeared to be the same age as his own daughter, though there any similarity ended. This one's eyes were the same colour as her father's, though of a darker, more inquisitive blue. Her hair owed much to the rich, honey colour of her mother's, yet it was much paler, leaning toward spelt straw. And there was no need to look far to see where she'd gotten the firm, determined set of her mouth.

Gaius turned his attention to the dark liquid, and hesitated. The drink had the brown, murky appearance of stagnant brook water. He sipped cautiously at the rim, and was surprised to find it was a pleasantly cool, thin-tasting ale. "Good," he said, and licked his lips, though he doubted she understood the word.

Coira smiled and coloured, which drew a growl from her brother, and she scowled at him. The woman muttered something to the pair, apparently telling the two to halt their bickering. Coira rose to her feet, sniffed her annoyance, and stalked outside. After a moment or two, the boy followed. The toddler, like a pup on a leash, trailed after his brother. The door swung shut of its own accord, and Gaius found himself alone with the woman.

He finished as much of the food as he could, chewing thoughtfully as his eyes followed her about the room. His thoughts wandered. It would soon be dark. The sun had started to set as the guards brought him from the walls, and the light would likely vanish earlier than usual, for the sky was heavy with cloud. Was escape possible? Or was he being tested?

A woman alone in the hut was less of a problem than a man, certainly. And once outside, dressed the way he was, he might lose himself in the night; he'd been given an old wool tunic and a set of cast-off britches, and could pass for one of the barbarians. Gain enough distance from the hut, and in the huge clutter of buildings he would be difficult to find. He could steal a horse—there were enough of them scattered about—and surprise might get him past the walls, and into the forest.

The bone-weary exhaustion that dragged at his body seemed to evaporate. He rose slowly, nodded to the woman as if in thanks for the meal, and stretched his arms lazily upward, yawning. A comfortable belch followed. From the corner of his eye, he measured the distance to the door.

Which was a mistake.

The woman caught the glance, and both moved at the same time. Gaius was two paces ahead, bracing his shoulder as he crashed against the door's planking. A red flash of pain stabbed down to his ribs as he bounced back into the room. The damned thing opened inward, though it probably would have made little difference. It was sturdier than it looked.

The woman pulled savagely at the neck of his tunic, sending him crashing backward onto the floor. Another shaft of pain lanced up his back, and, before he could move, she landed hard on his belly. The wind left him in a loud gust. He turned his head sideways as she rained blows onto his face and he tried to roll, but his half-healed ribs screamed in agony. He tried jerking and twisting, but she might have been glued there. He finally grasped one wrist, which just added to her rage. A moment later he managed to catch the other as her arm came crashing down on the side of his head. He held on, squeezing hard, as he tried to focus through pain-blurred eyes.

For a moment they were still, each glaring at the other, both panting. She seemed to realize she had lost some of the edge, and tried to pull backward and free her trapped wrists. Gaius pulled hard the other way, his weight and strength now the advantage, and she fell sideways. He quickly rolled over, fought his way on top, and forced her arms against the dirt floor, pinning them high above her head. She squirmed and bucked as if berserk, but it was of no use. As if realizing the futility, the woman stopped moving except for the rapid rise and fall of her chest. She sneered, her face twisted with hate, and snarled words in her own tongue.

"So what now, bitch?" Gaius grunted the words to himself rather than the woman. "How do I get out of here?"

He sat straddling her belly, rising and falling with her every breath as he stared down into her face. She stared back, her eyes unblinking. He glanced about the room, searching for something, anything, that might be of use. He didn't want to kill the woman, or even hurt her—if they caught him after that, he was as good as dead. And not very quickly either, he guessed. His eyes fell on the pole rafters, where a coil of cord dangled from a peg. It would do. Bind her, stuff something in her mouth, and leave.

He looked down again, trying to decide on the best way to grab the thin rope. Perhaps bring her arms down, pin them behind her back, then roll her over. Hold her while reaching upward for the rope, pull it down, tie her hands, stuff her mouth with …

It struck Gaius that the woman hadn't screamed or called out. Perhaps she thought she didn't need to. "Proud bitch, aren't you?" he muttered, then pulled one arm down behind her back, and held it there.

She grimaced, but still said nothing. Gaius glanced down, readying the next move. One shoulder had lifted, and the woolen dress was pulled tight about her chest; her breasts strained against the thinly woven fabric, heaving with every breath. An idiotic urge to grasp and fondle them crossed his mind, and he shook his head.

"Some other time," he muttered, his eyes catching hers as they moved upward to the other hand.

She snarled again, spitting words out as if guessing at his.

"Yeah, I'll bet you'd love to," Gaius said, guessing at hers, and quickly pulled the other arm down. The dress strained even tighter.

Grasping both of her wrists in one hand, he pressed the other on her shoulder, and eased himself slowly away from her belly. Again, he glanced quickly at her breasts, both straining against the soft wool, then upward to the rafters where the cord hung tantalizingly near. Slowly, he reached up with one hand…

Elena moved quickly. Jerking one leg upward until her knee was under her chin, she kicked out, hard. The bottom of her foot caught the Roman square in the crotch. He howled and fell writhing onto the dirt floor.

She lurched to her feet and glanced wildly about the hut for a weapon: a knife, a cudgel, anything to regain the edge. An axe caught her eye, a small one, embedded in a log by the fire. She jerked it free and whirled, ready to cleave the Roman's skull. The door creaked on its hinges, and Cethen stood framed in the opening.

"Where in a boar's bum have you been?" Elena yelled.

Cethen's startled eyes swept the room. They widened at the sight of his wife—gasping for breath, one hand propped against the side of the hut, an axe grasped low in the other. Her long hair fell in a honeyed tangle across her face, and her clothing, grimed with dirt from the floor, was bunched and twisted about her hips. Then he glanced down at the Roman, writhing and moaning on the ground. Both hands clutched his groin, his nose was bleeding, and his lower lip was split.

"Am I interrupting?" he murmured, his face breaking in a grin.

"Not at all, arsehole," Elena gasped. "We were just wondering when you were coming home to eat."

"Well, I'm here," Cethen said, gently reaching out to push the hair away from her face. "Are you alright?"

"Better than our Roman," Elena muttered, then gulped a deep breath and pushed away from the wall. The axe thudded back into the log.

"What was he bent on doing?" Cethen asked, his face turning grim. "Escaping or raping?"

"Escaping," Elena muttered. "It's why he's still got his balls to hold onto."

"Then I suppose we can't hold it against him. He has the right. Though he didn't hurt you, did he?"

There hadn't been time to dwell on that, Elena realized, but when she did, it was to understand that the Roman hadn't even tried. In fact, the man had gone out of his way not to. If that had been the aim, he could have smashed her head against the floor, and been gone. It galled her to admit as much, but it was true. "No, he didn't," she said, then added what was fair. "Though I'll admit, Cethen, he could have."

"Then he was thinking. If he had, it would have been repaid ten-fold. And the druids don't want that." He paused, then added, "And I don't suppose I do, either."

"Oh. Any reason why?" Elena asked, watching curiously as her husband grasped the Roman by the loose folds of his wool tunic and pulled him over beside the fire.

"Yes, there is." Cethen eased his charge up into a sitting position, and stood back to look. The man gingerly released his privates and lifted the hem of his tunic to clean his face. "Since he's here, I want to start learning his language."

"You what?"

"I said—"

"I heard you. What brought that on?"

Cethen looked sheepish. "It was Vellocatus."

"I see," Elena said, and paused, thinking it through. "It would be useful, wouldn't it? The way things are right now," she said finally, nibbling at her lower lip. "Who's going to lead the tuath is as yet undecided. And for better or for worse, the 'old bugger' seems to like you. It's as if you were one of his own. If we understood more of the Roman's tongue, it could prove very useful."

Cethen glanced up at his wife as he settled down in front of the Roman. The "we" hadn't gone unnoticed. The woman never ceased to amaze him. He'd had no need to explain the reasons Vellocatus had given; she seemed to have grasped them. Except perhaps one, which was personal. The one that goaded him to learn more than anything, and one that Elena would not understand. Or would she? Perhaps. For it would be sweet, very sweet, to have some grasp of the language when they took their village back. And the earlier he started learning it, the better.

He glanced at the Roman again and couldn't help smiling. Yes, his wife never ceased to amaze him. "I think we're going to need some water here, Elena," he said, "and maybe a cloth. You made a right mess."

Chapter XI

Gaius had been toiling at the ramparts for weeks, when the pattern was suddenly broken. That evening, when he was thrust inside the lodge, the children were no longer there. The druids Trencoss and Sorcha sat at the low table. Cethen was with them, all three nursing mugs of the brown, yeasty ale. Each looked comfortably fed. The usual platter of leftovers was not on the table, and his first thought was that the damned druids had eaten it all. He glanced toward Elena, who sat on the edge of the bed, making a red-dyed leather purse. There was no need to wonder where the material came from. He grew irrationally annoyed; he was damned hungry.

"Where—" he began, then just as quickly forced himself to remember his position, and fell silent.

The presence of the druids was not a good thing, he decided. Their being here was likely a greater concern than his belly, even if it was growling like a starved wolf. He stood patient, like a eunuch house slave, waiting to see which way the reed was bending. They kept him that way for a long time before deigning to speak, though Cethen cast the odd uncomfortable glance in his direction.

"Do you still not want to tell us why you came here?" Trencoss began at last, speaking Gaius's own language.

He shrugged.

Sorcha rose and stalked over until his thin, pallid face was less than a handsbreadth from his own. The young druid repeated the question, his voice a low, menacing hiss. When he offered the same silent shrug, Sorcha produced a short willow switch and swept it across Gaius's face. He simply flinched, as if it was nothing more than an annoying fly, which seemed to anger the young priest even further.

Again the question, followed by another asking what the Roman armies intended to do. The druid screamed, his voice filling the hut. The answer was the same, only this time Gaius contemptuously spat a glob of spittle onto the dirt floor by his feet. Enraged, Sorcha kicked the back of his knees. Gaius fell, and the druid delivered a tremendous blow to his belly. Trencoss suddenly spoke, rebuking the young druid in his own tongue, and Sorcha sullenly returned to the table to squat, sulking, in front of his mug of ale.

The old man calmly continued his questions, but in a manner that seemed to show concern for Gaius, who lay gasping on the rushes, eyes watering as he clutched his belly.

Elena angrily threw the leather to one side and, with a contemptuous glance at Sorcha, strode outside, slamming the loose-hinged door behind her.

Her departure was ignored. The questions continued to rain on Gaius, along with the occasional outburst from Sorcha. There was little response. It didn't even appear to be expected, Cethen noticed. It was almost as if a ritual was being played out, and he wondered why. Then he noticed something else.

Sorcha, when he returned to the table, picked absently at the dirt under his fingernails, as if the whole episode was nothing more than the end of a meal. He wasn't breathing heavily in anger, nor was his face red, as his own would have been if he'd lost his temper like that. It struck him that Trencoss was deliberately kind, and earned at least a small response from the Roman; whereas his young apprentice was deliberately cruel, and received no response at all. He wondered if it was worth their effort. He recognized such words as Cartimandua,

Ebor, Cerialis, and legions, but his learning had been slow, and most of the words were spoken too fast for him to grasp.

When Trencoss decided that enough had been done, the pair rose and left, beckoning Cethen to follow. Gaius remained on the floor, his knees drawn to his chest. When the door closed on his tormentors, he slowly straightened his legs and eased himself into a sitting position. He was gently rubbing his belly and deciding the battering hadn't been that bad, when the door swung open. He tensed, cursing himself for premature optimism, but Elena entered. He released his breath in a gush of relief. Her return probably meant the druids were gone. But his mood would have lifted anyway, druids or not.

The woman didn't appear to hold a grudge for the skirmish on the floor of the hut, though she hadn't thawed much, either. The time spent each evening learning Latin words had forced all three to speak with each other in a more or less civilized manner, if such could be applied to these barbarians.

Cethen, he found, had a greater struggle with the task than his wife, but was far more enthused. The tall Briton, while not particularly friendly, was an open man, and each step of his thinking was scribed on his face. When working at the meanings or pronouncing words, he'd laugh, or frown, or grow angry in turn. Elena remained impassive, saying no more than needed. Once in a while she might forget herself, but she'd quickly cover the slip. There would be the hint of a smile, or the start of a giggle—more so as the days wore on—but they were quickly stifled, and she remained aloof.

Gaius sighed. It was one thing to be cast into the field with five thousand men and no women. That was easy to handle. It was a different thing to sit next to one each night, close enough to touch. A lithe, sensuous woman, with a fist like a block of stone, and the scent of fresh-cut lilac. He grinned, remembering the military's mathematical proposition: desirability is an inverse ratio of availability. Or, the farther away from home …

"Not as bad as the last beating." Gaius spoke slowly, testing the ice while ruefully feeling his face.

Elena offered nothing more than a passing glance as she moved to the bench at the side of the hut where food was prepared. The leftovers had been made up after all, hidden under a damp cloth. She set them on the table without a word, added a slab of coarse barley bread, then resumed her seat on the edge of the bed to stitch the purse.

Gaius eased himself to his feet and made a show of hobbling to the table, groaning loudly with each step. He sat down with an even louder moan, tenderly rubbing his backside before settling it on the ground. Elena glanced up and, catching her eye, he winked and grinned. She snorted in disgust and bent her head to the stitching, but the faintest trace of a smile had crossed her lips.

"Hey," Gaius said. When she looked up, he gestured to the food and added, "Thank you."

The comment passed unacknowledged.

"You are," he continued, undeterred, "very beautiful." He meant the words to provoke a response, but as soon as he spoke, he remembered it was the first phrase a soldier learned when posted to a new province.

"I know," Elena muttered, not raising her head from the rich leather. "You're not the first rut-starved warrior to tell me that."

Cethen found Vellocatus waiting outside, perched on the top rail of the horse pen, his lean figure framed by the crimson orb of the setting sun. Dermat and Cian sat beside him, all three admiring the big chestnut, its head tossing as it picked at a pile of freshly scythed grass. The two druids followed as he crossed to the enclosure.

"So is the Roman fit to travel?" Vellocatus asked, swinging about and jumping down from the rail.

"Tired, but not injured." Sorcha grinned, his lean features ferret-like. "Just enough of a beating, though, to make him feel important."

"What do you mean, travel?" Cethen asked.

"Venutius wants him to escape," Vellocatus replied.

"Escape!" Cethen exclaimed, disappointed. "We just took him prisoner."

"It's politics."

"Strategy," Trencoss corrected, and turned to Cethen. "It's strategy."

"Whatever that means," he replied. "Why?"

"We can use him to our advantage," Trencoss explained. "The man likely knows nothing more about us than his friends already do. The ones who rode with him saw as much as he sees, or they must be blind. And who knows? Perhaps they were sent here merely to confirm information they already have. But if *we* let him escape, he will carry information *we* want them to have."

"Are you going to scratch it down, or ask him to remember?" Cian quipped.

Dermat chuckled, but Trencoss scowled and, deftly lifting the tip of his staff, jabbed Cian hard in the chest. His arms flew out, and he fell backward into the pen with a yelp.

"Since you ask, young man," the druid said, speaking through the rails to Cian, sprawled gasping for wind on the other side, "tomorrow he will learn that we've concluded a pact with our friends, the Selgovae and the Carvetii."

"The Selgovae?" Cian managed to gasp, incredulous. "You're not serious. We've been killing each other since the beginning of time."

"A common enemy makes a large circle of friends," Sorcha said piously.

"Did we really make a pa …" Cethen saw the familiar, mocking smile on Vellocatus's lips, and fell silent.

"It is enough that he believes we have," Trencoss answered. "He will learn as much tomorrow, for the story will be all about the fortress. And at the end of the day, he'll see the people celebrating the fact. It will be confirmation for him."

"But why? Won't that just make the Romans move faster?"

"No. It won't." The old druid's voice was patient. "The Romans are sure to know that we've been trying to get support from the stubborn, half-witted dullards. However, when the Roman escapes, it will be with the word that we will not unite until the end of summer, at which time we will attack their fortress. The one they call Ebor."

"But by then—"

"*Before* then," Vellocatus interrupted, "while they think we remain here doing nothing but practice our mock battles, we attack."

"He'll have a week to think it over," Trencoss explained. "Then three days at the most should see him back at Ebor. Two, if he rides fast and doesn't get lost."

Cethen's mind tumbled in confusion at the druid's words. When he'd left the meeting Venutius had held at Dermat's home, he had been sure that the king really intended to attack Isurium, not the place where his village had been. The plan to attack the larger fortress was surely thrown out as a ruse. Uncertain, he looked at Vellocatus with puzzlement on his face. The king's old shield bearer grinned as if reading his thoughts, then shook his head and winked.

"Cethen!"

He turned to see Trencoss staring at him thoughtfully. "Did the Roman ever ask why you pulled him from the river?"

He shook his head, remembering the awkward, stilted conversations since Gaius's capture, and the slow progress in learning the Latin words. "We talk, but that hasn't been a concern to him. Or he's too embarrassed to ask. I don't know which."

"That's good, because the day after tomorrow, when the time is ripe, he will be told the reason." Cethen glimpsed a thin-lipped smile, buried deep in the old man's beard. "It came when you looked down on the river where he fell in: a vision rippled on the surface of the water. You saw yourself with your sword raised to strike, the Roman helpless at your feet. You were on the burning walls of the fortress at Ebur. That's the reason he wasn't killed—to allow the vision to come true."

"Really?" Cethen thought that over for a moment. "He'll believe it?"

"If he doesn't, then at least he'll be thinking on it." Trencoss smiled and, nodding to Sorcha to follow, wandered off toward the older part of the fortress.

"Makes you think about the other visions they have, don't it?" Vellocatus murmured, as the pair disappeared into the darkness.

Almost a week later, at around midnight, the clamour of voices woke Gaius from a fitful sleep. Flames flickered yellow through the chinks in the wall of his prison, and the acrid smell of smoke filled the air. Suddenly alert to the danger, he fought panic. He was helpless, the chain that manacled his arm was secured to the wall of the tiny hut, and the fire appeared close by …

He pulled wildy at the iron fetter, and was for once grateful to hear the snarling of the dog outside. A grating noise followed, and the door swung open.

"Be quiet," a voice whispered. A dark figure stood framed in the glow of the fire.

"What's happening?" Gaius asked, suddenly unsure whether he was being saved or slaughtered.

"I'm here to help. Come on, there's not much time."

"I can't."

"Huh?"

"I can't, you fool. I'm shackled to this cursed place!"

"Shit. Who put a stupid set of sha—never mind. Who's got the thing that releases them?"

"I don't know." Gaius growled, anger uniting with his panic. "The guards outside? Maybe Cethen what-the-fuck's-his-name?"

The figure disappeared around the corner, leaving the door wide open. Gaius stared helplessly at the flickering glow that lit the night sky. He could see the roof of Cethen's lodge, dark against the light of the fire. The flames were farther away than he had thought. Even so, he resumed tugging at the long chain.

Vellocatus found Dermat waiting patiently behind the small prison, one hand gripping the reins of a horse, and the other the short leash of the slavering hound.

"He's got chains on," Vellocatus whispered angrily. "Who's got the damned thing that opens them?"

"I don't know," Dermat hissed, and turned to the two guards lying trussed on the ground. "Where's the opener for the—aaah, shit!"

He crouched down and released the nearest one's gag. "Where's the opener for the fool's shackles?"

The man spit dry wool from his mouth, his eyes rolling white in the dark as he tried to think. He was clearly not pleased with the finer details of the subterfuge. "The girl. The young girl has it. She uses it when she brings food in the morning."

"Dammit," Dermat muttered, and stumbled to his feet. "I'll go get it."

He began moving toward Cethen's lodge, but Vellocatus grabbed the back of his tunic and held him fast. "You can't go that way, the door to his prison is open. He'll see you."

"Then close the damned thing. Cethen's probably at the fire anyway, helping keep it under control."

"The girl is probably still home."

"You're not serious," Dermat exclaimed in a testy undertone. "All the brats within a mile will have pestered their das to let them go take a look."

"Don't give me flaming excuses, Dermat," Vellocatus voice snapped with impatience. "Find her. We need to get the man free."

"What do you suggest, arsehole?"

The hound growled again, a low rumble, and Dermat absently backhanded its muzzle. The animal yelped and snapped, drawing blood. Enraged, Dermat let go of the leash and aimed a steady barrage of kicks at the beast's head. The dog crouched, snarling and baring its teeth, but a boot caught it solidly under the jaw with a crack that almost snapped its neck. With a howl, it went yapping off into the night.

"Feel better?"

Dermat grinned darkly, nursing his bleeding wrist. "Better than the fucking dog."

Vellocatus took a deep breath to calm himself. "Look, I'll close the door so he can't see you. I'll talk to him, keep him calm. You go and find the girl."

Dermat nodded and tied the reins of the horse to the closest likely object, one of the guards' ankles. The man mumbled his displeasure, but Dermat ignored the protests and crept toward the lodge. He glanced in the direction of the fire and cursed. It had been set in a small hut not much larger than the one that held the Roman prisoner, and the flames wouldn't last forever. In fact, as he rounded the corner of Cethen's lodge, he saw several shadowy figures busily stoking the dying blaze

Readying his excuses, Vellocatus returned to the shed in time to hear the crack of breaking wood, and a sharp yelp of pain. He peered inside. Gaius lay flat on his back, cursing. The long chain lay loose between his legs, a splintered piece of board attached to one end. A jagged hole, lit by the glow of the flames, marked where the manacle had been secured to the wall. Blood streamed down Gaius's cheek where the shattered plank had struck as it jerked free.

"I see you're ready to go, then."

"I see you didn't find the 'thing' then," Gaius replied sarcastically, gathering up the loose chain as he scrambled to his feet. He rid the shackle of most of the wooden shard, then dabbed gingerly at the blood with his free hand. "It's called a key, by the way."

"I'll remember that, if I ever do this again. Now come on; we've wasted enough time."

Gaius hesitated. "What's going on?"

"I'm helping you escape. Risking my life."

"Why?"

Vellocatus sighed, having expected the question. "A couple of reasons, one personal." He closed his eyes as he delivered the lies, hoping they were more believable than they sounded to his own ears. "First there's the vision that Cethen had. Men will follow us, many men, if they believe they can make it come true. But for that to happen, you have to be at the fortress, alive, and not here."

"You're letting me go because of that foolish vision?"

"That's not the main reason, but as I said, men will follow what the gods foretell."

"I thought the druids were making it up," Gaius muttered, sounding unsure.

"I don't play games with the gods," Vellocatus said truthfully, for the tale was the work of the priests. "But there is also my wife. It is important that a message be taken to her. You will say that her husband sends his love. Tell her that before summer is over, she must return to her home at Camulodunum. I want to find her safely there by then. Stress the last words: at the end of summer I will find her safely there. Now come on—move."

"Was that really the reason he jumped in?" Gaius asked, still puzzling it through.

"Hey, I was there. Why else would he have done it?"

"She—he never said anything," Gaius said.

"Did you ask?"

"No."

"There you go, then," Vellocatus replied. "Besides, why would he? It's sacred. Now come on." He spoke the words quickly to end the discussion, and moved off to the side of the shed.

Gaius hesitated, then followed, first peering cautiously around the corner. A horse waited, bridled but unsaddled, and the trussed figures of the two guards lay on the ground beside it. As they neared, the horse whinnied and backed away. Both men were startled to see one of the guards slide with it.

"Shit," Vellocatus muttered, and dashed forward, which only made the animal drag the man farther. He decided to grab the guard instead and lunged out, catching the struggling man by his belt. The horse shied, but this time the weight was too much. "Stay still," Vellocatus hissed, crawling over the man to his ankle and releasing the reins.

Muttering damnation on Dermat, he led the horse back to the small hut, holding the animal still for Gaius to swing up. He tried, but the long chain and remaining splinter of wood made it difficult. Both men cursed.

"Here." Vellocatus cupped his hands, then hefted him upward.

"Who," Gaius asked patiently, once he was firmly seated and had the reins in his hands, "who is the lady who waits for this message?"

Vellocatus smiled. "You know damned well who makes her home at Camulodunum, Roman. And you surely know by now who I am. But if you wish it carved more plain, it's Cartimandua." He turned around and retrieved a large, oval shield and a bronze helmet from the rear of the shed. "Here. These will help you get past the defences. Ride through the rampart near the place you were working. The space will be guarded, but they'll be more concerned with who's coming in than who's going out."

"No sword? No spear?" Gaius muttered, as he hoisted the shield onto his left arm, and tucked the chain and splinter in behind

"I want you to escape, not kill my people."

"Then I still ask why ...Vellocatus. Your reasons seem short."

"You attach too much worth to yourself, Roman." Again he flashed his teeth. "I gave you reasons. Prime among them, though, is that I want my wife away from Ebor before autumn comes. But if you want another, let's say that I like debts—ones that are owed to me, and not vice versa. It's an advantage to have people in both camps when trouble arises. You might seek the advice of my wife about such politics."

With that, he slapped the rump of the horse and it leaped ahead, disappearing into the darkness to the south.

The Roman had barely gone when Dermat came panting back. "Here's the thingy-whatever," he said, handing over a short rod of iron, flanged at one end.

"It's called a key, you oaf," Vellocatus muttered, "and we don't need it now. He's gone. I just hope they don't get carried away when they chase him off the place."

"Who's looking after that?"

"Ebric."

"Oh shit." For a moment, Dermat stared into the darkness where Gaius had vanished, as if expecting to see something. Giving up, he glanced back toward the fire. The flames had all but faded. "What do you want to do, then? Go and help put it out?"

"You joke," Vellocatus said, moving off in the direction of Venutius's lodge. "I want to be as far from here as possible when Cethen finds we gave his chestnut back to the Roman."

Chapter XII

"In five days the column sets out from Isurium. The support elements from Ebor leave in four. You think you'll be up to it?"

Petronius stared skeptically at his senior engineer. Gaius knew what he saw. A dark, jagged scab from the wood splinter cut across one cheek, black with healing. One side of his face was bruised from the druid's beating, and the rest was covered in a web of scratches from the night ride through the forest.

Gaius gazed back at the legate with eyes that felt like they should be propped open, and managed a painful grin. "I can be ready tomorrow, if need be."

His return had taken less than two days, though it had nearly ended prematurely at the Stannick rampart. One of the barbarians standing guard had tried to ask questions, despite what Vellocatus had said. Another had tried to unhorse him, and when he managed to break free, a shower of spears had followed him into the night. Several had mounted and tried to follow, but they were slow, and he soon lost them in the darkness of the trees. Nonetheless, it was a heart-stopping race that lent credence to Vellocatus's words.

When daylight came he found himself miles south of Stannick. The weather had turned hard, with gusting winds and a steady, driving rain that quickly soaked his old woolen tunic, chilling him to the bone. The only solace was the animal warmth of Rufus's steaming back, and the fact that the big chestnut was once more where he belonged.

He crossed the path of a Tungri cavalry troop around midmorning. The dark beard and Cethen's wet cast-offs were an invitation to more rough handling, before they heard his voice above the steady drumming of the rain. Once he was recognized, his safe return was a matter of course. The decurio promptly decided the rescue—for that's how his report read—was a good enough excuse to call off the patrol and return to Isurium.

The small fort crawled with soldiers. Gaius had no need to be told that Cerialis's orders had been set in motion. A huge convoy of supply wagons, the slowest units of march, were parked in rows below the south ramparts. A good part of a Batavi infantry cohort was crowded inside the walls, and yet another troop of cavalry arrived late the same evening.

The rain ceased the following day, as if the gods were reminding him of their hand in his return. The debts owed on that field were piling up, and Gaius was conscious of the delinquency as he rode out early the next morning with the dispatch riders. It haunted him on the trek back to the fortress at Ebor. How much longer would fortune ride with him, if those debts were not paid? Yet, as the small troop of riders came in view of the stronghold itself, other matters began to distract.

Rufus splashed across the ford, now made shallower by a new bed of rock and gravel. The water ran swift, yet well clear of the animal's belly. Gaius counted eight ships crowding the north bank of the river, all but one cargo vessels. The fortress stood proudly above the river itself, its wooden parapets newly treated, the gates wide open. It gleamed with a welcome that filled his chest with pride.

The same afternoon of his return, Gaius was ordered to the legate's residence. The building reeked with the dank, heavy odour of fresh plaster. The grey coating clung damp on the walls, and until it dried, nothing would rid the building of the cloying stink. Petronius's quarters were sparsely furnished, but a meal had been laid on, served on two field tables placed end to end. More than a dozen officers were there. Petronius sat at the head of the tables on a soft leather folding chair, as did Gaius at the foot; the others made do with the rough wooden side benches.

"So tell me more of the barbarians' readiness," the legate said, his eyes surveying the table. He settled on a handful of shucked oysters, and arched his neck back to swallow the first.

"There's certainly enough of them there," Gaius said. "They practice daily on the fields around the fortress. Yet there's no appearance of an immediate campaign."

"Stores? Supplies?"

"There are lots of granaries and sheds, especially in the older part of the stronghold. But whether they're full or not, I don't know. There wasn't any hunger."

"No sign of hostile activity?" Titus asked.

"Just the opposite. I had the impression that nothing would be done until the northern tribes sent more men. Of course, perhaps that's what I was intended to think."

Petronius chased the mollusk with a mouthful of red wine. "You got this impression from the Cethen fellow?"

Gaius shook his head. "Definitely not. More than once I tried to steer the subject that way, but he would not be led. No, it was from the talk down at the ramparts where they had me digging." Anticipating the next question, he added, "I heard it from the slaves, and the barbarians' own plebes. Some of them were quite plumped up about it."

"Are any of our soldiers held there?" Titus asked.

Gaius grimly shook his head. "None from the legions. They prefer to parade our heads around. There were some auxiliary tribesmen, though. As to the slaves, I believe most were their own kind, probably taken during tribal bickering. A good deal of the work is done by their own plebes, though. I think the only reason I remained alive was because I was recognized."

"Which adds credibility to that ridiculous vision, I suppose," Petronius muttered. No one at the table believed it, yet not one of them felt comfortable about it, either.

"Standing in the cold, with an arrow pointed at you, is not the usual time for visions," Titus observed. "They arrive in the grey light of morning, when you're flat on your back, with a full bladder and a hard-on."

"And they're not about burning walls and sword-swinging barbarians," Salvius added, and leered.

"No," one of the senior centurions muttered sourly before draining his mug, "those come when you're trying to *get* to sleep."

"After the trouble they took to keep you alive, the escape seemed conveniently easy," Salvius commented.

"It struck me that way too," Gaius replied, thinking back to the flames and the broken shackle. "Though Vellocatus certainly didn't know I was chained. And the guard who almost unhorsed me seemed to be doing his best. I think I broke his nose. By the way, what did you do with the boy? Ethrin, wasn't it?"

"Him!" Salvius laughed. "Cartimandua took the waif under her cloak. It's becoming a habit. I think your lad has been going there as well, every chance he gets."

"He never mentioned it when I saw him," Gaius said, and shrugged. "I suppose he finds a sort of home there. Which reminds me, what about the message he wants me to pass on to her?"

"How does it go again?" Petronius asked, then provided his own answer. "She is to return home, and before the end of summer. He will come and find her there?"

"He'll find her *safely* there," Gaius corrected. "At Camulodunum. And he said he definitely wanted her gone from Ebor before autumn."

"Which seems to imply that she won't be safe here with us."

"Which reinforces the story about the northern tribes uniting with Venutius at the end of summer," Publius added helpfully.

"A story conveniently heard not long before your escape," Titus muttered.

Petronius leaned back in his chair, thoughtfully twirling an empty goblet in his hand. An orderly moved forward to fill it, but he waved the man away.

"I see nothing to halt the building of the old man's fort, though," he said at last. "We have word only two days old from Gaius that nothing is happening at Stannick. I'm inclined to take that as it is, but as always, remain alert. We'll move north as ordered. Step by step. I'm sure they're not expecting it. We'll have the ramparts up before they know we're there. It will be a critical staging point for the inevitable attack on the man's damned fortress." He turned to Gaius. "You haven't passed the message on to the woman?"

"No. Not without your permission."

"Then do so; it won't cause any harm," Petronius said, then frowned. "That woman always knows what's going on, sooner or later. And she always lets me know she knows." The legate mulled on the last comment for a moment, then added, "At least, I think she does."

"Gaius!"

He'd just left the commander's residence, and he turned to find Petronius framed in the doorway.

"A moment."

"Sir?"

"Thought I'd just see for myself how you're doing," the legate said, and stepped out onto the hard-packed dirt of the *Via Principalis.*

"As I said, fine. A few aches and pains, but I've had worse."

"And the boy? He's well?"

"Very," Gaius said, wondering what was really on Petronius' mind. "I still haven't decided on sending him back. I assigned him to Octavius Lupianus, a decanus of the fourth cohort. It'll cure the boy, or make him. If it doesn't kill him first."

Petronius chuckled, and said nothing more. Gaius frowned, puzzled, as they stood side by side, taking in the evening silence of the fortress. A shout rang out from one of the barracks, and an angry voice echoed sharply along the roadway. Across the street, the skeleton frame of a large stores building sat unfinished, the fresh smell of newly cut lumber wafting from the cream-coloured timbers. The soft scent seemed to reflect the mood of the camp as it settled down for the night.

Petronius gazed absently down the street, as if lost in thought. Gaius wondered if his mind dwelt on Cerialis's new fort. It was, after all, being built right under the noses of the barbarians. If so, was his opinion being sought?

"Four days before we leave here for Isurium, you said?" Gaius ventured in that direction. "I'll have to catch up on orders, though I imagine Titus has it all in hand. I presume he's going?"

"The new fort, yes—glad you brought that up. And yes, he is going, of course," Petronius murmured, seemingly relieved that the subject had been broached. Then just as quickly, he changed it. "You had quite a time while you were away, Gaius."

"It was different."

"We'd written you off as dead." Petronius looked sideways, studying Gaius, and added, "Everyone had."

"I know." Gaius smiled at the memory. "I had a long talk with Marc this afternoon. Though the boy claims he always knew I'd return."

"Yes, well, the whole thing was most unfortunate."

"I did follow your orders," Gaius quipped, beginning to feel as uneasy as the legate himself appeared to be. "I wasn't taking a piss when the barbarians charged. It made not a damned bit of difference."

Petronius' face was blank for a moment, then he laughed. "You do look badly mauled, you know. How do you feel? In yourself?"

"As I said, I'm fine," Gaius replied, wondering down what path the conversation was leading, "and in four days I'll be even finer."

"But the whole experience, especially after the first incident here, must have taken its toll. Not to mention the strain it's placed on your mind."

"My mind?" Gaius felt a sinking feeling in his stomach.

"This operation north of Isurium. I was thinking." Petronius appeared to be choosing his words carefully. "As you're the engineering officer, I would normally send you. You know, supervise the layout, look after the construction. I was thinking, though, that you might be more in need of leave. Perhaps even a journey home, take the family."

The legate again glanced sideways, but Gaius's mind was elsewhere, racing over the past few weeks. Was he being blamed for his own capture? He and Titus had certainly gone far beyond their orders. Was that the issue? It had to be. Yet the primus was still *in* favour; why should *he* be out? Perhaps it was personal. Was Petronius somehow aware of the subtle demands placed on him by Cerialis, namely to breathe down the legate's own neck?

"Have I shat in someone's platter of *puls*?" he demanded.

"No!" Petronius looked shocked. "Not at all. Your actions have been commendable. In fact, perhaps I shouldn't tell you this, but it's been recommended in dispatches that you be awarded a *corona vallaris* in recognition. No, no, it's simply that all this must have come at a cost. A long rest with your family would certainly be in order."

Gaius pondered the legate's words, but as far as he was concerned, there had been no toll on his well-being at all. Petronius was correct in one thing, though. Other than the march north to build the fort, there were no pressing duties. At least, not until late in the summer, when Venutius would be campaigning. Yet Petronius had suggested a journey home! There was no time to do that, and still be party to that campaign. And Helvia. She would surely not be in any hurry to return to Italia until winter. Not after she had just arrived. Though she had always professed to detest Britannia …

The legate spoke again. "How is your wife? Have you heard from her?"

"Yes, she wrote only once while I was away, to say she was settling in at Lindum. Then obviously she heard I was missing. She appears to be well. I'll write her tonight," he said and smiled, though he didn't relish the thought. "Let her know she still has a husband."

"Perhaps you should go yourself, and remind her," Petronius persisted.

Gaius again thought the matter over, but the new fort north of Isurium nagged at his mind. It was where he should be. And as to Helvia, dammit, he may have been lax there, certainly, but it was her own fault. He'd expected her to remain in Italia. Lindum was hardly a haven, even now, and Ebor was out of the question. Why hadn't she just remained at home?

"I will go back to Lindum," he began, and Petronius looked inordinately pleased, until he added, "but I'll wait until the initial defenses are completed on the new fort. That won't take long. I feel obliged to see it through. I know the land. I've seen the plans. It wouldn't feel right otherwise."

The legate sighed. "I imagine a few weeks won't make any difference. But I want you to leave as soon as you return from—well, from whatever we end up calling the place. That's one more thing to be decided, I suppose."

Petronius moved to go back inside, but Gaius had one more question. "There's the message to the woman. Where does she stay now?"

The legate jerked a thumb to the side of the building. "She's taken over the new barracks block next door." Petronius grinned as he lowered his voice. "There was a bit of a battle over the commander's residence, but the governor finally raised his sword on that one."

Gaius grinned, bid the legate good night, and went in search of Cartimandua. If the woman wasn't at the barrack building, then the message could wait until tomorrow. But as he turned the corner, he found himself half hoping she would be there. He wasn't disappointed.

The barracks block sat barely a wagon width away from the new residence. It was fronted by a planked landing, overhung by a roof extension set on raw timber posts. An iron bracket held a torch, and she sat quietly in the flickering glow of its light. Criff lounged on the floor by her feet, but as Gaius appeared, he rose and disappeared inside the building.

"Is Marc here?" he asked, wondering how much time his son was actually spending at the woman's household.

"He left not long ago. In fact, he bid me goodnight in my own tongue. The boy's a quick learner," Cartimandua squinted through the gloom at the damage to his face. "I see you've had another visit with my first husband."

"Your people seem to have nothing better to do than beat upon unarmed Romans."

"And Romans, of course, never beat upon unarmed 'barbarians'?"

Gaius ignored the comment, and instead echoed the obvious. "So he's not here, then?"

"He went back to the 'barbarian' you left him with when you went north to chase the faerie. He was more concerned with displeasing some slave driver called Octavius than he was about pleasing me. The boy has no sense of priority."

"I see," Gaius said, strangely reluctant to leave. "Well, thanks then."

"So, are you taking him with you?"

Feeling awkward looking up to her on the landing, Gaius climbed the steps and leaned against one of the support posts. "Haven't thought about it."

"Then you'd better hurry. You've only got four days."

The woman knew exactly when they were setting out, Gaius thought irritably, and she wanted to make sure that he knew she did. She was laughing at him.

"You know too damned much, for—for someone who shouldn't know anything."

"Too damned much for a barbarian?" Cartimandua cocked her head to one side in amusement. "You know, we're supposed to be on the same side, turd. Anyway, I think you should let the boy go with you. There will be a lot of troops, and it's not as if you're going out to do battle."

"Does he tell you everything that's going on?"

"Do you mean your son, the legate, or Petilius?" she asked, but didn't wait for an answer. "Not at all. In fact, they rarely tell me a thing. Certainly not this time, though the governor does let things slip once in a while. When that happens, I have to work out whether or not it was done on purpose."

"Then where do you get your information?"

"Oh, Roman," Cartimandua sighed, then laughed merrily. "Why don't you ask who I'm sleeping with, while you're at it? That would make two questions you'd give your sword hand to have an answer to. Is there a third?"

"There are probably a hundred, and I'm not sure you'd answer any of them," Gaius said. "I can tell *you* something, though. A message from your second husband. It was given to me while escaping from the first."

"You saw Vellocatus?"

"He's the only second husband I know of. Are there others?"

"There can only be one second, Archimedes," she snapped, surprising him with her knowledge of the name. "Do you need lessons in mathematics, too? What did he say?"

"I'm not quite sure. He said to tell you that he sends his love, and he wants you safe at Camulodunum by the end of summer. Emphasis on 'safe at the end of summer.' He says he doesn't want you here by then."

She shrugged indifferently. "So what do you make of that?"

"I'm still trying to decide where the message was directed—at you, me, or the legate? What do you make of it?"

"Is that the third question?" she said, and smiled. "If so, you won't get an answer to that one either, for I have no idea what he means. The second part, that is. As to the first part about sending his love, he's stretching his bowstring on that one. Especially if he's joined up with Venutius. How did you find him, by the way? My first one. How does he look?"

"Like a well-used, rust-pitted sword: badly in need of a new edge and an unguent," Gaius replied. "I think his scalp's going to flake right through to his skull. Though I didn't see too much of him. He lets his priests do the questioning. I think that priests are the same the world over. The gods will one day get even."

"They will do that with all of us," Cartimandua murmured.

"Better later than sooner," he said, and pushed himself away from the post. "I think I will take Marc with me. He wants to go. The experience will be useful."

"He couldn't do any worse than you did," she said, glancing at his skull as he stepped down from the landing.

Gaius didn't reply, but instead waved a hand lazily over one shoulder. The thumb and index finger were closed to from an "o" that was followed by a quick jab of his index finger.

He passed the end of the residence and had taken no more than a step or two onto the street, when Cartimandua spoke again. She didn't shout, but simply called his name in a voice only slightly louder than normal.

Without thinking, he turned back and peered around the corner. "What now?"

"It's amazing how voices carry when evening comes, isn't it?" Cartimandua had risen, and stood leaning against the wall of the barracks building, her arms crossed, her head flung back. She was mocking him.

"I suppose. But why tell me? As night falls, the more a voice will seem to ..." Gaius whirled about and found himself facing the front of the commander's residence. He and Petronius had been standing only a few paces away. "Damn!" he cried, and turned back. "What did you hear?"

Cartimandua was moving toward her door. "Just about every-thing, I think," she said. "You know, Roman, sometimes I think you are about as thick as this plank." She stamped her foot on the rough deck-ing, then disappeared inside, leaving him speechless. A single word drifted from inside the barracks as the door closed: "Turd!"

Chapter XIII

Venutius's army prepared to leave Stannick in the dim light of daybreak. It was almost midmorning, however, before the tail of the great column finally followed the head into the forest, tramping along the main track leading south. Even then, it was only because Venutius had meticulously set the order of march the day before. Each chief, with his warriors, had been ordered to camp outside the stronghold, ready to move with the dawn. And for the most part, they did; which was all the ageing king had hoped for.

The long, open slopes outside the fortress had the air of a summer fair, and by the time daylight came, every man, woman, and child had turned out to watch. The druids, Trencoss once again at their head, stood high on a wooden platform atop the south ridge, where the track disappeared into the trees. The structure faced the rising sun, where three bonfires were set in line to greet it. Each was lit as darkness faded, and three white bulls were sacrificed by the flickering glow of the flames.

The sun remained hidden behind scudding clouds, which at first made the omens indecisive. But the clouds were white, and blew more or less toward Isurium. The druids huddled and eventually found the signs promising. The chanting briefly resumed, but did not last long. Trencoss, under the glowering eye of the old king, soon ceased his pleadings with the gods, and nodded his approval to depart.

Venutius started the head of the column, and like a fat, glittering snake, the rest of the body followed. The lesser druids, their arms raised, droned their blessings over the slow-moving ranks of tribesmen. When the last warrior had vanished into the trees, over six thousand had walked by and received the gods' blessing.

Each chief rode proudly at the head of his own tuath. Most of the long, straggling army was on foot, though some rode and others, out of stubborn pride, drove their chariots. The small, agile carts would be useless against the walls of Isurium, but pride had taken priority. The attack was nothing more than a raid, Venutius insisted, and the column was unencumbered by excess baggage. The little that was needed had been stowed on a scattering of pack horses and small, two wheeled carts.

The strategy was simple. A long, forced march would end well after nightfall, placing them close to the ford at Isurium, where the river angled South. They would cross while it was still dark and storm the walls at first light, surprising those inside the fort. Once taken, the stronghold would be burned. There were no plans to hold it. The small army would then return north—perhaps. If casualties were light, more men might be called in from Stannick, and a push made on the new Roman fortress where the Eburi had once lived.

"The main concern with Isurium is the walls, which is why we're taking those ladders," Cethen told Coira as the kin awaited their turn to move out. He pointed to two of Maeldav's tuath who sat near a long, spruce rail laying flat on the grass. A series of crosspieces had been lashed along its length.

"It looks heavy, Da."

"It will be even heavier by midmorning, pigeon, but those two won't carry it all the way. Others will take turns."

"As long as someone's watching," Elena muttered, pulling at the pack tied to Rhun's saddle, making certain it was secure.

"Mam, it's fine," her son protested, glancing around to see if anyone was watching.

"Just be careful, and listen to your da," she replied, then embarrassed the boy further by pulling him close in a hug, and kissing his cheek.

"Mam!" he wailed, and pushed her away.

"Da, why can't I go too?" Coira pouted as she watched her brother swing up onto his pony.

Her mother glared at her. "If I hear that one more time, girl, your backside will be so sore, you won't be able to sit a pile of hay, let alone a saddle."

"Come here, lass," Cethen said, and lifted his daughter off the ground. "You look after your mam and your brother."

He whirled her about and set her back on the ground, then did the same with Tuis. As he put the boy down, he saw Cian's wife in the distance, coming back from where the head of the column had vanished into the trees. He waved, but she didn't wave back. Her arms were folded, and she looked unhappy.

"They're beginning to move. It's time," Cethen said, eyeing his own people standing impatiently in line.

It was a proud moment. The warriors from Maeldav's tuath were a hundred paces away, placed ahead of the Eburi. Those with horses were already mounted, and those on foot had bunched into a rough sort of order, jostling and joking as they awaited their turn to march. Maeldav's sons, Dag and Garv, stood restlessly by in the only chariots under Cethen's charge. Each youth was a heavy, black-haired image of his father. From time to time the pair glowered over their shoulders, clearly displeased at Venutius's choice of leadership. To make their feelings even more clear, the pair wheeled their chariots to the head of the tuath and, without waiting, urged the horses forward. The rest of their kin followed, but soon halted, for those ahead had yet to move.

"Those arseholes are going to be trouble," Cethen muttered as he climbed onto Flint's back. The gelding was a much sorrier mount than the fine chestnut Vellocatus had stolen from him, a fact he didn't hesitate to share with anyone who would listen. He kneed the horse close to Elena, and leaned down from the saddle. They kissed, long and hard. Rhun snorted in disgust..

"I thought you were going to forget," she whispered, clinging to his neck. Then, "Watch your back—and come back."

He caressed her cheek, his fingers lingering, then cantered Flint to a place at the head of Maeldav's kin. The horse squeezed in front of the two chariots, no mean feat in the densely packed column, and a few moments later Rhun eased his pony alongside. Almost at once, those ahead moved off and Cethen kneed the animal forward. The pace settled to a steady, easy walk, but once they had gained the ridge, the first hint of trouble started.

Garv urged his ponies to move faster, deliberately crowding the hind-end of Cethen's horse. The gelding, at best an ill-tempered, axe-headed beast with the mind of a mule, refused to be pushed. It dug its front hooves into the dirt, bunched its hind legs, and lashed out. Cethen made no attempt to stop it. There was a loud, solid thump that turned the heads of everyone within a hundred paces.

Garv's offside pony reared, squealing in pain, and veered side-ways, blood dripping from its mouth. It dragged the second animal with it, and both bolted in panic, tearing off across the open grassland to the sound of jeers and laughter. An angry, cursing Garv fought to stay inside the cart as it bounced across the rocky pasture.

"Son," Cethen said piously as the chariot hurtled into a distant clump of trees, "I can't say too much about having a well-trained horse."

"How's Cian?" Elena asked as Nuada drew level. "Or need I ask?"

"The usual," she replied, and turned to watch the long, colour-ful procession winding past. "Cawing like a crow because he'll be out in front when it all begins. And totally sure he'll take at least a dozen down before it's all over. The fool Luga that he's feuding with is just as confident."

"He's feuding with someone?" Elena asked innocently, and glanced sideways with one eyebrow raised, unwilling to admit to Nuada what she knew of the cause.

"Yes, I know, but—hey, it was Beltane," she said, then grinned imp-ishly. "Cian didn't know where I was, either. As to one killing the other, at the moment they're too busy trying to prove who's the better man."

Someone whistled and a loud chorus of yelps and whooping erupted from the column. A band of woad-painted warriors from the western hill country trudged past, waving their spears and thumping their shields. Most were nearly naked, though they carried cloaks and packs over their shoulders. All were in good spirits. Several made obscene gestures to the two women, and others bawled offers just as raw. Nuada laughed, waved, and, holding her arms over her head, twirled and gyrated. A roar of approval greeted the dance, and several men broke away, ready to give chase. She shrieked and ran giggling behind Elena. The chief turned and roared his annoyance, but the men had already started back, laughing as they went.

"You and Cian are a match," Elena said, not without disapproval.

"Especially when we're not together too long," Nuada replied, her cheeks pink with exhilaration. She was a pretty woman, several years younger than her husband. Like Cian, she was smaller than average, with a lively, elfin face, and a matching spirit. The pair were either deliriously happy, or arguing like two dogs on the same bone. There seemed to be no in between.

"Where are your wolf cubs?" Elena said, asking of her two children, two girls close to Tuis's age. Both took after their parents.

Nuada waved a casual hand toward the column. Hundreds of children walked and skipped alongside, wandering in and out of the crowd, chattering and calling to the warriors, and in turn being teased and chided. "With the rest of them, I imagine. They'll come back when they're hungry."

Elena glanced skeptically toward the ridge and found Coira's blond head bobbing up and down several hundred paces away. Tuis tagged along, not far behind. "I suppose," she said, then shrugged. "I'm hungry. As usual, everyone else had something to eat but me. You want to come?"

Nuada looked reluctantly toward the column, not wishing to miss anything, but the end of it, down by the ramparts, was stirring. They would be walking by it, anyway. "Sure, let's go."

Nuada's two children tumbled into the hut shortly after mid morning, along with Tuis, all three squabbling and shouting. The women gave them slabs of barley cake and some cheese, and promptly sent them scuttling back outside. The weather was good, the clouds beginning to thin, and outside was far better for the children—and for the women, as well.

Around midday, Nuada called them all in to eat, and Elena realized she hadn't seen Coira all morning. That wasn't unusual, so at first she didn't worry.

"Where's your sister?" she asked Tuis a while later. He sat sulking at the far end of the low table, still playing with his food, rather than eat as he'd been told.

"She went with Rhun," he said, reaching for a thick slice of ham, which promptly slid out of his plump fist.

"She what?" his mother demanded.

"She went with Rhun." Tuis reached down to the dirt floor, retrieved the meat, and carefully examined it. After a quick scrub, he found it fit to eat.

His mother slammed a jug of barley water back on the side table, slopping the cool liquid over her forearm. "I'll lop that man's stupid, sparrow-brained head off his shoulders," Elena raged, "if the damned Romans don't do it first."

"Who, Rhun?" Nuada asked in surprise.

"No, Cethen, damn him! The fool can't say no to the girl!"

"Da don't know she's there, Mam," Tuis mumbled between bites.

"Your da has to know, Tuis. You said she went with Rhun. He and Da were riding together. Don't tell me he's lost care of the boy, too!" She placed her hands on her hips and glared suspiciously at her youngest son. "What really happened?"

"Well, she wasn't *with* Rhun. What I meant was, she went where he's going. She was with Mioch. He gave her a ride."

"Oh, for the love of Dagda." Elena looked at Nuada in disbelief, then turned on Tuis. "Why didn't you tell me, boy? And who, in the darkest, dirtiest corner of the otherworld, is Mioch?"

Tuis shrugged. "I don't know, Mam. But Coira does. His da's a chief, I think. That's why he's got his own horse." Seeming to think that perhaps his explanations had been short, he added, "Which is how he could give her a ride."

"How old is Mioch?" his mother asked, her mind darting in all directions.

Tuis perked up, as if pleased he was able to answer the question precisely. "Sixteen this year. I heard him tell Coira when she asked, 'cause I was walking with them till she told me to go home. She told me not to tell you she was gone. That's why I didn't. Though I guess I must have forgot that part now."

"Children. Why do we have them?" Elena cried as Tuis contentedly went back to his piece of ham.

"You know why!" Nuada grinned, and raised her index finger.

Elena ignored the gesture. "Can I leave Tuis with you? Essa's somewhere lazing about, the gods know where. Make use of her, if you find her."

"Of course. You're going to fetch Coira, then?"

"What do you think?"

Elena wasn't interested in an answer. Jerking a cloth sack from its peg on the rafters, she threw food, soap, and a few items of clothing inside. Muttering under her breath, she took a sword and baldric from another peg, and finally stood by the door, looking around to see if she'd forgotten anything. Satisfied, she lifted the shield that always stood by the entrance, and opened the door. "With luck, I'll be back tonight."

Nobody saw any more of Garv after his chariot careened off across the field. Dag watched his brother's bouncing cart, mouth agape. A sly grin briefly lit his features as one of Garv's wheels spun away, just before the entire rig disappeared into the trees. He didn't go chasing after it. Instead, he settled down to driving his chariot, and after a few moments the sullen pout returned to his face. But he made a point of not crowding his ponies up against Cethen's horse.

The column marched south through the forest, crossing fields and meadows, marshes and becks, all green with the lush growth of summer. Those Britons who still remained on the scattered farmsteads came out to wave and cheer, and the men of the small army replied in kind.

But when the winding cavalcade passed under the dark, rustling canopy of the trees, they grew quiet, as if sensing the solemnness of their cause, and the presence of the forest itself. The chatter died, replaced by the soft, steady plod of hooves and the padding of thousands of feet.

Midday had come and gone by the time the head of the column reached the river where the Romans had scouted their fort. The small cluster of huts had been abandoned, and not a soul was in sight. Many crossed the river at places other than the ford, for the water was not high. The fast running stream hardly created a pause in the march, and they continued south. The afternoon was well on its way when, without warning, the column began bunching up.

At first Cethen thought a halt had been called, until he heard the faint sound of angry voices, farther along the track. They were in a densely wooded section of the trail where the path curved, and vision was held to about fifty paces. He turned in the saddle, finding the view behind little better. All that could be seen were a couple hundred warriors, either Maeldav's tuath or his own kin, and nearly all on foot. Just about anyone with a horse had gone ahead long ago, eager to join Venutius's mounted vanguard. There had been no stopping them.

As he eyed those under his charge, the thought crossed Cethen's mind that he should know exactly how many there were, though he wasn't sure why. It struck him that perhaps he should also have met with them all before the column left Stannick, maybe even days before, but again, what would that have accomplished? There was a gnawing feeling that something should be done—but what? Even Cian might have been doing *something* under the same circumstance.

Realizing just how much he was on his own, Cethen suddenly felt cold inside. The burden of leadership grew heavy, and he could cheerfully have done without it. He returned his attention to the trail ahead now crammed with impatient tribesmen, and sat thoughtfully pulling at his long moustaches.

"Da, can we eat too?"

Cethen came out of his reverie and looked down at Rhun, who stared back from the saddle of his smaller pony. "What is it, son?"

Rhun gestured to those behind. "Can we eat too?"

Cethen looked back again, and saw that everyone was sitting

down, busily digging into their packs for food. Dag had settled his rump on the back end of the chariot, chewing on a ham shank like a hungry dog. The two ponies had apparently adjusted to Flint, for they stood cropping grass well within range of a good, swift kick. There didn't seem to be a reason the boy couldn't eat, Cethen decided, and anyway, the shouting seemed to have died down.

"Go ahead," he said then, feeling something more should be done, he roared, "Everyone eat, but be ready to move. Pass it along." He felt self-conscious bellowing the order, but then he heard someone else doing the same up ahead, beyond the curve in the trail.

Rhun, who carried the midday meal, passed him two thick slices of bread, stuck to each other with a thick coating of honey. Both ate without dismounting. The gelding edged over to the side of the trail, and the pony followed. The animals cropped hungrily at the tall, sweet grass. After a while, even the birds resumed their trilling chorus.

They'd barely finished the bread when those ahead began shuffling forward again. The horses followed of their own accord, tufts of grass hanging from their mouths. A loud, grumbling chorus rose behind, as those of the tuath clambered to their feet and followed.

Faint cries again drifted through the trees, and soon after, the slow-moving ranks once more bunched up and halted. This time people began pushing and shoving as tempers frayed, and nerves became raw. Voices drifted through the trees from off to the left. A low, distant rustling of undergrowth followed, and the thudding of hundreds of running feet. Cethen shivered, then remembered a small track, a quarter-mile back, leading off into the forest. It was barely wide enough to take a single chariot. He decided that some of those behind must have taken it, but if so, it simply made things more confusing—and worrying.

Whoever was in front finally started forward, and the slow, steady shuffle resumed. They rounded another shallow curve in the trail. This time, once it straightened out, there was much to see. Cethen would have reined in his horse to look, if those behind hadn't kept pressing him onward. Flint grew nervous and he clucked soothingly, patting the animal's neck as it pranced sideways. He gaped down the narrow track, which ran true as an arrow for a good part of a mile. He could see elements of Venutius's cavalry far off in the distance, a dark mass of mounted men that plugged the trail like a bung in a wine jar. In between was a jam of foot warriors and cavalry, herded together like cattle in a pen.

A pair of riders burst out of the trees a hundred paces ahead, their faces scratched and bleeding from their ride through the thick undergrowth. Yet another appeared, even closer, and began yelling to the first two, motioning behind him. The two forced their horses past the crush, not caring who they trampled. When they reached the third horseman, all three vanished into the trees. Those on foot who were close appeared to do the same, and soon the column once more began moving forward. The pace was no longer a slow shuffle, but a good, brisk walk.

They reached a side trail, unseen until it was stumbled on. Like sheep, the tramping column followed the three riders down its path. The stumbling walk broke into a trot, and the distant shouting grew louder. Up ahead the treetops thinned, and bright rays of sunlight streamed through the branches. The harsh clamour of yelling and screaming grew to a roar. Above the din, Cethen heard the sharp clang of weapons, and drew his sword. The steady trot suddenly seemed no longer good enough, and everyone started to run.

The small track ended at a meadow, dazzling green beneath a sun that had finally won free of the clouds. Those ahead were running to the left as if they had a place to go, yet confusion reigned everywhere. Cethen wheeled Flint to one side, his first concern being Rhun. The others behind simply rushed on.

"There, boy! You stay right there, and don't move," he shouted, pointing with his sword to where the forest crowned the head of the meadow. Flint pranced nervously about the pasture.

"Da, I want to go with you," Rhun squeaked, his eyes bulging wide as he stared down the lea.

"Do as I say!" Cethen roared, yanking Flint's head about to face the confusion. As he rode away, he shouted for the lad's benefit, "We may need you to run messages. Don't move!"

He slammed his heels into the gelding's flanks, and the animal leapt forward. Dag now raced ahead of him in the chariot, which wasn't right; he should be at the head of the tuath. At the same time, his mind fought to understand what was happening, which was impossible. A fight seemed to be in full swing way up ahead, close to where the main trail erupted from the forest. Yet less than a hundred paces in front, those who'd been running were already fighting. Yet who?

No battle line seemed to have formed, just a confused mass of men on foot, slashing and hacking, yelling and screaming. Cethen took a firmer grip on his sword, braced his shield, and released a terrible, bloodcurdling howl, unheard in the midst of a thousand others. Flint, his blood up, redeemed Cethen's honour by charging into the battle a full length ahead of Dag.

Chapter XIV

The march north from Isurium was forced, and at an extended pace. A cavalry screen ranged a mile ahead, hurrying the column along in its wake. Seven troops of Tungri cavalry and an under strength auxiliary cohort of Batavi foot led the order of march. They were followed by the greater portion the Ninth's Fourth Cohort, squeezed in front of the baggage train, while the balance of it trailed immediately behind. Two more troops of cavalry formed the rearguard. A small force of service support regulars from the First Cohort travelled with the wagons, bringing the total number of souls in the force to just over twelve hundred.

The day itself was fine, and nobody was expecting trouble. A young Tungri trooper was the first to find it.

The man galloped past the Batavi cohort, shouting for space as his horse squeezed between the long ranks of foot soldiers and the dense undergrowth crowding the trail. He pulled up sharp alongside Titus, babbling his report before the animal had stopped. "Brigante tribesmen, sir. Horsemen. A dozen or more. We chased them off."

His horse lurched off toward the trees and turned full circle before settling down. Its flanks were lathered, and Titus frowned. "Calm down, trooper," he growled. "If there are only a dozen, what's the excitement?"

"I was sent to report, sir. A couple of them were painted up with that blue shit. They weren't out hunting."

"Fine, trooper. You've made your report. Now go back to your commander, and tell him it's noted," he ordered, then added harshly, "and don't flay your horse unless lives depend upon it. When you need the poor beast, it won't be there for you."

"Sir." The trooper saluted, then kicked the animal forward, this time at a sedate trot.

"Something must be going on, if they're painted," Publius observed.

"Absolutely," Titus said calmly. "But we don't panic. Or more important, we don't show panic. Gaius and I will ride ahead. See that the rest of the column is alerted. I'll get the Batavi to pick up the pace."

He turned and held two fingers in the air, gesturing forward. A pair of dispatch riders broke away and followed.

"Could be raiders looking for cheap horses," Publius called after them.

Gaius, the trials of the past several months on his mind, muttered under his breath, "And it could be Venutius with half of Brigantia behind him."

They halted briefly alongside the Batavi commander, a man called Marius Paulino, who was of the same age as Gaius. His face was sunburned below his plain helmet, and he looked up at them through a pair of startling, iron-grey eyes—Marius had chosen to walk at the head of his cohort, rather than ride. When he spoke, everything about the man exuded calm. "Thought you'd be coming up, sir. Good day, so far."

Titus nodded. "So far, praefectus. Place your men at the ready, though, and pick up the pace. There's either a barbarian raiding party ahead, or they're scouts for something larger."

Marius nodded to his senior centurion, and the man turned and relayed the order. Shouts echoed back along the line, and the subtle rustle and clatter of shifting equipment rippled along the trail as the infantry slipped shields and moved spears to the ready. Archers pulled bowstrings from the dry safety of their pouches, and looped one end over the notch in readiness. It was all done without breaking stride, or a second glance from the praefectus.

The Tungri cavalry, their rear ranks not more than fifty paces in front of the Batavi column, sprang to life and galloped off down the trail. At the same time, a second rider came racing back, laying into his horse even harder than the first. The trooper was an older man who had his mount well under control, despite the animal's breakneck speed.

"Contact with a large body of horse, sir. And chariots. I saw well over a hundred, but they were at a distance, coming down the trail. Could have been a thousand behind. I was with the screen. We fell back on the first of our cavalry as it was coming up on a meadow. If we can get there fast ..." He waved over his shoulder, and shrugged. "The Tungri are already moving their men up."

Titus turned to the Batavi commander. "Let's have them advancing at a run, Marius." Then, to the nearest dispatch rider: "Relay that back along the column. Tell them they're all needed forward, and fast. Then report back."

He urged his horse ahead at a canter, the trooper keeping pace. "Can Salvius hold them?"

"It depends how many there are, sir. The meadow's large with a beck running through, maybe a half-mile ahead," the trooper replied. "If he hurries, he might pen them up in the forest until the rest of our men arrive. If we can deploy and secure the meadow, it's a good place to stand and fight."

"I'd wager it's where we stopped to rest when we went scouting," Titus said to Gaius, spurring his horse to a gallop; then, to the Tungri, "Did Salvius say anything?"

A wry grin crossed the trooper's face. "He said, 'Go get some fucking help, Colm, and fast.'"

Gaius heard the yelling and fighting well before reaching the clearing. He and Titus burst into the open grassland pulling hard on the reins. Both horses slithered to a halt, skittish with excitement. The long meadow was chaotic. A mass of Tungri cavalry filled the other side, perhaps two hundred paces away, plugging the trail that led from the north. Beyond, as far as could be seen, the track was packed tight with Brigante horsemen.

Salvius's auxiliaries were holding, but his riders were a disorganized crush. Troopers rushed in and out tossing their spears, intent only on keeping the Britons from gaining the open ground. Most were ineffective, wheeling about on the grass, blocked from helping by their own men. Gaius could see that many of the Britons were edging off the trail, attempting to filter through the dense forest, and move in on the flanks. Skirmishing had already broken out along the tree line.

"Where the fuck is Salvius?" Titus muttered, cursing as he saw a decurio vainly attempting to beat his men into orderly ranks.

"It doesn't look good, sir," the trooper replied. "He was in the front ranks when I left."

"Shit!"

"They're going to flank us," Gaius said, and pointed to where a group of rider had broken free of the trees, farther up the meadow.

The frantic decurio had seen them too. Gathering as many of his troopers as he could, he galloped off to meet the threat.

"That man should be demoted," Titus snarled. "You can't plug a hundred arseholes with five fingers." He pointed off to the right. "Gaius, have the Batavi deploy over there, as soon as they arrive. I want them to advance in a solid front, and anchor on the East flank of the cavalry. If they look to be flanked themselves, have the right fall back against the trees on this side, and block that end of the meadow. I'm going to straighten that lot out."

Without waiting for a reply, the primus lashed his horse toward the Tungri cavalry, the trooper who'd brought word of the battle not two strides behind. Gaius was left by himself, for the moment perplexed. There was nothing he could do until the first of the infantry arrived, yet surely there was something. He gazed around the open grassland and saw at once that Titus was correct on one point. This was the meadow where they'd stopped to rest on their way north only a couple of months ago. He wished they'd ridden its length, at least to where it curved beyond the small farmstead. It probably ended at the river they had been shadowing.

The remaining dispatch rider coughed. "Sir."

Gaius had heard it too. The Batavi column was close, the steady thump-thump-thump of four hundred pairs of boots drifted through the trees as the centurions called out the time. The praefectus came first, alone, now mounted and trotting his horse through the long, trampled grass.

"Maintain your ranks, deploy to the right," Gaius barked, speaking before Marius had even stopped. He pointed to where the Britons were beginning to wriggle through the trees like perch through a pike net. "Advance toward the forest and form a front. Fall back on the right if they try and flank you."

The commander nodded, quickly assessing the lay of the ground for himself. His eyes narrowed as they took in the width of the field he was expected to cover. Behind him, the Batavi cohort spilled into the meadow in column of route, the senior centurion in the lead. Marius turned in his saddle as if the back of his head had eyes, and roared, "To the right, and mark time!"

"Good," Gaius replied, his eyes flashing back and forth between the Tungri crush in the centre and the Britons filtering through, now on either side. When he glanced back, the praefectus had galloped on.

Expecting the cohort from the Ninth to be close behind, he looked to see where it would be best deployed. There was little choice: anchor in on the other side of the Tungri cavalry, and eventually butt it up against Marius's left flank. Once in position, both infantry units would form a solid front all along the north side of the meadow. If there proved to be an overwhelming number of barbarians, the entire line could fall back against the trees on the south side of the huge open pasture, or form defensive square.

Satisfied, Gaius glanced westward, toward the head of the meadow. His eyes bulged. Hundreds of screaming barbarian warriors were erupting from the trees! How many trails led into this damned place?

Frantic, he turned looking for help, but the Batavis were still loping out of the forest, and moving in the opposite direction. He was tempted to break the cohort in two to try blocking the new threat, and saw Marius also eyeing the fresh onrush of barbarians. Then he noticed movement farther down the meadow to the east, beyond the curve where the farmstead lay nestled against the trees. Another raving horde was spewing out down there as well, including chariots and a scattering of cavalry.

"Oh fuck," Gaius muttered, his belly turning to ice.

"Where, Gaius, where?"

The voice screamed from behind, and he turned to find the last of the Batavi cohort leaving the forest, and Publius cantering his horse across the meadow. But there was no sign of the cohort to which he was attached. Gaius waved his sword toward the upper reaches of the meadow, fighting down his panic. "There. The moment they get here. Form a front and hold them back. Quick!" Gaius cried, then whirled to warn the Batavi commander of his own danger, but the man had already seen it.

The cohort had started its sweep across the meadow, and advancing steadily on the solid wall of forest to the north. Marius halted the advance on his right flank, and the rest of the line continued forward in a slow wheel. When it halted, there would be a diagonal wall of shields that rested against the rear of the Tungri cavalry; the right flank would be set against the forest to the south. Once in place, the entire cohort could fall back, and straighten out to face the new threat. But only as long as Salvius's force held in the centre—if, indeed, Salvius was still alive. Something that was growing more and more unlikely.

As the thought flashed through his mind, Gaius looked to see if Titus was having any success. It was easy to spot the primus's red-crested helmet in the sea of plain iron headgear. The primus had left the main group of riders, and was cantering over to another. Four troopers had knocked a Briton from his horse and were, incredibly, playing cat and mouse with him. Even at a distance, he could see Titus was livid.

Noting the progress elsewhere, Gaius allowed a sigh of relief. The decurios were getting a grip, and some of the Tungri had been ordered back to form a makeshift reserve. They sat, formed in line, holding their nervous horses well back of the fighting. But the meadow to the left was still wide open …

He was about to turn back to see where Publius was with the lead element of the Fourth cohort, when he saw Titus bark an order. The primus hit the rump of a trooper's horse with the flat of his sword to get him moving. Startled, the man spun about and, with his longer blade, caught the veteran a smashing blow on the side of his head.

"Oh shit," Gaius whispered, as what precious leadership remained with the Tungri cavalry crumpled in a heap in the grass.

There was no choice, he reluctantly decided. Someone was needed there, urgently, and there was no one else on the field. The flanks would have to be left in the care of Marius and Publius. There were still a few centuries of the Fourth Cohort yet to arrive after that, along with the support units from First. The commander, if the snail-paced bastard ever got here, would have to stumble through. Gaius checked both flanks and dug his heels into Rufus's belly, then promptly jerked back on the poor beast's reins, almost losing his seat.

"Oh shit!" he whispered again, as he saw Publius's men pour from the trees at a dead run, and head toward the west end of the meadow.

The four ranks of infantry were moving steadily up the open field in column, straight toward the enemy, instead of marching across to form a solid front, as his mind's eye had intended. It was understandable, though. Publius had seen the Batavi commander perform a similar turn on leaving the forest, when the man moved his command straight down the meadow to the east. Without thinking, the young tribune had done the same; but the situation had changed. The upper meadow was now teeming with barbarians!

Perhaps it wasn't too late. If they halted quickly and used the head of the column as a pivot, they might still wheel to face the enemy. Perhaps that was on the mind of the cohort's senior centurion, for the man seemed to be arguing as he ran alongside the young tribune. He was glaring at Publius, shouting, and gesturing with his sword. Whatever he said had effect, for the tribune pulled in his horse and pointed northward to the tree line.

Gaius again sighed with relief, a feeling that quickly turned to disbelief. Instead of halting to pivot and wheel, the centurion simply angled off to the north, and the column followed, snaking its way across the meadow. Gaius cursed. It would never reach the far side of the clearing before the barbarians struck. Digging his heels in once again, he sent Rufus racing forward.

"Pivot and wheel, pivot and wheel!" he screamed, oblivious to all else on the field.

Hundreds of Britons, howling in fury, struck the head of the cohort. The leading ranks, only four wide, began to disintegrate. Gaius's anger turned to rage, but he fought the urge to simply ride in and smash whatever came within range of his sword. Instead, he reined the chestnut in and sat taking stock, as the animal pranced impatiently in the long grass. The first part of the cohort had now cleared the forest, and was followed by a troop of Tungri. It was only thirty men, but they might help purchase some time.

"There's your enemy," he cried to the decurio, pointing to the head of the cohort, which had fallen into complete disarray.

The trooper looked uncertain, and for a moment Gaius thought the order was refused; but the man nodded, pale faced, as his optio formed his people into two ranks. It took only a moment, followed by a barely audible command, and the troop thundered across the grass toward the beleaguered centurion. At least something was being done, but where was the rest of the infantry? He eyes turned to search the empty trail that led south. The remaining troops were either behind or mixed in with the baggage wagons. Surely the commander had the sense to sort them out, rather than wait for the slow moving train to get here? And yet …

Gaius whirled about, and angrily shook his head. There were troops on the field that were idle! Half of Publius's men remained stranded along the south side of the meadow, halted when the head of the column had been engaged before it could deploy. But perhaps not!

The centurions, praise the gods, had them right face, presenting a solid front to the open grassland. One stood screaming orders at the four ranks, which now presented a front to the north. If they could march forward, and pivot at the point where the head of the line had crumbled, then it might stay the fight until the third …

The dispatch rider, sent seemingly an eon ago to hurry the column forward, emerged from the forest, jerking savagely on the reins as he pulled in beside Gaius. "They're coming, sir." The man's face registered dismay as he glanced about the field.

"How long?"

"A few hundred paces down the trail. Not long, sir."

Gaius whirled back to the field, and cursed. "Tell that centurion over there to advance on the…" he began the order, pointing to where the four ranks stood facing inward on the meadow; but there was no need to finish. The man had given the order himself, and the reduced column was advancing quickly across the field. As soon as it started forward, the rear rank slid off to the right, and reformed on the flank presenting a wider front. Gaius smiled grimly to himself. Roman discipline. The longer line was needed. But would it be enough?

Gaius glanced nervously to the empty trail, then to the battle whirling beyond the Tungri cavalry, and finally to the right flank. That, at least, was being competently held by the Batavi auxiliaries. All three fronts were engaged, but only Marius's command appeared to have matters well in hand. A mass of howling Britons were throwing themselves against the shields of his cohort, but the line was holding steady. The praefectus could use some cavalry to cover his flank, though. If only there were more cavalry.

Where was the last of the damned column?

Gaius, his belly hollow and his mouth dry, glanced once more to the empty trail. There was movement; he heard it before he saw it, and cursed in relief. Three men appeared on foot, and paused briefly at the edge of the forest. One ran toward Gaius, and he turned Rufus to meet him. He recognized Pedanius, senior centurion of the fourth cohort, which explained how the tribune Publius had been able to take charge and fuck everything up. Damn the youth! Damn both of them! The centurion's eyes reflected the same anxiousness as he trotted across the meadow.

"They're getting the best of us over there." Gaius pointed to Publius's column, then muttered, "Oh, shit."

The tail end of the Publius's force had moved forward with parade-like precision, and was wheeling to face the upper part of the meadow. Those Britons caught in front of the three solid ranks of shields and armour were swept back, as the infantry ruthlessly battered and stabbed its way forward. But at the point where the flank pivoted on Publius, the enemy had pried at the weakness, rushing in like water through a breached dam.

"Here they come," Pedanius growled, and for a moment Gaius thought he meant the barbarians; but the last of his force, the four centuries from the fourth cohort and the service support from the First, were streaming out of the trees.

"Straight across the meadow, and advance west?" The grizzled centurion had taken the field in at a glance and looked to Gaius, grinning darkly. "Relieve the unfortunate young tribune? If he can stay alive that long."

Pedanius led his command forward without waiting for a reply.

"Maybe," Gaius called out warily, and rode alongside, staring anxiously at Publius as he slashed and stabbed with his sword, "it might be better to form up first and wheel, or they'll catch you before you're able to fully deploy. That's the reason the 'unfortunate' tribune's in trouble to begin with."

"Only if you insist, sir." The centurion wiped his hand across his mouth, and grimaced. "It would be faster to head straight across the field. The stupid bastards are busy with the bear they've got in the trap. Their brains can't handle more than one thing at a time. They'll pick at the tribune's cohort until it's all gone, then look to see what else is coming."

The centurion moved off, running alongside his jogging infantry. The head of the column was already well into the open grassland, and his words proved correct. The Britons, sensing the collapse of Publius's cohort, fought on, hacking away at the broken ranks of infantry as more and more warriors poured in from the upper reaches of the meadow. Gaius bit his lip, staring anxiously at the screaming horde. Where were the bastards coming from?

Pedanius's column loped ahead, a mass of shields and helmets bobbing up and down, quickly closing off on the beleaguered Tungri cavalry. Gaius glanced along the rows of grim faces, and his mouth dropped open—he'd completely forgotten about Marcus! The lad had been placed toward the rear of the column, for his own safety. Now he was in the middle of the damned battlefield!

The boy's face was the colour of bleached linen as he passed, his eyes avoiding his father. Gaius flinched as if struck. His son was lightly armoured, wearing only a hard leather chest piece, and carrying a small shield rather than the much larger regular issue. He was helmeted, though, and armed. He was also alongside Octavius, and probably as safe in those ranks as anywhere else on the damned field. The old decanus saw his concern, and offered a thumbs-up as he trotted past.

The column turned and faced west as soon as it halted. Gaius was relieved to see Octavius shove Marc into the fourth, rearmost rank. Pedanius roared an order. The line began its advance up the meadow

at a steady, even pace, closing on Publius's desperate force as it fought
for its life.

The Britons, as if seeing the danger for the first time, broke off
piecemeal and charged forward. Gaius held his breath. But Pedanius
kept his men in tight formation, almost hidden behind a solid wall of
shields, and remained steady. With a sigh of relief, he turned to where
the cavalry still milled about in disorder on the far side of the meadow;
and the feeling of relief promptly vanished. The weakness that lay between the two battling lines of infantry was painfully obvious. How,
in the name of all that was sacred, had he allowed that to happen? The
deep chill that filled Gaius's hollow belly turned to ice.

Both fronts now brushed the protection of the trees on the south,
but on the far side of the meadow the forest was riddled with barbarians filtering onto the field. The infantry cohorts were supposed to join
ranks behind the Tungri, and form a solid wall of spears and shields;
but Publius's errant march up the meadow had not allowed that to
happen. In the centre, the few reserve troopers Titus had organized
before he fell had long since rejoined the fight; and Salvius's cavalry
were showing sign of failing. Many were now on foot, unhorsed, their
mounts cluttering the battlefield. The barbarians threatened to burst
from the forest in force!

Gaius looked wildly about for support, at the same time cursing
the lack. Then he saw the rearguard canter into the meadow—two
troops of Tungri cavalry. It was something. The gods, praise them all,
must have had a change of heart. He stopped cursing and pointed to
the far side of the field, where barbarian riders were squeezing into
the gap between the two lines of infantry. Caution made him hold one
troop back, though, ready for the next disaster.

Gaius relaxed enough to breathe. The supply train was unpro-
tected, and the main body of Tungri cavalry were for the most part a
mob with no direction, but for the first time he had a reserve, even if it
numbered only thirty.

The Tungri cavalry! Gaius sighed, even as he caught his breath.
They still hacked at the enemy in a wild brawl that so far showed no
sign of ending, which wasn't the role the damned cavalry was supposed to play! They were flank protection, and the eyes and ears of

the legions. The skirmishing was nothing but bloody attrition, and the barbarians outnumbered the troopers by the gods knew how many.

Yet to his right, Marius was holding well. The man had even commandeered a few of the Tungri to serve his flanks. Gaius wondered how he'd got them there, but then, the man seemed capable of anything. And Pedanius was advancing steadily up the meadow in classic formation, closing in on what remained of Publius's cohort, now scattered in more than a score of small, dirty fights.

Gaius smiled grimly, noting the progress. The old centurion's cohort moved relentlessly forward, leaving nothing behind that remained alive. The rear ranks stabbed, slashed, and hacked as they stepped over the huddled bodies of any wounded. Feeling a shiver of confidence for the first time, Gaius once more thanked his gods, and returned his attention to the Tungri.

As long as they held, all would be well. Pedanius, as soon as he'd salvaged what was left of Publius's cohort, would fall back on the Batavi force. Together they could all, in turn, fall back against the south wall of the forest, and present a solid battle front. The cavalry would disengage, regroup, and protect the flanks as they were supposed to do. Pedanius knew as much, too. Or did he?

To make sure the veteran centurion complied, Gaius sent the dispatch rider forward with the order. But no sooner had the man gone than a solitary barbarian broke through the whirling tangle of cavalry, riding a lathered white horse that might have been *Bucephalus*. The animal leapt clear over a dead Tungri and his fallen mount, and sent another trooper spinning even as he tried to turn. Gaius could have sworn the man in the saddle was Venutius. Other riders streamed close behind, each forcing a wider path through the breach. For the second time, a dam had broken.

"Push them back!" Gaius cried, signalling the decurio of the last troop to move forward. The man hesitated, staring skeptically at the mass of screaming barbarian riders pouring into the meadow.

"Now, trooper, now!" Gaius roared, and rode forward, ready to cut the man down and lead the charge himself; but the decurio nodded, and waved to his troop. It was at best a delaying action.

Alone in the centre of the field, no reserve remaining and the Tungri cavalry giving way before him, Gaius decided it was time to find shelter. He chose Pedanius. If the gods—and he cursed them for their fickleness—decided it was his time to die, then it would be with his son. He galloped Rufus to where the centurion directed the advance, which was now far enough up the meadow to have absorbed the beleaguered remnants of Publius's cohort.

Pedanius had also seen the breakthrough, and turned his two rear ranks. "Time to go back," he muttered as Gaius guided Rufus between the walls of shields. "I see my friend is of the same mind."

He nodded down the meadow toward Marius, also manoeuvring to battle on two fronts. His rear ranks had turned to face the breach, leaving the other two to deal with those swarming from the forest at the east end of the field. His one flank was against the tree line; the other, for the time being, was still being kept clear by Tungri cavalry. It was a protection that couldn't last long.

"He's advancing toward us," Gaius breathed, then searched his own line, looking for Marc. He found him in the middle rank, alongside Octavius, apparently unharmed.

Marius's cohort edged slowly across the field, struggling to maintain line. The centurions roared out the pace, running back and forth between the reversed ranks, screaming at the men to hold, and beating them back where they wavered.

"Or retreating," Pedanius muttered cynically, before issuing the same order.

The two battered Roman units gradually closed on each other, even as more and more Britons poured into the narrowing gap between. The shrinking battlefield became a wild, milling tangle of panicked horses and useless chariots. The Tungri cavalry, scattered and disorganized, simply fought to free itself from the barbarian crush. Horses fell on both sides, their riders with them, and the screams of both filled the field.

Gaius worked Rufus toward where he'd last seen Marc, then looked wildly about when he couldn't find him. The boy had moved to the forward rank and was fighting, Octavius protecting the lad's right. The centre ranks had thinned to almost nothing. They were nearing the Batavi cohort, though, for Marius's force, heavily engaged, was now less than fifty paces away. But the Batavi seemed to be falling in on themselves, as if the praefectus was trying to shorten his lines.

Or was he?

Gazing through a thicket of waving spears and swords, Gaius realized Marius was forming his men in square. Tungri cavalry were seeking shelter inside, with or without their horses, as the Batavi centre shuffled forward and the flanks fell inward, slowly forming solid walls, two ranks deep and thick with shields, on all four sides.

The man was a marvel! The manoeuvre instantly eased the crush of cavalry caught between the two cohorts. It happened just as the sheer weight of trapped and panicked cavalry threatened to overwhelm either side of the field. Once more, the gods seemed to have been there when needed. The gods, or Marius, or both.

A horse dashed wildly across Gaius's front, scraping against the forward rank, its heels kicking frantically at a tangle of entrails dangling from its belly. A path cleared, and for a moment there was a respite, when nothing seemed to move.

"Almost there, lad," Gaius called, edging his horse alongside his son. Marc managed a quick, pale glance at his father. The boy's face was splattered with blood and his eyes were wide as he fought his fear.

The throb and scream of battle suddenly rose to a deafening pitch, somewhere off to the right. It was a sound he had heard before. It was a cry of triumph—for someone.

He glanced over his shoulder in time to see Pedanius frantically trying to beat his men into line. Part of what was now the rear rank had collapsed. A gleeful horde of half-naked, woad-covered barbarians shrieked as they pressed into the gap, swinging and hacking every step of the way. Pedanius disappeared under a sea of swords and axes.

"Move it, move it," someone cried, as what remained of the line wavered.

"Steady, hold steady. Keep marching!" Gaius screamed. "We're almost there."

The Batavi cohort, still firm in its square, loomed only yards away, like a battered harbour in a deadly storm. Octavius added his angry roar as discipline began to fracture, but the noise behind rose to a fever pitch. Orders passed unheard. Men rushed forward, tearing through the chaos of barbarian riders and crazed horses, slashing wildly at whatever lay in their path.

Gaius cursed as all around him men broke and ran. Orders were useless, and there was Marc, confused, still standing firm alongside Octavius. He quickly edged Rufus between the two. "The cinch," he cried. "Grab the cinch!"

Octavius dropped his shield, Marc his sword. Each wedged a hand against the sides of the big chestnut's sweating chest, and grasped the strap that held the saddle. Gaius slapped the animal's rear with the flat of his sword, and it leapt forward, forcing a path through the crush.

The distance wasn't great, and Rufus plunged gamely on. Faces appeared, surprised faces covered with blood, contorted and confused; faces that disappeared as the chestnut, wild and panicked, rode or kicked them down. Gaius felt a jarring shock as the animal stumbled over the twitching carcass of another horse; then the firm, steady ranks of the Batavi auxiliaries were suddenly there, a grim-faced wall of blood-spattered faces.

"Go, go," Gaius yelled as a space opened up. Marc and Octavius released their grip and sprinted forward.

Something struck Gaius high on the back of his armour and he whirled, slashing with his sword. A mounted Briton, his mouth flicking foam through a blood-matted beard, lunged with a spear. Rufus shied, and Gaius hacked wildly at the man's weapon. The blade caught the shaft, forcing it downward. The tip sliced into the chestnut's flesh ahead of the saddle, not more than a handsbreadth from his groin. Rufus squealed in pain, lurched sideways, stumbled, and went down.

Gaius rolled free, and ran blindly for the Batavi square. One of the auxiliaries hefted a spear, and his mind registered disbelief as the man drew back his arm and threw. But the shaft whistled past his head just as a tooth-jarring blow struck the back of his helmet, and he pitched forward onto the churned and bloodstained grass.

Chapter XV

Dag survived the day's fighting relatively unharmed, but lost his chariot. It lay on its side, barely thirty paces from the Roman square, one wheel smashed, and both ponies dead in the harness. One had been impaled on a spear, the other killed by Dag himself when he finally managed to break free, and found the animal squealing in pain. The hilt of a Roman sword grew from its belly, the owner dead alongside with no face, for he had fallen beneath the animal's flailing hooves.

Dag limped slowly up the meadow, favouring a twisted ankle. He'd also sprained a wrist and had no weapon, for his own had broken in the fall from the chariot. At the time, he hadn't felt like picking up another and starting over again. It was a feeling shared by many of the tuath after the Romans formed a square, and the frenzied rage of battle cooled.

Venutius organized two more attempts to breach the stubborn defences before evening fell, and both were fiercely repulsed. But each took a Roman toll, and for the Britons, the odour of defeat did not hang in the air. As night began to cast its cloak, the feeling was that tomorrow would be a far better day. The enemy were outnumbered, trapped, and going nowhere. There was nothing but advantage in waiting.

"Lopping heads off is not only messy but, at this time of year, it brings more flies than a pile of shit," Dag muttered. He flopped down beside Cethen and stared morosely at a woad-daubed party of hill men moving among the dead, each trying to recall which of the Romans he had killed. Once identified, the dead man's head was hacked off amid great whoops of triumph. A pushing match had erupted between two of the hill men, and both argued as they straddled the corpse of a particularly large Roman decanus.

"Not only that; the damned Romans cut their hair short, and it makes them hard to carry," Cethen quipped in turn, and both men laughed.

The two sat cross-legged on a red cloak retrieved from a Roman corpse, and ate for the first time since the hastily snatched bite of food earlier in the day. Around them the tuath took care of itself, and since no kin close to either had been badly hurt, both men left well enough alone.

Cethen had grudgingly formed the opinion that Dag, without Garv, could be almost human. They had fought side by side when Venutius had twice decided the Roman square could be taken, each staying close to the other as if in unspoken agreement. Both of them missed a brother who should have been there, and while it was like yoking an ox and a mule together, the partnership had not felt uncomfortable.

"Da, why do they do that?" Rhun asked, staring in fascination as one of the hill men completed his grisly task, and jammed the severed head on the end of his sword. He waved it gloatingly at the Roman lines.

"It's to make their piss boil," Dag answered, watching curiously as several arrows arched lazily from the square, falling close enough to send the hill men running. "I think it's working."

"No, I mean why do they cut them off at all?"

"It's where a man's soul lives, son, and remains even after he's dead," Cethen explained. "They say if you take a head and hang it up, it brings lots of good things—luck, power, courage. Especially if the enemy fought well before he died."

"So why don't we do it?" Rhun asked, wincing as the man pulled the grisly trophy free of the sword and tossed it into the air before finally placing it in a leather bag.

"I suppose we do, son, but in a different way. We carve heads, or paint them. You've seen them—etched into metal, made out of clay. We just don't bother cutting the damned things off."

"Because they stink," Dag added helpfully.

"And bring flies," Rhun said, giggling.

Cethen playfully pushed his son sideways, preparing to wrestle with the boy when he bounced back, but he saw a familiar figure riding carefully through the sea of warriors and horses that now filled the meadow. He rose, grunting at the stiffness that had settled on his legs.

"Cian. Over here." He waved as he yelled the words, and saw his brother change direction. There was another man with him, and they were towing an unsaddled horse.

"Came to find out if you were still on the green side of the weeds," Cian called as he neared.

"Takes more than a Roman army," Cethen replied cockily, but his attention was on the horse. It was Gaius's chestnut. There was a flesh wound at the base of the animal's mane, which explained why there was no saddle. But the cut was not deep, and seemed to be causing the beast no great discomfort.

"So. What are you doing with that, Cian?" he asked cautiously, pleased to see the animal, but afraid his brother had claimed it himself.

Cian grinned, reading his thoughts. "Don't worry; it's a gift, from Vellocatus. He recognized it when they were gathering the strays."

"Gift, be damned! The man stole it from me, and gave it back to its owner," Cethen complained, then glanced up, startled. "Is he dead? The Roman, I mean."

The man beside Cian kicked his horse forward and answered. "You know that can't happen," Luga said, his deep voice slow and confident. "You're the one that will kill him. The druids have said so."

"But they lied about the vision ..." Cethen began, but gave up when he saw Luga's expression tighten. "So how did the man lose my horse? What happened?"

"I saw a spear bounce off his back like it was magic," Luga said, pleased to be asked the question, his great, bearded face full of awe. "Another was pushed away even as it was driven into his belly. Then he was thrown from his horse, and still he wasn't hurt, so another man rushed in to kill him. But a spear came out of *nowhere* and took *him* in the throat, just as he struck the Roman on the back of the head with an axe!"

"An axe in the back of the head will usually do it," Cethen suggested dryly. "It works well with goats and chickens."

"That's just it," Luga cried, pleased at the example. "It does, doesn't it? But with this man, it merely knocked his helmet off in pieces. After that, he crawled forward until several Romans rushed over and pulled him into their miserable square. I tell you, the gods have charmed his life. There's a spell on him."

"If you took a spear in the throat while trying to brain someone, your aim would likely be off a hair too," Cethen observed, then another thought struck him. "Shit, that's three helmets the Roman's gone through since spring."

"As you can see, Cethen," Cian said, changing the subject with a sly look sideways, "Luga's got nothing better to do on a battlefield than watch others fight, and tell stories."

"That's not true," Luga protested. "You were there too."

"I was too busy doing the fighting. Never saw a thing."

"I was fighting too, curse you. It doesn't stop a person seeing things."

"Exactly!"

Luga's mind pondered the comment, then he growled, "What do you mean by that?"

"Dammit, you two," Cethen interrupted, "I thought you weren't supposed to fight until after the battle."

Both men glared at him, then Luga spoke slowly, with just the trace of a smile. "Cethen, that doesn't make any sense."

For a moment there was a pained silence, then the two brothers roared with laughter, both surprised at the big man's wit.

"Come on, you fools, get down and eat," Cethen said.

Luga started to dismount, glad of the invitation, but Cian waved him to stop. "Better not," he said. "There's the other thing. Vellocatus said sending the horse might calm you down when I told you what else has happened."

"And what was that?" Cethen asked, suddenly wary.

"Coira. She joined the column right after your part of it left Stannick," Cian said, unable to keep the amusement from his face as he gestured toward the far side of the Roman square. "She ended up riding with the mob that took the trail to Bran's farmstead. Gutsy little vixen, isn't she?"

"How is she?" Cethen cried in alarm.

"Unhurt, except for maybe her backside."

"Damn!" Cethen yelped. "What was her mother doing?"

"Actually, Elena chased after her all the way here. In a temper that would put a sow bear to shame, I might add. Last time I saw them, they were at the farmstead down the meadow, not speaking to each other. Or anyone else, for that matter."

"Shit!" Cethen cried again, and threw his hands up. "Shit!"

"Can I come too, Da?" Rhun asked. He was holding Flint's reins ready, even before his father whirled around looking for the animal.

It wasn't true that Elena was not speaking to anyone. Cethen found her near Bran's farmstead, using her saddle as a seat as she savoured the warmth of a small fire with Vellocatus. It was one of hundreds glittering about the meadow. The air was cool and damp, and quick gusts of wind rustled through the treetops carrying with them the threat of rain. The pair were sharing a warmed jug of wine, and a litany of the day's frustrations. Neither lacked for words.

Cethen's temper had cooled during the long ride around the Roman square. He dismounted, his body tired and aching from the day's pounding. He dropped Flint's reins and limped to the fire, sitting down beside Elena without speaking. Vellocatus wordlessly passed the jug. It was accepted with a grateful nod and all three sat in silence, staring into the flickering embers. Rhun, not sure of the sudden, unusual quiet, decided it was best to go and find his sister.

Elena finally spoke, angry at the reproach she found in her husband's silence. "Go ahead and say it."

"Say what?" Cethen asked mildly, sipping at the warm wine.

"That I should have kept a better eye on the girl."

"You should have kept a better eye on the girl," he said, and shrugged. "Is there anything else you want me to say?"

"Arsehole!"

"Bitch." He grinned and playfully pushed her shoulder. "Where is the lass?"

"Over by the farmstead. I think. Though you never know, with that girl. Probably sulking, and as scared as a trapped rabbit. The boy she was riding behind got his arm sliced off by one of their horsemen."

"How is he?"

"Where is he, is more the like. Somewhere in the other world, I'd guess, after leaving most of his blood spread all over Coira," Elena said then added with a mother's logic, "That'll teach her to go wandering off with the first boy who's willing to take her."

Cethen and Vellocatus exchanged silent glances, the latter vainly suppressing his habitual grin.

"Yes, well, I'm sure the lad got the point of the lesson too," Cethen murmured.

Elena snorted and called out to the dark, "Coira!"

Her daughter stepped immediately from the shadows with Rhun in tow. One side of her dress was black with Mioch's blood, and a large, purple bruise shone high on her cheekbone. Her small jaw was clenched and her head held high as she walked in front of the fire and stood before her father. Cethen decided that there wasn't much of the trapped rabbit to be seen.

"What have you got to say to your da?" Elena demanded.

After a long moment, Coira sighed, then forced a sheepish grin, and nodded toward her mother. "She should have kept a better eye on me," she repeated, and turned to Elena. "Is there anything else you want me to say?"

Her mother began to rise, growling her anger, but Cethen held her back. "She's still here, love; let her be." He stared intently at his daughter, then down at the stains on her dress, and spoke gently. "I'd guess she's seen enough for one day. How are you feeling, lass? Being in a battle's a lot different than the tales they tell when it's over, isn't it? You going to be alright?"

Coira stared blankly at her father for a moment, then her eyes began to water. "Oh shit!" she cried, then whirled about and disappeared into the shadows.

"Rhun!" Cethen called as her brother turned to follow; the boy stopped, and he continued, his voice still gentle. "And you?"

"Can't wait until tomorrow," he said, and shrugged. "You never know, there might even be something for me to do."

"Everyone seems to be in a foul mood," Elena muttered, staring after Rhun as he trailed behind his sister.

"That's because we didn't finish it today," Vellocatus offered, then gloomily spit the dregs of his wine into the fire. "If we had, the only ones in a foul mood would be the Romans. If any still lived."

"Even Coira might be on your sunny side," Cethen said to Elena. "Are you taking her back tomorrow?"

She shook her head. "Now I'm here, I'd like to see it through. Venutius said that one well planned attack in the morning should do it. I'd like to see that."

"That's the plan," Vellocatus said, though he didn't sound totally convinced. "But it has to be over by tomorrow. Or at least before the sun rises the next day. Relief could arrive any time after that, if they have the soldiers for it. Which they do."

"So will Venutius be sending to Stannick for more men?" Elena asked.

Vellocatus snorted his disgust. "The stubborn old bastard figures five to one is more than enough. It's a matter of pride. Though I suspect his pride will be wearing thin if we haven't cracked them apart by midday."

"You don't think he'll send for more help then?"

Vellocatus smiled cynically. "I think he should send for more help *now*."

"But will he?" she persisted.

"Let's put it this way," Vellocatus said, suddenly serious. "If the Romans aren't broken by this time tomorrow, you and your lass mount up, and ride home."

"I'll add my voice to that." Cethen took a last sip of wine, then stood, nodding toward the farmstead where a flickering yellow light shone through the open doorway. "You staying inside tonight, love?"

"It's crowded, but I found room. It's going to rain." Elena glanced at the rolling black clouds closing from the south. A flash of lightning glimmered on the horizon.

"It won't be here for a while yet," Cethen said, his mood changing as he spoke. He added a grin. "You want to go for a walk?"

"Nothing better to do." Elena smiled, and held out her hand.

"Neither have I," Cethen said, feigning a grunt as he pulled her to her feet.

"Fickle females," Vellocatus muttered, staring balefully into the fire as he took the warm wine jug from Cethen, and raised it. "I asked the woman earlier, and she said no."

"Probably nothing personal," Cethen suggested, draping an arm around his wife's shoulder. "It's all the other stuff. Age. Good looks. That kind of thing."

Darkness arrived on a damp, cloying wind that threatened rain. Inside the Roman lines, it also brought a respite from the barbarians. Hundreds of exhausted men began digging a ditch that, under more orderly conditions, would have been dug ahead of everything else. They piled the sodden earth behind the muddy trench, forming a rampart that was the first line of defence of any marching camp. When finally completed, the ditch was almost chest deep, making the berm that backed it appear twice as tall.

Gaius was unhappy with the sparse ridge of stakes that topped it. Only the Batavi cohort had marched into the meadow with its men carrying their kit. The packs, each with a single stake, had been abandoned where the cohort formed up to fight. Yet a small part of their luck was holding, Gaius conceded. For when Marius formed the square, a good deal of his cohort's kit had been recovered, including most of the stakes. There was food too, though very little. But above all else, a decent portion of the shovels had also been recovered.

The defenses were complete by midnight. The beck that meandered through the centre of the square had been nothing but a nuisance during the battle; but now, thanks to a fresh cut channel, the water rushed into the ditch, filling it to the brim. Soon after, it began to rain.

Gaius and Titus called an orders group in the final hour before dawn. Officers of all rank met in the centre of the Roman square, with no shelter from the drizzle, and no fires to ward off the bone-chilling cold. The centurions crouched on the sodden ground, one knee in the mud as they huddled about the four senior commanders. Gaius, his hair plastered black against his skull and the long scar glistening white in the darkness, detailed their options. Only one seemed feasible.

"We simply wait them out. Two days. Today, when it finally dawns, and most of the next. Petronius should be here by then, probably before evening falls. All we have to do is hang on."

"The worst will be their first attack. Survive that, and we'll make it," Titus added, his voice betraying the pain that racked his body. "It will come at daybreak, and from all sides. Most of their men are down meadow to the east, so the brunt of it will fall there." The primus winced as a he pointed to the first traces of dawn showing above the trees. His left arm had broken in the fall from his horse, and the right side of his face was gashed and bruised where the helmet had taken the Tungri's blow.

Gaius suspected that every bone in the man's body ached. Two dismounted troopers, fighting as they fell back, had dragged the unconscious primus across the meadow by the ankles. During the bumpy passage, no one on either side, man or horse, had been careful where they set their feet.

One of the medici had cleaned the primus up, clucking to himself as he stitched the wounds. He set the bone, then splinted the arm with a broken spear shaft. The man left as soon a the job was done, commenting that it was now up to the gods, and wasn't it a bitch that all the supply wagons had been lost? Titus had finally awakened when it started raining, silently wishing he'd remained in the arms of Morpheus.

"The ditch and the water will come as a surprise," Gaius said.

"No doubt it will," Marius agreed. He was the only officer not nursing a badly bruised or perforated body. "But then, the gods give and the gods take, don't they? We'll have to wait and see how they roll the dice. Will it be Petronius first, or Venutius?"

"Venutius is already here," Gaius said, puzzled.

"Yes, but what is he doing? He has us outnumbered, certainly, but we're dug in. On top of that, well—we're us! If I was wielding his sword, I'd send to Stannick for every man I could summons. It's close, closer than Ebor. He should try and crush us with numbers, while we're still vulnerable."

"True, I suppose," Gaius muttered, his thoughts dark and bitter with memories of his talk with Cartimandua, "but what really pisses me, is they knew we were coming."

The attack didn't come at dawn, as expected. Venutius appeared to be taking no chances. He spent the first part of the day positioning his army, placing most of his men down the meadow from the Romans, as expected. The open grassland offered a broader and more open front. Even so, a strong force was positioned at the upper end, ready to block the Romans' escape when the square broke. During the attack, it would harry the enemy's rear as the main blow was struck from the east.

Cethen was given responsibility for that portion of the meadow. It was where Maeldav's and his own tuath were located, and where each had fought the previous day. The task was one he didn't relish, for it would be like cajoling a herd of swine to pull in harness. When he reflected on it, the task had likely been assigned due to his own poor timing at the farmstead.

He and Elena had returned as the rain started falling, both of them flushed and happy. They entered the hut at the very moment that Venutius was placing his chiefs about the meadow. The old king glanced up as the pair walked in, and Cethen suddenly found himself leading not only the tuath, but everyone else positioned at the western end of the field.

Elena hadn't been so sure about the details, though. She noted that the old man said Cethen was "responsible" rather than "in command," and cynically offered the difference. There were at least a dozen chiefs at the same end of the meadow, she pointed out. Without Venutius right there to sort things out, it would be akin to ordering a pack of deer hounds to sit down and quit yapping. She opined that Cethen would have to wheedle, defer, cajole, and beg to get them to attack anything other than a good meal.

The battle finally began at midmorning, following the lumbering effort of raising more than five thousand warriors to a state of frenzy, every last one standing in a fog of drizzling rain. Most of the younger druids had marched with the small army. Their task was to harangue the king's piebald army, goading the tribesmen to a high pitched state of battle fever with shouts, screams, threats and exhortations.

The druids shrieked their loathing and danced their spite, gradually inflaming the shivering Britons to a crazed, violent hatred. They bawled out the terrible wrongs inflicted by Rome, and roared the vengeance that was about to fall. They called on the spirits of the dead, evoked the power of the gods, and conjured the dreadful magic of Mother Earth. All about the meadow, warriors beat shields with weapons already dark with blood, and screeched their hate until hoarse.

The noise slowly swelled to a thunderous, ear-piercing roar. The shields beat faster and louder and stronger, until the meadow itself seemed ready to erupt. Then, when the druids judged the howling screams had crested, Trencoss himself turned to Venutius. The king roared an unheard order, and pointed to the Roman square. The horde surged forward.

It was as Titus said, Gaius thought, the first attack was the worst. The Britons hadn't balked at the barrier of mud and water. Those in front were forced through the ditch by the unrelenting pressure of those who followed, or they died. And many of them did. The frenzied horde surged forward, spurred by the weight of its own numbers. Down through the muddy water they slid, up the slick rampart on the other side, and onto the sodden, stake strewn crest.

Gaius, standing behind the first ranks of defenders, watched in dismay. The barbarians themselves hardly realized what was happening. Shock filled the faces of those who led the charge as they plunged down into the narrow moat and fell, or, with no will of their own, were flung upward against the wall of shields and iron. Hundreds were crushed and drowned as others behind pushed on, screaming wildly even as they trampled their own men underfoot.

Shield to shield, the Romans fought back, slipping and sliding in ranks three and four deep atop the makeshift rampart. The centurions paced the rear, bawling and shoving, every second word a curse. Men were shoved forward to brace those in front with shoulder, shield, and with whatever footing could be found. Gaius paced back and forth with the primus, their pain numbed as they balanced the precious reserves, and frantically plugged each hole as fast as it appeared.

Near the centre of the square, Publius was on his feet. The young tribune had hardly spoken since the collapse of his cohort. When found, he was only half conscious and bleeding from a dozen cuts that had passed unnoticed when received. Pain had followed with a vengeance, as the medici stitched and bound each wound, stanching the flow of blood. The renewed attack came as a welcomed penance for his blunder.

As night fell and the troops dug in, he had remained silent and morose. During the orders group in the final hour of the dark night, he hadn't opened his mouth, and no one had encouraged him to do so. But with the dawn, he ignored the hurt and placed himself at the centre of the square with Gaius, commanding nothing but his injured pride.

The barbarian breakthrough came at the height of the attack: that terrible moment when every man is committed, and no choice remains but triumph or defeat.

A score of barbarians, their horses skidding, sliding, and twisting, gained the east side of the rampart. The animals were crazed, beaten and spurred by their riders until mindless with fear. A dozen screaming warriors followed in each one's wake, clinging to the cinches, the tails, the saddles, and each other.

The lead horse skewed sideways on reaching the ditch, and most the others went down. But the first to top the rampart slipped, and rolled over its rider as it tumbled inside, scattering the ranks of defenders. Those that followed hurdled the fallen beast with no thought to the man who was down. A great roar of triumph echoed from behind. A sea of warriors charged over the ditch, the path made easier by the bog of broken bodies.

The centurions screamed orders. Infantry rushed forward. But the barbarian charge had gained a momentum of its own. The wall of shields clashed and closed, and at first held. Then gradually, hacking and stabbing, the solid ranks of Roman infantry were pressured back, sliding over the treacherous earth as more and more tribesmen rushed through.

Publius swung onto his horse. The leaderless remnants of a Tungri troop stood nearby, like a flock of lost sheep; perhaps a half-dozen were mounted, and five times as many were on foot. The tribune waved his sword and pointed.

"Come on," he screamed, wheeling his mount. "Do something, dammit, or you'll die!"

Then, not caring whether they followed or not, Publius spurred the horse forward—not at the mass of Britons battling inside the defenses, but at the breach itself.

The animal charged forward ramming with its chest and flailing with its hooves, as it ploughed through the stream of warriors pouring through the gap. The beast lurched drunkenly onto the rampart, where Publius hauled back on the reins, stabbing wildly at whatever moved. One or two Tungri riders were suddenly alongside, then miraculously, several more. A score of dismounted troopers followed, each mad with battle fever and fear. At their heels ran a decanus, bringing with him the dregs of one of the last reserve squads.

Each man crawled bravely onto the earthen mound, ignoring the flailing hooves. A line took form, back to back, stubbornly linking up to plug the gaping hole. The Tungri wheeled their horses and rode back, as more infantry rushed from the far side of the square to take their place.

Publius vainly tried to do the same, but both reins were slashed and he no longer controlled his mount. The animal splayed its forelegs, squealed, and shook its head in confusion. Then it skidded sideways and slid into the ditch, the tribune tumbling with it.

The filthy water was ice cold and black. The horse rolled and staggered to its feet, leaving Publius winded, his face underwater in the trench, his mouth plugged with slime. Something heavy fell hard on his back, pinning both his legs. Publius twisted and writhed, blinded by mud and panic; his mind flashed red, and his chest felt ready to burst.

One leg suddenly pulled free. He kicked wildly, and found a place to brace his foot. Whatever it was felt soft. He pushed hard, freeing the other leg at the cost of a boot, his lungs bursting for air. One hand slid along the slime of the ditch as he rolled, kicking wildly backward. His head broke the surface, gasping and spluttering, both eyes blurred and raw. A dark shape loomed above, vague and threatening, and his mind screamed.

Publius lifted his free arm, the sword still clenched firm in his fist. A crushing blow jarred the blade and he fell backwards, his mouth once more full of the foul water. He tensed, waiting for the final blow, but instead a great weight fell on his chest, forcing him farther under the filthy water. Then, equally fast, the weight was gone, and someone was lifting him by the neck of his leather tunic.

The roar of battle once more filled his ears. He stood in the ditch shaking, thigh deep in water on a shifting bed of sunken bodies, wiping both eyes in an effort to clear them. Beside him stood the decanus. Close by, the body of a huge barbarian sank slowly under the muddy surface in a swirl of dark crimson.

"You still alive?" the decanus asked, and offered a hideous, blood drenched grin.

Publius nodded, gave a dry heave, and tried to focus. Other shapes moved in the ditch, and more on top of the rampart. As his eyes cleared, he saw they were all, thank the gods, on the side of Rome—soldiers who now stood in rank, shields up, gamely fighting a thinning horde of barbarians. Desperately wanting to redeem himself, Publius stumbled from the ditch onto the churned mud of the meadow.

"Sir!" the decanus warned.

Publius ignored the cry. Raising his sword, he yelled, "We have them. They're ours."

Several infantrymen, waist deep in water, waded up into the meadow and formed a line. A second rank atop the rampart descended and, using the dead as stepping stones, deployed behind.

"Sir, sir!" the decanus cried again, but once more his voice was lost in the uproar.

The Britons seemed confused, hesitating as the ranks of Roman infantry stepped forward to flank Publius. None of it made sense. Most of the barbarians stopped and stood cautiously watching, their frenzy now drained and cool. The moment did not last long. Venutius's warriors did not turn and run. They simply turned and slowly, reluctantly, began to quit the field.

Titus climbed onto the rampart, leaving Marius to deal with the few barbarians who remained alive inside the square. Gaius joined the primus a moment later, after first making certain that Marcus survived, and was again safely under Octavius's wing. When Publius and the ragged ranks of infantry deployed in the meadow began slowly moving forward, both men started in surprise.

Gaius quickly called one of the surviving dispatch riders to his side. "Give the young tribune my respects, trooper, and order him to fall back. Fast! It's enough that the enemy has called off the attack."

The man departed, and Gaius shook his head. "We just might get the silly ass back before he gets himself killed."

"Or fucks up a second time," Titus muttered.

"They'll attack again tomorrow, only earlier," Gaius concluded moodily. "As yet, there's no sign of his reinforcements, but I'd guess they'll be here sometime tonight. They have to be coming, or he'd attack again while he can. The man can count the time as well as we. He can figure out when we might expect help."

The four officers sat on sodden, bundled cloaks, absently picking with their fingers at a tasteless glue of barley meal cadged from the Batavi. Nightfall was not far away and the evening was bleak, but no barbarian appeared ready to threaten any part of the meadow. There were no fires either, which offered Gaius a grim satisfaction: the enemy would be just as wet and miserable as the men in the square.

In the meantime, the defences had been renewed. The ditch was cleared and its depth restored, the beck flushing the foul, crimson water off down the meadow like a barracks' latrine. The bodies of the Britons hauled from the square were cast well back on the muddied grass, both as an object lesson and an obstacle. The Roman dead were laid out in neat lines inside the square, the heads, thankfully, still attached.

"I doubt Petronius could get troops away from Ebor until this afternoon," Marius ventured. "Maybe as late as this evening, or worse still, tomorrow morning. Dammit, he might not have heard we were even in trouble until this morning."

"I should have dispatched a rider as soon as I saw what was happening," Gaius said.

"I did," Publius, in better spirits despite the pain etched on his face, spoke unexpectedly.

The other three stared at him, and Titus asked cautiously, "You did?"

"Yes. As soon we entered the meadow," Publius said, and added to make light of it, "The man was damned pleased to go."

"That could give Petronius an extra half-day!" Marius said, his tone lighter. "Though we'll still have to hold out for most of tomorrow. It's going to be tough slogging for any relief though, with the bastards expecting it. But that was good thinking, Publius."

The tribune smiled wanly, then lowered his head and stared at the mushy barley. "Actually, one of the senior centurions suggested it as we entered the meadow. May the gods be kind to him. I was too busy fucking things up."

There was a pained silence at the words, because everyone knew they were true. There was nothing more to be added. Even so, Marius tried. "Look on the plus side, Publius. You tried to get yourself killed this morning, and you fucked that up too." He chuckled. "And it's lucky you did. It was the turning point."

"And if you can do the same again tomorrow, we'd be grateful," Gaius added, stuffing the last of the paste into his mouth, and licking his fingers. "I doubt they'll be back today."

He'd barely spoken the words when a ripple of movement ran through the ranks on the down meadow side of the square. Voices called orders, as others groaned their frustration. Men sitting cold and wet under the sodden shelter of their cloaks began clambering to their feet. The clatter of weapons rang through the evening gloom as shields were retrieved, and spears and swords gathered.

A decanus came splashing through the mud. "Riders, sir. Lots of them. Coming from downfield."

"Shit," Gaius muttered.

They climbed to their feet, Titus and Publius helped by the others, then stumbled across the muddy square and onto the rampart, where they gazed out across the meadow. Gaius cursed the gods, convinced they were making sport of him, and only him. His optimistic prediction had barely fallen from his mouth, and the barbarians were attacking!

Or were they?

Across the vast expanse of meadow, the sea of barbarian warriors remained huddled in their ragged, makeshift lines. In their own way, they appeared little different than those inside the square, only there were far, far more of them. Yet beyond, vague and grey in the drizzle of the waning day, a mass of horsemen, deployed in line, trotted across the open grassland. The Romans watched as the distance rapidly closed, and the faint yelp of voices drifted through the rain.

The advance was a puzzle. Tactically, such a charge made no sense. Venutius's army had not prepared itself. It lay idle, resting between the advancing line of riders and their own defenses. Yet the cavalry rode onward as if—

"They're ours!" Titus voiced the impossible, his bruised and bloody features breaking into a broad smile. "Where, in the dark pits of Hades, did they come from?"

"Who cares?" Gaius laughed as the first wave of troopers fell on the farthest reaches of the barbarian camp. "They're here."

※

"Da!"

Cethen sat hunched over with his knees clutched against his chest, half dozing as the heavy drizzle fell on his back, soaking the cloak that covered his chilled shoulders. Rhun's urgent voice penetrated his torpor, which he'd been enjoying despite the soaking rain and the cold, bone-cutting damp.

He'd been musing on going back to Bran's farmstead, whoever Bran was, or had been, and making sure that Elena had taken Coira back to Stannick. His wife had promised to leave by midafternoon, but he knew she'd been reluctant because of the downpour—not to mention the chance that the Romans might be overrun. It was warm and dry inside the hut, and a lot was probably happening there. There would also be many whom he knew. Vellocatus would likely have returned from Stannick as well, with word of sufficient warriors to roll over the Romans like a herd of stampeding cattle.

"*Da!*"

"What!" Cethen shook his head to clear the cobwebs, and looked up to see Rhun standing before him. The lad was soaked through as well, his features pinched and pale. A hard gust of wind might have knocked him over. When he went to the farmstead later on, he would take the boy with him, perhaps leave him there. After all, he *was* supposed to be a messenger for Venutius.

"Something's happening, Da! The Romans are moving."

The boy seemed really worried. He held the reins of his pony, and he'd also brought Flint with him. Cethen looked about and saw that only a few others were still resting on their rears. Everyone else was on their feet, staring off toward the far end of the meadow. He held out his hand and Rhun pulled him to his feet, a chore that took a good deal more effort than he'd imagined.

"What are they doing?"

"I think they're leaving."

Cethen swung up on the gelding's back for a better look, but it wasn't enough, so he climbed unsteadily on top of the saddle. Everything grew suddenly, startlingly clear. The Roman force had abandoned its makeshift camp, and was deploying in four ranks, facing the far side of the meadow. Beyond them, all across the open field, there was absolute chaos.

The main part of Venutius's army, camped in clusters all over the open grassland, milled about in confusion. A large force of Roman cavalry was on the move, driving his hard-pressed warriors backwards, sideways, all ways, as if they were nothing more than a herd of cattle. Those Romans who had been in the square, the ones who were supposed to be swept away the next morning when help arrived from Stannick, were slowly marching forward to meet them.

"We're in trouble, son," Cethen muttered, sliding down to straddle the saddle; he sat there, dumbstruck, pondering what to do. Rhun was wondering the same thing, and gave voice to the question. It prodded his father to a decision.

"Son, ride back toward Stannick as fast as you can, and tell Vellocatus the Romans have been reinforced. They're breaking out." His mind was more concerned with the boy's safety, though; any relief force was surely too far away. "If you meet Vellocatus on the way, tell him, and keep on going to Stannick to warn the others. They'll need to know, and be ready. Do you understand? This is very, very important."

Rhun nodded. "What about you? And Mam?"

"She's likely halfway home," Cethen said without confidence. "Just listen to me and pay heed. It's important you deliver the message. Now go. And here, take the Roman's horse with you."

Rhun climbed onto his pony, grim faced, and pulled its head around until the animal was facing the trail north. Cethen handed him the chestnut's reins. The lad nodded to his father, unable to hide his fright, then lashed at the pony's flanks. It broke into a fat, loping canter, the larger horse following at a quick trot, its head high in the air. Cethen couldn't help wondering how long the smaller beast would go before it, too, fell into a trot, and then to a walk. The boy would probably have to beat the creature all the way home.

What next? Only the gods knew how many of Venutius's warriors were at this end of the meadow, for Cethen certainly didn't. Five hundred? Seven hundred? A thousand? Again, he had the gnawing feeling that he should have been doing something about that earlier, but again, what? The important thing was that they should probably be attacking the rear of the Roman infantry. There was no better time than when their long, even ranks were moving forward to close with the cavalry. It had to begin with the tuath. And with Dag. And the other chiefs.

Cethen raced Flint frantically from one group of tribesmen to another, screaming and cajoling, reminding them all of Venutius's orders, anxiously trying to stir each one to action. Some did finally begin to move. It took time, but a ragged, halfhearted charge did fall on the rear of the Roman line as it engaged those at the other end of the meadow. The assault lacked the screaming, blood-crazed rage of the morning. The Romans were the ones now primed for battle, the ones who could smell victory. The two rear ranks simply about-faced as their officers halted the advance, and almost casually repelled the attack. The battle proved no more than a skirmish.

Cethen ordered those who remained of the tuath to return to Stannick as best they could. He abandoned them in the forest at the place where the trail from Bran's farmstead met the main track. Both paths were crowded with Venutius's people, all running from the meadow, many badly hurt; but he no longer cared. As far as he was concerned, Dag could take over the whole damned tuath, which was exactly what he'd told him to do. He pushed Flint hard through the stream of men fleeing north, fighting to get back to where he'd last seen Elena.

Long before he could break free of the forest near the farmstead, the angry clash of fighting filtered through the trees. Roman cavalry appeared farther down the trail, pushing their way in from the meadow. For a moment Cethen considered the odds of riding on, but a pinprick of sanity prevailed. Cursing both earth and sky, he wheeled Flint about and dug his heels into the tired animal's flanks. Heedless of others escaping down the same track, he whipped the animal forward, praying to any god that would listen that Elena had left the field with their daughter as she had promised.

Chapter XVJ

Cerialis held his own debriefing several weeks after the battle, on his return to Ebor. It was a good deal less cordial than the earlier one ordered by Petronius. Until the governor's arrival, the legate had considered the costly engagement to be more a victory than a defeat, though not particularly decisive either way. He was rapidly apprised of the difference. The first hint was when Cerialis informed him that it would be held in the commander's residence, because "it's too damned embarrassing to hold in the fucking headquarters building."

The session was more a post mortem than a debriefing, Gaius decided, only it was one performed on live bodies. The autopsy took place in the building's courtyard, where the governor's voice at times reached such a pitch that he might just as well have conducted it in the headquarters building. He spared no one, even those who hadn't marched with the ill-fated expedition. But the four surviving senior officers received the deepest cuts, along with the vicarious sympathy of those who witnessed Cerialis's vicious necropsy.

Titus stared grimly ahead, one arm slung across his chest, his face so battered it might have been used for sword practice. Gaius sat alongside, his shaved head topped by a new row of stitches where the third helmet of the year had been smashed against his skull. Publius was allowed the privilege of lying on the floor with his back propped against the wall. Bandages swathed both his legs and one arm, and he was in

251

a good deal of pain. He could have remained in the hospital, but he insisted on being brought to the residence out of a masochistic need for atonement. The only one of the four unhurt in the battle, Marius, sat by himself on a bench. Ironically, three fresh stitches decorated his forehead, closing a deep gash acquired the night before, when he accidentally walked onto the pointed end of a spear. The weapon was battlefield salvage, carelessly stored on a rack alongside one of the storehouses.

The new Tungri cavalry commander, a man called Quintus Babarus, sat beside Marcus Aurelius, the camp praefectus. Petronius himself had not taken a seat, preferring to stand behind Cerialis, as if trying to lose himself in the shadows of the veranda. Everyone wished they were somewhere else, but especially Petronius, because regardless of any circumstance, he was ultimately responsible.

Cerialis began his tirade in a low, hissing voice directed at Titus. "Over five hundred casualties, primus! Five hundred! I send you out to build a plain, simple fort, and you come back with five hundred casualties. And no fort. And no supplies, either! An entire supply train lost! How long have you been in the army, soldier? Twenty-five days, or twenty-five years? It is not, sir, the duty of the legion's primus pilus to charge into battle every time he sees a herd of Gallic horse humpers tripping over their own cocks!"

Just the mention of the Tungri seemed to infuriate him, and he turned on the new cavalry commander. Quintus had led the relief force in its assault from the east end of the meadow. The entire strategy for the lightning rescue had, in fact, been his idea. The praefectus had been miles away, back at Ebor, when the two armies had first collided. He'd cajoled Petronius into rushing help north, a move that proved wildly successful. His jaw dropped in shock as Cerialis took him to task, no longer hissing, but in full voice.

"They behaved with as much discipline as a mob of Dacian donkey drivers. And they were just as effective. I don't blame the men—it was their lousy leadership. On one edge of the blade is the primus, who sees a fight and decides he wants to be a decurio. On the other side is Salvius whatever-his-damned-name-was, who sees a barbarian advance party and thinks he's a fucking trooper! And look what it got him! We don't pay our senior officers to fight, we pay them to think. It's the damned men we pay to fight!"

"And speaking of Salvius—" Cerialis paused for breath, then suddenly fired a question from out of the air. It was a habit that Gaius was already beginning to recognize; the general's mind flitted from one arena to another, as if by whim. "By the way, what happened to his brat?"

Everyone looked puzzled, except perhaps Quintus. "A small, tousle-haired boy? A barbarian?" he asked.

Cerialis raised his eyebrows at Titus. "That the one, primus? Salvius promised he'd see to the boy."

Titus offered a painful shrug. "I think so, sir. Name began with an E—Ethnio or something."

"Ethrin," Quintus said coolly, his face reflecting the unfairness of Cerialis's barb. "He's been in and out of the officers' quarters, hanging around the men. Someone said he was Salvius's. Don't know what to do with the boy now."

"If he's a thorn in the arse, let Catey keep him. Permanently. She always has space." Then, changing colour as fast as a chameleon, Cerialis's face turned red as his voice grew to a roar. "As I said, speaking of Salvius, he should have sent his decurios forward, dammit! The commander is needed alive to command. If he's killed, everyone's buggered! I'm warning you now, young Babarus," he shook his finger in the praefectus's face, "you ever do that to me, and I'll have your balls nailed to a cross!"

He whirled again on Titus. "And you—not only do you never, ever fart off again and leave your command like that, you don't leave it to a damned engineer!"

Cerialis turned angrily on Gaius, shaking his head in disgust. "Engineers—what do you do with them? What are they good for? Shit all!"

He turned his back, waving one hand in exasperation, as if he found it too painful to look at his senior tribune. His eye caught that of Petronius, off in the shadows, and he winked. Gaius saw only the legate's jaw drop, and wondered what dire exchange had just taken place.

The governor whirled back again, shaking his finger. "Linear thinking. One think at a time. It's all an engineer can handle! Perhaps that's why they send troops into battle one useless unit at a time. Like building bridges, one span first—ah, here it is. Now where's the next? Oh, and maybe one more." Cerialis paused as if trying to control his temper. "Well, it doesn't work that way, tribune! You do that with men, and it's like feeding meat piecemeal to a butcher! Here's the first slab. Oh, not enough? Then here's another, and another, and another. Great new tactic! Choke the barbarian son of a bitch to death before he can digest all your troopies!"

The governor threw both hands in the air, as if in despair. "Mind you, should our man Gaius have known any better?" he asked, his voice dripping bewilderment as if begging for the answer. When none was forthcoming, he turned and bellowed at Petronius. This time the legate's jaw fell to his chest. "He's your man, dammit—your responsibility! Yes, I know he's only a fucking engineer, but that doesn't excuse it. He wears the uniform of a Roman officer. He's a trained soldier, dammit. There is no excuse!"

The harangue continued, and Gaius seethed. It was all true, yet all so unfair. For the hundredth time, his mind returned to the meadow. When they had gone in, the fight had looked to be a simple skirmish. Matters had simply escalated. What more could have been done? And for the hundredth time, he replayed the battle in his mind, grudgingly admitting that some things could indeed have been done differently. In fact, a lot of things.

Yet if only they had known thousands of barbarians were coming down that trail.

If! Gaius sighed. There was no such thing as 'if' in a battle. They should have been prepared. The entire force should have assembled in the meadow first, dammit, and let the cavalry hang for a while. Act; don't react! But then, they had not known what was happening. Perhaps …

Some of Cerialis's diatribe penetrated his thoughts, something about the casualties being ten percent of the Ninth legion's strength. Even that wasn't fair, he thought, because some of them were auxiliaries, and the entire strength of the Ninth, with its support groups, was nearly ten thousand. But the governor's numbers spun in his mind: *a tenth of the Ninth, a tenth of the Ninth*. This, from a man who had lost an entire attack force to an Iceni mother and her two daughters!

That thought boiled through his mind as he sat brooding. Ten years ago, Cerialis had done the same thing, only worse. Half the Ninth, not a tenth, and all from not being prepared. And why? Carelessness, overconfidence. More than two thousand men lost, and he was bitching about five hundred! And that other thing in Germania, against Civilis—total carelessness there! And the man had the nerve to accuse the Tungri of stepping on their own pricks! The greatest hypocrisy, though, was that the man had lost half the Ninth in this very same province, and was throwing shit, in this very building, for losing less than a tenth of it.

Less than a tenth! Gaius continued brooding, half listening, until he realized the pace of the governor's words was slowing.

"Of course, we really expect nothing from tribunes, especially the young ones. And you know what? They never disappoint. Nothing is exactly what they give, and they give it in abundance. Usually, though, young Publius, they don't go off, half-trained and quarter-brained, thinking they can do a better job than their own senior centurion—who is no longer here to tell us what happened!"

He threw up his hands once more, and turned to Petronius. "I've had all I can stand, legate. Get this—this rabble out of here, and see if there's anything you can do with them. Dammit, I want an army, not a nest of vestal virgins leading lambs to slaughter. Do something!"

Cerialis dropped back into his seat. A table stood beside the chair with an assortment of food and drink, none of which had been offered to those present. He poured himself a beaker of a thick, brown wine, and sipped moodily as he stared down into the contents. Everyone, including Petronius, began shuffling out, Marius and Quintus supporting Publius on either side.

"By the way," the governor said. He didn't look up. The clatter of hobnailed boots stopped and, to a man, they all turned uneasily back. "Marius, you did a damned fine job commanding the east flank. We'll see what we can do about a decoration."

The Batavi cohort commander flushed. "Sir!"

"And Publius."

After a long pause, the young tribune finally spoke, his voice tentative, "Sir?"

"You did finally do some good, when you jammed a bung into that hole the barbarians punched in our line. Well done."

"T-thank you, sir."

"In fact, if you'd been killed, I'd have seen you were decorated for bravery," Cerialis added benignly.

Another long pause followed as Publius digested the dubious honour, then he again muttered, "Thank you, sir."

"No need." The governor waved his hand in dismissal. "It would have been the least I could do for your father. He's a good man."

Once more the boots clattered across the wooden floor, and once more Cerialis called out a name, without bothering to raise his head: "Trebonius!"

Gaius muttered under his breath and stood frozen in the doorway as the others clumped off to safety. He could almost feel the embarrassment of his fellow officers, each drawing his own conclusion and thinking, *There, but for the mercy of the gods, march I.*

"Sir?"

"Come over here," Cerialis said, gesturing toward another chair at the far side of the small table. "Sit down."

Mutely seething, Gaius obeyed, slumping down into the seat. He'd taken enough abuse. What more could the general do? If it was disgrace, then dammit, he'd fight it. He'd done his best, and it hadn't been that bad. His brother in Rome, edgy as his position was, might still have some influence. Though it didn't matter anymore; there were other things a man could do. An administrative post in Gaul, perhaps, up by the northern border …

"Have a drink." Cerialis nodded toward the table, smiling. "There's a heavy, sweet fig concoction that I had sent in. It's a bit early in the day, but then, it's been a long one, hasn't it?"

Gaius glanced warily at the governor, then poured a healthy dose of the brown liquid into one of the mugs. "Thank you," he murmured, feeling like a rabbit he'd once seen, frozen in front of a weaving cobra. The snake had been deceptively calm, right up to the moment it struck.

"Well, that should give them something to think about, eh?" Cerialis grinned.

The comment so astounded Gaius that all he could stutter was, "Uhhh …"

"I can sympathize with both of you, you know," Cerialis went on, though at first Gaius barely heard a word as his mind struggled with the quick shift from one cart track to another. "Sometimes shit simply happens. And when it does, it always runs downhill. That's my job. I've been on the other end of it often enough to know how it works. You too, I suppose—you were with me once. Similar circumstance: poor intelligence, hasty response to a threat. Oh, that was a bad day."

Cerialis sighed and leaned back, his eyes half closed. "The only word we received was that *some* of the Icenii had revolted. Some! It was the whole fucking tribe, with half the province behind them. All waiting in one great, bitching ambush."

"There were a lot of them," Gaius agreed, opting for cautious understatement until he knew where the governor was headed. The man's mind seemed to fly from one plane to another, with the flitting wings of Mercury.

"No doubt, no doubt. But I got sucked into a whirlpool, just like you fellows did. Scouts hit their cavalry first, and we chased them until they caught us. Like a flock of fucking ducks charging down a crocodile's throat. The rest is history—bad history. Not that there was anything I could do. Much like you fellows."

"Sir?" Gaius whispered hoarsely. Was this the same man who'd just flayed his senior officers alive?

"Well, in my little foul-up, there were so many barbarians after our skins, the only way we could escape was to outride them all the way back to Lindum. And as to the soldiers of the Ninth, we all know a man on foot can't outrace a horse or a chariot. Just like we know Romans don't run away either, eh, young Trebo?"

"Never, sir," Gaius muttered, thinking that the governor was pouring the *garum* a little heavy in the soup. Not just the running away bit, but the "young Trebo," as well.

"Pshaw!" Cerialis snorted. "That's shit. Of course they run, if there's no other choice. That's how I got away. There was no cavalry to rescue us then, let me tell you. I and about a hundred horse 'fell back' in a dead panic. Even then it was a close run thing. You think you had a tongue-lashing from me this morning? It was nothing to compare with the one I received from Paulinus. At the time, I could cheerfully have fallen on my sword, like that gutless bastard from the Second, who wouldn't creep out of his fort and fight at all. But Paulinus had to do it." He shook his head, and stared wryly down at his empty mug of wine.

Gaius sat waiting, still unsure if the sword was going to fall, but growing less uneasy with each passing moment.

"Let me tell you, Trebonius," Cerialis said, turning to look him straight in the eye. "Fate, shit—call it what you will, it simply happens. But officially, there is never an excuse for a legion's defeat in battle. Officially. Like me, you made mistakes. And like me, yours showed up like shit on a sheet. But only later, with the luxury of a spy hole to the past. Unfortunately, the politicos who judge such events judge them through that same hole."

"Sir," Gaius agreed cautiously.

"Here, fill it for me, Trebo. And take some more yourself." Cerialis held out his mug. "Politicos! Damned leeches. But they're a fact of life. What's really important is this: what we did wasn't stupid at the time. It only proved stupid when it went wrong. Had I succeeded with Boudicca, I would have been an idol, a hero. My name would probably be remembered a thousand years from now. Only I didn't. I certainly could have handled things differently; you certainly could have handled things differently. So learn from it."

"Yes, sir," Gaius said, realizing that not only did the governor's mind flit from one swing of the plumb to the other, so did his own opinion of the man.

"I'll give you an example of the politics, and a damned big one." Cerialis chuckled, and crossed his legs as he eased back in the chair. "Quintus pulled your arses out of that cow pasture because, believe it or not, he convinced Petronius to take a chance." He thought that over for a moment, and shrugged. "That didn't surprise me, you know. I figured our fearless legate was prompted."

He leaned back with his drink as if mulling the thought, then con-

tinued. "You may or may not know this, but the first of Salvius's cavalry dragged their whipped tails back to Isurium not long after you
found yourself penned up in your square. The commander there had
the sense to immediately dispatch riders to Ebor, and continue to do
so every time he got a report on what was happening. Before dark,
Petronius knew most of your force had survived, but were trapped.
The decision he had to make was simple: abandon them to fight their
own way out, or send cavalry—it had to be cavalry. There was too little
time for any infantry we might scrape together. So Petronius, pushed
as he was by Quintus, agreed to send the cavalry."

"It seemed logistically impossible, sir."

"Yes, I know." Cerialis smiled at the assessment. "But he did it
anyway. A couple troops of Tungri were here at Ebor, and of course, the
Ninth's own complement of riders. We scraped together well over a
hundred, and immediately packed them off to Isurium, with Quintus in
charge. It was dark when he left, carrying orders to commit every horse
there, including those Tungri who'd come back with their pricks dragging in the mud. I think he had over four hundred with him, finally."

"There looked to be more than that," Gaius said, his mind returning to the long lines of cavalry sweeping across the meadow like a gift
from the gods.

"There were. At the same time that Petronius sent Quintus to
Isurium, riders were sent to *Derventio* with the similar orders. There
were well over three hundred troopers to be had there."

"But how …"

Cerialis beamed at the question. "Apparently there is an enormous
hill between Isurium and Derventio, only a bit further north. Next to it
is a great crag that can be seen for miles. Quintus suggested it, for it's
known to all the patrols; stands out like a beacon, and they use it as
such. There's a barbarian village close by the foot of it, and they made
that the place to meet. Quintus had his men in the saddle at dawn, the
commander at Derventio the same. When they met up later in the day,
the plan was to get within striking distance, rest up, and attack the next
morning."

"But they didn't—"

"No, they didn't, did they? There was a shred of daylight left, so our bold commander decided to go in right away rather than risk discovery. Both the animals and the men were exhausted. I'm not sure if, had I been there, I wouldn't have waited." Cerialis paused and glanced at Gaius with his tongue in his cheek. "But it was the correct decision. Why was it the correct decision, tribune?"

Gaius smiled. "Because it was a successful decision."

"And Petronius's decision to send Quintus in the first place—because, ultimately, even though he was pushed, it was his decision—why was that correct, tribune?"

"Because it was a successful."

"And at Stannick, why wasn't the primus pilus told that it was not his place to go farting off on a hare-brained patrol, when he'd been sent north to carry out an entirely different task?"

"Because it was a successful decision, sir," Gaius said with a smile, and added, "at least for the most part."

Cerialis grinned. "No, dammit. It was because he's the primus, and he's allowed one fuckup. And besides, I wasn't here when he got back. Though, believe me, he heard about it when I did. But you're getting the hang of it. Let me ask you one more question though, young Trebo. Had the relief force failed to put the barbarians to flight, and been hacked to pieces …?"

"Then it would have been a terrible decision, sir."

Cerialis nodded his approval. "That's what my dear father-in-law would have said. And I would have been telling Quintus, if he were still on the green side of the dirt, that his balls should indeed be nailed to a cross for attacking too early. Tired horses, exhausted men, daylight fading—a terrible decision!

"There's the art of soldiering, Trebo," the governor continued around a yawn; he unwound his legs and stretched them. "And then there's the politics of it. When there is less than a total victory, the politics become a far more formidable foe than the one we fight on the battlefield."

Cerialis sighed and slumped back again, staring thoughtfully into his empty mug. As the moment dragged on, Gaius wondered if the discussion was over, and he should leave. He cleared his throat, and the governor sat up, biting his lip.

"There is another matter I wanted to speak to you about, Trebo." He paused, choosing his words. "It's really why I held you back when the others were leaving. Though the embarrassment didn't do you any harm."

Gaius nodded, remembering the sympathetic glances. Cerialis still seemed hesitant, drumming his fingers on the arm of his chair. It struck Gaius that he was behaving as Petronius had, during their strange talk after his flight from Stannick.

Cerialis's voice was just as gruff, when he finally spoke. "I'm ordering you and your son back to Lindum for some leave. Thirty days. You'll go as soon as possible."

Gaius clenched his jaw, distressed that the conversation had once more turned sour after seeming to go so well. He mumbled a toneless response, and the governor sighed again.

"It's not a punishment, Trebo. It's a recovery period. I mean, look at what's happened this year. Injuries. Wounds. A couple months as a prisoner. It's all been …well, I'd say, perhaps …" His jaw clenched as tight as Gaius's own, and he suddenly slammed his right hand down on the arm of the chair. "Dammit, I'll be blunt. Why do we treat these matters as if they're hot coals? You need to pay more attention to your family affairs—your wife, to be specific—rather than leaving such things in the province of the legate, Catus. It's a damned embarrassment!"

It took a few moments for the words to penetrate, and when they did, Gaius leaned back in his chair, stunned. His mind galloped wildly, angrily, in every direction, before slowing to a canter and clearing enough to think. And with it came icy contemplation: the ebbing flow of correspondence; Helvia's constant, fluttering commentary on the legate's oily solicitousness; the vague, bumbling words of Petronius when he'd "suggested" Gaius take leave; Marc's sudden, brooding appearance, and his reluctance to go home. *Marc—shit! Marc knew, too!* He wondered how he could have been so obtuse.

"Yes, sir, perhaps that's best," he whispered.

"Yes, well, that's good then." Cerialis seemed relieved that the matter was over, but added, "Oh, and one more word about politics. When you get to Lindum, Trebonius, do not forget one thing: Lucius Catus *is* the legate there. He *is* the general in command of the Second. Remember that, *Tribune* Sabinius."

"Yessir," Gaius mumbled, and forced himself to his feet.

He stumbled from the atrium, literally, for his foot caught against the walkway by the main entrance, and he caught himself against one of the supports. It struck his numbed mind that he must present a pitiful sight, and he tried to force himself into some state of normalcy. The only thought that came to mind, however, was another matter still unresolved, which he realized was inane and out of place the moment he brought it up.

"By the way, sir, I haven't had any time to run down the other matter you asked me to pursue. The boy. Your son. I suppose it will have to be put off a bit longer."

Cerialis's eyes widened in surprise and for a moment he seemed lost for words, then he raised a hand in dismal. "Oh, that! Don't bother. I had words with the woman herself. It's no longer relevant."

Gaius nodded, but didn't move; he wondered dully if the answer cleared both issues, or just one of them.

Cerialis mistook the hesitation as curiosity, and growled in irritation, "I saw the boy. Best left where he is." He coughed, again waved a dismissive hand, then thought fit to add, "And the son of a bitch up north has the gold torque. Or at least, that's what *she* claims. Now get out of here, and have a good, stiff drink."

Gaius left the commander's residence feeling angry, humiliated, and damned foolish. At that particular moment, there was no one, absolutely no one, he wanted to talk to. He simply wanted out of the fortress, to where he could find a deep, quiet hole, and bury himself inside. With nothing definite in mind, he started for the south gate, his mind a fog.

He had gone no more than a hundred paces, head lowered, eyes glued to the ground, when he stopped. Something didn't feel right. It took a moment to realize what it was. One hand went instinctively to his bare head. No helmet. He was in full uniform, and felt naked without it. Then he remembered that he hadn't been wearing one. The damned thing was somewhere up north, on a lousy, stinking-rotten battlefield, and the new one was late in the making. Its lack was yet one more damned problem to address.

Angry, he kicked out at the nearest object—an amphora, one of several full of olive oil, stacked in a row outside one of the supply tents. The vessel keeled over into the mud, which spared the contents, but excruciating pain shot through his foot, as if the toe had broken. The hurt offered a perverse feeling of relief.

"Some days nothing goes right, does it," a cheerful voice called from inside the tent.

Gaius turned to find the source, and saw the Brigante queen in the shadows of the open flaps, two of her menials behind her with their arms full of supplies. Army supplies! The sight annoyed him further. He bent his head to acknowledge her presence and continued on, favouring his right foot.

"I would guess Petilius is in a foul mood this morning," she said as she caught up. Gaius offered nothing more than a sullen grunt as the woman fell in step alongside.

"Or perhaps it's simply a bad mood of your own making, and you are abroad spreading its evil seed?" Cartimandua suggested, and offered a smile. She dismissed the menials with a wave of her hand, and gathered her long dress with the other, lifting its hem above the ground. Gaius glimpsed a pair of slim, pleasantly formed calves. She noticed his glance. "Not bad for a woman of my age, wouldn't you say, tribune? In truth, I've been truly blessed. Look!" She halted and pulled the hem to mid thigh, angling one leg from side to side, the foot arched. "No ugly blue lines, either. What do you think?"

Gaius sighed at the intrusion, but stopped and studied the limb. His answer matched his mood. "You're right; it's not bad, for a woman your age." He continued toward the gate.

"Oh-oh. Twice!" Cartimandua said, and followed, seemingly unperturbed. "I'll wager Petilius's tongue was really aflame this morning. Did you deserve it?"

"That's not the problem," Gaius snapped, and immediately regretted the words. But her voice, with its lilting accent he might once have found vaguely attractive, was suddenly irritating. He forced himself to remember that while she might be a barbarian, she was also supposed to be a queen. Though of what, no one was sure.

"Then why is that despondent mind of yours so damned—" She began angrily, then suddenly fell silent.

The distance to the south gate narrowed. Beyond it Gaius saw the mast of a single ship, and its crew busily piling stores on the dock. Gaius's thoughts turned to more pressing matters, and he wondered when the vessel was leaving. He'd have to make arrangements for himself, and soon. And he'd have to tell Marcus. The boy was still in the hospital with a deep slash on his thigh, received when the barbarians had broken through the square. Some sort of invalid transport would have to be arranged for the lad, if he could be moved at all ...

Cartimandua's sudden silence made him turn. She had stopped speaking in midsentence, which was odd for her. It wasn't like the woman to aim a barb, then not throw it. It suddenly struck him why. "Shit!" he cried, throwing up his hands. "Does everyone in this stinking province know what's been going on, but me?"

Cartimandua considered the question seriously. "No, probably not. Petilius knows, of course, but he's not a man to gossip."

"Petronius knows."

"Of course; he's your commanding officer. It's his job to know. But he's not going to mention it either. Does Titus act as if he's been filled with such gossip?"

Gaius thought that over, and answered fairly. "No, and neither does Publius, I suppose. Or anyone else, for that matter." He continued toward the gate, grudgingly accepting that she was likely correct. "So what have you heard?"

"Not much, actually. It seems this man Catus pays a lot of attention to your wife. But how much attention, no one knows but the two of them."

"And the entire Lindum garrison. Damnation on him! How could the bitch be so stupid?"

"A bitch, is she now, this mother of your children?" Cartimandua's eyebrows arched. "And you, of course, are beyond reproach."

"As a matter of fact, yes, I am." He hurled the words at her, but she simply shrugged.

"Of course, lately you haven't exactly had much choice in the matter, have you?"

"That has nothing to do with anything." Gaius brooded on Helvia, and the harrowing thought that everyone and his lowest slave at Lindum probably knew about her involvement with another man. And he was going there. It was damned humiliating. And soon everyone here …

"How did Petilius learn of this …this indiscretion?" he asked.

She smiled, her eyes glinting with amusement. "I told him."

"You! How could you possibly know?"

"Oh, Roman, this is my country, not yours."

"Yes, I know," he sneered, "yet you didn't seem to know there was a barbari—that Venutius's army was marching down from Stannick, bent on destroying Isurium."

Gaius's first conclusion, that their column had been ambushed, had been put to rest when the first of the prisoners was interrogated. The Britons' true destination had been Isurium, not Ebor, as might have been expected.

The chance encounter had once again set him wondering about the whims of the gods. Were they taking a special interest in Gaius Sabinius Trebonius? He remembered the so-called vision, which was rubbish, of course—yet his destiny did seem to be tangled in some small way with that of the tall, hairy Briton who'd pulled him from the waters of the Abus. Or had the collision between the two armies been planned? No, it could not have been; Venutius had been as unprepared as the Romans. It had to be fate. Yet surely this woman, who seemed to know every other damned thing that was going on, would have known of her own former husband's plans.

"How would I have known what the fool was doing? I don't even know what my present husband is doing," she said, and laughed at the thought. "I suppose that's a condition you and I both share."

They passed through the gate and onto a dirt road that, so far, was nothing more than packed soil, pounded out of the pasture by the boots and carts of the legion. Gaius halted and looked in both directions. Upriver was the ford, and beyond it the thick, cloaking forest of the north. Men were working there, logging and clearing, and he clung to the need to be alone. Down river, the sloping pasture led to the mouth of the Fosse, where trees and shrubs still covered the smaller stream in a canopy of green. A slow, circular path would bring him back through the north entrance and, if he dawdled long enough, might be stretched out for most of the day.

"I'm going that way," Gaius said curtly, and pointed. " It's been a pleasure."

"Wonderful," Cartimandua said, ignoring the dismissal. "That's the same way I'm going."

He shrugged, deciding it made little difference, and said as much. They set out along the bank of the Abus, and for the longest time neither spoke. Gaius went back to his brooding, and Cartimandua followed, cheerfully humming a low, lilting melody, a blade of grass dangling from the corner of her mouth. The walking was easy, across open pasture, and through grass cropped short by the horses. In no time the riverbank dipped to the low, bushy ground that marked the mouth of the lesser river. They turned and followed the trees along the banks of the Fosse.

"We'll be clearing this area soon," Gaius said, compelled by the silence to say something.

"Uh-huh." She continued humming.

The low, steady thrum was beginning to grate. Gaius was sure she meant to annoy him. "The side stream will provide a sheltered area for docks, where ships can unload freight," he explained, wishing she would stop. "The current is much easier here."

"Fascinating," she replied. "I can't wait to see it."

Gaius's irritation started to fester. "There's no need for sarcasm. You wanted to walk this way. I'm trying to be pleasant."

"Then don't be so damned stiff. And don't carry your problems as if they're a plough hitched to your brain. Seize the day. One never knows if it will be the last." She bent and picked up a flat, rounded pebble, and threw it over the trees to splash into the river beyond.

"I'm not worried on that account," he complained. "I have lots of days left. The gods wouldn't let me off that easily."

"Ah, it's to be self-pity, is it?" Cartimandua's voice held its own current of irritation, and Gaius was irrationally pleased. "Very well, Roman. Show me where you plan to build this wondrous place to land your precious freight, and I'll leave you to enjoy your misery."

"Look," Gaius said, stopping to face her. "What do you want me to say? Yes, it is *indeed* a glorious day? The birds are singing. The insects buzz with joy. The rabbits blissfully fornicate in the fields, even as we speak. Aah, it is *so* wonderful to be alive." He spread his arms, looking upward to the sun. "It is so wonderful that I hope to have many, many days like this. In fact, today will be cherished forever in my memory as the standard, the benchmark—no, the very *pinnacle* by which all others shall be measured from hereon in. There, how was that?"

"Hmmph. From wallowing pity to full-blown sarcasm. I suppose it's a step in the right direction." She walked ahead, following the narrow path into the trees.

"Thank you. I might point out that I was recently taught the subtleties of sarcasm by a craftsman—or craftswoman," he replied snidely as he fell in behind her.

Her shoulders stiffened, telling Gaius he'd gone too far, but he didn't care. He'd wanted solitude, time to ponder the journey to Lindum, to consider his options with the legate when he got there, and how to approach Helvia. In fact, he needed time to decide how he even felt about the woman, for in all honesty, things had long been cooling on both sides of that fire. But to offend this barbarian queen who, in all honesty, had only been trying to lift his mood …

He caught up with her, ready to fumble some sort of apology, but she spoke first.

"It is truly regrettable that sarcasm is all I can teach you, Roman." Her face radiated controlled anger. "If that's all you can find in me, so be it. As I said, show me where you plan to build this damned dock, since I'm here anyway, then I'll leave you to your pitiful solitude."

Any words of regret were suddenly tasteless, so Gaius grunted and moved ahead. He would show her what she asked, then she could resume her own rose-petalled path. He paused, realizing the precise place for the structure had yet to be selected, then shook his head. He was thinking like an engineer. Anywhere would do.

He moved farther into the trees, stumbling to the edge of the slow-moving Fosse. The river was perhaps twenty paces wide at that point, and the water flowed dark, a foot or two below the grassy bank. It was a quiet, restful spot; at any other time, Gaius might have found pleasure in it. "Somewhere about here," he said, turning about and gesturing vaguely with his hand.

"Then be the first to enjoy it," Cartimandua replied, and pushed firmly against his chest. Gaius caught a glimpse of her face as he tumbled backward. It wore a sharp, fiendish grin of satisfaction.

There was barely time to gulp a lung-ful of air before hitting the water with a tremendous splash. The weight of his armour pressed him downward, and he squirmed onto his stomach, pushing away from the soft, silty mud of the riverbed. Without pause, he began swimming downstream, pulling himself over the tangle of waterlogged flotsam that fouled the bottom, gaining as must distance as possible before rising for air. When his lungs threatened to burst, he swam even farther, then clawed to the surface, close under the bank.

Exhaling as quietly as he could, he peered back through the thick grass and the low-hanging branches of the trees. There was no sign of the woman. Had the callous bitch simply abandoned him? He might have drowned! He pulled himself farther onto the bank, staring angrily upstream, and saw a spot of colour. She stood away from the river, gazing back at its still surface.

For a moment, nothing happened. Then she muttered a low curse, ran back to the bank, and stared down at the murky water. Another curse, much louder, and she unbuckled the silver belt around her waist, then jerked her long dress to her midriff, and over her head. She wore nothing underneath. As she leapt naked into the water, Gaius couldn't resist the thought, *Not bad, for a woman her age.*

He pulled himself clear, feeling inordinately pleased with himself. Crouching low, he circled back through the trees, pausing only once as her head broke the surface, then quickly disappeared again. He crept to within a few paces of the riverbank and lay still, waiting for the quick intake of breath and the splash that told him she had again dived. It didn't take long. When the small clearing once more fell silent, he hurried to the edge of the river and sat cross-legged on the bank, a huge grin on his face.

Cartimandua never surfaced.

Gaius rose uneasily to his feet, peering intently into the slow-moving current. The dark water revealed nothing. The riverbed itself was probably three feet of soft, oozing, clinging mud, riddled with water-logged trees and branches. It was a web of death. Anxious now, he began loosening the straps on his breast plate, cursing silently. One side of the breastplate came free. He dropped his belt, squeezed out of the armour, and quickly pulled off his leather tunic. At that moment, it occurred to him that she was playing the same game.

Clutching a tree limb, he leaned out over the water, looking carefully down river. He even ran a dozen paces or so that way, but saw no sign of the woman. Cursing again, yet at the same time calling on the gods to be kind, he pulled the wet linen tunic over his head, gauged where she had entered the water, and jumped in. Down, down, hands groping through the brown murk, he kicked toward the soft riverbed, and began feeling around the tangle of rotting logs. Nothing.

When he broke the surface for the third time, gasping for breath and paddling like a dog, Gaius was desperate. The woman could not possibly be there; she must have floated farther downstream. He swore, and was about to once more plunge below the surface when he heard a faint cough. He turned in the water, relief mixing with anger as he blinked to clear his eyes. She was resting against a tree, her long legs casually crossed, a blade of grass again dangling from her lips. She was as naked as the day she was born, and not at all self-conscious.

"Fishing for something, turd?"

"How …?" Gaius began, but he knew.

She told him anyway. "I reasoned you were bright enough to look downstream, but not bright enough to look upstream. You Romans may be organized, but oh, you are so predictable!"

Gaius trod water, wondering where events were leading. In this shady green oasis, she looked like Aphrodite. He smiled at the thought, and at the next one: she was a damned sight more stunning than in full daylight—though, he had to admit, he'd never seen her naked in the full light. Mottled sunlight speckled her pale skin, and her pose could tempt Tantalus. One arm rested across her lap, barely covering her right breast, and the other was folded in such a manner that it hid most of the left. Her legs, long and slim, were coyly crossed so that her bare feet hid the centre of her. Despite the chill water, he felt himself responding.

"So what are you going to do?" Her eyes narrowed and her smile taunted him. "Float around until you sink, or keep dredging the bottom until you find some hidden treasure?"

"I was just considering the best way to get out," Gaius said, his wit completely abandoning him.

"That's easily solved," Cartimandua said, and rose lithely to her feet. She walked to the bank and stood with her legs slightly apart, one hand on her hip, the other extended toward Gaius. His groin responded faster than his brain and he froze, choking on the silty water as he slipped below the surface. A peal of laughter rang out as he spluttered upward, vainly trying to clear his eyes.

"Come here, fool, before you drown," she said, sounding pleased at his response. She knelt and reached out over the water.

Gaius swam to the bank, grasped her hand, and kicked his way onto the grass. He didn't let go after she helped him to his feet, but stood facing her, close enough to sense her warmth. An amused glint in her eyes stayed him, though.

She stepped back and looked down. "Those under-breeks look ridiculous. A grown man in a bairn's nappy. Though a bairn wouldn't stretch the linen like that."

"That's easily solved," Gaius said. Without releasing his grip, he clumsily pulled the drawstring with his free hand, then kicked the garment free.

He stepped forward, clutching at her, eager for the feel of her cool breasts against his chest. He bent to find her lips, but her impatience was greater. She reached down and grasped him, sliding toward the ground, eager to guide him inside her. He was there, even before her long, black tangle of hair came to rest on the grass.

Their coupling was violent and faceless, each one's mouth buried, gnawing, biting, suckling at the other's neck, one body pounding the other in a mad, breathless race, as if both were intent on beating the other. It was a wild and frantic chase, and did not last long. Gaius shuddered, moaned, then cursed quietly under his breath.

They rolled apart, panting, and lay back against the cool grass. After an amused, self-satisfied glance at his glazed expression, Cartimandua nestled her head on his shoulder and settled her body comfortably into the crook of his arm. For a time they both lay quietly staring at the soft, rustling sway of the treetops, each chasing their own thoughts. Then, just as Gaius was drifting off into what promised to be the first blissful moment of the day, Cartimandua spoke.

"Remember what you said earlier?" she asked, her purring voice smug. "The bit about being above reproach? I was wondering about your thoughts on that now."

"Shiiiit!" Gaius wailed, adding under his breath. "Women!"

"I guessed as much. But be honest—you wouldn't have done this with me if, for example, that was your wife standing over there looking at us."

"What?" he yelped, jerking upward in alarm.

Across the river, an equally startled doe stood in the trees, its enormous ears erect. It bounded off, a young fawn hopping unsteadily behind.

"Don't do that," Gaius grumbled, and settled back down.

"See? It's your guilt. The point is, you wouldn't have done it, any more than your wife would, if you were still at Lindum, or if she were here. How can you blame her any more than she can blame you?"

"So, she is fornicating with that prick, Catus?"

"And you're fornicating with that bitch, Cartimandua." She chuckled, then her voice grew more reflective. "To be honest, I don't know if she is, though it's more than likely. The point is, though, how is that any different? You know, Roman, I feel lucky. We 'barbarians' are far more pragmatic about such matters than you 'civilized' people."

"In my case, there was a naked lover standing in front of me, flaunting her assets. Which, I might add, are not inconsiderable. What did you expect? A limp prick?"

She rolled over and gazed into his face, her breasts swaying tantalizingly near, and he was surprised to find himself already responding. Her face had resumed its malicious grin. "And if she had a naked lover standing in front of her, with not inconsiderable assets? What would *you* expect?"

"Oh, the gods protect me, must I picture it, too?" Gaius groaned. "It wouldn't be a limp prick, I suppose. And pricks, incidentally, make babies. There is a difference."

She snorted. "A bairn is a bairn is a bairn—you tell me the differ-ence. Just take to heart what I said." She leaned forward and rested her head on his chest, her breasts cool on his belly.

Gaius cursed, because she'd again made him focus on his wife and what waited at Lindum. They both lay with eyes closed. Then she asked, "When are you going to Lindum?"

Once more, he wondered if the woman could read his thoughts. "You know about that?"

"No, but it's obvious that if Petilius has been talking to you, you must be going."

"I see," he said, and gave the question some thought. "I don't know. In a day or two, I suppose. What are you going to be doing?"

"Not any more of this, my fine Roman, that's a certainty." She raised her head and smiled down on him. "I never make my whims an obsession. Especially when it might imperil what little status I have left in my own land."

"Oh?" Gaius replied cautiously, disappointment failing to dampen his ardour.

"Not in the foreseeable future, anyway," she murmured, and bent forward to nibble at his lower lip. "But there is today. Let's make the best of it. Last time it was for you. This one's for me." The nibbling slid sideways to his neck, and she took one of his hands, guiding it downward.

"Aaaah, that's got it," she whispered a few moments later, then added, "And slower this time—turd."

It was midafternoon when they started back to the fortress. Cartimandua left first, following the path along the Fosse as it wound its way through the trees. She would enter the fortress from the north. It wasn't much of a ruse, Gaius supposed, for if anyone did place them together, it made little difference. Certainly as far as he was concerned.

He shivered and cursed as he strapped the armour back on. His clothes were close to dry but cold, and the linen tunic held a brown tinge from the muddy water. Metellus could tend to it. He started back by the shortest route to his quarters, which was through the east gate. Something was happening just outside the rampart, though, and he slowed his pace. Soldiers crowded the area, and the cause took a few moments to register.

A good many prisoners had been taken in the battle, of which about four hundred had been deemed worth keeping—those either unhurt or only slightly wounded, and of an age and condition suitable for use. Most were prime warriors who would likely end up in the arena, or who might gain a chance to enlist in the overseas auxiliaries; the civil war in Germania had created a critical shortage of troops, due mostly to the shipping out of the rebellious Batavis to less volatile parts of the empire. The rest of the warriors caught in the net had, of course, been culled on the battlefield.

Four large temporary pens had been staked out in the ditch surrounding the fortress, with one side abutting the east wall. Gaius himself had approved the construction, and had been there when the first of the prisoners had been interned. At that time a temporary forge had been set up close by the gate, and the smiths had been busy shaping the neck irons and chains necessary for transporting the barbarians. The pens had been only half full that first day, but seemed to be serving their purpose; he had paid little attention later as the remaining captives were brought in—such details were the province of the *procurator* and his staff. Now, however, civilians were going in and out of the pens under escort, and just as many scribes trailed behind, scratching their styluses against an endless supply of wax tablets.

One of the civilians, a paunchy, well-dressed man who seemed to be in charge, responded to Gaius's query. "Getting ready to ship them. The *procurator* wants them tallied and valued." The man nodded toward the river, where the merchant ship still sat by the dock. "The first shipment will be loaded tomorrow."

Gaius nodded his thanks, satisfied, and continued toward the gate. He was about to pass through when it struck him that the barbarian Cethen might be among those taken. The fellow hadn't been there when the first of the prisoners had been marched down from Isurium, but he could have been brought in since. This might be his last chance to find out, though what he would do if the man was there, he had no idea. He turned back, and beckoned to one of the decani to provide escort.

The enclosures were in an abysmal state. No shelter had been provided, and the latrine was nothing but a pit. The food was dished out onto a long, troughlike table lashed to a series of stakes driven into the ground. The water situation was little better. A barrel sat on a sled hauled from the river, and a single ladle hung from the side.

Gaius paced quickly among the prisoners, searching for the long tangled mop of fair hair and the drooping moustaches. Many fit such a description from a distance, but none had the lazy blue eyes and sandy lashes that were the mark of his man. Most of the Britons refused to meet his gaze, choosing instead to stare at their feet or the ground. He peered up at those perched higher on the earth rampart, but again, none looked familiar. He was in the fourth pen and ready to conclude that Cethen hadn't been taken when a shock of yellow-blond hair caught his notice.

His attention so far had been focused on the barbarian males, ignoring the few females scattered about the pens, all of them grimy, bruised, and poorly dressed. But the golden mop stood out like a familiar jewel. Gaius dropped his gaze to the face and found Cethen's daughter, Coira, staring back with icy blue eyes. His gaze moved to the woman sitting next to her; she quickly looked away, but not before Gaius recognized the wife, Elena.

He stood staring at them, biting his lower lip. They appeared healthy enough. Their fate would be service on one of the estates, he supposed, his mind refusing to address any seedier probability. They would at least be protected there, he reasoned, if they behaved. He nodded, deciding that was enough; it was, in fact, more than enough. Such a life would be far better than living the way they did here. And a lot safer, too, considering what probably lay in their future. He again nodded to himself. It was all for the best.

Gaius's expression must have mirrored his thoughts, for a sneer crossed Coira's lips. She spat her contempt onto the dirt. He shook his head slowly from side to side, smiled coldly, and turned to go.

He'd barely taken two steps when a voice called, "Roman!"

He hesitated and almost kept walking, but something, perhaps the memory of the barbarian queen, made him turn. Elena had scrambled to her feet, and stood with one hand propped against the wall of the pen. With the other, she gestured toward her daughter.

"You ...owe him," she said slowly in Latin. "Help ...the girl."

One of the guards started toward her, but Gaius barked an order and motioned him away. He turned to the decanus. "Do you know their speech?"

"Mostly, sir."

"Good. I have a little of it, but I want her to clearly understand. Tell her they'll come to no harm, if they behave. Their life will not be bad."

The guard translated, then gave Gaius her reply. "She said that she might expect as much from a Roman, sir. She seems to think her husband saved your life. She says you thank him by selling his wife and daughter into slavery."

"Shit, that's not my fault," Gaius muttered, half to himself and half to the guard. "She was taken prisoner while trying to kill us." He sighed. "Tell the woman that there is no debt. Her husband took me prisoner. He would have seen me worked to death, if I hadn't escaped."

Elena snorted angrily when the decanus finished speaking. He translated her response word for word, then bit his lip to prevent a smile: "She says, tell the fool that we let him go."

Gaius glared at the man, though her reply came as no real surprise. He had always felt his escape had gone too easily for Vellocatus to have done it alone, despite the eagerness of the guards to spit him when fleeing the rampart. The confirmation annoyed him, though, for they had played him for a fool—something that seemed to be happening a lot lately. *Wrong thing to say,* he thought as he turned to leave. "Tell her I know, and I don't care." he said.

"Ask him if he's paid his debt to the gods yet," Elena shouted. Gaius stopped dead in his tracks as the words were translated, and she added, "Tell him they have a part in this too. Does he dare anger the gods by selling into slavery the daughter of the man they chose to save him from the river?"

When Gaius still hesitated, her voice rose to a near-scream. "The daughter of the man the gods chose to set him free!"

Gaius turned slowly, reluctant to acknowledge the truth of what the woman said. She knew of his debt, a debt still unpaid. He'd spoken of it at Stannick, during the long evenings when each had fumbled with the other's language.

He scratched thoughtfully at his cheek, staring blankly at Elena as she stood glowering, her eyes angry, yet pleading. "Tell her I'll try to place the girl in my own household at Lindum," he said finally. "She'll be well looked after."

From the expression on the woman's face, he saw it wasn't the answer she wanted. Surely she hadn't expected him to release the girl? Gaius continued on his way, angry at the ingratitude, yet in some small manner haunted by it.

That evening, Gaius sat with Publius in the large command tent that now served as the officers' mess. The tribune was tossing the wine back freely, as much for his melancholy as the pain, but Gaius picked at his food and sipped his wine. When Cerialis entered, Gaius didn't seek him out but waited, still not sure of his promise to the barbarian woman. Had it been too much? Might it have been too little? The gods would decide, he finally reasoned: if the governor spoke to him, then he would raise the matter; if he didn't, then he would let it slide. His path would never cross the woman's again, and when all was said and done, dammit, she was a prisoner taken in battle—a battle in which she had been trying to kill Roman soldiers. She deserved no special consideration.

It was dark when Cerialis rose to leave, and Gaius sighed. He found himself looking down on Publius, making his excuses as if rising against his will. He caught up with the governor as he lifted the tent flap.

"A young barbarian girl?" Cerialis asked, raising his eyebrows, his mouth an irritating leer. "That was quick."

"What?" Gaius blinked in surprise. "No, sir. Not for me."

"Oh," Cerialis almost seemed disappointed. "The boy, then?"

Gaius blinked again. That thought hadn't occurred to him either, yet the suggestion had merit. Marcus was fifteen, and nearly grown.

But then, his sister was at home, and they were living in close quarters; and of course there would be his mother to contend with …in more ways than one. He felt the familiar depression well up, and brushed that thought aside. He decided the truth was the best course.

"She's the daughter of the Eburi chieftain, that Cethen fellow. The one who pulled me from the river. She and the man's wife were both taken. The …uh …" Gaius coughed, suddenly embarrassed, "the mother reminded me of debts unpaid."

"I see." Cerialis looked thoughtful, and actually smiled. "You feel you owe it to the man. And his wife too, I should think. She fed you while you were prisoner, did she not? Treated you well?"

"Uh, yes. I suppose she did," Gaius mumbled, realizing that, in seeking her daughter's freedom, Elena had not mentioned her own. And the woman *had* treated him well. He smiled ruefully, remembering the fight on the floor of the hut.

"The father's not here too, is he? I'd like to meet him."

"No. He didn't fall into the net. He's probably dead," Gaius said, and wondered if that was why the woman hadn't cared what happened to herself.

"Well, it's a reasonable enough gesture, under the circumstances," Cerialis mused. "Some would say it speaks well of you. You'll be wanting to 'rescue' the man's wife, too, I imagine. Two females, and both prime, I suspect. The *procurator*'s not going to like that."

"Uh, I …" Gaius suddenly felt trapped. The idea hadn't occurred to him, but Cerialis seemed to think it was natural. The reply fell almost involuntarily from his lips. "Yes, I suppose so, sir."

"Where are you going to place them? That could be a problem."

"I thought the girl could be sent to Lindum …er, household help, company for my daughter." The improvisation came easy. "It would also be surety for her mother."

The woman herself couldn't be sent. Certainly not to Helvia, not with everything else happening. The arrival of a tall, attractive, honey-haired barbarian female would be misconstrued. "She can help around here," Gaius said numbly, his mind barely ahead of his words. "My manservant Metellus can train her. Perhaps she can help at the mess, too."

"Arrange it with the *procurator*'s staff, then," Cerialis said, and peered owlishly along his nose as he added with the trace of yet another leer, "Make sure the woman doesn't cause any trouble, though, or it will be on your shoulders. Remember which direction shit flows, young Trebo."

Cerialis slapped him on the back and left the tent. Gaius stood by the flap completely lost for words, and wondering what, exactly, he had just done. He glanced over to where Publius sat at the table, somdrely refilling his mug with wine. After a moment's reflection, he went over and joined him.

Chapter XVII

Cethen stumbled back to Stannick the evening after the battle was over. He led Flint through the gates of the gloom-ridden fortress as if in a daze, both animal and master dead tired and limping awkwardly. Two horses trailed wearily behind: one was the Roman's chestnut, a slow, crimson trickle oozing through the blood caked high on its withers, and the other Rhun's small pony. The boy swayed in the saddle, barely awake, and quite willing to be led like a child as long as it was in the direction of home. Cethen had found his son waiting on the north bank of the ford where the Romans had once planned to build their fort. The lad would likely have remained there, too, until the last man had passed him by.

Cethen's body might have been bone tired, but his mind was wide awake, for he was worried. The lodge was empty, as half expected, so with a sick feeling low in his belly, he limped over and tried his brother's. Nuada stood outside, her two children and Tuis playing listlessly nearby. The answer to his question was in their faces, especially that of Tuis as the boy peered anxiously past his father, searching for a glimpse of his mother and sister.

"She's not here, then?" Cethen asked, letting the reins fall to the ground. Flint simply hung his head.

"No. And Cian?"

Cethen shook his head. Nuada bit her lip, unable to halt the tears

279

welling up in her eyes. Her two children clung to her skirts. The youngest began to sniffle.

"I haven't heard he's dead. There's still time," he muttered, not believing the words, though it was possible. Cian had been at the end of the field where the Roman cavalry struck. So had Elena and Coira.

"Well, you're here now," Nuada said, suddenly determined. "Tend the children. I'm going to look for him."

"I've already done that, lass," Cethen murmured gently, and shook his head. "If he's coming at all, he'll make his own way back. Going looking won't do any good, either for you or for him. There's still some coming in. He might have stayed to help—he would do that."

Cethen waved a hand vaguely southward. He had seen hundreds filtering back along the trail, though for the most part they were wounded. The more able had been wending their way back into the fortress since midnight the evening before. Cethen had spent the rest of that night, and most of the day after, vainly searching for Elena and Coira in that same stream of stragglers. He'd found neither. The only place left to look was the battlefield itself, and that was out of the question. Perhaps in a day or two, when the Romans had left. But by then, there would be only bodies to find.

Earlier that afternoon he stumbled across Balor, who was resting up a few paces off to one side of the trail. His back was parked against a tree, his right arm sliced to the bone. Nearby was a stranger, an older warrior who lay sprawled on the grass with skin the colour of ash. Even though wounded, Balor was doing his best to comfort him. The older man had walked as far as he could, then collapsed in exhaustion. He appeared to be bleeding to death inside, for his belly was a hard, bloated purple. Several of Maeldav's tuath stood in the middle of the trail numbly watching, a couple of them hardly in better shape.

Cethen had remained, feeling a certain responsibility, and eventually it became something to do: try keeping what was left of his own and Maeldav's tuaths together. In truth, it was difficult to know how many of them were left. Those with a good pair of legs, or a horse that could stand being ridden, were already gone. To his surprise, he found Dag had lingered, even though he had in some manner acquired another chariot. The youth had packed it full of those most hurt and driven back, mindful of the uneven track. You just never knew, Cethen mused.

He told Nuada of the confusion that waited in the dark, and she seemed to waver. The woman needed something to do, though, or she'd convince herself that going to find Cian was the proper thing. Cethen moved to the pony and lifted Rhun from its back, then motioned her over. The boy had fallen sound asleep, but groggily opened his eyes when he realized where they were. He leaned unsteadily against his father.

"Where's Mam?" he asked, peering blearily about the faces hovering in front him. "Hey, Tuis. Where's Mam?"

The tot looked to his father with the same question, but Cethen spoke gruffly to Nuada instead. "The boy's hardly slept since the night he left here, save dozing on his pony. Lend me a hand, will you? He'll be hungry, if he's not too tired to eat."

A hot stew simmered over the fire and, though meant for Cian, Nuada had them both sit down, and readily ladled it out. Rhun took several mouthfuls, then stared glassily about the hut, as if ready to flop forward into the steaming bowl. Cethen lifted the boy and would have taken him back to his own lodge, but Nuada insisted he be placed on her own cot.

"I'd rather we be together," she insisted. "When Elena returns, she'll know where we are. I think both of us could use the company. And I want to know what happened."

Nuada spoke rapidly, her eyes moving to the door with every sound that seeped through. Cethen eased himself down again, crossed his legs, and told how the fortunes of the previous two days had swung back and forth, like the cutting edge of a farmer's sickle—only every time it turned, people fell, not tall, waving stalks of spelt. When he got to the part where the Roman cavalry appeared as if by magic, Nuada interrupted with a question.

"I saw him last on the morning of the day it finished," Cethen answered, "but I had to return to the tuath. Venutius ordered me there."

"He was safe then?" Nuada asked hopefully.

"Aye, he was safe then," Cethen replied, and remembered their other meeting, the one following the first day of battle. "The evening before, Cian and that great oaf Luga came by and let me know Coira was there. With Elena." He suddenly grew angry. "She promised, Nuada, she promised! She said she'd take the girl, and leave before nightfall. Damn her!"

"You said the Romans attacked first where Cian was," Nuada mumbled, more to herself than Cethen, as she took his plate and ladled another helping of stew. "He probably didn't stand a chance."

"Venutius got away. I heard that," Cethen offered. "Cian had been with him not long before."

"Kings and their kind always get away," Nuada observed bitterly. "It's because there are a thousand other fools who risk their lives to help them do it. The idiots believe it's important."

"You sound just like Elena," Cethen said, and smiled tiredly.

"That's only because it's today." Nuada smiled sadly in return. "Elena sounds like that all the time. You know, I—"

A deep male voice outside shouted, "Hellooo," and the door swung open. Nuada turned eagerly, but a tall, heavyset warrior, one neither had seen before, filled the entrance, huge and dark against the crimson glow of the failing sun. The weather, which might have made a difference during the past two days, had perversely turned fair again.

"The name's Bruga." The man squinted into the dim lodge, looking hesitantly at Cethen. "You—you're Cian?"

Cethen shook his head without rising, his gaze slowly taking in the scruffy figure. The man reminded him of someone, but he couldn't think who. The blood of battle crusted his tunic, and his right forearm was bound with a grey linen cloth blotched dark with blood. He looked as exhausted as Rhun. "No, I'm his brother. Cethen, of Maeldav's tuath." Cethen had thought more than once that he'd have to stop using that name, for Maeldav was dead; but what else was he going to call the people, until someone else was elected? Clearly not Cethen's tuath, though he seemed to be responsible for the damned thing.

"Good," Bruga grunted, and glanced covetously at the simmering pot. "That's two heads with one swing of the axe. I need to see you, as well."

Nuada gestured toward the stew. "Are you hungry?"

Bruga thought the simple question over with what seemed a great deal of effort, then said, "Yes, but I want to get home and find sleep. Thanks anyway. You Cethen's wife?"

"No, Cian's." Nuada rose and ladled out a steaming bowl of stew anyway, and added a slab of warm bread.

"Have you seen him?" Cethen asked.

"No. I've seen neither my brother or Cian. That's one of the reasons I'm here." He scooped a great mouthful out of the bowl, ignoring the scalding heat. "I'm getting worried, too."

"About Cian?" Cethen asked, his tired mind puzzled by the man's concern.

"You need sleep too, Cethen," Bruga said with a tired smile. "No, what I meant is, I'm also worried about my brother, Luga. The two were together. When did you last see yours?"

"Yesterday morning. Early. He was with Luga. And you?"

"At the end of the day, when the Roman cavalry struck. Luga and Cian were sent to fight them off, along with the rest of Venutius's riders. I would have gone too, but the king needed protection."

Cethen and Nuada glanced at each other, she with bitter, humourless vindication.

"Did you see a woman and a young girl?" Cethen asked. "The girl has yellow-blond hair. About fourteen years old. They were at the farmstead."

Bruga shook his head. "Bran's farmstead! Last I saw it, Bran was dead in the doorway, and the place was in flames. Everything was in flames. It was after dark. I went back for a look. The bastards were even burning the dead. In piles. They'll pay for that."

"You went back? You actually left Venutius unattended?" Nuada asked, her voice scornful.

The sarcasm passed unnoticed. "No. We met up with Vellocatus, but by then it was too late. The force he brought with him was too small to start it again—perhaps a couple of thousand. Earlier it would have been enough, but the rest of our people were scattered. Venutius had them all turn back. Which reminds me of why I wanted to see you, Cethen. There's another council meeting. Midmorning tomorrow."

Bruga scooped one last mouthful from the bowl, then wiped it clean with the remains of his bread. It seemed impossible, but the whole meal had been wolfed down in a matter of moments.

"I'll be there," Cethen said.

"And bring a tally. Venutius wants a tally: dead, missing, and wounded. And he wants to know what you're going to have left to fight with. There's a chance the Romans will retaliate, and quickly."

"How …" Cethen began, then fell silent. That was probably one more thing he should have done.

Luga's brother grinned his understanding. "Take a count of who you've got left in any sort of condition to fight. Then find out who's wounded too bad to be up and about in the next few weeks. Take the total away from what you started with, and you've got your dead and missing. If there's anyone important you can't find, bring their names, too."

"Fine," Cethen said, but he frowned.

Bruga's grin broadened. "And in the event that you misplaced the count taken before you left, then do what the blushing bride did: make believe you still have it." He left without closing the door, and they heard him calm his horse before mounting.

Cethen called after him, belatedly struck by the odd hope in his question, "Do you think the two are still going to fight each other?"

The reply drifted back over the pounding of hooves: "Only if they're both stupid."

Nuada and Cethen's eyes met, the same thought in their minds. She was the one that voiced it, laughing bitterly as tears once more welled in her eyes. "That doesn't disqualify Cian, does it?"

"Heard anything at all?" Vellocatus asked the next morning as the two men walked along the damp gravel path that led past the great hall, and up to Venutius's lodge.

Cethen shook his head. "Nothing. It's been two days now. I'm going to see who wants to go looking with me."

"And Cian?"

Cethen simply shook his head.

"There's still time," Vellocatus said lamely. "Luga's missing as well. The pair of them are probably in a clearing somewhere, trying to bash each other's brains in." He pushed through the door of the lodge, walking in as if he lived there.

It was the first time Cethen had been inside, and his eyes slid sideways, covertly taking it all in. A high roof protected the huge interior, cross-timbered with enormous oak rafters. A tall stone fireplace stood at one end, and at the other a large double door led to Venutius's own quarters. Smaller rooms were tucked under the eaves on both sides. A long, low table sat before the empty fireplace, and lesser eating platforms were scattered about the rush-covered floor, along with hundreds of thickly piled pelts. "You could settle more than a hundred in here," he murmured, hesitant to enter.

Vellocatus grinned. "If you could get that many to sit still at one time."

Both men laughed, for they had just left a council meeting that might well have been a bear baiting. Those who had fought at Bran's Beck—the now popular name for the battle—spent their time shifting the blame, while those who hadn't been there found it far easier to assign. No one offered an opinion in a voice that was less than a shout. Venutius had sat through it all, saying nothing as his chieftains worked out their grievances. When it was over nothing was new, only a solemn promise to avenge the "forced withdrawal" from a battle "lost through duplicity."

Or, as Vellocatus had observed when informing Cethen that his presence was required in the lodge after the council, "It's the old bastard's way of saying we'll get even, because they got there before we thought they could."

Vellocatus nodded toward the stone fireplace. "Over there."

Several men squatted at one of the lesser tables, close by the hearth where a log fire burned. It cast barely a flicker in the huge, lofty hall, though Cethen found the interior grew lighter as his eyes adjusted. He trailed behind Vellocatus feeling like a minnow in a school of pike.

Cethen knew why he'd been invited. Over the past several months, he had drawn attention by being conspicuous—or, as Elena might have needled, by doing a few things very well that hadn't gone too badly wrong. Which was a curse, Cethen had decided. When those higher up the hill notice somebody doing something well, they expect more and more of the same. His newfound esteem wasn't unwelcome, but sometimes he felt like a man drowning in a river, unable to swim, while those onshore saw nothing less than an otter.

"Hey, Cethen," a pair of deep voices rumbled, and he was pleased to see Ebric and Dermat seated there.

"This is Loskenn," Dermat said, gesturing to a thickly bearded man with an unusually large head and the neck of a boar, most of it hidden under a long tangle of black hair. It was the same man he'd met at Dermat's lodge. Loskenn replied with a grunt and nothing more.

"He's here," Dermat whispered, glancing warily to the entrance of the lodge.

Cethen took the words as a warning, for he'd been about to offer his opinion of the council meeting, and ask a few painful questions concerning the previous three days.

All eyes turned as Venutius approached. A slim figure, too slight to be a man, trailed behind, walking with the loose, confident saunter of a warrior. As they drew near, Cethen recognized the Carveti woman. She was even more attractive than he remembered, though the word seemed hardly fitting to describe someone who looked capable of lopping a head off with one blow, and taking an arm on the back swing. Yet the pleasant scent of lavender preceded the pair's arrival, and Cethen was damned sure it didn't come from Venutius.

"Morallta," Venutius said casually, should anyone not know.

Food and drink had been placed on the nearest table, and both helped themselves before sitting down. The others belatedly rose and did the same, for it was apparent there would be no invitation.

Venutius scratched at the angry flaking on his scalp and he glared about the table. Some of the scale fell into his lap and onto his plate, but he didn't seem bothered. Instead he glared pointedly at Vellocatus. "We had no information the enemy was taking to the field. None. Yet they were planning to build a fort a few miles from our main gate!"

"They didn't know we were going to raid Isurium, either," Vellocatus countered. "And it was more than a few miles."

"Is this the only reason we're here?" Morallta asked, blandly raising her eyes from a half-eaten pigeon carcass, one finger remaining deliciously in her mouth. Cethen noticed an appealing spatter of freckles on either side of her nose.

Venutius scowled. "Huh?"

"Are we trying to assign blame, so that one or two might feel better? Or are we here to solve our problems?"

Venutius's face turned as red as the scalp he'd been bothering, but surprisingly, he held his temper. "We are here to determine our deficiencies. And to do something about them," he said testily.

Morallta appeared to think about that, then nodded. "Good. I just want to be sure that was the reason ."

Cethen glanced back and forth, marvelling at the woman's disdain and Venutius's unusual control. He knew the cause—the old man was after the support of the Carvetii. In the hills of Cumbria, Morallta would be considered a queen. The word she took back was likely critical. Had the attack on Isurium been an outright success, it would likely have brought her people's quick and total commitment. Yet the battle had not been a total rout either, so the possibility was still there. Most of Venutius's army had managed to crawl back from Bran's Beck, and the Roman casualties had been high. But there was no getting around the fact: it was a long, long way from a victory.

Still scowling, Venutius turned to Loskenn. "Speak. Tell them your plan."

Loskenn's great bulk didn't stir. Only his eyes moved, dark and moist, as if greater motion was too much effort. His huge moustache bobbed up and down as the words fell from his mouth in quick bursts. "We must learn from the Romans. They patrol. We don't. Not with any order. They have discipline. We don't. They fight together. They train their soldiers. We don't—not together."

Morallta sneered, barely audible, "You've only just realized that?"

Loskenn's watery eyes moved her way, but he didn't blink as he continued. "Our people are braver and stronger than the Romans. We must work with that. Train them, as we have started to do. As Caradoc did. Then strike hard. But don't be afraid to run. Like wasps. We can't beat them in open battle. But we can sting. Make them bleed. Lose enough blood, and you die."

"When I get stung by a wasp, I get pissed," Morallta muttered. "Then I swat it."

The dark eyes again flickered in her direction and the heavy lids narrowed, but Loskenn didn't let the barb draw his anger. "Bad comparison. I should have said wolf. You don't swat a wolf. Or wolf packs. That's more what I had in mind."

"It would be something like what we did by Isurium that first time." Ebric sounded eager, as if trying to cover the tension. "We killed those Tungri warriors. Remember, Cethen?"

"I remember," Cethen mumbled, for the actual fight was still something he'd rather forget. He had bumbled badly, though the others seemed to think he'd done his share. Then he realized Ebric was not speaking of the four unsuspecting riders, but of the ambush, when the large Tungri patrol had been wiped out.

"You did well on that, Cethen," Venutius added, seemingly eager to speak of better times. "As we all did. And Ebric, you grasp what Loskenn says, only we must do such things with greater numbers. We need to pick the best warriors from among our people. All our people." He nodded to Morallta for emphasis. "They must be properly trained and properly led. Like the Romans. It is what has disadvantaged us against them."

"The Roman auxiliaries are tribesmen," Vellocatus pointed out. "They're well trained."

"And they have no chieftains amongst them, " Loskenn growled, finally heaving his great bulk forward to emphasize the point. "Only warriors. Chiefs always want to lead. Most of them can't lead a hog to its slop. But to get their warriors to join us, we need to do more. We must make it an honour to belong. A great honour. And they must learn to be loyal to each other. Not to their tuath. It is how the Romans do it." Loskenn fell back with a grunt before finishing what had sounded like a speech for him: "The battle frenzy of our people is the first enemy we must defeat. Then we can meet the real one in battle."

Morallta's tone was again sardonic. "And if we do find enough material to forge this brilliant force of champions, how many do you propose?"

By the gods, she's a nay-saying bitch, Cethen mused, his eyes darting back and forth between Loskenn and the Carveti woman. He could see where she'd earned her name: "Great Fury." Had she finally squeezed his balls hard enough that he'd kick?

When Loskenn spoke again, his voice rumbled with barely hidden annoyance. "That is for those who are with the plan to discuss. I can only guess. To start—what? A hundred? Two hundred? Perhaps more. I see long months of training. Many will fall out. But after that, given time, who knows? Maybe an entire army. We have to build. We have many good people. Right here at the fortress." He slumped back as if tired by the effort, ponderously waving an enormous hand to show that the matter could be decided later.

"And who would lead this fearless band of heroes?" Morallta asked the question in the same snide tone, glancing first at Cethen, then one by one at the others. Her gaze finally came to rest on Venutius, one of her dark copper eyebrows raised in question. The look left no doubt that she found them all wanting.

"That depends, *my dear*," Venutius replied, laying his tongue heavily on the words; the king appeared to have been pushed to his limit. "If you were willing to give your heart and mind to the force, then I would choose you to lead these *heroes*. If, however, you only want to lead for the power and the glory of it, then I would choose from the others gathered here." The two glowered at each other, and he added, "Whether now, or later!"

Morallta's eyes clouded, and her head tilted thoughtfully to one side as she stared at Venutius, reminding Cethen of a young wolf gauging the pack leader. Everyone watched in silence, wondering if she would have the sense to roll over and bare her throat. A touch of pink coloured her cheeks, then faded.

Slowly she bowed her head to show acceptance. "The idea has much worth," she said carefully, the sarcasm gone. "I would be pleased to accept the task—providing everyone here has no objections and will follow," she gave the rest of them a forced smile, "*my dears!*" The geniality moved no further than her lips, as her cool eyes narrowed on each of them.

One by one they mumbled their acceptance. Loskenn was last, announcing in his deep, rumbling voice that he was pleased with the choice.

Satisfied, she turned to Venutius. "I gather this force is still early in the womb. What work has been done?"

"It's just an idea as yet," Venutius mumbled, as if uncomfortable with the admission.

Morallta raised a hand, as if to halt further words. "That is good. I prefer it that way," she said brusquely. "A sword is best forged by the one who wields it. I'll think tonight on how it will be done. Tomorrow we begin—at the great hall, shortly after the rooster crows. I expect you all there, prepared for anything."

Morallta stared them down as each confirmed his understanding. All of them were struck by same thought: what had the old bugger set loose on them? Even Venutius appeared uncertain, for when she rose and offered her final comment, he almost choked.

"There is one more essential detail that separates us from the Romans, and it's of prime importance." She directed the words to Loskenn. "Theirs is a professional army. They pay their soldiers. Regularly." She swung her glinting eyes to Venutius. "I'd like to know by tomorrow how you're going to handle that."

Two days passed before Cethen managed to leave Stannick and search for signs of Elena and his daughter. In his heart, he knew the journey was hopeless. Nuada insisted on going as well, and he didn't protest. The pair took the longer way to the meadow at Bran's Beck, switching to the east bank of the river when they came to the place where the Romans had planned to build their fort. It was of some consolation that Venutius had at least stopped them putting the damned thing up, though the small village was now marked by nothing more than dark circles of ash.

When they drew near the battleground, they both hung back in the shelter of the trees, quietly watching the meadow from across the river. The long, open field sat empty, and all that could be heard was the chirp of birds, and the soft hum of insects. Yet the pungent smell of old fires and the stink of carrion hung in the air, urging caution. When a vixen ambled from the trees carrying a kit in its mouth, there seemed no further point in lingering. They pushed their horses across the shallow river and up onto the grassy bank. Almost at once, the air grew heavy and fetid.

There was nothing left of Bran's farmstead save a pile of burnt and blackened wood. Oddly enough, the toppled log and the dark circle of ashes where he had sat with Elena and Vellocatus remained untouched. Cethen half expected to find the wine jug on the ground, but it was not there. Farther up the meadow, a huge black circle burnt in the trampled grass confirmed Bruga's words. In the centre stood a huge pile of ashes pocked with dark, rusting globs of molten iron, and littered with splintered bones and the chalky mounds of a thousand skulls.

"Bastards!" Cethen muttered.

"At least they could have let us bury our dead," Nuada said bitterly, her eyes searching vainly for anything that might speak of Cian.

The leaves shivered on the trees in a sudden gust of wind. It carried a faint, yet powerful stench of death from the forest.

"The gods know how many crawled away to die," Cethen muttered. "Do you want to go look? See if any of them are ...you know."

Nuada's expression turned grim, but she reined her horse toward the forest and urged it forward with a vicious kick.

It was dark when they finally returned to Stannick, and once back, they said nothing more of searching. The next day, Nuada moved into Cethen's lodge with her own two children and began looking after him and Tuis and Rhun. It was the practical thing to do. Within a month, she was sharing his bed.

Chapter XVIII

The path to Lindum was busy, and Gaius's small party met many other travellers during the three days he took to reach the fortress. Where the river Abus flowed past Petuaria, it was a wide tidal estuary; an expanse of water that, once crossed, was as different as night from day. A Roman travelled with far less fear of barbarian attack. The countryside exuded an air of latent prosperity, if for no other reason than by comparison. Heavily loaded wagons rumbled over the hard-packed track, dispatch riders hurried by, and the road itself was being widened and paved.

They reached the north gate of the fortress at the end of the third day, and Gaius eyed the gate tower with trepidation. Had they been alone, he might have halted to gather his thoughts before entering, but a small escort marched behind, trailed by a party of walking wounded that had been granted permission to recover at Lindum.

Marcus had to be considered, too. The sooner the boy was resting in his own bed, the faster his recovery. His son had made the journey in a crude litter slung between two horses. Metellus guided the lead animal, walking alongside and setting the pace. The long poles of the stretcher gave the rig an enviable sway, and Marc slept for a good part of the journey.

The girl Coira walked alongside the second animal, one wrist shackled to one of the stretcher poles. She had hardly spoken during the journey, not even aboard the ship that ferried them across the Abus, though it had obviously roused her interest. When she thought no one was watching, her large blue eyes slid sideways to take in the vessel's broad deck, and the long, rhythmic flash of its oars. Yet she remained almost mute, muttering words in her own dialect only when necessary.

Marc seemed amused by her sullen interest, and watched quietly during the two days on the road. He stared covertly at her grim features, as if trying to fathom the girl. At first he had tried to talk, but her replies were one-syllable grunts, and he finally abandoned the effort. Sleeping seemed a far more pleasant way to pass the journey.

The streets inside the fortress were almost empty. Gaius wondered vaguely where the troops were, and if the legate was with them. That might not solve his immediate problem, but its postponement held a certain appeal—not that it outweighed his anger and impatience to get the matter out in the open, but ...

With such thoughts distracting him, Gaius soon found himself at the headquarters building. Leaving the senior decanus to take care of the escort and telling Metellus to take Marc and the barbarian girl to his home, he strode inside, deciding a bold face was the best course.

At any other time, the clean, hard clatter of his boots on the stone floor would have been exhilarating after months of treading nothing but mud and plank; but the pleasure was lost as he braced for the sight of Lucius Catus, with no idea what he would say. The only officer present, however, was the praefectus castrorum. Gaius watched his face for the slightest change of expression as he reported in. The man's lips tightened and his eyes dropped briefly before they met Gaius's. It was enough.

"He's around the garrison somewhere," the praefectus said, glancing toward the door as if afraid the legate might enter.

"Then give him my respects," Gaius muttered, startled to feel warmth creeping into his cheeks. "If anyone needs me, I'll be at my home."

Cursing himself for a fool, he turned and strode from the building, crossed the courtyard, and walked out onto the street. His belly felt cold and his chest as tight as a drawn bowstring. If it weren't for the shame running would bring, he would have climbed on his horse and returned to the cruder comforts of Ebor. Perhaps Cartimandua might even welcome his return, he thought wistfully, though the possibility that he had been used there, too, had occurred to him more than once.

He paused, staring down the *Via Praetoria* toward the south wall, struggling to find the will to continue. The house he had taken for Helvia stood beyond the gate, on the steep slope that fell away from the other side. He only half remembered the place, for he had seen it but briefly earlier in the year, when he was recovering. It was owned by a trader who had been only too happy to lease it, what with Ebor about to be built, and Petuaria growing. The house had been vacant and made ready for his wife's arrival, but by then he had already returned to Ebor. If only he had remained, perhaps matters might have worked out differently. Or perhaps they might have been even worse …

Gaius growled to himself. He might be reluctant to go there, but he had to do it. With a sigh he glanced to either side, and was about to continue down the street when a figure dressed in a pale blue *stola* caught his eye. He watched as a small woman with black hair piled high in a knot made her way toward the west wall. There was a casual, appealing sway to her walk that Gaius found all too familiar.

Helvia. Gaius's chest tightened. He watched with an odd, mild curiosity, but didn't call out. She passed from view, and he stepped out into the street and followed, maintaining the distance between them. When she reached the west gate, instead of passing through, she turned and climbed the steps to the rampart. She paused on the walkway running behind the wall to look over her shoulder, then disappeared inside the gate tower.

Gaius quickened his pace, his eyes moving to the very top of the gateway. The blue clad figure appeared briefly, then quickly vanished as it moved off to the far side. What was she doing there at this time day? If indeed it was her. Both the south and west walls were popular with the garrison as evening fell, he knew that. To the south the land fell steeply away, offering a breathtaking view of the lush countryside for miles about. And to the west, if the day had been pleasant and a low haze of clouds clung to the sky, the sunsets were spectacular.

Gaius realized he was dawdling. He climbed onto the rampart and faced the entrance to the gate tower, debating whether to enter. Part of him was ready to walk the wall to the south gate and go home. Yet the tower itself seemed empty and no sound came from below, which was unusual. From long experience he suspected why. If a senior officer decides he wants privacy, then everyone finds a reason to be elsewhere. With a sigh he opened the door and started upward.

When he thrust his head through the stairwell at the top, he found just two people there: Helvia, and a man who had to be Lucius Catus. Their backs were turned as they gazed at an evening sky already aglow with scarlet tinted clouds. It was a glorious sight, but as Gaius stepped quietly onto the plank decking and saw nobody other than the two of them there, it served only to fuel his anger.

"Lovely view, isn't it?" he said.

They both whirled. *Keep the advantage of surprise,* flashed through his mind. It was the basis of all tactics, but after the initial comment he was at a loss. Helvia was taken aback, but didn't appear particularly horrified. In fact, Gaius decided, she looked damned good in the long, flowing *stola.* The man with her looked decidedly annoyed, though, his eyes glinting as he took in the intruder's uniform.

"And who do you think you are?"

Gaius ignored the question and crossed to Helvia. He took her gently by the shoulders, and kissed her softly on the lips. She stepped back and gazed up at him, her eyes confused.

"You are well?" he asked. She simply nodded.

A harsh cough broke the silence, and he turned to find Lucius glaring at him, chin angled upward like a dog sniffing the way of the wind. Gaius glared back, his mind taking the measure of the man, and finding pleasure in the fact that he himself was a full head taller.

The legate was dressed in a loose linen tunic belted tight about a thick waist, and wore a pair of open sandals. He might have been a wine merchant. In fact, he looked Greek—or Macedonian. Gaius knew Catus had been born in Rome, but the straight, broad nose of the peninsula Greeks dominated his face. That, and the fellow's oily, swarthy complexion, coupled with a pair of curved, sensuous lips that Gaius personally found womanly, made the man look damned unpleasant. The general was certainly no Apollo. What grabbed the woman's attention?

"I'm this woman's husband," he said, and because the legate had undoubtedly not meant his question to be literal, demanded, "And just who do you think you are?"

"Careful, soldier," Lucius growled.

Gaius fought to keep calm. Ignoring the comment, he addressed Helvia. "So what is going on here?"

"Lucius was—we were looking at the view." Helvia lowered her eyes. It was a weak reply and she knew it.

"And this is a regular occurrence?"

Helvia looked up and Gaius saw the strain in her eyes. She glanced sideways. "Lucius is, well, he is an amusing man."

"And ...?"

"And ..." Helvia dropped her eyes again. "And he can be very persuasive."

Gaius swung back to the legate, his anger rising.

"I said be careful, tribune," Lucius snarled before he could speak. "Remember who it is you address."

A similar warning from Cerialis leapt into Gaius's mind, but he pushed it aside. Only the anger remained, and the insulting posture of the legate. "And you remember who it is you dishonour, you Peloponnesian pig!"

Lucius Catus appeared momentarily baffled at the description, but he shook his head and replied in a low, rumbling growl, "You will apologize, soldier, for your career is fast disappearing."

The arrogance only made Gaius angrier. One small part of him whispered caution, but the other screamed at the man's pretentiousness: caught with someone else's wife, yet roaring his outrage. "Don't threaten me," he snarled. "I have the right, not you. First you demean my wife, and now you would demean me further!"

"And now it is gone. As you will soon be. Like that." Lucius snapped his fingers, and moved his head slowly from side to side as if in pity. "And as to demeaning your precious wife, don't make me laugh. That's impossible."

Gaius turned to Helvia. "Tell me, how—persuasive—has this greased ape been?"

Helvia, though, was looking at Lucius, her face scarlet and her mouth tight with anger. Then she turned, and once more dropped her eyes. It was answer enough. Gaius sighed, almost with relief; at least he now knew. The image of Cartimandua flashed into his mind. Would she have mocked him at the irony? What had she once said? People make their decisions based on what their needs and conscience dictate—at the time—and usually in that order.

"And your choice in this thing?" he asked in a voice far from steady.

Helvia looked up at him with a resigned, helpless expression. Her eyes moved to Lucius, and saw no encouragement there. Then, as if remembering his slur, her mouth tightened. "There is only one choice."

Gaius closed his eyes, feeling overly obtuse, and drawled, "And what, my dear, is that?"

Her eyes widened. "Why, you, of course."

Gaius whirled back to Lucius and spat at his feet. "I will have redress. Unless you are a coward, too."

"What?" the legate exclaimed. He laughed. "A lousy engineer? With a whore for a wife? Oh, you stupid man!"

Gaius saw the man's chest heave upward as he drew breath—Lucius was about to call the guard. The gesture heated his anger to a boil; without thinking, he drove his fist hard into the legate's belly. Air whooshed out as if blown from a bellows, and the general doubled over. Gaius savagely grabbed his head, and jerked one knee upward to smash against the man's forehead. There was a sickening thud, and the commander of the Second Adiutrix fell like a block of granite.

For a moment Gaius and Helvia stood in numbed silence. Then Gaius dropped instinctively to his knees, peering wildly about the fortress to see who might have seen. But the upper level of the gate was as high as anywhere else in the stronghold, and the blow had passed unnoticed. He rose slowly to his feet and stared dumbly down at Lucius.

"Is he dead?" Helvia asked, one hand to her mouth.

Gaius turned to his wife with a sigh, then slumped down on the legate's back. "Probably not. Though I might as well be."

"Oh dear."

"We appear to have a problem." Receiving no reply, he looked up. "Helvia, I want the truth. Has this man been playing the bastard, or were you really …" Gaius couldn't bring himself to use the word, not with his wife. "Was there really something going on between you? It's important that I have the truth."

Helvia sank to the decking in front of her husband and she, too, sighed. "Sort of. I suppose," she began, her voice assuming a sobbing tremor. "He was very nice at first. And I thought it would be good for your career to entertain him, feed him. I thought I might even arrange for you to transfer back here. But then …"

Cynically wondering at her newfound interest in his career path, Gaius prompted, "But then …?"

"Then a few weeks ago—no, a month. Or was it two?" She looked at him as if helpless. "I suppose it was probably before that. The journey from Rome is long. One night, I couldn't get him to leave. And he—well, he forced himself on me!"

"He forced himself?" Gaius asked skeptically.

"Yes. He forced himself." Helvia nodded emphatically, as if reinforcing the truth of it. "It began on a night when others were there. We all had too much wine, I suppose, and then everyone else left. He remained. And yes—he forced himself on me."

Gaius fought back an almost uncontrollable urge to shout at the woman and curse her duplicity, but he pushed the impulse aside. There was a crisis here, for both of them, and for once Helvia seemed willing to talk. He knew damned well that if it were left to time, the truth would never come. He continued to push. "Well, it must have happened more than once. After all, you were meeting him up here—what, every …?" He gestured about the top of the gatehouse with one hand, then suddenly stopped, shocked. "You weren't actually doing it on top of the fucking gatehouse?"

Helvia looked shocked in turn. "Of course not. What do you think I am?"

Gaius, with a good deal of effort, let that one pass. "But it was ongoing?"

"I had no choice." Helvia sounded contrite, and her eyes were again downcast and full of tears. "Once it had been done, he seemed determined to continue. As I said, he's forceful. As a compromise, I insisted that the meetings be away from the house—he wouldn't come there and …and force the issue. I wanted to protect Aelia and Marc.

And hush the servants and the slaves."

"So you were here this evening to—"

"No," Helvia said sharply, then added in a softer voice, "It was to
…he wanted to arrange another meeting."

Gaius again sighed, deciding he'd heard better excuses on sick
parade. In the meantime, there was the pressing matter of the legate.
His career with the legions lay sprawled under his hind end, like a
fire about to flare. Lucius was obviously a vengeful man, in a fortress
where he reigned like an emperor. A very angry emperor.

The body beneath him stirred. With a groan Gaius leaned forward,
elbows on his knees and his head cradled in both hands, vainly trying
to think. Part of him wished the man dead.

"He called me a whore," Helvia whispered, as if hearing the word
for the first time.

Gaius grunted, privately deciding the legate was not far off the
plumb. Forcing himself on her! Probably seven days a week, just like
the Brigante woman had "forced" herself on him. As that thought
struck, the notion that Helvia had likely been as ready and compliant
as Cartimandua angered him even more. Yet what to do?

The choices raced madly through his mind. The legate had been
fornicating with his wife, dammit. A man was still entitled to claim his
honour! Who was going to dispute that? Especially under Vespasian.
And Helvia, after the slur about being a whore, was certainly going to
hold to her story. Forced! That was a laugh.

Gaius began to rationalize. Lucius hadn't been in uniform; it wasn't
as if he'd struck an officer in uniform, or in the course of duty. It was an
off-duty affair of honour. The man had influence, certainly, and he was
well known, but Cerialis was known as a fair man. Most of the time.
Though the governor had warned him. Damn!

Gaius rose slowly to his feet and scratched at his ear under the side
of his helmet. Lucius groaned, stirring again as the weight lifted from his
back. The swarthy face rose slightly, and the legate blinked as if trying
to make sense of his surroundings. Gaius decided he wasn't yet ready
to face the man. He grasped the general's head in both hands, raised it
about a foot in the air, and slammed it down on the wood decking.

"The bastard won't know the difference between one thump and two," he muttered, feeling a whole lot better. His mind made up, he started toward the stairs.

"Gaius!"

He ignored her and headed down the steps.

"Gaius, what should I do?" Helvia wailed.

"Whatever you like, my dear. To be perfectly honest, I don't give a damn," he called, then, more to himself than his wife, he added, "If nothing else occurs, try telling the truth. You might find it refreshing."

For the second time in nearly as many days, Gaius found himself stalking the inside of a fortress with no other desire than to be alone. He left the gate tower the same way he had entered, but instead of retracing his steps, he turned south and followed the intervallum running behind the rampart. There were no people there and he wanted to think.

The only course of action was to return to Ebor. He would throw himself on Cerialis's mercy before Lucius could lay his angry, perfidious hands on him. Once safely back at Ebor, the worst that could happen, surely, was the loss of his career—which wasn't exactly the end of an empire. There were always other paths to follow. That administration post was the likeliest choice, though a far lesser position than he might otherwise have expected. Perhaps politics at some junior level, though a dangerous enemy now existed in that arena—or would, once the general regained his wits. *If the man had any to begin with,* Gaius thought as he quickened his pace.

It was all over with Helvia, he was certain of that. All that remained was to get back to Ebor, posthaste, and report to Cerialis before the legate regained his feet.

Gaius hurried through the south gate, nodded a salute to the decanus in charge of the guard, and continued along the main road. The house lay only a few hundred paces down the slope, and he tried not to break into a run as he drew near. He burst through the door looking for Metellus, but not a soul was in sight. The two pack horses stood in the courtyard, bare of their burden, and with heads bent low over a pile of hay.

"Damn, damn, damn," Gaius muttered, and roared the slave's

name. It seemed to take forever, but the man finally came running. "Saddle my horse—or better still, a fresh one, if possible. Quick. I have to return to Ebor."

Metellus bit off the question that came to his lips and disappeared, leaving Gaius to pace the small garden, fuming and slapping his fist in the palm of his hand.

"What's the matter, daddy?"

Gaius turned to see Aelia framed in the doorway, her face concerned. Had he been so wrapped up in his own matters that he'd forgotten to greet his daughter? He clenched his hands, trying to settle his mind. The situation felt worse, far worse, than a full-blown battle with the barbarians. At least there, a man had a reliable enemy and a measure of control over his fate.

"Urgent matters back at Ebor," he replied, hugging her to his chest, and wondering how all this would affect his daughter when it finally spilled out. "I have to leave."

"But you've only just got here."

"I know, I know," he said, and stared down into her soft brown eyes, feeling like a common criminal. "I have to go. Mother will explain."

"Mother?" Aelia pulled back, her voice suddenly as full of concern as her clouded expression. "Where is she?"

Gaius groaned. Did even their daughter know? "She'll be along soon; she's at the fortress," he said, and turned, looking anxiously for Metellus. "Where has that damned slave got to?"

"Are you in trouble?"

"Nothing that can't be resolved, my dear. It will sort itself out."

"Daddy, is Mother alright?" Aelia stared at him accusingly.

"What?" Gaius exclaimed. "Of course she is. I left her—well, when I left her she was fine. I met her on the *Principalis* when I first reported in. She was fine." Aelia said nothing, so he asked, "Marc—is he being looked after?"

"He's in his old room, awake, but I doubt for long. How long will you be away?"

A damned good question, Gaius thought, and said, "Not long, sweet. Ah, good!"

He turned at the clatter of hooves and saw that Metellus had brought Helvia's mare from the stable. The slave handed him the reins, and bent to pick up the saddle Gaius had used for the journey down from Ebor. It still had the pack tied to the cantle.

"Hurry, man," Gaius urged, though the poor fellow was threading the cinch as fast as he could.

"Daddy," Aelia said anxiously, and stepped forward as he prepared to mount. "I don't know what has happened, but be careful."

Gaius held the mare to a fast trot, fervently trying to push the horse without attracting attention. Clattering back to the south gate, he debated whether to take a shorter path through the fortress itself, or ride the longer way around to the west, where he would pick up the road again on the north side. Like so many things of late, the decision seemed to run a course of its own. A small crowd had gathered in front of the gate where a rider sat his horse, speaking and gesturing urgently with two other troopers. From the squared plume on his helmet, Gaius saw he was a centurion—a senior centurion.

Surely word was not out already? Or—the thought struck him sickeningly—had Helvia betrayed him? Again? Cursing events that were moving far too fast, Gaius urged the mare forward, forcing himself to remain calm. He turned the animal's head to the west, hoping to slip unobtrusively past. In his heart he knew it was useless, but he had to try. Perhaps he should have slipped out of uniform; without it, the man wouldn't know him from Hermes. But he had not, and now it was too late. The horse had barely taken a dozen steps when the centurion's voice rang out.

"Sir!"

Gaius ignored the call. He edged the mare through the crowd, intent on spurring the animal forward once it broke free. The voice rang out again, and out of the corner of his eye, he saw the centurion spur his horse forward.

"Sir!"

Gaius sighed and pulled the mare to a halt. The centurion cantered his horse alongside.

"Sir, don't want to bother you," the man said, and saluted, "but perhaps you might not want to leave at the moment."

Gaius stared wearily at him, wondering exactly what the man's orders were. "Why?"

"It's the Legate Catus, sir. I believe he might be dead."

"He's what?" Gaius felt his heart jump as if pierced by a knife. Surely he hadn't slammed the man's head that hard? The second blow had been less heavy than the first, and Lucius's skull was as thick as a plank anyway! Though when the fool's head hit the decking, he had gone out like a wet candle. Gaius tried to remember: had the legate still been breathing when he last saw him? Shit! This was murder!

" ...the west gate. From the top."

Gaius glanced up, suddenly aware the centurion had been saying something. "Er, I missed that," he mumbled, then cautiously asked the expected question: "How did he die?"

"As I said, sir, one my men here just brought the word. There's been an accident of some sort at the west gate. They say he fell from the top. I saw you riding by, and thought you should know as well."

"He what?" Gaius yelped.

"He fell from the top of the gatehouse. They said some woman was up there, too. Absolutely hysterical. I don't know what the story is, but I'll wager it would make Ovid blush."

So do I, Gaius thought as the words sank in. Baffled, he leaned back in the saddle as the centurion again saluted, then wheeled his horse and rode inside the fortress.

The funeral of Legate Lucius Catus was an elaborate display of the pomp and power of Rome, put on as much for the locals as the man himself. Every available detachment was recalled to the fortress, and full dress was the parade order. The Second's eagle was marched, along with the standard of each cohort and those of the auxiliary regiments. Armour was burnished, linen was washed, horses were brushed, oiled and plumed, and hooves painted a glossy black.

Massed on the parade ground with the legion itself, the Second's band led the long funeral procession from the field. A dozen ranks of musicians headed the column, playing a wailing dirge on the *tubae and corni*, as the drums trailed sombrely behind, tapping the slow tempo of the funeral march. The interment was a quarter-mile from the west gate of the fortress. The oration took place at the grave site, delivered by the legate's younger brother Demetrius, a tribune serving with Agricola's Twentieth legion. The funeral had been held in abeyance, pending his arrival.

The man's presence surprised Gaius, though he had found no cause for concern. He felt comfortably blameless in what had obviously been a murder, despite Helvia's creative account of the legate's death. He marvelled at her grief-stricken story, which he was forced to hear in greater detail at the reception that followed the burial.

Cerialis hosted the gathering at the Lindum headquarters building. For the most of it, Helvia and Gaius stood apart. Due to the size of the crowd, the food was served on portable tables and eaten standing. The fortress belonged to the Second Adiutrix, and there were many faces present that were familiar. Gaius's service with the legion had been brief, yet he was well known; he simply did not feel like renewing old acquaintance. And Helvia, he thought cynically, appeared of the same mind Even so, more than a few officers did come over to greet him, but most did not remain long. Once the platitudes were offered, each seemed in a hurry to find someone else to talk to. Gaius found their reaction only reasonable.

More than one glanced covertly in his direction, though, with an odd look which was as first indecipherable. Only later did he realize what was on their minds. Each likely suspected foul play, surmising he was the one who had contrived it. More than once veiled admiration flickered in their eyes, for there was no doubt his honour had been offended. It probably helped that Lucius Catus had not been a popular commander.

During one of the long moments when he and Helvia were alone, Cerialis wandered over, as if by accident. Demetrius walked at his side. The man might have been chiselled from the same block of marble as his brother. Cerialis made the usual introductions, but Demetrius did not offer his hand. Gaius offered a short, stiff bow, and expressed his condolences.

"Thank you," Demetrius said, his voice hollow, and he looked to

Helvia, spending no time on formalities. "I understand you were with him when he died?"

He dragged out the last word in a manner that invited further response, but Helvia simply said, "Yes. I'm sorry."

Demetrius nodded, but seemed unwilling to let it rest, and spoke bluntly. "Such a death is not what I would have expected from my brother."

There followed an embarrassed silence. The young tribune looked down his nose in the same canine manner as his brother, as if sniffing the air.

"In many ways, it didn't surprise me at all," Helvia said.

Demetrius showed his surprise, and his nostrils flared. "Oh?"

"Just what I said. It didn't." Helvia appeared to be choosing her words carefully, but Gaius could see the blood flush below her chin. His wife was nettled. "He was a strong man. But—how should I say it? A forceful one, too. What he wanted, he took. He was—and I say this not to malign him—he was often contemptuous of those who stood in his path. He often held them in ridicule, and it contributed to his death, I regret to say; in fact, it caused it." She paused, then added with seeming reluctance, "Though perhaps in some manner, so did I."

There was perhaps a trace of acknowledgement at the words in the slight incline of Demetrius's head, but his jaw tightened at Helvia's final comment. "Oh?"

Gaius groaned inwardly, wondering where his wife was leading the man. His belly was growing cold, and he stifled the urge to grab her arm and pull her forcefully from the building.

"I hesitate to say this, for it seems inappropriate, certainly at a time such as this." Helvia gestured to the crowded room, and wet her lips as if embarrassed to go further. "But perhaps I must, for you are obviously pushing for the truth. Lucius was a burden to me. A burden I did not ask for. He was told many times. The day he died, I threatened him." She inclined her head toward Gaius. "I told him I would inform my husband of his unwelcome attention. Unfortunately, I also told him my husband would resort to violence if he did not stop. That's what helped speed his death."

Demetrius's eyes swung to Gaius with the same contemptuous stare as his dead brother.

"We never really knew each other," Gaius murmured, angered at the unspoken contempt, yet twitching with apprehension over what Helvia would say next.

Demetrius snorted. "I doubt that Lucius would have felt threatened."

"Exactly, for he did not know my husband," Helvia said loyally, then suddenly grew more animated. "You see, he actually seemed to find the idea amusing. He laughed. In fact, he roared with laughter, and I grew angry, which simply made him laugh more. His contempt was his downfall. He ridiculed Gaius, pretending he was terrified for his life, and he began clucking like a chicken. He waddled about the gate tower aping a rooster, something like this ..."

Helvia pulled her hands over her breasts and flapped her elbows in imitation of a bird, looking down at her feet as if recalling the vision. A dozen people standing nearby peered sideways, at the same time pretending not to notice.

"Then he turned about like this, and hopped onto the wall where it meets the corner. But his foot ..." She moved her right leg. "Yes! It was this foot. It slipped on the edge and he tumbled backward."

Helvia straightened up and looked directly at Demetrius, her great brown eyes wide in amazement. "You know, I would have thought he'd cry out, but he didn't. He just disappeared. One moment he was there, the next he was gone." She shook her head and delicately wiped one eye, as if the memory was too much. Gaius watched in slack-jawed astonishment.

Demetrius had been studying his face as Helvia spoke. "Quite a thing to happen, don't you think, Sabinius?"

"It's—it's the first time my wife has been willing to recall the tragedy in such great detail," Gaius said, then, unwilling to give any ground, added, "I had not realized the humiliation he had put her through. Or me, for that matter."

The tribune stiffened but said no more, and the remark seemed to end the conversation.

"Ma'am," Demetrius said, bowing stiffly at the waist. "It is most unfortunate that we could not have met under less distressing circumstances."

"I again extend my condolences," she murmured.

Demetrius then did a strange thing. He turned to Gaius and placed a beefy right hand on his shoulder, and stared up into his face with eyes that were two thin cuts of Tuscany marble. "We shall meet again, Gaius Sabinius Trebonius. Perhaps then, we will go over the matter once more." He turned stiffly and walked off into the crowd.

Cerialis had stood silently by, carefully watching the play of words. The governor simply shrugged in response to Gaius's unspoken question, as if to say he had no idea what was on the man's mind. A few moments later he, too, departed.

Gaius stood numbly digesting all he had heard, and finally exhaled a huge breath. He glanced down at his wife, and said in hardly more than a whisper, "You're a strong woman."

"Sometimes, life requires iron determination."

"I have never doubted you possessed that particular quality, Helvia. What I meant , though, was strong in body. The man was solid. And he was heavy," Gaius murmured, then another thought occurred to him. "You know, he could have survived the fall."

Helvia shook her head. "Only the gods can give life to the dead."

"But he was alive when—" Gaius began, but his wife interrupted. "Not when I last saw him."

The night before Gaius returned to Ebor, he found himself alone with Aelia. It was after the evening meal, and he lay on the dining couch, eyes half closed, studying his daughter as she embroidered the neck of a white stola. How much did the girl know about what had passed, both before and after his arrival? Had Helvia enlisted Aelia's help for her betrayal, or had the two quarrelled? He realized that the girl was growing up very quickly, and yet he knew so little about her.

As if sensing the scrutiny, his daughter set the garment on her lap and looked up at him. "You are staring," she accused. "What is it?"

Faced with the question, Gaius hesitated, unsure where to steer the conversation. "Just wondering …have you heard anything? Rumours? That kind of thing?"

Aelia stared back, studying her father's face with soft, unreadable brown eyes. She seemed a lot older than her fourteen years. It dawned on Gaius that she might be wondering how much *he* knew about what had been happening.

"I know that Mother was there when he fell off the top of the gate, if that's what you mean," she ventured.

"True, true," he hedged. "Was that all you heard?"

She chuckled. "Megg says there are rumours that Mother pushed him off." Megg was the youngest of the slaves, purchased for Aelia when she was a toddler. They had grown close, though the girl was perhaps eight or ten years older.

"Do you believe that?"

"Father! Of course not!" Aelia sounded shocked. "When just the two of them were there, someone was bound to say it, weren't they? If they stopped to think, how could she have? The general would have had to have been drunk, or half asleep."

"True, true," Gaius said, and almost added the words "or half dead," as he recalled Helvia's terse account. He reflected on Aelia's reply and wondered why he'd started down the path he had, but he was unable to resist one or two more steps. "There were just the two of them, were there not? Did you hear anything else said? About anything?"

Aelia seemed to ponder her father's words, then sighed as if exasperated. "What you really mean is, did I hear if she and the legate were 'doing it' with each other, don't you."

Gaius feigned surprise. "You heard that?"

"Father, I'm fourteen. And that's not what I said. I was asking you what you really mean. If you have a question, then you must ask it."

"I just did," he said, deliberately obtuse.

"Then it was not well put. And the answer is yes. I have heard that. But that's not what you are really asking, is it?"

The girl is certainly her mother's daughter, Gaius thought, *at least when it comes to verbal swordplay.* He was walking on quicksand. Both of them knew it, but he found it perversely difficult to pull back. "So do you believe it?"

308

"You are not being fair," Aelia cried. "If you're going to disguise your questions like that, then I have one that should be answered first. What do you believe has been happening while you were away?"

Gaius leaned back on his couch, momentarily dismayed. He could not tell his daughter what had been going on. After all, Helvia was the girl's mother. It could be devastating if it proved that she was, indeed, unaware. He also realized, and it came as a revelation, that for the same reasons, Aelia could not bring herself to tell him what she knew. After all, Helvia was his wife. He smiled at her conundrum. He gazed at his dark-haired daughter with a sudden, unexpected burst of warmth. A frown wrinkled her forehead as she waited for a reply.

"You know, my little bear cub," Gaius said, "it really doesn't matter. The important thing is, how are you coping? Are you alright?"

Aelia tilted her head with a smile that would last an entire campaign. "Daddy, don't worry. I'm fine. I am coping quite well." Then the smile turned to an impish grin. "But I will try to take better care of Mother, next time you go away."

Gaius smiled and nodded, and decided it was time to change the subject. "Tell me. The barbarian girl, Coira. How is she fitting in?"

Chapter XVIIII

Morallta's force numbered less than two hundred when it crested the bracken-covered ridge, in search of more sheltered ground. The valley that lay below might have been cleft from the land by the single swing of a blunt axe. Thick forest coated the slopes, falling to a broad basin scattered with lush, green trees in full leaf. A shallow stream glittered like a silver ribbon along the valley floor, bubbling its way eastward to the upper reaches of the Abus. Much of the bottomland had been cleared and cropped, but it appeared to have seen little use of late, except for pasture. The grass was chewed, but not short, and the ground was dotted with dung.

Morallta decided the long, secluded valley was ideal ground for the final week of training. Her small force had been in the field for a full month, and it was nearing time to return to Stannick. The leaves would soon be on the turn, and help would be needed in the fields long before winter settled. She told them all as much the next morning. It was the first mention she'd made of when they would be returning home.

"There is no need to know," she'd snapped when asked the question on the very first night after departing Stannick. They were huddled around a score of tiny campfires in the cold, windswept hills west of the sprawling fortress. "A Roman warrior follows without question. Time and home do not matter," she glared at them with contempt, "and if it does to you, then you don't belong with us."

Three hundred warriors were there to hear her words, and now a third were gone, most in the first few days. Some had been turned back for simply not being good enough; others had grown disgusted with the endless practice and the constant demand for discipline.

They spent five days in the valley, and the fifth began the same way as the previous four. Two troops were dispatched to patrol, replacing the one on duty for the last half of the night. The remainder, four in all, were detailed for yet more instruction.

Cethen rode upstream with Borba, whose duty was to protect the upper reaches of the valley, and patrol the rim. Dermat rode downstream with Borba's twin, Luath. Morallta had placed Cethen with the two troops to watch and to teach the pair, a chore that was hardly needed. In fact, he continued to wonder what he was doing there at all, for he had no more skills than the others, and in many ways felt he had less. Only Dermat and two Vangione slaves traded from the Deceangli had any real knowledge of Roman drill. And drill it was, so much so that Cethen chafed under the repetition, yet he was supposed to be part of its instruction. Borba, on the other hand, had taken to Morallta's rigid schedule like a duck settling on a pond, as had his brother Luath.

Borba the Red had been one of Cethen's own finds. He had stumbled across the pair during the first days of recruiting. Thousands of warriors would have answered the king's call, for Morallta asked only for the bravest. A single restriction, however, slowed the rush from a torrent to a trickle: none of the chieftains, or any of their sons, would be accepted.

"Use the chieftains?" Morallta had scoffed, when someone suggested that at least their close kin be allowed to join. "We're trying to get rid of the disease, not foster it."

Sufficient volunteers had eventually arrived, but in the beginning Cethen and many others rode into the hills, spreading word of the elite force in hope of gathering the cream. Cethen found the twins on one such trek, at a farmstead tucked, half hidden, at the head of a sheltered ravine. He found the small cluster of buildings by following the yapping of dogs; and what first caught his eye were the horses herded into a pen close by. Four solid bays stood in the enclosure, larger than the other animals, and almost certainly owing their ancestry to Rome.

When their owners came warily out to greet him, Cethen thought he was seeing double. Each man's appearance was average in every way, except for a crop of bright red hair. The belligerent flash in their eyes reminded Cethen of his brother, and he smiled at the thought, wondering briefly if the gods had led him there. The pair also wore the same thin, scraggly moustaches as Cian, which would never fill and grow, and walked with his same cocky air of confidence. Their long hair was pulled back and tied the way Nuada had liked to see it, and each bore a broken nose that looked like a carved turnip. It was the sole feature in which they seemed to differ. On one the break angled left, and on the other, right. Cethen would later use the difference to tell them apart.

Cethen told the pair who he was, and who had sent him. They at first appeared more interested in the big chestnut than Venutius's call to arms, but each nodded gravely. One said his name was Borba; the other, Luath.

"The Swift and the Proud," Cethen translated, and grinned. "Are you correctly named?"

"It doesn't matter," Luath said. "One follows the other. He who is swift is also proud."

"And your wives? How do they tell you apart?"

They both grinned, and Luath made a point of scratching his nose before speaking. "Well, one has a scar across his arse, and it's not Luath the swift."

Borba laughed. "Of course, by the time it's noticed, it's too late to bother."

Both roared at the joke, though Cethen guessed it was an old one. He dismounted and followed the pair to the larger of the huts, where they offered a seat under the shade of an apple tree, laden with the harvest. One of the wives, he didn't know which, but according to the twins it didn't matter anyway, brought several cool draughts of ale and a platter of bread, cheese and cold meat. Cethen sipped the liquid as his eyes slid eastward to where the ravine widened and fell away to a broad valley.

The lush green slopes were a peaceful sight. Tiny figures worked the fields, scything an early hay crop that was as high as their bellies. They moved slowly across the hillside in even rows, the sea of tall, swaying grass retreating slowly ahead of them. In a way, it reminded him of the Romans and their own orderly, relentless advance. Perhaps Morallta and the old man were right after all. If those labouring in the fields could maintain such steady lines all day long, then surely …

The comparison was suddenly incongruous. The business of fighting seemed foreign and tiresome in this quiet haven. Cethen sighed. He was going to press the matter home anyway.

As he suspected, the twins eagerly embraced the challenge when he voiced the idea. Summer had been at its height then, and life was growing boring. Two weeks later the pair rode down from their hills, and into Stannick.

The Carveti woman's method of weeding had been ruthless and effective. The final recruiting took place at sunrise, on the slopes outside the fortress. Any who showed late were excluded, and they had been warned as much. Any who failed to bring the weapons they had been told to bring were also rejected. And those with weapons in poor condition were told they were not needed.

Cethen watched in alarm as more and more disgruntled warriors walked away, and began to wonder if Morallta would keep any at all. With a dour grin, Dermat told him how it worked. Morallta had decided she wanted three hundred, and kept stiffening her standards until that number remained. Cethen nodded, then listened with amusement to the arguments put forward by the last would-be trooper to be ordered on his way.

He was a young man with a friendly smile topped by a blond moustache with the depth of a cobweb. His horse and equipment were both in excellent condition, but his age and build were not what Morallta sought. He was far from tall, and was as spare as a sapling. There was a hard wiriness to him, though, that Cethen picked up on the longer he watched.

"If I'm no good after I've been tested," the youth persisted, "you can toss me out with the rest of the dross. But don't let appearances fool you. I can be a real bastard when I want to."

Morallta's voice echoed her exasperation. "What are you called, boy?"

"Ligan. Ligan Tren-fada."

Cethen and Dermat laughed, and for the first time a genuine smile seemed to cross Morallta's face; but it was fleeting, and no longer there when she answered. "And who gave you such a name, Ligan Strong-arms—yourself?"

"Of course myself," the youth replied, as if there could be no other way. "My enemies cannot give it. They are all dead."

Morallta's tongue pushed into her cheek. "And how many have you slain?"

"Every last one I ever fought," Ligan replied with a similar suppressed grin.

"And how many—" She suddenly stopped and shook her head. She pointed to where those selected were being sorted into troops by Loskenn and Ebric. "You'll do, boy. For the time being, anyway. Off you go."

Ligan quickly showed that he had his wits about him, for he had been carefully watching those selected. Most others had their eyes on those being whittled. He scurried off before she could change her mind, and sidled into the group where Borba and Luath had been placed.

Morallta spent the first two months near Stannick, for an attack had been expected ever since the fight at Bran's Beck. Instead came only reprisals: small raids, stolen stock and grain, random burning and killing.

As the weeks passed, more and more Britons poured into the fortress, looking to Venutius for both aid and vengeance. Morallta found herself increasingly pressed to counter the attacks with her own raiding, but she insisted her small force wasn't ready. Despite the king's grumbling, Vellocatus agreed. Venutius's old shield bearer had been working with the Carveti woman, for his knowledge of the Romans was critical; perhaps he, more than anyone, knew that much remained to be done.

Following yet another stormy meeting with Venutius, Vellocatus pulled Morallta aside and suggested she simply take her people and leave. It was about time they took to the field anyway, he reasoned, and if they were out of sight, then they would be out of the old man's mind. So at the beginning of the third month, she led those who had survived the early culling southward, following the high, windswept ridges that ran down the spine of Brigantia.

And when she was through pushing them hard in the barren wilds of the high country, she led them down to the lush, wooded valleys that poked into the hills like long, fat fingers of green. From dawn to dusk, and at times all night, she kept them on the move. The drill was simple: maintain formation, defend each other, and follow orders. The lesson was equally plain: learn anew how to fight, how to ride, and to follow orders. And the cost was also clear: go without food, go without sleep, and follow orders; learn to be at the correct place, learn to be on time, and learn to follow orders; learn that all must attack as one, all must defend as one, and all must follow orders.

Borba's small troop followed the stream west, toward the head of the valley. Almost at once, he dispatched four riders to the heavily wooded slopes on each side. The men nodded silent understanding and disappeared into the trees, following a spider web of paths more fit for a deer than a man on horseback. The patrol continued upward along the narrow path, the only sounds the hushed thump of hooves and the soft jingle of equipment.

Twice more riders were sent out to scout the flanks, and when the trail finally opened onto the treeless, windblown hills beyond the upper reaches of the dale, only Cethen, Borba and three of his people remained. Two were women, the only ones in the twin's troop, and he pointed them toward a scatter of low bushes that clung like lichen to the nearest rise. A pair of riders burst from the cover of the same bush and galloped toward them

"Someone's too damned eager to be off their watch," Borba muttered, and shook his head as if much better could be expected from his own people. "Go and relieve them before they trample us."

Cethen coughed as the two women prepared to leave, and Borba snapped his fingers. "Yeah, that's right. Ficra, you'll be in charge. Are there any questions?"

It was part of the lesson pounded into all their minds over the past months: someone should always have command; no questions should be left unanswered.

Ficra grinned impudently as she wheeled her horse. "No. Do you?"

Cethen followed the trail back down the valley with the two relieved riders. Borba was left to circle the rim on either side with young Ligan who, despite Morallta's earlier doubts, had earned himself a place of favour.

At the halfway point, where the second set of riders had disappeared into the web of game trails, Cethen dismounted. Leaving the two night pickets to return to the camp, he eased the cinch on the saddle, and stood back to admire the magnificence of the chestnut horse. It was something he did a half-dozen times a day. The animal was a constant source of pride. He had named it Gadearg, which meant "red javelin." He slumped back against the gnarled trunk of an oak tree and watched the beast fondly as it lowered its head to graze.

He was half dozing when the thudding hooves of a single horse brought him to his senses. He rose stiffly, gathered the chestnut's reins, and stepped from the trees. The rider was Ficra. Startled, she pulled her own animal in hard, and the beast skidded to a halt.

"There's a Roman patrol," she gasped, almost whispering the words as her horse, its blood running hot, circled nervously in the narrow trail.

"How far?" Cethen asked, and glanced quickly up the track as he tightened the cinch on the chestnut's saddle.

"They were coming down from the hills, across from where we were hidden in the bushes. Elna saw them first."

"Where is she?"

"We both came back, but she stayed hidden in the trees at the top, to warn us if more come."

"That's good." Cethen swung up into the saddle. "How many did you see?"

"Two came first, then the rest appeared. Perhaps thirty in all. A single troop, moving at a walk." Ficra's forehead furrowed as she recalled the Roman formation, and its disposition. "The scouts weren't riding as far ahead as they should have been."

"That's good for us," Cethen said, and smiled at her criticism. "Let's tell the others."

They rode into the meadow at a full gallop, and raced down its length to where Morallta had split the force into two groups. Loskenn was drilling the larger, cantering in column, then turning in three solid ranks that thundered gleefully across the open stretch of pasture, spears level and voices screaming. Those with Morallta were dismounted, set like a flock of roosting hens on the grass as they listened to her speak.

Everything came to a halt as the two riders thundered across the clearing, and reined to a halt. Loskenn, curious, urged his horse closer.

"Quiet!" Morallta shouted when Ficra finished her report, and a loud muttering followed. The silence came at once, something Cethen still wasn't used to. Morallta glanced up the valley to where the trail entered the field, then down to where the foot of the long clearing blended with the trees. Her green eyes glinted as they swept back again, taking in the forest on either side of the long pasture. The decision was quickly made.

"Loskenn, take a third of the troops and set them in two lines, hidden behind the trees over there." She pointed downstream to where the forest closed the bottom of the meadow. "Completely hidden! Ride out again and see for yourself that it is well done."

She turned to Ebric. "Take another third and do the same in the trees that run along the north side of the meadow. I'll take the last third into the forest across from you. Form a long, single rank, but hold a few riders back to make sure none of the enemy escape. If we can lure them even halfway down the pasture, we will all burst out, and catch them in a net."

She'd given the orders so quickly that at first no one moved. "Hurry, dammit, hurry. Get your people separated. And get back here as soon as it's done!" She turned to Borba's brother, who stood by with the reins of her sorrel. "Luath, count off my third and see they're prepared."

Cethen's spirits sank as Morallta spoke, and he grew more bitter by the moment. Loskenn and the other two moved off, leaving him sitting his horse feeling like the hind tit on a boar. He was wondering which way to go when Morallta appeared alongside.

"We have a problem," she muttered, her eyes taking in the trampled expanse of grassland. "There are tracks and horseshit all over this place. It will shy them off if they get time to look at it, and if that happens, it will be at best a poor run fight. We need bait to take their eyes away from what can be seen." Suddenly suppressing amusement, she turned to Cethen and Ficra. "It will have to be you two," she said curtly. "Strip off your clothes."

"What?" Ficra blurted. She was a small girl, tough as iron and as wiry as a weed, but now she looked horrified.

Morallta studied her face with a long, hard stare, and bit her lip. "No, I suppose that won't do," she murmured. "You're not—well, you're just *not*. Find Luath and send him here. I'll take your place. Cethen. Follow me." She swung onto her horse and looked up and down the field.

Cethen sat the chestnut, once more feeling confused, but a sliver less bitter. Loskenn and Ebric rode up and reined in alongside. Mounted riders milled about the meadow in a fury of movement, but three distinct groups were gradually taking shape. The animals seemed to sense the excitement. The rich odour of horse sweat hung in the air like an invisible mist, and the tension could almost be touched.

"Luath," Morallta cried as the twin cantered his horse over. "You will take the third group. Not me." She turned to the other two. "Cethen and I will be the bait. When I yell the order, all three forces will charge from the trees. Luath, Ebric," she pointed farther up the valley, toward the spot where the Romans were expected to enter, "the far end of your lines will close together, and trap them inside. Loskenn will charge from the south, and seal their fate. Questions?"

"When?" Ebric asked.

"I expect the two scouts to come first. Cethen and I will lure them in, then take care of them. When the rest of them arrive, they will chase us. We will lead them to Loskenn." She turned to the huge man sitting impassive astride his horse. "Be ready, but don't move until I say. Or unless we fall. Understand?"

All three voiced agreement as Cethen slowly absorbed Morallta's words. He repeated them under his breath, unsure if he understood. The two of them would take care of the scouts, she had said, the words dropping from her mouth as casually as a falling leaf. What, in the name of Dagda, did she have in mind? And the rest of it: but if we fall, go ahead. What did the woman expect from him?

"Agreed, then," she said. "We only move when all the Romans are in the clearing. And only when I say. If you see I'm unable, then use your own judgement. Understood?"

Again the low rumble of assent, and Cethen nodded, reluctant in front of the others to ask any of a dozen questions flitting through his mind.

"I need a few extra spears," Morallta cried. "Anyone?"

At least a dozen were offered, and she tucked four under one arm. Then, with a nod to Cethen, she kneed her horse forward, trailing after Loskenn's riders as he led them down the meadow. Cethen followed, his mind racing and his belly cold.

Morallta dismounted a good hundred paces upstream from where Loskenn's force melted into the trees. Cethen did the same, leaving the horses side by side, reins dragging the ground. A fever of excitement seemed to have taken hold of the Carveti woman. Her breathing had grown short, and her cheeks glowed a bright pink. The heat of battle was on her, Cethen decided, before it had even begun. That came as a shock. With himself, it took either a long warm-up by the druids, or a personal slight that picked hard at his anger.

"Strip," Morallta hissed as she unbuckled her belt. Her fingers moved to the lacings that held her tunic. Cethen stood as if rooted. "Come on, man. Come on. There isn't much time," she urged, and pulled the garment over her head.

A linen undershirt followed, and Cethen's jaw again sagged as he found himself staring at two pale, perfectly rounded breasts with just a sprinkling of freckles above their lush cleavage. Tiny goose bumps peppered her skin. Both mounds fell deliciously forward as she bent to remove her boots.

"Come on, come on, come on," she snarled, and the tone finally snapped Cethen from his torpor. He began shedding his clothes as if they were in a race.

"Into the stream," Morallta ordered when they were both naked. "Bring your weapon with you."

Cethen's whirling wits were sufficient to question which one, but his spirit too subdued to ask. He grabbed the sword and hobbled behind, cursing as his bare feet slid on the shifting gravel of the streambed. He fell, sprawling on the rocks with a painful grunt. The water was ice cold.

"Stop playing the fool and hide the sword in the grass," Morallta growled. "I'll set the spears beneath the bank." Then she stumbled and fell sideways, cursing in turn as the spears fell into the stream.

Cethen dropped his sword and lunged forward, plucking the shafts from the water. He hid them on the rocks below the grassy bank. "Shit. We should have kept our boots on," he grumbled.

Morallta giggled. The noise startled Cethen and he stared hard, wondering if she might be giving in to nervousness. Her cheeks had flushed a deeper pink, and her eyes were bright. They were totally focused, though, thank the gods. She seemed to be out of breath.

"That would look ridiculous," she said, and sniggered at the notion, "to die stark naked, but for a pair of boots."

Cethen straightened, looking to retrieve the sword, which had fallen into the water when he fell. Instinctively he moved one hand to cover his ice cold manhood.

"That's hardly worth the bother." She giggled again.

"Th-the damned water's cold," Cethen muttered, strangely embarrassed and tongue tied. He found the blade and pushed it into the grass, leaving the hilt comfortably outlined against the pale grey of a large rock.

"Lower yourself into the water so the top half of you can be seen by the scouts when they arrive," Morallta said. "It's important they see us right away, for they need distracting. They're not here yet, are they?"

Cethen glanced up the valley as he sank back in the water, but there was no sign of the Romans. When he looked back, he couldn't keep his eyes off the woman's wonderfully rounded breasts, each hovering above the water and not an arm's length away. The dark, honey-coloured nipples were small, and puckered as tight as if suckled.

"The two scouts will find us seemingly busy," Morallta said. The giggling was gone, but her speech was quick and ragged. The excitement had her firmly in its grip, Cethen realized, and wondered if it might mar her judgement. "They will likely wait and let their eyes search the trees. I don't want them to do that, for they might see something that doesn't belong."

"So what do we ...?"

"You will pretend to notice them as soon as they see us. You will panic, run for the horses, then run back for me. They'll charge as soon as they see us trying to flee. The sight will be too ripe an apple not to pluck."

Except for the panic part of it, the plan didn't sit well with Cethen, when he carefully thought the sequence through. Morallta's judgement certainly was not at fault on one point: the scouts would charge. But if *he* was a Roman bent on charging two naked Britons, one pink and gorgeous and the other tall and hairy, which would he kill first? "And then?" he asked, his mouth dry.

Cethen could see she was living the plan in her mind, for as she spoke, her words came faster and her breathing grew deeper. The prospect of danger seemed to arouse all the woman's senses. "It will be you they go for, as they will see you as the threat," she said, casually ceding his unspoken point. "You will climb on your horse, and be ready to receive them. But stay close by me."

"That's a bitch of a way to die," Cethen said involuntarily, and wondered if it was the prospect of his own death that excited her. "Stark naked, and no boots."

"Some of the tribes still fight that way," she snapped, then licked her lips.

"Not without boots," Cethen muttered with feeling.

"When the scouts close in, they will pay no attention to me. That's why you must remain close." Again Morallta's tongue ran across her lips. "I will appear to be unarmed until the last moment, then leap forward with the spears. We'll take one down as surely as murder, and in the confusion, the other will follow."

"Confusion!" Cethen glanced to the head of the clearing, finding himself as chilled on the inside as he was on the outside.

The pathway was still empty. Morallta saw him look, and decided to rise from the stream and see for herself. Her body remained facing his, her head turned to scan the trees bordering the pasture. Cethen watched in fascination as the water ran down her pale, smooth belly—there wasn't a pinch of fat on her body, except for those rigid, wonderful breasts—and into the tiny triangle of copper hair, all only a hand's grasp away.

"It's good. Not one of our people in sight," she murmured, and her hand moved absently to the dark triangle and began to scratch. No, dammit, the hand began to rub, and not half a pace from his nose. The faint scent of her womanhood drifted to him, and Cethen's eyes popped wide as the tip of her middle finger seemed to disappear.

"Do you realize," she breathed, finally sinking back down in the water, "there are close to two hundred people watching us at this moment?"

As Morallta stared at Cethen, her mouth partly open, he wondered if she was waiting for him to say something, but her breathing seemed to have grown even more laboured. He suddenly noticed that his had too, and the thought struck him like a thunderclap: *Shit! This can't be happening!*

"A Roman patrol will ride down that trail. Doesn't that send your blood racing?" she asked.

It was happening, Cethen decided, and the icy water be damned. He reached down to confirm the impossible, but found her hand was suddenly there first. She grinned in triumph, her breathing as ragged as that of a winded horse.

"Lean backward, dammit. Lean back," she gasped, "and keep your eyes on those trees."

Cethen almost whimpered as Morallta slid forward in a single lithe movement, her hips thrusting as they straddled his own. She quickly drew him inside her, urgently working her body back and forth, hard and bruising, panting and cursing with every breath. The green eyes rolled, half closed, and her mouth opened in a contorted smile.

One arm pushed hard against Cethen's chest, holding him at bay. He realized, with a start, that the gesture was for those watching. They would see only two people frolicking in the water. The woman had a grain of sense, he thought, but it was still like clinging to a raw, unbroken colt.

Morallta's laboured gasps grew louder and shorter while Cethen's mind, the saner part of his body, kept wandering to the trees as if pulled there. The wild, frantic pleasure was all hers, for the violent movement was like thrusting at a cold, wet sheath of leather. Then, in one of his many glances, he saw two riders, half hidden in the darkness of the forest where the trail entered the field. One of them was pointing.

"They're here," Cethen hissed, almost glad of the interruption. "Two of them."

"Yes, yes," she moaned, and simply moved faster. "What—what—what are they doing?"

It struck Cethen that, despite the danger, Morallta wasn't going to stop, and he found that suddenly arousing. Tremendously so. The danger, the woman, her excitement, was suddenly hot oil on a cooling fire. Before, his mind had been intent on holding on until she finished. Now he responded, madly thrusting harder, wilder, louder, and with more urgency. Amazingly, he found himself almost there. She sensed it too, and answered with a violent, thrusting burst of her own.

"They—they are pointing," he gasped.

"Yes—well—just …"

"Oh yes—just …"

A low, screeching wail began, as if something had gone terribly wrong. At first Cethen didn't know where it was coming from; then he realized Morallta was climbing to wherever she was trying to reach. A final, powerful, sobbing embrace followed as their hips clung together, bound as if by iron. Then she leapt off, leaving Cethen throbbing and bent, spewing what was left of his seed into the ice cold water.

"Quick. Stand up and notice them," she hissed between panting breaths, staring toward the head of the clearing.

"I can't stand up."

"Shit!" Morallta grabbed his scrotum and squeezed.

Cethen yelped and leapt to his feet. The pain only partially solved the problem.

"Look at them, dammit, and point."

He did, and it happened just as she had said it would. Both riders kicked their horses to a canter, and the animals loped almost casually across the field. The two men readied their spears as they came, each shifting the weapon to his right hand, but holding it easily upward at a slant.

"The sword. Pick up your sword."

Cethen grasped the hilt. Oblivious to the stones, he jumped onto the grassy bank and edged toward the horses. Glancing down, he noticed his manhood was still twice the size it should have been under the circumstance. *Perhaps three, considering the cold water.* This time it was he who almost giggled.

"Stop admiring your prick, and tend to your front," Morallta snarled.

He looked up. The two riders had seen the sword and quickened their pace. He moved to grab the chestnut's reins, but the animal had its ears pricked toward the Roman horses and shied away. Cethen cursed and followed.

"Not too far," Morallta yelled.

He glanced back and saw she was out of the water, but still close by the bank where the spears lay hidden. Or did they? "Have you got the spears ready?" he called.

She glanced down at the water. "Shit!"

Cethen muttered the same word as Morallta jumped back into the stream. Deciding that there was no reliable help in that direction, he again lunged for the chestnut. Mounted, he might stand a chance against the first rider, and if not, he could run the damned horse in circles. By then the woman might be of some use. Gadearg, though, had grown nervous at the pounding of hooves. The animal lifted its head high to clear the reins from the ground, and trotted toward the trees. The sorrel did the same.

"Shit! Shit! Shit!" Cethen almost sobbed, and glanced frantically toward the stream. All he could see was a pale pink bottom sticking up in the air. The stupid woman couldn't find the fucking spears!

He cursed Morallta, for he knew what had dislodged them, then whirled around. The lead rider was close. The man had a huge grin on his face, already savouring his victory. Or perhaps savouring the second thing he was going to do, Cethen thought, falling to a low crouch and bracing the sword in both hands. The Roman kicked his horse forward to gain speed, and lowered the spear.

A voice screamed behind him, "Down. Bend down. Low!"

Cethen cringed and crouched low; so low that he felt his belly between his thighs, and grass against his forehead. Later, he would relive the moment, and the sight he presented to Morallta, completely nude, and she standing behind with a spear. But at the time, all he could feel was ice cold fear as he waited for the blow to fall.

The Roman sensed movement over by the stream, and his eyes widened. Too late, he tried to bring his shield across, but Morallta's spear thudded solidly into his chest, just above his belly.

"To the right. Move to the right."

Cethen skittered sideways like a crab, his eyes fixed on the second rider as he spurred his horse on. The man was now alert but hesitant, suddenly unsure of his target. The spears or the sword?

A flash of pink moved off to Cethen's left, and he knew Morallta was still there. The Roman made what seemed the logical choice: the spears. There could be no turning his back on them. At the last moment he swerved away. Cethen wildly swung his sword, his long arms stretched, but the Roman was too far away. The blade grazed the man's shoulder, cut across the saddle, and sliced down the animal's belly.

The second spear hummed by his shoulder, but the trooper was ready. The point caught his shield and stuck, dragging it down. He spurred his horse forward, then just as quickly jerked savagely back on the reins. Morallta had planted the butt of the third shaft in the turf, the head angled upward. The animal stopped short, the sharp tip a hand's breadth from its chest. Its rider, unsure, pulled hard on the bit, and the horse backed away.

Cethen circled, closing in from the side as Morallta moved forward. The Roman seemed hesitant to turn and run, for his back was too ripe a target for the spear. He hefted his own weapon and reined his horse sideways, but the animal whinnied in terror and began to buck.

"It's guts are hanging," Morallta cried as entrails belched from the wound left by Cethen's wild slash. She lifted her spear and threw it hard at the beast's rump.

The horse squealed at the new terror, whirling in a tight, frantic circle. Morallta ran for the river bank to recover the remaining spear. The animal kicked wildly at the stabbing pains ripping its guts and goring its rear. The Roman tried vainly to hold on, but the last spear thudded home, catching him high in the shoulder. The man sprawled forward as his mount stumbled and pitched on its side. Cethen and Morallta were on him before his writhing body struck the dirt.

"Are you alright?" Cethen stuck the point of his sword in the ground and leaned on the hilt, gasping for air.

Morallta rested a hand on his shoulder while she caught her breath, then slowly lifted her eyes. They paused as they passed his groin. "I see you're back to normal," she said.

They both stood silent for a while, giving their blood time to cool.

"I'll put some clothes on before the rest of them arrive," Cethen said at last, then grinned. "Unless you want to try the same trick again."

Morallta started to laugh, then grasped his arm. "Look," she whispered, and inclined her head toward the top of the valley.

The troop of Roman cavalry had entered the clearing and sat motionless. The decurio, one hand shading his eyes, peered down the meadow. Cethen looked nervously for their horses, but both grazed peacefully over by the edge of the forest. The first Roman's horse was the only one close by, gently nudging its dead owner with its muzzle.

"Let's double," Cethen said, and walked carefully toward the animal.

The movement seemed to decide the decurio. His voice echoed across the meadow, and the entire troop began to gallop down the pasture. Cethen fought the temptation to run the last few paces, instead whispering soothingly to the horse. The animal seemed unconcerned, and remained steady as he reached out and grasped the reins.

"You first." Cethen helped Morallta into the saddle, then passed her the sword. She reached down with her free hand and swung him up behind. "Come on, come on," he hissed in her ear, "they're damned near here."

"I want them chasing us," she said, and turned the horse down the valley with infuriating slowness before kicking it to a canter.

Cethen held tight to her waist, his head turned backward to watch the thundering troop of horsemen. The Romans were gaining at an alarming pace. He kicked the flanks himself, and the animal broke into a gallop.

"Don't panic, we're almost there," Morallta shouted, and looked over her shoulder. "See? They're in the net. They've taken the bait. They've taken the bait!"

She threw back her head, raised the sword, and screamed, "Now, Loskenn! Now!"

For one dreadful moment, Cethen thought nothing was going to happen. The horse closed the end of the open field and started down the pathway into the forest. It was as if the two of them had been abandoned. Then the undergrowth rustled and crackled, and further back in the trees dark shapes began to move. Scores of riders spilled from the forest in two long, ragged lines, thundering upward through the pasture. The huge figure of Loskenn rode at the centre, roaring, "Keep the line straight. Keep the line straight."

Morallta turned the horse back up the trail, but when they came to the open field, she reined in. Cethen, sitting close behind, wondered why they had stopped. Morallta leaned forward as if to watch, her hands resting on the animal's withers.

"Maybe we should help," Cethen muttered, and halfheartedly made to kick the animal forward.

"No, no," she said, and absently moved her free hand against his belly to stay him. "You and I have no shields, and only one sword between us. Let our warriors earn the glory. Look, the Romans make their first mistake."

When Loskenn's force burst from the trees, the patrol had reined in as the decurio assessed the threat. When Ebric and Luath's riders burst into the clearing on either side, the troop quickly lost all direction.

"Their only chance was to hold their pace, and charge right through us—keep on going down the valley, and don't stop for sur-

vivors." Morallta seemed angry. "Damn, I should have given Loskenn
twice the number."

"But you didn't, and they held back," Cethen said. "Look."

"Yes, yes, they did." She leaned forward again. "Look at them.
Look at Loskenn. By the gods, look at that one there ..."

Cethen felt her intake of breath through the hands that clutched
her narrow waist. Morallta called every blow as it struck, and the death
of every Roman as he fell, her voice rising to a fever pitch. Each crash of
a sword or thrust of a spear seemed to make her squirm, and the velvet
warmth of her pink rear rubbed back and forth against his groin.

Even so, he almost toppled from the horse when her hand dropped
the sword, slid down his belly, and once more grasped his manhood.
She glanced quickly over one shoulder with her mouth half open and
her eyes half closed. Bracing herself on the pommel, she eased over the
back of the saddle and down again, uttering a long, drawn-out moan
as Cethen once more slid inside her.

His hands slid carefully upward to clasp her breasts, then quickly
down again as he began to lose balance. Instead, he clung to the soft,
rhythmically twisting hips, which were close to the rigid safety of the
cantle should it be needed.

The battle was almost over when Morallta's body heaved with
a great shudder. She sighed, and without a word slid forward again.
Almost immediately, hooves pounded the trail behind. Alarmed,
Cethen turned his head.

Dermat reined his horse in alongside, his dour features split in an
enormous grin as he stared out across the littered battlefield. "You get
a lovely view from here, don't you?" he said cheerfully.

Chapter XX

Cartimandua shivered and leaned back against the wall of the barracks, wrapping her cloak tight about her shoulders. The evenings were fast growing cold, and the small pleasure to be found sitting under the covered porch-way as the sun fell across the Abus would soon end.

Gaius studied her features, cynically wondering if she sat there for the sake of the crimson twilight, or the chance of eavesdropping on words from the headquarters building next door. Even so, time spent lingering was pleasant enough, for the bard Criff's soft tunes soothed, and the talk often intrigued. He was grateful that she hardly ever raised the matter of his wife, or of the brief coupling by the Fosse. The barbarian queen was never, however, short of subject matter.

"Your problem is, you've acquired a she-wolf that you're trying to turn into a lap dog," she suggested one evening, yawning as if the matter was of little interest.

"She's a slave. You don't want she-wolves for slaves," Gaius replied, no longer bothering to question the source of her information—at least where it concerned his private life, which was growing increasingly tense. On this particular issue, Cartimandua's arrow fell far wide of the target. Elena was anything but a lap dog.

"Perhaps not. But I don't think you want a drooling, tail-wagging house hound, either." Cartimandua said, seeming pleased with her analogy. "Not on an ongoing basis, anyway. Take a horse, for example.

You may want to ride it, but you certainly don't want to kill its spirit."

"I'm not riding it, dammit," Gaius growled, and took a long sip at his wine; the liquid had been heated and spiced, and he cupped his hands around the warmth. "And I'm not trying to, either."

"Then what did you get *it* for?" Cartimandua asked, archly emphasizing the word.

"I told you before, I got *it* because *it* asked me to prevent her daughter from being sold off to some greasy Alexandrian whoremonger."

"You could have done that without keeping the mother. It's not as if they were sold as a matching set," Cartimandua said, amused by his discomfort. "And I'm surprised she knows about Alexandrian whoremongers, greasy or otherwise."

"My words, not hers," Gaius sighed. "For all I know, the woman knows nothing about anything. She barely talks—surly as a whipped cur. Only she's not been whipped. Perhaps it's about time it was done."

"And her surliness bothers you?" She chuckled. "It shouldn't. She's just a slave."

"Exactly why it should bother me," Gaius said, and then laughed bitterly. "I mean, it's not as if I was married to the woman, is it? Then I might expect it."

One moody woman had been bad enough, and now there were two. Gaius often brooded on that of late. The main problem was living inside the fortress. If she'd been on his brother's estates in Italia, Elena would have melted in with the other slaves. Or would she? Wherever she was, the woman stood out like Rufus in a herd of barbarian ponies. And that was another matter that rankled—he missed his horse!

He was going to have to do something about the woman, though. She was making his life miserable. She'd shown no gratitude for what he'd done for her daughter, and he'd expected none; and using the girl as a hostage was only reasonable, was it not? After all, it permitted the woman to remain relatively unconfined, as long as she remained inside the walls. And she well knew her other choice: a consignment abroad, possibly to the brothels. That would prove a brutal lesson, though the bidding would be low at her age—or perhaps not. The woman had a good deal of appeal, even though she was certainly less marketable than the daughter. The *procurator* had wielded a sharp blade on that one!

He'd been shocked at the depth of Elena's hostility, the day before her daughter had been taken to Lindum. Metellus had brought her to his quarters that evening, wearing the same bloody, tattered clothes she'd been wearing when captured. A stale, unwashed odour had filled the small room. The woman's face was grimy, and her hair hung in loose, oily strands across her face. Yet she stood defiant, her head held high.

Gaius had been seated, and deliberately remained that way. He leaned back against the wall, set his feet on the low table in the centre of the room, and peered down his nose. The pose was meant to annoy, and the clench of her jaw showed that it did.

"The girl is safe," he finally said. Criff, standing by the door, translated the words with no trace of expression. When there was no response, Gaius added, "She will be with my own daughter."

The grimy features remained impassive, so he spoke again. "She is at Lindum. No harm will be done to her."

Elena finally nodded her understanding but remained infuriatingly quiet. Gaius raised his voice in irritation, and Criff raised his eyebrows. "That is, no harm will be done her as long as you stay here. If you flee, she will be sold. And I don't care where. Do you understand what that would mean? Where she would go then?"

Again the nod, and she finally spoke. "For this I am to give thanks?"

He pondered the question, then quite seriously said, "Yes. You probably should. Had I not paid good money for her, very good money, she would be in chains and on her way over the sea."

"You got good value for your money," Elena sneered.

"Certainly. And I could make a good profit if I sent her to Rome and sold her!" Gaius barked, allowing his anger to show, and turned to Metellus. "Wine, dammit. I could use some wine."

The slave bobbed his head and busied himself at the side table; the moment dragged on, the gurgle of the liquid the only sound in the room. He returned carrying three goblets. He handed one to his master, one to Criff, who raised it and winked at the slave, and set the other on the table.

Gaius glared at the third goblet, then at Metellus, and was about to curse the man for his presumption, then stopped. He recalled the cool mugs of dark ale that had been set before him each night in that crude hut at Stannick. Was his own slave, who must have overheard the story several times, sending him a subtle reminder? Perhaps. Yet he couldn't bring himself to tell the woman to pick up the wine and drink it. Instead, he sipped slowly at his own. Criff solved the problem by handing the goblet to Elena, who drained half in one gulp.

"You will serve the officers' mess," he said, and waited for the translation. The word came out as "barracks-house" instead of "mess", for Criff was unable to find the right word, and he mixed up the others.

Elena curled her lip and threw the goblet at Gaius, barely missing his head. Slamming his feet to the ground, he rose and lurched toward her; she fell to a crouch, a low growl rumbling in her throat. Criff cried out in alarm and threw himself between the two, waving his arms in agitation as he spoke rapidly back and forth, some in her tongue, some in his.

Gaius hesitated as some of the words penetrated his flaring temper. "She what?" he asked, and Criff managed to explain the misunderstanding.

"Shit," Gaius said in disgust, and sank back into the chair. "Tell the stupid bitch what a mess is. And tell her that serving means she has help give out the food and drink, and clean up. I'm not sending her to be *used*. And tell her if she thinks every officer in the Ninth lives only to plough a barbarian woman, then she's deluding herself." He gestured to Metellus for more wine, and muttered under his breath, "And I'll have the balls of any bastard that tries."

Elena rose warily to her feet as Criff translated, including the final comment. When he finished, she resumed her sullen stance. Gaius groaned. The pose was hauntingly familiar. "Metellus, arrange to have her bathed, then find her some clothes. Those look more fit for a hog pen. In fact, they stink as if they've been there. Try the quartermaster; he'll have cloth and thread. In the meantime, the barbarian queen might be of help."

Metellus nodded and made to leave, but Gaius stopped him. "You can pour her another glass of wine on the way out."

The slave filled another goblet and held it out to Elena. Criff spoke, his voice quiet and persuasive, and she reluctantly took it. She cupped it in her hand, not drinking. Again Criff spoke, this time his tone flippant and amused. Elena stared at him, then smiled, shrugged, and took a sip of the wine.

"You are correct," she said slowly in broken Latin before taking a longer drink, her words meant for Gaius rather than Criff. "It is good. I *would* be the one to suffer if I let it go to waste."

She turned her eyes to Gaius, staring at him with an expression bordering on contempt—or perhaps simply disdain. Whatever it was, over the following weeks the woman learned to balance it perfectly. While 'The Look' did not cross the line, it bordered heavily on insolence. And Elena kept it that way, along with a surliness that simmered, but never boiled.

Eventually, the mere sight of her dull, glowering features was enough to plunge him into a similar sour mood. Yet there was nothing else, really, for which he could fault the woman. She performed whatever task she was given, usually well. In fact, quite well, which led to another matter that rankled of late, for no good reason other than knowing it was intended. When she worked in the officers' mess, the bitch could be downright pleasant—to everyone but Gaius.

"I *asked*," Cartimandua said, breaking into his sudden fit of brooding, "since you raised the subject of marriage, how matters stand with the other bane in your life—if I can hold your attention long enough to have you tell me." She flashed the same malicious smirk he had seen before being tumbled into the Fosse. "You do seem to have trouble with your womenfolk, don't you?"

"Ha!" Gaius muttered, gathering his wits. Criff had broken into a soft lullaby, or perhaps a love song. "That one is more a problem than even you can conceive. She will be leaving Lindum at the end of the month to go home for the winter. I doubt she will return next year, after what happened."

"Doubt? I thought she said she was never coming back."

"Only a thousand times. Which is why I say I *doubt* she'll return." Gaius laughed. "Helvia never tells the truth."

"Is she taking the woman's daughter with her?"

"I suppose so. What else can be done? The girl certainly can't come to Ebor. If I placed mother and daughter together, they'd fly so fast, they'd beat a hawk to the horizon."

"So what does she say about her daughter going?"

"Huh?"

"You amaze me, Roman," Cartimandua sighed, shaking her head. "You haven't told the woman her daughter is going to Italia?"

"Never thought about it," Gaius muttered, and ran his fingers across his chin. "I suppose I should. Sometime."

"I wouldn't doubt she has some idea. The slave Metellus, for example; he talks to her?"

"Yes, but I doubt he'd say anything."

Cartimandua clucked at him. "He wouldn't have to." Again she slowly shook her head. "The woman isn't stupid—you should know that by now. If she knows your family is going to Italia, then she knows it's likely her daughter will be going too." Cartimandua paused to draw a deep, despairing breath. "Men! Have you talked to her about the girl at all? Ever?"

"Why should I?" Gaius shrugged, then said indifferently, "She's never asked."

"Roman, from you, I doubt she would ask for a drop of water, if she were dying of thirst." Cartimandua snorted. "And you wonder why she's sullen."

"I haven't treated her badly," Gaius retorted, his annoyance growing.

"What are your plans this winter?" Cartimandua asked, seemingly changing the subject. She rose from her seat as if ready to leave, wrapping the cloak tighter for its warmth.

"If everything's quiet, I was thinking of taking winter leave myself this year," Gaius said, and frowned, for he was as yet unsure. "If I did, it would probably be sometime in November. It's been a while since I've been back home, and with Vespasian wearing the purple, matters may have changed."

"Then you might consider taking Elena with you. It would almost certainly cure the problems you seem to find in her."

"To Rome?" Gaius said, startled.

"Unless you are going somewhere else."

"Out of the question," he said, for such an idea was absurd. "Besides, Metellus and I would be going overland at the same pace as the dispatch riders. She's a only a woman. She couldn't ..."

Cartimandua smiled as Gaius's voice faded, for he knew full well the 'woman' could probably ride at least as well as he could. She opened the door and disappeared into the barracks, but not before tossing off a final dart that was left to find its own mark.

"If you don't take her, you can always leave her working in the officer's mess."

Gaius watched with ill-concealed amusement as Elena moaned, her glistening skin the colour of chalk. A thread of bile drooled past her lips, only to be plucked away by an ice-cold gust of the north wind. He knew her stomach had long since given up anything that lay on it, and suspected that, if offered the choice, she might cheerfully have died. She had no energy remaining to lean over the rail of the tossing ship, and instead sat huddled on a pile of cordage at the foot of the mast, head bowed low over a bucket.

"I can see *Gesoriacum*," Gaius cheerfully shouted over the creaking roar that filled the ship's deck. The Gallic port lay directly ahead, almost lost in the mist of bow spray, the drizzling rain, and a sea of windblown whitecaps. "It won't be long now. Later this afternoon!"

Elena heaved, clutching the slick wooden pail tighter between her knees. She mouthed two words that he could not hear, but which he certainly understood. They simply caused his grin to widen. Gaius found enormous satisfaction in finally seeing the woman's hard, unbending countenance sink to a pliant weakness, even if took the might of Neptune to do it.

Elena had grown ill even before the ship left the waters off Petuaria, where the estuary flowed calmly down to the sea. The passage down the east coast had been fast, for a following north wind blew them most of the way, easing the vessel's constant pitching. Even so, the first rolling wave emptied her stomach, and every succeeding swell kept it that way. By the time they reached the heavy chop of the ocean channel, the woman was in a pitiful state, far worse than the evening Metellus had brought her to his quarters.

The slave seemed to have grown attached to the woman, though by race they were as different as stag and hound. Metellus had been taken from the Parthians as a child, two decades before, and had no idea where his ancestry lay. Certainly in the east, for his skin was a rich olive, and his hair black as jet. His time in Britannia had given him yet another language, and he knelt beside Elena's hunched form, offering words of comfort. Gaius doubted she heard them.

He looked from the two soaked figures to the coastline. The ship would soon make landfall, and her recovery would be quick. He had seen it often enough, though Elena had been far sicker than most. He had not thought to warn her of the malady, though doing so would have done little good. Besides, the idea that such a crack might appear in her armour had never occurred to him. That stolid control had been constant, and especially rigid when told where she would be going. Yet it was also the first time Gaius had seen it soften, even if for only a moment.

"We will be leaving for Rome in about a month," he had said. "Your daughter departed a week ago, with my wife."

Gaius sat in the same chair as when Elena had first been brought to him, filthy and stinking from the pens; she again stood before him with the same impassive stare. At least this time, he thought, she looked presentable. Her sleek, honeyed hair was combed and wound into braids, which she had brought forward to circle her head like a crown. Her skin had a fresh glow, and she wore a calf length *stola* of dark green cloth, presumably a hand-off from Cartimandua. It had certainly not found its roots in the quartermaster's stores. A faint perfume hung in the air—a fresh, garden-like scent.

Elena nodded to acknowledge the information, but otherwise said nothing. Gaius grew instantly annoyed, as usual, but this time decided he was in no mood to take any more of the glowering silence. He waved his hand, angrily dismissing her. "Fine, then! Just go. You'll be told it's time on the day we depart," he snapped, then muttered under his breath, "Miserable, troublesome bitch."

By this time, both understood a good deal of the other's words, and when spoken aloud, they were deliberately intended for hearing. Losing his temper was a weakness, Gaius knew, but dismissing her with nothing more to go on than an expletive was worth its loss. He rose, turned his back to her, and poured himself a goblet of wine, instantly annoyed that Metellus was not there to do it—but then, he had sent the slave away. He drained half the goblet, waiting for the sound of the closing door. It never came. Instead, to his surprise, she spoke.

"Coira—will I see her there?" she asked, her voice still sullen.

"Of course you will, you stupid—" Gaius caught himself and assumed the same indifferent tone that each had grown accustomed to. "She will be there."

"Do you intend to sell us both, then?"

The question was a further surprise, but Gaius was too annoyed to totally deny it; in fact, it provided opportunity for a further threat. "Not Coira, certainly. My daughter seems quite taken with her. You, however, are another matter. Your attitude offers no reason for keeping you. I'm forced to draw the conclusion that being sold elsewhere is precisely what you wish."

Elena ignored the invitation to deny the statement. "Will we remain there when you return?"

Gaius hesitated, weighing whether or not he should reply, but the question set his mind to wandering. What would he do the following spring? The girl Coira would probably stay, but what about Elena? Would he bring her back? Which led to the other problem that had to be faced when he arrived in Rome: Helvia. Despite the cooling of the marriage, the barbarian woman would have to be explained. Damn Cartimandua and her meddling! Perhaps he might claim he had bought her as a mate for Metellus. Gaius grunted aloud. That thought suddenly struck him as distasteful, though his mind didn't explore why.

"Not unless my posting is changed, but I don't expect it to be."

"Posting?"

"If I come back here, and if you are not sold, then no, you won't remain in Rome," he said with exaggerated patience, deliberately omitting Coira's name.

Elena thought the matter over, then asked, "How far is Rome?"

"A thousand miles," Gaius said carelessly, then, seeing her blank expression added, "Much, much farther than the length of Britannia itself. Yet there are good roads across Gaul, all the way to Rome. We will travel fast once we land there, changing horses as we go. At the most, three weeks. If you can keep up."

She grunted as if the idea of not keeping up was beneath her. Her next question came in a tone that was at least neutral. "Perhaps, before we leave, you might tell me what it will be like?"

Both the weather and the roads improved as they rode south, travelling light, and resting at any of a hundred inns, forts, and outposts along the way. The closer they rode to Rome, the more Elena was filled with wonder. She gaped at the sprawl of the cities, which grew larger, the farther they travelled. She stared at the marvel of temples and amphitheatres, paved roads and stone walls, tall aqueducts and towering, snow-capped mountains. And at the end of the day, when Gaius turned her over to their care, she revelled in the ever-present bathhouses.

When they finally rode into the great city itself, crossing the Aemulius Bridge into a huge forum filled with chattering, teeming crowds of people, Elena was awestruck. They rode slowly past shops and markets crammed with goods she had never seen before, sold by people she hadn't even known existed.

Gaius led their small procession on past the enormous length of the great Circus Maximus, then under the lofty arches of two huge stone aqueducts, and onto the Appian Way that led south to the family home. The journey had taken them through only a fraction of the massive city. The surrounding hills, packed with endless rows of buildings, loomed up on all sides as vast, unexplored wonders. Rome was the most awe-inspiring and, at the same time, the most unsettling vision Elena had ever seen.

Gaius explained it all with the pride of Roman ownership, yet pretended indifference in the telling. His own unsettling vision waited when the tired travellers arrived at the family estate, on the slopes above Aricia. Helvia greeted him with a belly as ripe as an Autumn melon. He asked the inevitable question, counted backward on his fingers, and decided the timing might well be called by a throw of dice. Provided, he thought glumly, the same dice were not already loaded. It was, after all, Helvia who had provided the due date. An astute gambler might wager on an early birth. He remembered the old adage: babies usually take nine months to arrive, but the first may come at any time. The trouble was, this was the third.

Chapter XXI

Tests! Quests! They were well and good in the telling, Cethen brooded, but such deeds were best performed by heroes and ancestors. He didn't consider himself one of the former, and was in no hurry to join ranks with the latter. The Carveti woman had kept them hopping like rabbits all winter with patrols, practice, and mock fights on the slopes outside the fortress, and they were fit to drop. Now she wanted them to prove themselves.

"Get bloodied," she had called it. "I want heads. The old man wants heads. A half-dozen from each troop!" And the long-haired, heavily whiskered heads of the Roman auxiliaries were not good enough, she added. She wanted the close-cropped skulls of the legion infantry. As if the difference mattered!

She decided Cethen would lead two troops, nearly sixty in all. Reluctantly accepting the inevitable, he had asked for the territory around the Roman fortress that now stood in place of his village, for it was familiar. There were places to hide that the enemy did not know existed, and Morallta had agreed, adding that it only made sense. Cethen had then asked for the twins, Borba and Luath, and she had agreed to that as well. Lately she seemed ready to agree to most of what he asked. It was probably due to her condition. Or possibly because she was finally warming to him as her belly grew larger, though she had yet to acknowledge he was the cause.

340

In fact—and it was a sore point—when it came to that side of her life, she hardly bothered to acknowledge him at all. Her disposition remained as cool as a mountain stream. She'd shown no further interest—not carnal, anyway—which left him baffled. It seemed that only the mind-boggling danger of battle, or seeing men slaughtered by the score, aroused the woman. And if that was the way of it, Cethen didn't think his heart would stand another such ploughing. Though looking back on it …well, there had never been anything quite like it.

Nuada became moody when he told her he was leaving for a few weeks, which surprised him. The bond that bound them together had grown out of need, rather than the lust and love that had tied her to his brother. She tended the children, looked after the food, and took care of the small lodge; he provided the means to do so. She had other needs as well, of course, as did he, and he tried his best to satisfy those, too. For the most part he succeeded, but there were times, usually late at night, when the memory of his lost brother gained new levels of respect.

"If we get to Bran's Beck, I'll look around a bit more," Cethen had promised the morning he left, hoping to lift her from her moping, "see if I can at least find trace of what happened to them."

"And if *you* don't come back?" Nuada demanded.

"Cheerful bugger," he muttered with a lopsided grin.

"He's coming back," Rhun said firmly. He sat on one of the hides strewn by the table, his ears and eyes following the bickering.

"That's what Cian said," she grumbled, her words meant for Cethen.

"In a few weeks. I promise." He turned to Rhun. "You look after everyone while I'm gone, son. And bide by what Nuada tells you."

Rhun nodded solemnly, ready to assume the burden, though he was no longer quick to ask his father if he might ride with him. Cethen knew the bloody, hard-fought battle at Bran's Beck had stayed on his mind, especially the time that followed: the panicked flight from the battlefield pulling the big chestnut; the night and day spent anxiously waiting for his father by the river; the wounded and the dying struggling by in endless procession. When Cethen found him, he'd been sitting the pony with an expression that clearly revealed the gut-twisting panic inside. He'd greeted his father with a relief that told Cethen he was convinced his da would not return.

That, and the sight of full-grown men hacking each other apart on the battlefield, had taught Rhun caution. Yet the boy had not withdrawn inside it—every day he joined others his age in the walled part of the fortress, where the older warriors taught the youngsters how to fight. Cethen was often there, watching the process with a newfound disdain, and telling Rhun that the old warriors were simply teaching the same old mistakes. But for the time being he let it go on; the discipline taught by Vellocatus and Morallta would come later.

"A lass like you will have no trouble finding another," Cethen told Nuada, finally answering her question when they were alone outside the hut. Her ill humour was drawing him into the same bitter cauldron.

"I'm sure," she carped, "and look where it'll leave me. If the next bugger has five brats himself, that will be ten I'm looking after. I'll be a hunched crone before my time."

"Rhun's no bother," Cethen retorted, feeling he deserved a better send-off than this, "and Tuis can help. He's getting old enough. And anyway ..." he swung into the saddle, where he paused for a moment and sat slowly counting his fingers " ...if the next bugger has five, that'll make nine, not ten."

He started the chestnut on its way feeling pleased with the calculation, then suddenly reined in and turned to stare at Nuada. She gazed balefully back, her arms crossed over her chest.

"Ten?"

"At least."

"Aw, shit!"

Nuada showed no inclination to say more. Annoyed, Cethen dug his heels into the chestnut's belly and cantered off to meet the twins and their riders. It was the woman's own fault, dammit; she had no reason to whine. She was always at it, wouldn't leave him alone, sometimes. Look what it had got her!

And what had it got him? Now he had two of them baking bairns at the same time. Two! He shook his head, then a moment later shook it again, and chuckled. Two! In separate pots, yet! That was surely something. By the gods, Elena would kill him. That thought was instinctive, and immediately followed by regret. She would have killed him for certain—if only she were alive.

Cethen took the same path south that Morallta had taken the previous autumn. They rode along the great, treeless ridge of hills that broke Brigantia in two. Winter still clung to the north slopes of the valleys in the shape of wind-carved snow banks, that hid the gullies and ravines under a heavy crust of drifts. Yet here and there, the green of early spring bravely forced its way through, wherever the earth had blown clear.

He rode much farther than Morallta had, the week they ambushed the Roman patrol, intending to circle back on the fortress from the southwest. The path offered a safer prospect. Over winter, the Romans had turned the track from his old village to Isurium into a well-travelled road, much too dangerous to use. Even the trail north from there now belonged as much to them as to Venutius. Yet Cethen had another reason. A small village he wanted to visit, a settlement much like his own, lay in that direction. It was home to the Cloghan, a people named for the stones that crossed the river there. Kemoc was head of the kin, and might offer information.

Yet when they neared the tiny village several days later, approaching from the cover of the forest, Cethen saw immediately that something was wrong. Most of the huts had been burned, including the largest where Kemoc once lived. It had happened some time ago, for the wind no longer held the bitter scent of charred wood. The few pens that remained were empty of livestock, and at first glance the village appeared abandoned. Then Borba pointed to a faint wisp of smoke drifting from two of the smallest huts, close by the river.

Cethen rode cautiously up on the rear of the small settlement, drawing his sword as he closed on the back of the huts. He called a warning, and a few moments later the stooped figure of a woman peered fearfully around the side of the building, two children clinging to her skirts. For a moment Cethen didn't recognize the wizened features, for Kemoc's wife had aged far beyond her years.

"Alva?" he finally asked, though it had to be her.

"Who is it?" the woman quavered, and stepped into the open.

"Cethen. Of the Eburi. What happened here?"

He swung down from the saddle, and when she stumbled forward, he lifted her up and clutched her against his chest. She started to cry. After a few moments she looked up, squinting through a white scale that mottled her eyes. The tears ran freely down both cheeks, and Cethen brushed them away with his fingers.

"Easy lass," he murmured, staring over her shoulder at the two children standing uncertainly under the eave of the rotting thatch. "Whose are the bairns?"

"My son's, but he's gone. So is Kemoc. Cethen, they're all gone."

"Where?" he asked, though he was certain of the answer.

"Before winter. They took everyone who was strong. The few they didn't want, they let be. Unless," her fingers moved by reflex to an angry red scar that crossed her cheekbone, "unless they tried to stop them."

"Everyone's gone?"

"Some fled—those who could." She looked anxiously over her shoulder. "Perhaps you should come inside. The Romans have placed us on a path to somewhere. Small armies of them often come through."

He demurred. "No, Alva. I'm less trapped in the open. If anyone comes, I'm sure we'll hear them first."

Cethen glanced toward the river, where the main track passed through the middle of the settlement. It was muddy, and churned by heavy use. He edged over for a closer look, and saw it had been gouged deep by the passage of shod hooves, many of them fresh. "When was the last time they passed here?"

"Yesterday. In the morning," a new voice answered.

Cethen turned, startled. A boy stood by the hut, a young lad probably the same age as Rhun. "You are?" he demanded.

"Ilbric."

"And how did you escape the Romans, Ilbric?"

"I was upriver, toward the falls. Tending cows."

"Your mam? Your da?"

"They took Mam, but Da was killed. He tried to fight them."

He spoke the words in a dull, matter-of-fact way that brought a lump to Cethen's throat. The boy could have been Rhun, using the same hard self-control to tell the same tale about his own da. "How many came through the other day?" he asked.

"Over a hundred. There was a proud-looking pig riding in front, with armour on his chest that shone like brass. They came from that way." Ilbric pointed westward, toward a distant shadow of hills.

Alva spoke. "Since spring started to show, they've been coming and going like rabbits on a run. Mostly a few at a time. Sometimes they drag extra horses."

Those would be messengers, Cethen thought, pulling at his moustache. That was probably where to find the heads that Morallta was set on getting—at least a couple of them. More, if they were lucky. She'd also said Venutius wanted to know what was happening at the fortress itself, which was almost a half-day's ride farther.

"Things will change, Alva, things will change," he murmured, trying to offer comfort.

"Will they, Cethen?" Alva's voice actually held a quaver of hope.

"They will, lass, they will. I'm riding in that direction," Cethen lied, nodding westward to where the Romans had come from. His eyes caught a stone pillar standing beyond the last hut. "What is that?"

Ilbric answered, "The Romans put it there, and told us anyone that moves it would be killed."

"That still doesn't tell me what it is."

"They carved what they call us on it," Alva muttered. "The soldier said this place is known as *Calcaria*."

"Bastards." Ilbric spat. "They won't even let us keep our own names."

"If I hadn't seen Stannick, I would have thought this place huge," Innsa breathed, staring down on the fortress.

"When I left here a year ago, my home was right in the middle of it," Cethen said wistfully, but he couldn't decide where. The stronghold was crammed with wooden buildings, some large and some small. A grid of roads crisscrossed the inside, and neat rows of tents were set up in the few open spaces remaining in between.

"It is huge," Ligan, Luath's second-in-command, muttered in awe.

"The Romans are busy," Borba observed, pointing to the field east of the fortress.

The pasture had been enlarged and cleared, except for a thin belt of trees that lined the winding banks of the Fosse. Row upon row of stakes had been pounded into the open field and hundreds of soldiers were hacking at them, presumably at sword drill. Elsewhere, troops were marching in formation, wheeling and turning without pause.

The four were across the river from the fortress, kneeling behind a tangle of flotsam left by a bygone flood. It lay in the cover of the trees, a few paces back from a long meadow that ran along the south bank of the Abus. Luath, too, had wanted to come, and was irked when Cethen had selected his brother instead; but Borba had won by drawing the longer stick, and the bickering was only halfhearted.

"Their ships are huge," Innsa said. She was from Borba's troop, a dark, attractive woman of the Carvetii tribe who reminded him of Nuada. Lately, any woman with hard opinions and a flash to her eyes seemed to remind him of Nuada. He hoped the choice wasn't a reflection on Borba's judgement.

"They're bringing in all sorts of scurfy trash," Ligan muttered, eyeing the supplies packed into the grassy area between the fort and the river.

"Aye, they're planning something," Borba said, then sneered, "The fools think they're here to stay."

Cethen studied the meadow immediately in front of them with a dull ache of familiarity. Their hiding place lay on the southern, inside bank of the river's curve. Off to their right, the field ran straight, following the river itself. Only an abandoned log hut remained standing, about two hundred paces off to the left, close by the road that led to the ford. It had probably been left there as a shelter of convenience. Almost directly below them, the Romans had set up a raft-like ferry; though the ford was clearly still preferred when the water ran low. It had been used all afternoon, while the ferry sat idle.

"Are we going to use that?" Innsa asked, seeing Cethen's eyes fall on the building.

"Why?" Ligan asked. "We can see all we need to see from here."

Cethen was about to agree, impressed with the lad's levelheaded-ness, when Borba offered his opinion. "There's no glory in that. Anyone can hide in the woods like a rabbit. Down there, we'll be closer. We could probably listen to them as they ride by tomorrow. I can hear the telling of the tale now."

"The bugger even acts like Cian," Cethen murmured to himself, then said, "Aye. The tale will be named 'The Beheading of Borba the Blue.'"

Borba had been given the name "Blue" for the cloth ribbon he wore around his neck. His brother Luath had been given a red one. At first the twins had worn them so others could tell the pair apart, then Luath's entire troop, followed quickly by Borba's, took to wearing rib-bons of the same colour. Morallta was at first irked by the gesture, then noticed the effect that such a small emblem had on the spirit of the two units. Subtle hints were given to the others, and now each troop wore tokens to set its members apart from others.

Borba grinned. "That does have a fine ring to it, no?"

Cethen snorted. "Only to your grandchildren. Ligan has a good point. I fail to see how being a couple hundred paces closer will help. If we did hear anything, we couldn't understand it anyway."

"But it would be a brave thing to do," Innsa enthused, and Borba grinned again.

"Haven't you learned anything these past months, woman?" Cethen demanded irritably. "What of the words of Morallta, your own chieftain? We are trained to carry out orders, just as the Romans are. Not to run off doing things that are brave."

There was a long, chastened silence, then Borba spoke. "So we don't do anything brave?"

"That's not what I said—not what I meant."

"Then we should go and see what's in there, then."

Cethen sighed. "We'll see."

By the time it grew dark, the pair's nagging was eroding his will. They would go down later, he finally agreed, after midnight, when the sky was black, but just for a quick look around. As Borba pointed out—more than once—there might be something of use inside. Besides, he knew the family that had lived there; they were kin and had made the trek to Stannick. Any small item he might take back would be of value, if not to him, then at least to them.

Cethen decided it was best to take Borba with him to the hut. The decision was not due to the twin's constant harping, but rather because of Ligan's common sense. He felt more comfortable leaving the younger man in the trees as a backup. The twin would be a stalwart reserve, certainly, but he still seemed prone to impulse. Not only that, if he was as much like Cian as he seemed, then he was probably randier than a humpbacked wolf hound. The idea of leaving him alone in the dark with Innsa, who had been goading him all day, was simply plain stupid.

The pair entered the hut well past midnight, both doubly nervous: there were a thousand Romans to worry about, plus the countless demons of the forest. Nobody really believed in the demons, of course, but they still had half the night left in which to prowl.

The door creaked shut and both men paused, testing the air inside the small building. It should have stunk of must and staleness, but it didn't. Their eyes adjusted slowly—at least for one of them; Cethen found it difficult to see; Borba seemed to have little problem.

"There's a loft," he whispered, and made his way across the dirt floor.

Cethen followed and banged his knee against something that crashed to the ground. He cursed, then followed Borba up the ladder to what had been the children's sleeping area—there were several small cots with rope mattresses woven across the rough frames, still holding bits of bedding.

"Here, let's take this out," Borba said, and began tearing at the boards that shuttered a small, square opening cut into the end wall just below the roof pole.

"What are you doing?" Cethen asked, deciding that Borba had the eyes of a cat.

"Come here and look at this."

Cethen slid across the loft and put his head to the opening. It was lighter outside, but only when compared to the tar-like blackness inside. The river was off to his right; he could feel the cool chill of its presence. At first he saw nothing, then he made out a thin, grey ripple where the water tumbled over the ford and, as if by magic, heard the low, rushing gurgle of its passing. "A good view of the crossing," he said, "but so what? As Ligan pointed out—"

"But here. Look here." Borba edged over to where the sloping roof met the floor of the loft. He pulled at the reeds, slicing at the binding with his knife. Cethen joined him as the hole grew larger, though the twin kept it screened from the outside with a thin curtain of thatch.

"I can't see a damned thing," Cethen complained, "and again, so what? When it gets light, we'll be able to view the fortress from five hundred paces rather than a thousand. It makes little difference."

"Ah, but the thrill. It gets you right here." Borba clasped some part of his body that Cethen couldn't see, nor did he want to.

"I know. I know," Cethen lied. "It gets me like that, too. But that's not why we're here. Anyway, I don't want to go all day without food and water. We've seen the place. It's a good spot. Now let's go."

"Ah, thirsty are you? Stay here." Borba scuttled down the steps and soon returned to press an earthen jar into Cethen's hands. "There's a whole row of them," he said. "Inside, just behind the door. I noticed them when we came in."

Eyes like a cat! Borba had picked out the jugs and Cethen had not even seen whatever it was he had tripped over—even after he tripped. His hands grasped the rough pottery flask which was stopped, from the feel of it, by a bung and beeswax. It wasn't the sort of thing that would have been left by those who had once lived there. He cut away the seal and pried the bung loose. It was wine, and not a bad one, either.

"Here." Borba fumbled with his leather pouch and produced a rock-hard barley cake. "Chew on that. They go well together."

Cethen knew what was happening. The twin was biding his time, hoping to remain until it was too late to leave, and they would have to stay there all day. That was not going to happen. A quick drink, something to eat, and they would be on their way. And it wasn't going to be much longer, for when he next peered through the hole in the thatch, the dark outline of the fortress was beginning to form in the night shadows.

"Gather what you have," Cethen said, stuffing the balance of the cake in his mouth, "we're leaving."

He turned away from the small hole, then stopped at a muffled sound—a single set of footsteps approaching from the direction of the river. He grabbed Borba's arm, and peered out through the hole in the thatch. A bent, cowled figure materialized from the darkness not ten paces from the hut, walking straight toward the door. When it got there, it did not come in. Instead it remained outside, as if guarding the small building.

"Shit, we've been seen," Cethen whispered. "There's someone outside the door."

"Only one?"

"Yes."

"Then let's kill him," Borba said, moving toward the ladder, "before others begin to—"

Borba had barely started down the wood ladder when they heard another sound, this one from the direction of the ford. At first it sounded terrifying, as if a whole troop of cavalry approached. They edged nervously back across the loft, and peered out. Only Borba was able to distinguish what was galloping through the darkness: a single rider cantering his horse down the pasture. But behind him, like a stallion leading his mares, two strings of horses followed, a half-dozen to each.

Cethen finally saw the rider for himself as he drew close to the hut: a huge man, almost a giant, who sat his horse as if it were a hill pony. He dismounted, almost stepping from its back, and began releasing the animals, one by one. The figure outside the door moved to help, and the small herd was soon grazing peacefully alongside the hut, each horse dragging a length of rope from its halter. There were only two men, and more than a dozen horses. And the night was still fairly dark....

"Do you have the same thoughts as I?" Borba whispered.

Cethen grin was as wide as Borba's. "If we can get the animals to the trees before daylight, the four of us can take them from there. It would work out to ..."

"About three each," Borba murmured as Cethen ran his thumb across his fingers. "It can be done. What are they doing?"

"They've gone," Cethen whispered in alarm, then heard someone outside the door. "Quiet, they're coming in."

"Even better," Borba hissed, and slithered to the edge of the loft. Cethen followed, and lay alongside.

The two Romans entered the hut, talking as easily as if inside the fortress itself. Cethen nudged Borba, and held a knife up to show it was his weapon of choice. He could barely make out the shape of the twin, but then a long blade appeared out of the gloom, a mere finger's length from his nose. They were ready.

Cethen waited nervously for someone below to kindle life into one of the oil lamps, but nothing happened. Perhaps there were none there? Borba would know, but he certainly couldn't ask him. The two Romans continued to chat, now almost whispering. When Cethen's nerves finally eased long enough for him to listen to the voices, he froze. One of the voices was familiar. It belonged to Criff.

He reached sideways and grabbed Borba's arm, feeling the muscles already bunched as if ready to leap. Cethen shook his head vigorously, and sensed the twin easing back. He gestured to the two figures below with his index finger, and then to himself. Then, placing his hands side by side on the rough planking and using the first two fingers from each, he moved them across the floor to show two people walking together. Borba nodded his understanding, and slipped back from the edge of the loft.

Again they waited, but this time with a good deal more impatience. Dawn was not far away, and the small rectangular opening at the end of the loft was growing lighter. Moreover, strange things were happening on the floor below. At first it sounded as if Criff and the huge Tungri trooper were scuffling, but their words were not harsh. In fact, they were just the opposite, soft and intimate. Borba nudged Cethen hard on the shoulder. The twin's face showed dimly in the growing light, and the two men stared at each other in shock. Then, despite their predicament, each grinned knowingly at the other.

They both retreated silently to the back of the loft, convulsing with laughter. A crash suddenly filled the hut, as if a piece of furniture had tipped, followed by a groan of pleasure from Criff, and a loud curse from the Tungri.

Borba nudged Cethen and, mimicking Cethen's earlier gesture, walked his fingers across the planks. He pointed downward, then to Cethen, and raised one finger and his eyebrows in question, with a wide smirk on his face. Cethen jabbed his own finger under the twin's nose, then rolled over, one hand covering his mouth in an effort to contain himself.

The hysteria was short-lived. Cethen glanced at the opening, where the dark of night was fading to grey. Daylight seemed only moments away. By the time Criff and the Tungri finally spent themselves, he was almost frantic. Finally, he heard footsteps crossing the floor. The door creaked, followed by a long silence. Cethen sagged with relief.

Holding the dagger ready, he peered over the edge of the loft, Borba at his shoulder. The huge Tungri stood in the open doorway with his back to the room and a wine jug in one hand, staring quietly into the half-light of the meadow. Criff was still inside lacing his britches, but his eye caught Cethen's movement and he started.

Cethen quickly put a finger to his lips, at the same time readying himself to jump, should Criff raise the alarm. The expression on the bard's face was beyond price. When the shock finally vanished, he looked quickly to the Tungri, then back again, offering a bewildered, questioning shrug. Cethen pointed to the Tungri and made a gesture with his hand, as if waving the man away.

Criff understood, and nodded agreement. A few moments later, peering from through the small hole in the thatch, they watched the huge fellow walk over to his horse. He was a handsome man with long, sandy hair, thick moustaches and a beard; a man who looked as if he could do battle with three at once, and walk away none the worse.

"You just never know," Borba whispered as the trooper swung onto his horse and urged it forward, herding his drifting charges down the pasture.

"I suppose you've been here all night?"

Cethen turned to find Criff peering over the edge of the loft.

"We were here first," he said defensively.

"Shit!" the bard muttered, then crawled the rest of the way up the ladder and squatted on the floor. "The trouble with this place is, there's no damned women."

"I don't see any sheep, either," Borba said helpfully, but received only a scowl.

"What are you doing here?" Criff demanded. "Stealing horses?"

"We were thinking about it," Cethen admitted, "but then I realized who it was down there. We're really here to spy, though."

Criff's reply stunned them both. "You, too? Has the crafty old bastard changed *all* his warriors into spies?"

Cethen and Borba looked blankly at each other. "What do you mean?"

"Dermat. You know him?" Criff shook his head, and answered his own question. "Of course you do. I heard he was with you that time at Isurium. Anyway, it seems he's taken to wheedling secrets as well."

"From you?" Cethen cried. He found himself both angry and shocked. Dermat was supposed to be at Isurium. Did Morallta not trust him? Was she sending others to see he did as he was told? "He's not supposed to be here. He's—" Cethen blurted, then closed his mouth.

Criff looked amused. "A-hah! Rival spies. Keep everyone honest, hey?" He laughed, and clapped Cethen on the shoulder. "Don't worry. Your territory's safe. I saw him two days ago at Isurium. In fact, I only just got back at dusk. I ride back and forth with the Tungri. I, too, like to stay informed."

"Dermat was there?" Cethen asked skeptically, even though that was where the stolid chieftain was supposed to be.

"To be precise, he was in the stable at the back of Catey's old compound. Not officially, of course. But yes, he was there."

"What did you tell him?"

"Not very much. There was nothing really to tell," Criff said, then added mysteriously, "then."

Cethen rose to the bait like a trout to a fly. "And there is now?"

Criff nodded and smiled. "There's a big meeting going on. The legate from the Twentieth legion is here, though not for long, I'm told. I said to Dermat I'd meet him again tomorrow night, and let him know what I found out."

"Here?" Borba asked.

"Well, close by." Criff gestured vaguely toward the other side of the river.

"So are you going to tell us?" Cethen asked heavily.

"Of course, though I don't know how accurate the information is. What I hear sometimes comes too readily, so I'm never sure if it's being fed to me." He frowned. "It could be accurate, though, because it comes from Catey herself, and fits in with what I hear about the fortress."

Borba snorted. "If information comes from her, then it's a lie."

"Possibly, but *you* have to judge." The truth was obviously not a deep concern for Criff. "Mind you, she never actually tells me. It's as if she's just gossiping, loose with her tongue. She speaks of Roman plans in the same manner as deciding what food to select for the evening meal. It's a quandary."

"So what did she tell you?" Cethen pressed.

"Oh." The bard looked surprised, as if the information was of little concern. "The legion here is supposed to march out in about four weeks. With the auxiliaries. Together they should number eight or nine thousand. They're to attack Stannick—at least, that's the obvious choice. But I'd guess they'll make one of their marching camps first, probably where they were going to build, or maybe the place where you bumped into them. Everyone now calls it Bran's Beck, you know."

"What about that legate that came here?" Borba asked.

Criff shrugged. "There was no mention of him, so tell me what that means."

"What do you think?"

Again Criff shrugged. "His army will either join up with this one somewhere else, or it will come here and they'll march together. But then, if I was being fed information, it could mean they won't do either."

"There's a road they've been using to the southwest," Cethen whispered, recalling Alva's words. "A lot of messengers have been riding it. They will probably come from that direction, and unite their armies."

"If they come at all. I also heard the other legate was to take his army up the west side of the hills, and come in that way when this one strikes at Stannick. That didn't come from Catey, though. I heard it somewhere else." Criff looked puzzled as he tried to remember.

"That's a long march, and it would split their army," Borba said skeptically.

Cethen glanced at the twin, impressed. Then another thought struck him, one that seemed to come from nowhere, but one about which he was oddly curious. "The Roman Gaius, the man who almost drowned here. Is he still around?"

"Mmmm?" Criff muttered, his mind shifting. "Yeah, Gaius. The one with a scar across the top of his head, as if his skull was a cracked egg?"

Cethen nodded.

"Can't say for certain. I haven't seen him yet, but as I said, I only just got back. I think he's due to return, though. Catey mentioned as much a week back. She seems to have taken an interest in him." He frowned, trying to recall what else he might know. "The man wintered in Rome. And yes—oh yes, he—he ..." Criff's voice picked up eagerly, then just as suddenly faded as his mind caught up with his mouth.

"Yes, yes, he what?" Cethen persisted, his interest inexplicably roused.

The bard shrugged, as if deciding the information was harmless. "Well, I guess he took your wife with him."

"Elena?" Cethen yelped. When only a nod came in return, he added, "She's alive?"

"The man's a Roman, but his tastes aren't that depraved," Criff sniggered. "Of course she's alive."

A shocked silence followed, then Cethen quietly asked, hardly daring to hope, "My daughter? Coira?"

"I suppose that's her name. She went back to Rome earlier with the man's wife. The girl was first sent to Lindum after Bran's Beck. I gather she was some sort of hostage for her mother—who remained here."

"Elena was here?"

"Ever since the fight at the beck," Criff said, again frowning. "They left for Rome ...when? I think it was not long after Samhain."

Cethen slumped back against the wall of the hut, his mind racing. Both of them alive, and he had spent most of a year grieving! Yet, when he thought about it, what difference did it make? They were as good as gone.

But no! If they were alive, they were not gone. There must be a way to get them back. He would challenge the man! But no—no Roman would accept that. Buy them back? That was something a Roman would understand: buy them back! But how to go about it? And what would the man want? What in the name of the gods did a slave cost?

A discreet cough made him look up. Criff was watching him thoughtfully, his index finger scratching at the side of his nose. "I, uh, I suppose you don't know your brother lived through it either, then?" he asked.

"Cian?" Again, the yelp.

"I think that was his name."

Cethen uttered the first thought that came to mind. "Shit! I'm ploughing his wife."

Criff shrugged indifferently. "I wouldn't worry about that. He got sent out on one of their ships. Probably dead in the arenas by now. He was brought in a day or two after the fight." Criff suddenly grinned. "The yappy bugger would have stood out anywhere, which is why I remember him. He kept demanding to see the Roman Gaius. At the top of his voice, I might add. As if he could demand anything! They finally chained him up in one of the barracks until he was shipped, just to keep him quiet. Insisted on telling everyone he was your brother, and he'd helped save the Roman chief."

Cethen could think of nothing to say, and slumped over on his back, staring at the roof. Borba, though, had rushed to the window. The thunder of galloping horses drifted through the small opening, and he turned anxiously to Cethen.

"Ten, twelve riders, and a hundred horses," he said, "all coming this way."

Cethen fought to drag his mind back to what was happening, but he remained stunned, his next question as casual as if inquiring whether it was raining outside. "So, Criff, what are this bunch here for?"

"They're moving horses this side of the river to pasture. Nothing unusual. You should be safe if you stay up here. They'll move them back later in the day."

"Nothing unusual," Borba snarled. "Why didn't you tell us earlier?"

"I forgot? You didn't ask? We were busy talking?" Criff shrugged disarmingly. "It's what they do. My, uh, friend is part of it. He simply came here early. Hey, come on, Cethen; it will make a good tale later, hey?" The bard punched him on the shoulder, then started down the ladder.

"Is it safe to let him go?" Borba asked.

Criff dutifully stopped on the second step, waiting for the response. Cethen could have laughed. In so many ways, the bard was as innocent as a lamb. Regardless, the man had held Cethen's life cupped in his hands once before, at Isurium. He hadn't let it loose then, and there was no need for him to do so now. "Yes, it's safe."

Criff disappeared and Cethen rolled once more onto his back. "Let's get some sleep," he muttered.

Cethen took a long time to drift off, for his mind would not stop working. When he finally did, it was to a restless, groaning sleep. When he awoke it was sudden, and with a grubby hand clasped firmly over his mouth. Borba's face loomed above, with one finger to his lips in a call for silence. When the twin was sure he understood, he let go and held up two fingers, then pointed below. Someone was talking, in a dialect that neither of them understood. It was broad daylight; whoever was there had obviously found a use for the hut. The wine jars should have told them as much.

The door opened and swung shut and two more people entered. Borba rolled quietly toward the ladder, taking advantage of the clump of feet on the floor and the banter they brought with them to cover any sound. The door opened again and someone left, probably the two who had been there at first. The loud plop of a bung sounded, and for a moment there was no further noise but the gurgle of liquid. Soon after, the chatter resumed, but not for long. The door crashed open, an angry voice bellowed an order, and the door slammed shut again.

Borba grinned and mouthed the word "Morallta," then sliced his finger across his throat. Chairs scraped on the hard dirt floor as those below clambered to their feet, their grumbling plain in any dialect. A few moments later the door again opened and creaked shut, followed by silence. Both men sighed in relief, and Cethen rolled forward to lie alongside Borba. The motion prompted further movement from below, though, and the two looked at each other in alarm—they'd thought the hut empty! The loft suddenly dipped as the weight of a foot fell on the first rung of the ladder.

"Criff?" a deep voice asked, and an enormous, bearded face appeared above the floor of the loft. The large blue eyes had barely a chance to register surprise before two knives struck, digging hard into each side of the man's throat.

"Grab him," Cethen yelped as the huge Roman swayed backwards.

Borba grabbed the man's long hair, and Cethen a piece of his chain armour where it hung loose above one arm. Blood gushed from the Tungri's throat in a fountain as he slithered to the floor, his great weight dragging them both thumping down the rungs of the ladder. The pair crashed on top in a mess of arms, legs, and blood-soaked Tungri. Each of them held his breath, nervously awaiting the consequences.

"This is not good," Cethen muttered finally, when nothing happened. He pushed himself free of the tangle and rose, hands and arms glistening crimson.

"Criff is going to be pissed," Borba panted, and wiped his sleeve across his forehead, leaving a long, dripping streak of red.

They stared at the huge body lying on the floor, the last of the blood feebly pumping from the gash in its throat. It was as if someone had cracked a vat of dark, sticky wine.

"Over behind the door," Cethen said, snapping from his stupor. "Someone else will be in looking, as sure as worse luck follows bad."

He knelt down beside the Tungri, his mind churning, wondering if even the gods could sort this one out; but slowly his thoughts settled, and reason seeped in. The man had a horse. It was outside. There might still be a way out: a mad dash, riding double.

But what if they were seen right away? Two on a horse was a race already lost. Yet Ligan and Innsa were hiding in the forest with four horses, weren't they? Surely they hadn't given up and gone. The pair had to be there. If they could gain the tree line …

The same angry voice again bellowed outside the door, and an instant later it was flung open. Cethen whirled as a short stocky trooper stepped inside. The man's ugly snarl quickly turned to surprise. Borba slid from behind the door and grabbed the collar of his tunic, even as the man's mouth opened to shout the alarm. In the same motion the twin's other hand slid forward and sliced the Roman's throat, as neat as gutting a trout. More blood, this time like spouting water.

"I believe," Borba said calmly, "that even if the noisy fool had yelled, it wouldn't have alarmed anyone." He wiped the blade on the sleeve of his tunic, and slid it back into its sheath.

Cethen closed the door, but not before cautiously peering outside. The horses had drifted farther down pasture, where they peacefully grazed, scattered haphazardly along the length of the riverbank. Most of the Tungri riders sat on the ground talking, but two had remained mounted, one at either end of the herd. Most important, two saddled horses stood barely ten paces from the door, their heads down, each one pulling quietly at the fresh grass.

"The chain," Cethen whispered, closing the door. "We'll put their chain tunics on." Perhaps from a distance, he reasoned, the deceit would pass.

Without a word they both began tugging at the sticky clothes. The result was not impressive. The twin took the smaller of the two chain mail coats, the one belonging to the decurio with the loud voice. It stretched tight across his body, and fell short across his buttocks. In contrast, Cethen, despite his height, found his to be baggy, and even when cinched about his waist, its hem fell almost to his knees. But perhaps from a distance …

The large Tungri's helmet lay on the table; Cethen put it on. It was a surprisingly good fit, though the cheek pieces felt uncomfortable and restricting. But that left Borba with no head cover. His bright red hair would not be mistaken for the smaller dead man's black hair. Though perhaps from a distance …

Cethen peered cautiously outside once more. The herd had not moved. Stepping carefully outside, the two walked over to the horses. Borba quickly took the dead man's helmet from the saddle and jammed it on his head. It was much too small, and sat balanced like an apple on a turnip. Cethen thought it looked ridiculous, but the headpiece did hide most of his bright red hair. Perhaps, from a distance …

Both men resisted the urge to kick their animals to a gallop, each softly reassuring the other that it was the worst thing to do. They plodded across the pasture toward the patch of green forest where Ligan and Innsa were supposed to be hiding. As they moved along the edge of the trees, Cethen called out, as loud as he dared, and two sounds rang back at the same time. One was the hoarse caw of a very sick crow, which had to be Ligan. The other was a loud cry from farther down the pasture.

Borba glanced over his shoulder. "It's one of the Romans." A herder, less than a half mile distant, was riding toward them at a fast trot.

"Wave him off. Anything. Yell," Cethen urged. "You're his master."

He turned away as if the man was Borba's responsibility, and kicked his horse to a canter. At the same time he called out to Ligan, telling him they would meet him on the trail that led south, and away from the ford. The sick crow again cawed from the trees.

Borba half turned in the saddle and roared a long, garbled command that echoed down the pasture like a death rattle. Waving the man off, he turned back and urged his horse into a canter that matched Cethen's. The Tungri herder pulled in his mount and stared. Whatever the reason for his ride, it was apparently not that important. Throwing his hands up as if in disgust, the trooper turned back.

Cethen and Borba continued along the fringe of the forest until they reached a wide, well-travelled track that led to the south. Moments later they were riding beneath the tall canopy of the forest, each grinning like cream fed cats.

Cethen chuckled. "She'll be pissed we didn't bring the heads."

"She only wanted ones from real Romans," Borba replied.

"We could have cut their hair off, and given them a shave." Cethen laughed out loud. "She'd never know the difference!"

With no further prompting, both men threw back their heads, raised their voices in a yell of pure triumph, and kicked their two new, well-fed Roman horses to a gallop. Life did not get any better!

Chapter XXII

"The assault will be two pronged. The Twentieth will advance from the southwest, and the Ninth will march at the same time in the east. In other words, this attack will be coordinated, gentlemen." Cerialis held a long pointer, and bent it like a drawn bow between his hands as he glared around the circle of faces. His eyes rested pointedly on Agricola. "That means that both forces will not only converge on Stannick at the same time; they will strike at the same time. Understood?"

A low rumble of agreement followed the words, and more than one pair of eyes slid sideways towards the Twentieth's legate. Agricola grunted his understanding along with the others, but he wore the trace of a smile.

Cerialis nodded his satisfaction, and turned his attention to the huge flour paste model of Brigantia that filled two tables along the east wall of the headquarters building. It had been painstakingly built by the Ninth's clerical staff, who viewed it with the same pride of ownership as the governor who ordered its creation. The large, contoured map was built to emphasize the ruggedness of the north country. The craggy hills running down the centre were painted brown, as was the moorland to the northeast. The lowlands, valleys, forests, and marshes were splotched shades of green, and the long blue ribbons that crisscrossed the model like a web of diseased veins were obviously rivers. The centurions had unanimously decided that, if nothing else, the layout was colourful.

"The Ninth Hispana will assemble here in full force, arriving from three directions." The pointer fell to a spot where the brown paint met the green north of the fortress, and the moors dropped sharply off in the shape of a small, broken nose. "You should find it familiar, Quintus."

The cavalry praefectus bent his head in acknowledgement. It was the place where his own force had assembled before joining the battle in which his predecessor had been killed.

"The full strength of the Ninth legion will march from here at Ebor," Cerialis continued, the long stick hovering and darting over the contours like a hummingbird, "and the auxiliary units will depart from Isurium and Derventio. At the same time, elements of the Second Adiutrix will march north from Lindum to hold the fortress here while we are in the field. One artillery unit will be attached. It will consist of only the lighter *ballistae* for quicker movement. They will be drawn from …

The governor droned on and Gaius forced his tired mind to concentrate, but it was a one sided battle. He was worn down, and feeling both angry and vaguely guilt ridden. He had arrived at the fortress only days before. There had been no word sent that Cerialis intended to begin his campaign so early in the year, dammit, and he had felt no urgency to return to the province before spring. For once, winter in Italia eventually had proved to be more than pleasant, and there had been more than a trace of reluctance in his leaving. Yet when his boots again trod the long walkways behind the parapet at Ebor, he'd found the familiar echo of their hobnailed soles surprisingly refreshing.

The night before had found him doing exactly that, pausing by the westerly gate to reflect on the months that had passed since last standing there. Leaning against the wall of the tower, he watched the great red orb of the sun fall softly behind the glittering Abus. Much had happened during the past winter, some for the better, some for the worse, and he was still trying to sort out which was which.

At first the excuse for remaining so long had been a perverse determination to see Helvia's baby. The event caused no delay, though, arriving earlier than expected in mid February. Once back in Rome, Helvia had shed the heavy cloak of remorse worn in Lindum, and after its birth, any pretence of the child's parentage. He had half-expected the child to be named Lucius, which would have been too much to tolerate, but when she suggested Gaius, he found the idea even more repugnant. Annoyed, he had sarcastically tossed out the name Publius, and to his surprise, she picked it up and used it. Later, his shock-wary mind wondered if there might be someone of that name in her sordid past; he also began to wonder if that same mind was breeding a permanent state of persecution.

Cartimandua's insistence that "a bairn is a bairn is a bairn" were remembered more than once, but the words were sour. What Venutius would have made of that philosophy strained the mind! Which was something, he realized with a start, the man might well have once dealt with if Cerialis spoke the truth. More than once he wondered who the governor's boy actually was.

And the winter had led to a further surprise. Both children had taken paths that proved the opposite of what might have been expected. Aelia had become a staunch ally, which was strange, for the girl usually tried to walk the middle of the road. Yet he seemed to have lost Marcus altogether, and his mind constantly pondered on the cause: the boy's return to the coddled familiarity of Rome; his brutal encounter with the Britons; or merely being back with his childhood friends, none of whom lacked privilege. Whatever the reason, Marc had displayed absolutely no willingness to return to Britannia. He was determined to remain with Helvia, and at first Gaius wondered why, for the boy had been set on becoming a soldier. In fact, he had been openly proud of the scratches received in his first battle.

Only later, on the passage back to Britannia, did Aelia unburden herself and offer the likely cause. Marcus simply did not want to leave Rome. His friends were all there, many of them; and his daughter's tone implied that little good would be found in their companionship. Yet Helvia had willingly approved, both of Marcus and his friends. In fact, if he correctly surmised the words that Aelia left unspoken, his wife had encouraged the boy. Certainly she was coddling him, and he could guess the reason: it was nothing more than spite—and one more point upon which to brood.

Yet the questions and doubts were almost nothing when compared to the trouble caused by the wife of the hairy barbarian. He sighed and placed his elbows on the parapet, half blinded by the dull glow of the fading sun. The low crimson circle had all but disappeared, casting long, dark shadows across the forest where the trails lost themselves in the gloom of twilight.

The slave woman possessed a monumental stubbornness. At first he'd wondered what perverse streak had stopped him from having her beaten into obedience, but the winter had been long, and it had been as well that she remained unpunished. It would have been like thrashing a horse simply to speed its breaking. Though sometimes, of late, he wondered which one of them had eventually been broken.

The thought brought a smile, just as a flicker of movement in the trees caught his attention. He leaned forward over the parapet, eyes straining, and caught sight of a dark shape slipping from the forest close by the trail that led north. Another shape, almost impossible to see in the gloom, flitted back into the woods as the first came into view. Gaius slipped back into the shadows and waited, watching the man walk closer to the wall. The guard shouted across the space that separated the two and the figure started running, hurrying inside before the gates closed.

Gaius recognized the man as he walked past the flickering light of the torches. He waited a few moments, then followed. The street was almost empty, but it was of no matter, for he suspected where the man was going. When he was certain, he called out a name: "Criff!"

The bard halted, startled, one foot on the landing outside the barrack building taken over by Cartimandua. He peered into the dim light, trying to see who had called. One hand moved to the hilt of his dagger. "Who is it?" he croaked.

Gaius drew closer and saw hesitation reflected in Criff's eyes, as recognition came. The man completed his step then turned his bearded face to peer down from the vantage of the plank deck. "It's you," he said, and when Gaius said nothing, added, "Welcome back."

The street was absolutely quiet. Gaius walked the last few steps, unsure of what to say. Should he accuse the man? Summon help? March him over to Cerialis? He placed his hand on the hilt of his own blade, and hedged. "Beautiful sunset, no?"

Criff also hedged. "Aye, the gods are the finest of artists."

Gaius climbed warily onto the landing, placed his back against one of the support posts, and faced the bard. "Their work is best seen from the top of the ramparts, though. Not from the shade of the forest."

It was an invitation to speak, but Criff instead became defensive. "Is Rome now dictating where a man must go to watch a sunset?"

"No. Not to watch a sunset," Gaius growled, "but when a man slinks about the forest to meet others, yes, Rome does get somewhat dictatorial. This is a military post, not a barbarian fair."

Criff said nothing, his eyes reflecting confusion as he struggled to find an answer. They glanced downward, upward, then into the distance, until his mind finally seemed to find a roost. He tugged nervously at one of his moustaches. "Well, it wasn't really—"

The door suddenly opened and both men, each wound tighter than a loaded ballista, whirled toward it. Cartimandua stood in the opening, a broad smile on her features.

"Gaius!" she cried, and moved forward to embrace him. "I'm pleased to see you again. What's going on here? Is Criff defending my door, or my honour?"

Gaius frowned at the queen's timing. She must have heard every word, he decided, appearing only when they grew difficult. "We were discussing his nocturnal wanderings," he growled.

Cartimandua glanced to the west, where the low scattering of clouds glowed a dark crimson. "It's hardly nighttime."

"The time of night isn't the problem," Gaius said, growing angrier by the moment, "it's who he meets when it starts falling."

"O-ho, you are discovered, Criff," Cartimandua cried immediately. One hand moved to cover her mouth in mock horror. "You had best go inside while I explain. We don't want to embarrass you. Go, go." The bard quickly disappeared, as if glad of the excuse. She called after him, "Have someone send out some wine."

"Can't the man tell his own story?" Gaius growled.

Cartimandua walked to the same chair where she had sat the previous autumn, and waved a suggestion that he should also make himself comfortable. Gaius allowed his back to slide down the support post until he sat facing her, one leg dangling over the side of the landing.

"He could," she said, "but I prefer to tell it. It saves the poor man a certain amount of discomfort."

One of the menials came out bearing a tray with two goblets and a glass jug full of wine. Cartimandua leaned back and stretched her long legs across the planks, regarding Gaius with a look of amusement as he took the proffered drink. He noted she had seen fit to bring a wool shawl, which she drew about her shoulders. No doubt she would have brought the wine, too, had she been more prepared.

"This is serious," he growled. "And as for discomfort, I fail—"

"What you say is true; the matter is serious," she cut in. "And so is his discomfort, for it is real. Tell me: if you had an assignation and came slinking back before the gates closed, would you not feel a certain discomfort if you were accosted on your return?"

The image did not fit what Gaius thought he had seen, but he replied to the question anyway. "Criff is a free man. I see no reason for the discomfort. In fact, he's surrounded by soldiers, most of whom would boast of an assignation."

"If they were meeting a Tungri cavalryman?"

Gaius almost choked on his wine.

"And from what my women tell me," she continued, smiling as she shook her head ruefully, "it's the biggest waste of gifts ever granted by the gods."

"Criff? He's a ...?"

"Let's say he's an open minded poet."

"And the Tungri," Gaius insisted, to be sure of what she was saying, "he's a raving poet too?"

"Let's say the embarrassment would be greater for the Tungri than it would be for Criff, should it come to the attention of his superiors. Or his equals, for that matter. Personally, I don't give a lump of pig dung one way or another. Though your comment does raise a question, Gaius Trebonius."

"Which is?"

"Do all soldiers boast of their assignations?"

"Of course not. A man of honour does not do such a thing," Gaius said stiffly, remembering their languid moments by the Fosse.

"I'm so relieved," Cartimandua replied, then raised her brow. "So tell me, how have you been? You have kept well over winter?"

"Yes, thank you, and you?" Gaius replied, only mildly irritated when he realized her diversion. "Did you pass the winter here?"

She shook her head. "No. I spent most of it at Camulodunum. My own people are there. It's where I was needed, I suppose. But Petilius seems to think I might still be of use, once he's taken Stannick. Not to him, but to my people, though I think the governor just likes to keep me around." She shrugged, and her expression grew sardonic. "There are times when I'm able to soothe his angrier impulses. When that happens, my people reap the benefit."

Without doubt, Gaius thought, his mind turning back to Criff's abrupt dismissal. He opened his mouth to speak, but the woman was there first.

"So tell me about the woman Elena," she said breezily. "I hear she is now sharing your bed."

Gaius raised his head and snorted. "A few moments ago, you looked surprised to see me."

"I was being polite. What did you expect me to say? You have been back for more than a day, and you haven't dropped by to pay your respects—turd!" She tilted her head to one side. "So what happened? Last time I saw the woman, odds were two coins for one she'd slit your throat. Tell me."

Gaius smiled, and told the story. Or at least, the bare bones of it. But as the words fell from his mouth, they were only a small part of the tale that ran through his mind. A tale that had come to a head less than a month after arriving at his brother's estate. He had gone looking for Elena on his return from a journey to Rome, and found her missing.

"Where is she?" Gaius demanded.

Helvia rested comfortably on a long, padded couch, carefully shaded from the sun by a painted awning. The tentlike cover had been raised on the highest terrace, which looked down on the villa below, and the broad valley beyond. Gaius knew damned well she had climbed there to avoid him. It merely added to his anger.

"I wasn't expecting you back so soon," Helvia murmured, ignoring his anger and rubbing her eyes as if disturbed from sleep. "How did matters go in the city?"

"I asked where she was!"

"Who?" Helvia asked with feigned innocence, then recoiled in shock when her husband strode forward. Grasping her by one arm, he jerked her roughly to her feet. She instinctively clutched at her swollen belly with one hand, and tried to steady herself with the other.

"One last time," Gaius snarled in her face. "Where is she?"

"You mean your slave woman?" The pretence turned to a sneer. "How would I know? You're the one who should know where she is. Perhaps she's run away."

"Her daughter's here. This is Rome. She has no reason to run." One hand slid up to her throat. "What have you done with her?"

Helvia licked her lips as her mind struggled with the truth, then the pressure against her windpipe increased ever so slightly. "I—she—she's gone."

"I know that, bitch. Where?"

"I don't know where. Honestly."

"Then what? Did you kill her, too?"

"No. No!" Helvia appeared genuinely alarmed at the suggestion. Words tumbled from her mouth as he eased the pressure on her throat. "I sold her, you bastard. What did you expect me to do? You dare call me a bitch? She's the bitch, the sullen little whore. I won't tolerate that sort of behaviour from any slave, especially one that's spreading her legs for my husband. And in my own house!"

"*You* dare to talk about spreading legs!" Gaius shouted, not releasing his hold. "And I have told you a hundred times, I am not ploughing the b—the woman. Do you understand? Who bought her?"

"I placed her through the market."

"You what?" Gaius had an unsettling vision of the auction blocks, the leering bidders, the lewd crowd. His hand squeezed almost involuntarily. "In Rome?"

Helvia gasped, and managed to nod.

"When?"

"Two days ago. When you left."

Gaius threw her back on the couch, but she scrambled ponderously to the other side and crouched with one leg on the padding, glaring and rubbing her throat.

"Bastard!"

"You call me a bastard," he shouted. "What about killing a legate, and parting a mother from her daughter? What other deeds have I missed?"

"You should have thought about the girl before you brought her here."

"I did, dammit. It was one of the—it was *the* reason I did bring her here. To see her child. It did wonders for the woman's behaviour."

"I'll wager it did," Helvia sneered.

"Ahhh, what's the use?" Gaius cried, throwing up his hands. He whirled and stalked toward the villa.

"Where are you going?" Helvia asked, moving awkwardly after him.

"Where do you think?" Gaius broke into a trot and reached the villa long before his wife, who simply returned to the couch and lay scowling.

He found Elena late the next day, in the dockyard at the busy, silt-ridden port of Ostia. The place exuded the stink and bustle of seaports everywhere, made all the worse by its position downriver from Rome. He caught up with her as she was being marched onto the deck of a grubby merchant vessel, almost lost amongst a score of other slaves. They were nearly all younger women, every one consigned to Neapolis.

A good deal of bargaining took place under the impatient eye of the ship's master, who loudly voiced his irritation as Gaius haggled with the trader. Elena watched too, and sighed in relief when the bargaining finished. He parted with three times the sum the oily merchant had paid for her in Rome. When the transaction was complete, she followed him down the gangplank and across the quayside. Neither spoke until they arrived at the hostler's, where he retrieved his horse.

"We'll have to ride double," Gaius said tersely as the animal was brought from the stable.

"It wasn't my fault," Elena said, interpreting his foul mood as annoyance, and remaining remarkably subdued.

"I'm not angry with you, I'm furious with my wife," Gaius snapped, turning to look at her for the first time. She was clad in a short, grubby tunic of cheap sackcloth, and wore rope sandals on her feet. Her hair was as wild as a hag's.

When she saw him grin, she scowled her irritation. "You find my appearance amusing?"

"I was admiring the improvement. It's far better than when I purchased you the first time," he said. "Have you been ill used? Abused?"

"You mean, has someone been fucking your property?"

"No. I mean have you been beaten? Hurt in any way?" Gaius said, surprisingly patient.

"I was pushed and shoved, but not beaten. Or abused," Elena muttered. "I've received far worse hurt in the past, without having to do battle to get it."

"I'm glad to hear that," he said, and after a moment's hesitation added, "and I'm glad to get you back."

"I would imagine. It would be a tragedy to lose your money."

Gaius shook his head at the response, and raised his arms in helpless surrender. "I rode my arse sore last night and again today, to get here. I then paid triple what you're worth to keep you out of a Neapolitan whorehouse, and you accuse me of not wanting to lose money!"

"Then why did you?" Elena asked, squinting upward against the falling sun to look directly into his face.

"Because Helvia got my piss boiling with what she did, and I wanted to get even! What do you think?" Gaius grumbled, and turned to his horse.

"Tribune!"

He scowled back over his shoulder.

"I can't say I'm glad to still find myself a slave, but thank you."

Gaius grunted acknowledgement, then placed one foot in the

cupped hands of the hostler and swung up onto the horse. He hesitated for a moment before reaching down to pull Elena up behind. The hesitation was instinctive—it was not fitting for a man of rank to ride with a slave tucked behind his saddle, even if he wasn't in uniform.

Elena had been around the Romans long enough to recognize why he paused. "I can walk," she muttered, and turned to do so.

"Ah, get up," Gaius muttered, and grasped her hand. "The day won't last much longer. There's little time left to walk."

Elena swung up with the ease of a cat and settled down behind the saddle, clutching the leather cantle rather than his waist. Gaius guided the horse slowly across the dockyard and turned onto the main road leading to Rome.

"Do we ride through the night?" Elena asked, as if it was of little matter.

Gaius didn't answer, for he was unsure of his plans. The horse wasn't going far, that was certain. He'd spent most of the day riding down from the city, and even so, the way back was not safe at night—at least, not without an escort. He knew people in Ostia with whom they both might stay, but he rationalized that arriving at their door with a female barbarian slave on his saddle would be misconstrued. And the more he convinced himself of the premise, the more certain he was of its truth.

"This place holds promise," Gaius said a while later, as they passed through the outskirts of the city. A lofty gateway marked the entrance to a large inn. With a flick of the reins, he rode through.

The hostel was overtly expensive. A row of fountains played in front of a white, two-storey building set back in a lush garden rimmed by a small forest of trees and shrubs. Small villas dotted the grounds, each with its own terrace discreetly hidden by a low wall of bushes. The two slaves who guarded the gateway carefully eyed the horse and the man who rode it, and skeptically allowed them to pass. Nonetheless, one trotted alongside as Gaius made his way to the main building, just in case their judgement proved faulty.

The villa Gaius took was much larger than it appeared from the outside. A huge room took up the greater part of the building, and a single bedroom most of what remained. A small bathhouse that opened onto the terrace contained two pools, the first cold and the second heated. A pair of long marble tables set nearby held towels, oils, and scented unguents.

A half-dozen slaves quickly filled the villa, each rushing to an appointed task: heat the pool, light the score or more lamps ranged about the terrace, fuss with the main table and couches, stock the room with food and drink, set the perfumed hangings, and place fresh linen in the bedroom.

Elena had been in Rome long enough not to be surprised when the bustle settled down and four slaves remained, two women and two men. One of the men came onto the terrace, where she sat with Gaius under the glow of a dozen flickering torches. The slave poured a very good wine and they sipped it, picking absently at a bowl of dried figs and honey-roasted almonds. Neither spoke as darkness fell, choosing instead to watch the sun disappear beyond the cypress trees as both of them tried to divine Gaius's true motive. Elena, who was carelessly drinking far more wine than she should, was probably having more success.

"You will bathe before your meal, sir?"

It was hardly a question, and Gaius rose and followed the slave inside. The scent of lavender hung in the air above the cold pool, where the two female slaves—small, olive-skinned women with warm, dark eyes—waited on either side of the marble steps. Gaius turned, saw Elena watching with hazy eyes, and wrinkled his nose, one eyebrow raised. "I think you need it more than I," he said.

"I suppose, but that's all I need."

"I wouldn't say that." Gaius grinned. "There's your clothing—it's filthy. And your hair is even worse. Now come on, or they'll have to change this place into a sty."

He moved to the edge of the cold pool, where the two women removed his clothes, then he stepped down and plunged into the water. It was nowhere near as icy as the bathhouse at Ebor, but after the heat of the day and the long, tiresome ride, he found the brisk waters invigorating. The brief soaking felt good, but his mood had fallen when he finally rose and moved to the hot room. Elena had disappeared.

A blast of warmth blew through the door as he slipped inside. The low marble benches, stone pillows chiselled into either end, glistened with moisture sucked from the damp air. Gaius sprawled on one, resting his head on the hard pillow and one foot on the floor, and brooded. He could have ordered her, of course, but that was not what he wanted. Yet if not, what exactly did he want? He was still wondering when the door swung open, then quietly closed.

In the dim light cast by the lamps, Gaius saw Elena settle on the other bench, either nervous or simply unsteady, he couldn't tell. Her hair was wet and coiled atop her head, and both cheeks were heavily flushed from the wine. A white towel covered her body, tucked into itself above the rise of her breasts. She seemed unsure it would stay there, for one hand clutched the fold as if holding the makeshift garment in place. She ignored his nakedness, her eyes reluctantly meeting his.

"So what happens next?" She asked the question as if it was a chore, tossing her head as a damp strand of hair fell across one cheek.

Gaius answered the question at its face value. "The two women will apply a perfumed oil. They will provide massage at the same time, if you like. Or the men, if you prefer—stronger hands. Then they will remove the sweat and grime. I prefer they do it with a wooden strigil, myself. It's warmer, and I find it more pleasant than the brass. That's followed by some time in the hot pool, to cleanse the body. Not for too long, though I do like to relax there for a while. Then back into the cold pool to tighten the skin, get dried off, and then we eat. So you see, there's nothing terrible about it, is there?"

"I don't know," Elena murmured. "I'm not too sure about the man giving me a massage."

"The idea of a male slave doing that bothers you?" Gaius asked, and chuckled.

"Any slave being forced to do that bothers me," Elena snapped back. But a few moments later, as if the day's strain had been far too much, she yawned and lay back on the marble slab with a tired smile.

"Here," Gaius murmured, and carefully swung his legs off the bench to sit upright on the damp surface. When Elena said nothing further, but simply stared at him with large, hazel-green eyes, he rose cautiously to his feet. "Perhaps I might help."

Gaius remained at the villa for a week at considerable cost, which he didn't regret. When he returned home, Helvia had moved to the house his brother kept in the city, taking Marcus with her. That suited him admirably, for it solved the sleeping arrangements. There was no point in subterfuge anyway, except perhaps for the sake of Aelia, and he supposed Coira as well. Though when Gaius took time to reflect upon it, Coira was probably the only one who might balk at the new arrangements.

What was left of winter passed quickly, and at its end, Gaius's only real problem lay in what should be done with the two girls on his return to Britannia. His first thought had been to leave them both in Rome, but as the time to leave drew closer, the idea offered less comfort. Helvia would no doubt find some way to exercise her spite on Coira. The small, blond Briton would probably be sold before he'd left the outskirts of the city. After the incident with Elena, he had no doubt of it. He would have to part the two girls, and take her back.

Aelia was no concern, of course, for Helvia was her mother; if nothing else, his wife had been a good mother. And Rome was, after all, his daughter's home. She would definitely not like the arrangement, though, for over winter she had grown close to the Brigante girl. And when he put the notion to Aelia, she came close to a tantrum, which was uncharacteristic; but he was surprised to learn that her distress was due not to parting from Coira as much as remaining behind herself.

When the time came to leave, all three women came with him to Britannia. They started the journey earlier than usual, for with the two younger girls, progress would be slow. On their arrival, Gaius left the pair under the care of Metellus and a female house slave at the resort town of *Aqua Sulis*. They would move north to the house at Lindum once the blossoms were falling from the trees. With Elena at Ebor, Gaius didn't think losing his manservant would prove much of a hardship. The fact that Coira remained under his control elsewhere, however, was a truth that remained unspoken.

Chapter XXIII

"It doesn't sound as if you heard it right," Venutius muttered, scratching first at his chin, then at his scalp, as he stared at Dermat and Cethen. "Why would they split their army in two?"

"Maybe he's learning from you?" Dermat offered dourly, without cracking a smile.

Venutius simply glared.

"We're not certain they're going to do that," Cethen said, glancing sideways at Dermat for confirmation. "When I talked to Criff, he said he'd heard as much, but wasn't sure."

"Criff told *me* he overheard two of their officers talking about two different armies," Dermat said, his dark brow furrowed as he tried to recall the bard's exact words. "One moving up the west side of the hills, the other to the east. The officers didn't like the idea of splitting their people either, which places the ring of truth around it. I would guess they're so confident, they plan on using one part of their force to cut off our retreat. Did Criff mention the day to you?"

"Not exactly. About four weeks. He seemed anxious to be on his way," Cethen said, biting his lip as he remembered the huge Tungri they had nearly decapitated. He looked at Dermat. "That reminds me. Did Criff appear upset?"

"No more than anybody else sneaking off into the forest to tell secrets." Dermat smiled as if recalling the meeting. "He wanted back before the gates closed. He said the same thing to me, though: about four weeks. When was that, about three days ago?" He turned to Vellocatus. "You said they have a way of working it backward from the day itself."

"They plan it all out," Vellocatus explained. "If four weeks was true three days ago, then the attack is set for twenty-five days from now. That's a big if, of course. They work it out so both armies will have done something or be somewhere by a certain day. For example, if Dermat does have the right of it, then tomorrow is day twenty-four from the attack. Three weeks from now it will be day four. Or will it be day three? No, it'll be four. Anyway, their armies will have started out about then. Certainly the one in the west will, because it has farther to go."

"So is this bard lying?" Morallta asked, shifting uncomfortably in her seat, a move that prompted several pairs of eyes to shift to her belly. No one present knew for certain who had put the child there, including Cethen at times.

"Criff isn't lying," Dermat said firmly.

"But he doesn't know if he's telling the truth, either," Cethen added, then climbed to his feet and walked to a side table where a pile of food and ale waited. He'd had no choice but to come to Venutius's lodge on his return, and he was hungry. Piling his dish high, he stood watching the others as he ate for the first time that day.

"If a second force from the west is involved, then its commander visiting the fortress lends truth to the fact," Venutius murmured.

"Send someone down the west side of the hills to Cornovii territory," Morallta said. "If a legion is preparing to march, it will show signs of readiness. Especially if they are far enough away that they don't feel the need to hide what they're doing."

"But what to do in the meantime?" Venutius mused, his eyes half closed in thought.

"Two armies," Vellocatus said quietly. "That's close to twenty thousand men. We cannot meet them in the field. Boudicca taught us that. Even Caradoc taught us that, in the long run."

"But half the army—ten thousand, caught unawares," Morallta replied. "That was how Boudicca did it; she caught them by surprise."

"Two thousand," Vellocatus corrected. "She didn't wipe out a legion, only part of one—a couple thousand soldiers at the most. The rest of the time she spent slaughtering civilians and old men, most of them Britons. In the end, less than ten thousand Romans wiped out her eighty."

"But—"

"Look it in the eye and accept it," Vellocatus said firmly. "The Romans have not lost a single battle *where they had time to deploy their troops*. Surprise has given us every one of our victories. But I will warn you, all of you, that if we try for surprise and don't have it, then we have done nothing more than grab a wild boar by the tusks."

"So you suggest we skulk in the fortress and let them starve us out?" Morallta jeered.

"No. I'm just pointing out a basic truth," Vellocatus replied. "As yet, I don't know what to suggest."

"A fortress might be a safe place to hide," Loskenn rumbled, "but it, too, can be a trap. Personally, I prefer the wide open spaces."

"I agree." Morallta scratched at her stomach. "The Romans don't fight in their fortresses, they use them as a place to sleep. They fight in the open."

"That's because they're always on someone else's land," Vellocatus pointed out, "which is the reason they're good at it. They've had lots of practice, and they have no place else to run."

"That's enough," Venutius growled, and his fingers rose again to worry at the red rash. His entire scalp was angry with the scratching it had received lately. "We need to know more—a mountain more. And we need warriors, too. Dermat, Vellocatus, we have to call in more of the people. One thing's certain, the Romans are going to move early this year. If Criff said almost thirty days, we'll figure on twenty. I'll travel north again and treat with the Selgovae. It's a long, hard ride, but it's in their own interest to help and they know it. The fools have been dithering all winter. With luck, twenty thousand of the bastards will be here when the Romans come. Which leaves the Carvetii."

"They are preparing," Morallta hedged.

"Not good enough. I need them in the field, as early as possible. I must know."

"They will be there."

"But when?"

"They are preparing. But in twenty days? Yes, some will be down here; how many, I don't know. I'll leave tomorrow and hurry them," Morallta replied, sounding unusually indecisive. As if to turn attention away from the matter, she looked at Cethen. "The patrols will go out tomorrow, of course."

He groaned, not only for himself but for Borba, Luath, and the others who had returned with him. He doubted they would be in any condition to depart the following morning. Certainly he was not, with his aching body, sore legs, empty belly, and a need to sleep for a week. The others would surely be the same, though on reflection he decided it was more likely they would need two days just to sober up. Their small success at the Roman fortress would be celebrated as a triumph.

Yet he had Elena and Coira to think about, which *was* a good reason to go back to the fortress. He could seek out Criff. The bard might be able to speak to the Roman about a trade. Of course, there was no guarantee the man would sell, and he himself had no idea of a fair price. Perhaps Criff could help there, too. Why, oh why, had he not gone over that when Criff was in the hut? Now, with the death of the man's hulking partner, the bard would surely be angry, and offer no help at all.

Cethen sighed and stared blankly at Morallta. She winked, and he sighed again. Was the gesture an invitation, or a sign that she had not been serious about the patrols leaving the next morning? Surely not an invitation. The woman had grown extremely touchy about the arrangement with Nuada of late, which was damned unreasonable, all things considered. He never pried into what she did with her idle time. Besides, Morallta was getting on the large side for that sort of thing.

He decided the wink was to let him know that she was baiting him about leaving tomorrow. To get even, he leered back and casually dropped one hand to his groin when no one was looking. Morallta smiled and nodded agreement. Cethen groaned, and suddenly felt very old.

Nuada was in a foul mood when he finally came home, long after darkness had fallen. The inside of the hut flickered with the dim light from only a single small lamp, for the children were asleep. They must have been, for no one friendly seemed about to offer a greeting. Nuada herself sat quietly on the end of the bed by the flickering light, sewing pieces of a small, lambskin jerkin together. She did not look up and Cethen sighed at the familiarity of it all. It was as if Elena was home again, and brooding. Why did women pretend to be preoccupied and overworked, he wondered, when they were really full of piss and provocation?

Normally, Cethen would have played the game of "who'll be first to speak," which he usually won, because he was hardly ever the one who was particularly pissed. Tonight he was tired, though, and he also had much to tell—so much, he didn't know where to start. It might have been best to begin by telling Nuada that Cian had survived the battle, but since she was obviously sulking, he decided to leave that for last.

"I have to leave again," Cethen said, sounding like he was grumbling, though realizing with some surprise that he was not. "Could be gone for another twenty days or more."

Nuada shrugged as if it didn't concern her, and studied the jerkin.

"Back to the same place." He squatted on a rough-hewn log and tugged at his boots. "Venutius wants us to go back to the fortress and keep an eye on the Romans. They're supposed to be getting ready to move." He paused, then shot his first arrow, which was deliberately oblique. "I'm hoping I'll catch a glimpse of Elena, though I doubt there'll be a chance for us to speak."

As he said the words, Cethen wondered what would happen if he did see her. Might he simply ride up to her, unarmed? It would be a ruse similar to that he and Vellocatus had used with success at Isurium. Not with the big chestnut, of course, for it was far too conspicuous, but perhaps with one of the ponies. Which brought another idea to mind— how much would the chestnut weigh against the price of a slave? Yes, the horse was probably the answer. He might negotiate a settlement through a messenger. Criff perhaps …

Nuada's silence was suddenly an overpowering presence. He glanced up and saw her staring, open-mouthed.

"Elena?"

"Yes, Elena. She's being held at the fortress with the Romans." Cethen tried to sound casual, yet found himself speaking slowly, for his voice felt ready to crack. "Or she will be, after she gets back from Rome with Coira."

"Coira too?"

"Uh-huh."

"Rome?"

He nodded. "Rome. Wherever that is. It's where the bast—where she seems to have passed the winter."

"And she's coming back?" Nuada sounded doubtful.

"Criff says she is. He's Cartimandua's bard."

"Hmm." She thought that over, then snorted. "I'll wager two goats to a grain of barley that your Roman is the one who took her there."

"That's who Criff said she went with," Cethen replied, puzzled at her magical leap of logic. It was as if he were speaking to Elena herself.

"Hah!" Nuada said derisively, the implication clear.

"The man has a wife," Cethen said, though the words sounded hollow. Nuada's disdain sent his mind plodding down a trail that had been well travelled the past few days.

"Oh, of course. That should make all the difference, then. Never mind." She returned to her sewing, but a few moments later shrugged philosophically, and said, "It probably evens out, I suppose. You're ploughing her sister by marriage. And seeding, too, I might add."

"That's not fair," he mumbled in protest. Finding no fault with her logic, though, he decided to retaliate instead. "I trust Cian, if he ever finds out his wife's being ploughed by his brother, will be just as understanding."

Cethen couldn't contain his smirk when he saw Nuada's jaw drop a second time. He realized he'd been hanging onto his boot, so he let it fall to the ground and began tugging at the second one.

"Cian's coming back too?" she breathed.

"Aw, shit, no," Cethen whispered hoarsely, his tone suddenly one of shame, for she had heard a message in his words that was not there. "He survived, but was sent away in one of their ships. When that happens they don't come back. At least he's probably alive." Cethen fell silent, keeping Criff's words about the arenas to himself.

"So he isn't coming back," Nuada snapped.

Cethen didn't know what to say, so he simply shrugged. The inside of the lodge grew quiet again except for the soft breathing of the children, and the occasional crackle of embers dying in the fire pit. He continued removing his clothes and Nuada went back to the jerkin, though her needle no longer darted in and out of the soft leather. After a few moments she gave up the task altogether and simply gazed at the embers, lost in thought. Cethen stared at her through half-lidded eyes, absently pulling at his moustache. After a while, her features creased into an impish grin, and she turned to look at Cethen.

"We are a pair, aren't we?" she giggled.

"Aye," he agreed, "a pair of rutting hedgehogs."

Morallta departed the following morning for Cumbria, but before going, she dispatched a small force down the west side of the mountains to Cornovii territory, where they could spy on the Romans. Venutius also departed, heading north to treat with the Selgovae. Dermat's two patrols left four days later to prowl the woods around Isurium, the same day that Loskenn took his riders to cover the new road the Romans were cutting between Ebor and Derventio.

Almost three weeks remained to the date that Criff had set for the Roman attack, and about ten days to the more cautious deadline set by Venutius. Cethen himself felt in no hurry to depart for a day or two. His people had been the last to return to Stannick so he felt justified, and besides, he was still struggling to work out what to do about Elena.

The druids held a small ceremony in the old part of the fortress to speed Loskenn and Dermat on their way. When they finally finished, Cethen found himself alone with Vellocatus, each standing close to the sacrificial bonfire as it burned itself out.

"Have a feeling we're getting near the end of it?" the older man asked.

The familiar mocking smile accompanied the question, yet Cethen felt a sudden kinship with its owner. "Aye. But not with an ending on which I'd care to place a wager."

"Dermat tells me your wife is held by the Roman." Vellocatus eased himself down on the grass, and held his hands out to the warmth. "The gods do play their games with you, Cethen Lamh-fada."

"I'm not flattered by their interest," Cethen grumbled, and slumped to the ground alongside. "I doubt my wife and daughter are either."

"And you worry about that."

"It's occasionally on my mind," Cethen said, and smiled at the understatement.

"And ...?"

"I doubt the bastard will fight me for them like a man of honour would," Cethen muttered, irritably tossing a half-burnt stick back into the flames, "so I had thought of doing it his way—buying them back."

"With ...?"

"You know the Romans better than I." He turned to look at Vellocatus, unable to keep the anxiety from his face. "What's the value of a good horse compared to a female slave?"

"There's a certain fairness in such a trade, I suppose," Vellocatus said carefully. "You have his horse, and he has your wife. I suppose it would depend on which he values the most." He suddenly grinned and opened his mouth to say more, but he quickly shut it again.

"What?" Cethen demanded.

Vellocatus shook his head, though the corner of his mouth twitched. "Nothing."

"You might as well say it, you prick," Cethen muttered. "You were going to say: it depends on which gives the better ride."

Vellocatus didn't deny the words. "If we fight the Romans off and follow up with an attack on their fortress, you still might get her back alive."

"I thought about that, too," Cethen sighed. "But Coira's held at some other place. The bastard has done that so neither one will run. I think the best way is to try and buy her back. How would you go about it?"

Vellocatus bit his lip as he gave the matter thought, and ended up confirming what Cethen had in mind. "Criff. Go through Criff. Dermat has some manner of meeting with him."

"Criff wouldn't give me the pickings from his nose," Cethen grumbled, "not since Borba and I killed his …his friend."

"His friends come and go," Vellocatus scoffed, "though not usually quite the way this one did. Anyway, for Criff, the story's probably better for its tragedy. Hey, speaking of Criff, maybe he'd get Catey to look after it? In fact, that's probably even better, though I'm damn sure it'll take more than a chestnut horse. On principle—the Roman probably still thinks the animal is his."

"And I think Elena's still mine."

"But you're the one who wants to buy." Vellocatus paused for a moment, then added softly, "And is she still yours?"

"What do you mean?" Cethen demanded, his voice a growl.

"Cethen, I don't mean anything by it, but she's been gone for— what? Nine, ten months now? Look what you've been doing in that time. You've been ploughing Nuada, just for a start. Then there's Morallta. Everyone pretends not to know it, but she's carrying your brat. So what do you think Elena's been doing all this time?"

Cethen clenched his jaw and said nothing.

"Not only that, she has been to Rome."

"The Roman's wife was there, too," Cethen muttered weakly.

"Aye, but I tell you, that's not the point." Vellocatus climbed to his feet with a look that said there was no use in saying more, but he would anyway. "Cethen, I've talked to men and women who've been taken as slaves, from all four corners of Rome's lousy empire. I've spoken to people who once lived in mud-walled huts, one-room hovels, and desert caves pried from the animals that lived there; folk who shit in holes five paces from their doorway, washed in water two steps farther on, and drank from the stream it all trickled down to. And every one of them, when they see whatever there is to see in this place they call Rome …well, I'll tell you, Cethen. They change."

"Elena wouldn't," Cethen persisted.

"Then talk to Dermat," Vellocatus said, throwing up his hands. "See if he can set up a meeting with Criff. Anything's worth a try, I suppose."

Venutius returned three days later in a black mood. The Selgovae were willing to help, but it would be another two weeks before any kind of force would reach Stannick. If Criff's prediction was correct, then they would be in time, and it could mean the difference in defeating the Romans. At least fifteen thousand had been promised, though of that, perhaps only a half, and more likely a third, within the time that mattered. Even so, his own people were gathering, and given another ten to twenty days, they would outnumber the Romans by at least three or four to one. It was uncertainty that plagued the aging king, though, and made him increasingly edgy.

Cethen, who had been set to leave anyway, decided he was overdue, and left the next morning. His small force again travelled south across the upper reaches of the valleys, using the hidden trails that joined one rugged hill to the next, for the more direct path was no longer safe. The patrol turned eastward down the same valley where they had slaughtered the Roman patrol, and Morallta's bairn had been bred in the brook. They reached the Abus as evening was falling, cutting the road to the fortress a few miles south of Isurium.

Darkness had fallen earlier than usual, for clouds blackened the sky. It had started raining in the late afternoon, soaking clothes to the skin, and chilling bodies to the bone. Makeshift pine branch lean-to's were built as shelter against the night, each set deep in the forest. Sputtering fires were coaxed to life under the dripping canopy of the trees, but provided little warmth. It was a cold, tired, surly group that woke the next morning to greet yet another dark and rainy day.

Hoping to meet Criff, Cethen wanted to reach the fortress as soon as possible, but they were still on the west side of the river. The small force could have continued downstream and watched from the forest, but for Cethen, that placed them on the wrong side of the swollen Abus. He might see Criff or Elena, but it would be from a distance, and there would be no chance to talk. Though if he saw Elena, would she even want to talk?

Cethen suddenly realized that the prospect of catching a glimpse of his wife, or meeting Criff, was now governing every action of the patrol. Not that it changed matters, but it certainly made them more complicated. He was contemplating what to do should he see his wife when Luath, who had been scouting the river, ducked his head under the pine bough shelter.

"If we're going across, the only way is farther up river," he grumbled. "The water's rising fast. There won't be a chance for long. I'd guess that once there, we'll be stuck on the other side." The twin's red hair was plastered dark against his skull, and his thin moustaches dripped like leaky thatch. He shook himself like a dog and rubbed his hands together, searching vainly for warmth in the dead fire. With daylight, each one had been smothered.

"Too much smoke," Borba explained as he edged in alongside his brother. He stamped his feet to force feeling back into them.

"No sign of anyone?" Cethen asked.

"Not even a fresh track," Luath replied, "though you can't hardly tell, in this weather."

"We'll cross over," Cethen decided, as another forlorn measure of hope came to mind. "We might come across Dermat."

Borba frowned, puzzled. "Why would we do that? He's supposed to be watching north of Isurium."

"Yes, I know," Cethen muttered, groaning as he picked up his saddle and threw it over his shoulder, "but he's also in touch with the bard at the fortress."

They crossed the Abus using an old ford not far downriver from Isurium. Another half day of rain, and they would have been swimming. The horses waded across with the current driving hard against their bellies, staggering onto the eastern bank of the river like a pack of wet hounds. Everyone needed a rest, and it seemed ages before they moved off again. Cethen decided the whole day had been wasted, for it was evening when they finally neared the fortress. They made camp in the dripping forest, and tried to rest.

The next morning he left the two small troops with Luath, and walked the last half mile through the trees with Borba. They hid in the dark cover of the undergrowth, soaking wet, and dwarfed by the closeness of the Roman fortress.

"The buggers have the sense to stay inside," Cethen muttered, gulping for breath as he pushed the foliage aside and peered through the heavy rain.

The long wooden palisade stood black against the dark overcast of the sky. There were no soldiers outside the stronghold, and farther along the wall the gates were closed. Only the shadows of a half-dozen guards could be seen through the drizzle, patrolling the top of the ramparts. The forlorn hope of seeing Elena or Criff appeared to be exactly that: a forlorn hope. Even the gods would not have stepped outside on a day like this. He was about to say so when Borba spoke.

"They've got different guards," the twin murmured, almost indifferently.

Cethen peered through the rain, unable to see anything other than dim shapes atop the wall. *His eyes again,* Cethen thought; *they're like a cat's.* "How so?" he asked.

"The ones who built the place have red shields with yellowy wings."

"They do?" Cethen stared a while longer, mulling over what that meant. If different soldiers were guarding the fortress, they were either reinforcements, or the others had left. The thought struck Cethen like the blow of an axe. If they had left, then surely there was only one place they would be going—north! Yet there had been no sign of movement, anywhere.

"What else do you see?" he asked.

"Nothing."

"Exactly," Cethen whispered.

There *was* nothing more to be seen. No horses grazed in the pastures, no auxiliary cavalry came or went through the gates, no soldiers were outside the walls. At Stannick, there was always some movement during the day, and the weather be damned; here, surely, it should be no different. Even the riverbank was empty. A half-dozen ships were moored by the dock, certainly, but he saw no trace of the cargo they had seen stacked along the waterfront when they were last here. The fortress reeked of desertion.

"They've pulled a sack over our heads," Cethen muttered, drawing back into the trees, gripped with a sense of urgency. "They've left by the back gate."

The two quickly withdrew, and hurried back to the others. Both troops were soon backtracking to the only other possible path: the new Roman roadway cut to Derventio. Yet even as the horses crashed off through the trees, none of it made sense to Cethen. Derventio lay at the edge of Parisi territory, miles to the northeast; Stannick lay north too, but it was further to the west. He felt an icy coldness inside; a dark, hopeless feeling that filled his stomach, for he had no idea what was going on.

Such heavy rain usually would have washed all sign of normal traffic from the unfinished surface of the road. It was soon apparent, however, that whatever traffic had passed this way was not normal. The deep ruts scarring the forest floor could only have been carved by loaded wagons, scores of them, possibly hundreds; and only an army of hooves and boots could have left the rest of the roadway in such a quagmire. Every trough and hollow overflowed with water, the edges already rounded by the downpour.

Yet the direction made no sense! Why march eastward to Derventio, if the destination was Stannick?

They soon found the answer. Farther along the roadway, where the soggy surface rose to higher, firmer ground, another crude track had been hacked quickly from the forest. The telltale ruts and the chopped, pounded mud showed that an army had travelled this way, over a trail carved mere days ahead of its passing.

"They did not come through here yesterday," Luath said, staring down at the mutilated earth. "The rain would have made it far too deep a bog to pass through."

Ligan knelt beside him and probed the muddy water in the ruts. "It was at least the day before, and ahead of the rain. It was as dry as a dead man's throat then. The wheels dug in some, certainly, but the wagons would still be here, had they tried this morning."

"They could have two days on us," Cethen muttered, and glanced up at the rolling clouds; not even a patch of dull light showed where the sun sat.

"Two days at least," Borba said. "They could be attacking as we speak. For certain, they'll be in position in the morning."

"Surely Venutius will know where they are," Cethen murmured, as much to himself as the others. "Loskenn may have seen them and taken word. He's been down here almost a week now."

Several others muttered their assurance, but Borba voiced their doubts. "But maybe not. He could have been closer to Derventio."

"Aye, maybe not," Cethen sighed, and turned the big chestnut back the way they had come. "If we ride like the wind, we might get there before dawn. We'll likely kill the horses, but we have to try."

They pushed their mounts as hard as they dared, then goaded them even faster, galloping over the slick trail without care for life or limb, rider or beast. They slowed to rest only when the horses laboured too heavily, and began to falter. Even then, they walked, pulling the reluctant animals along by their reins.

They passed by Isurium early afternoon, cautiously walking the animals along the back trails away from the bank of the swollen river, which cost more time. Yet the caution seemed unnecessary. The fort, glimpsed from the far side of the river, had the gates firmly closed. Even at a distance, the stronghold reeked of the same emptiness as the fortress at Ebur. Only a few guards walked the parapets, and if they saw the dim shapes of riders amongst the darkness of the trees, they showed no concern. Which only confirmed that the Romans were on the move. Cethen fought the puzzle with the same frustration: if so, where were they?

There was no sign the Isurium garrison had taken the path north, if their troops were indeed on the move. Nor was there any sign of Dermat. If he had seen the Romans leave the fort, he would have surely ridden ahead with the warning. If not, then more than likely he was camped somewhere, simply watching.

They passed the eerie stillness of Bran's Beck as evening was falling, and later, with both horses and riders spent, arrived cautiously at the burned-out village where Rhun had waited for his father. The night was well on its path, and still they had found no trace of the Roman army. Its absence where the village had once stood put the lie to what Criff had told Dermat: the site would likely be used as one of their marching camps to strike at Stannick. Which led to the second lie: Criff had also said the Romans would not move for another ten days!

Cethen cursed as Gadearg waded the stream. Who was lying to who: Criff to the Britons, or the Romans to Criff? Lies or not, Cethen would have wagered a cow to a cockerel that the enemy was somewhere close by. Probably to the east; or possibly, may the gods strike them all dead, farther to the north.

They'd covered most of the distance that remained when they again rested, for the horses were of small use, and the riders little better. Nearly half of them were now scattered back along the trail, the horses blown, splayed, or broken. The twins still set the pace, their fine animals reduced to a state of exhaustion. Ligan sat wearily on his big bay, its head hanging low. Three of the women had kept up, as had a score of the men. All needed rest, yet not one grumbled when they moved off again.

Once more they went on foot, slogging forward at a giddy, weaving trot, tugging at the reins to make the horses follow. For the moment it was faster than riding the tired beasts, and if the animals had anything left, it was best saved until the end.

As the night wore on toward dawn, the trail began to show familiar signs, even in the blackness of night. Cethen recognized landmarks while still unable to see them: a dip where the track crossed a small beck; the black shadow of a large rock on top of a ridge; and at last, the ghostly pale trunks of the birch stand that marked the end of their path. Stannick was only a half mile away, on the other side. He breathed a sigh of relief. A long night of a hundred pleadings to the gods had been answered. They had arrived before the Romans, and it was still dark.

The few who remained paused a final time to catch their breath, then climbed onto their spent animals for the final leg of the journey: a dark trail that wound through the thick cluster of birch trees. Exhaustion suddenly disappeared, replaced by a tight-stomached tension.

Cethen rode silently at the head of the small line of riders as they crested the tree covered rise that looked down on Stannick. He reined Gadearg back as they broke from the birch stand, a cold shiver running quickly down his spine. Something in the night air gave him pause, an eerie sensation that caused the hair to rise on the back of his neck. The chestnut halted of its accord, and Cethen listened.

At first it was a soft, steady rustling that whispered through the trees, as if the forest itself were coming alive. The sound grew steadily stronger, suddenly becoming horribly familiar: the low creak of straining leather, the rhythmic pad of plodding feet, the soft whinny of a horse, and the dull, heavy jangle that armour and weapons make when warriors are on the move.

"Shit," Borba whispered, then uttered the word again.

Cethen's eyes were far less keen than the twin's, but even he could see the hundreds—no, thousands—of dark shapes moving across the slope barely a spear throw away. Cethen closed his eyes and cursed the gods; sometimes, they could be greater shits than the Romans. Perhaps the gods were Roman!

His heart sank deeper into despair as more and more dark shapes passed beyond the shadow of the forest; a slithering, ant-like mass of movement that made the earth itself appear alive. His mind turned to Rhun and Tuis, both boys asleep inside the false protection of the fortress lying lost in the blackness below. Nuada and her two children would be there too, along with all the other kin. Cethen's chest felt as if a band had tightened around it, and he could hardly breathe.

Fighting panic, he swept his gaze over the shadowy flow of the Roman army. For a moment, barely the blink of an eye, a break appeared. Cethen hesitated just long enough to believe what he saw, then quietly urged Gadearg forward. A moment later he was lost among the moving shadows.

Chapter XXIV

Elena sat patiently on a bench in the courtyard of the headquarters building, sheltered by the portico that ran around the inside of the walls. The courtyard itself was a clutter of clerks all perched behind tables, each with a restless line of soldiers standing in front. Others moved back and forth in a steady stream throughout the building, with heads down and expressions serious. Elena knew above all that interruptions were the last thing that Gaius wanted, especially for personal matters, but be that as it may—some things were of graver importance.

The garrison's morning clatter had started unusually early, waking her long before dawn to find Gaius gone, his side of the bed already cold. She normally slept lightly, and wondered how he had managed to steal away without disturbing her. A quick glance outside showed it was still dark, but soldiers filled the street. Oxen-drawn wagons creaked by the open window, and she saw light flickering in the upper openings of the headquarters basilica.

For a while Elena had thought the legion was moving out, launching the assault they had all known was coming, but that was not supposed to be for another two weeks. Anger that Gaius had kept it from her was followed quickly by anguish when she thought of her two boys at Stannick. She knew that Cethen would do his best to protect them, but had he survived only to die alongside the children when the Romans struck?

As daylight came and the morning advanced, it became apparent that the legion was not going anywhere, though she could tell that it was getting ready to move out, probably the next day. Scores of wagons laden with supplies had been parked unharnessed in orderly lines on the streets. Wherever she looked, soldiers were drawing field rations, inspecting kit, or honing their weapons. When Elena looked in on the courtyard in front of the headquarters building and saw the clerks setting up their tables, she knew it was almost time.

Centurions from the legion were there, along with officers from the auxiliary and cavalry regiments, all reporting unit strengths and receiving final orders. If she needed any further confirmation at all, she got it in the troop transports arriving on the tidewater, ferrying the two replacement cohorts from the Sixth Adiutrix at Lindum. The Ninth was moving out, and with it, all the troops that could be mustered. Elena had walked with grim determination to the quadrangle in front of the headquarters building, where she sat down to wait.

It was approaching midday when Gaius came out of the building with Titus and the quartermaster, all three arguing. An entire shipment of arrows for the auxiliary support troops should have been aboard the last supply vessel to unload, and it was not. A heated debate followed as to whether the missiles were necessary, or if the archers—all eight contingents of them—could get by with what they had. The commanders said they could not, which was to be expected. Titus decided they could, if the damned archers were damned careful and didn't shoot their damned arrows off like they were hunting hogs …and there were not any more to be had anyway, were there? And if they damned well advanced like they were supposed to, they could retrieve the ones they had shot! Or at least, the ones that missed.

The quartermaster went back inside, ready to pass the word to the next man who complained about arrows. Titus, after a few more words, left the courtyard, leaving Gaius to scratch at the hidden scar on the top of his skull, and decide what to do next. His glance caught Elena as she rose to her feet under the portico, and he frowned. Then something else seemed to tug at his memory and ease his mood.

He smiled and walked over to greet her. "Have you been here long?"

"A while," she said, suddenly uncertain. The welcome was less than the impatient dismissal she'd expected.

"Want to go for a walk?" he asked, and moved toward the street without waiting for a reply.

Elena followed, wondering why he seemed so at ease with himself. Under the circumstance, the army readying itself to move and a hundred distractions on all sides, she had expected to find him doubly irritated at the interruption. Instead, Gaius turned left on the *Via Principalis* and made his way through the dense traffic to the east gate, his mood almost cheerful. She trailed behind for the most part, because the street was jammed with soldiers and rows of waiting wagons. It seemed like a score or more had been added during her wait in the courtyard.

Outside the walls, the fortress seemed just as busy, with the fields full of auxiliary troops, and men of the Sixth moving in their gear under the shadow of the palisades. "Where are we going?" she asked as they threaded their way through a full cohort of Tungri cavalry sorting through its equipment. The odour of horses was sweet and pungent, the smell of the creaking leather rich and warm. Everyone seemed occupied, and other than the odd salute thrown Gaius's way, neither animals nor men paid them the slightest attention.

"I want you to see something," he said as they neared the green curtain of trees that hid the smaller river Fosse. "Something I had to deal with before going to Rome last year. It was necessary, and long overdue."

"There's also something I have to tell you," Elena said, falling in alongside; she had decided that firmness was her best approach. "I'm going with you tomorrow."

Gaius glanced sideways and frowned, but did not slow down. "What have you been told about tomorrow?"

"Nothing. Nothing at all," she said, and swept her hand about the field and back to the fortress, "but I'm not blind, either. You leave tomorrow, or you're going to a lot of trouble for nothing."

Gaius said no more and quickened his pace.

"I have two children at Stannick, and I want to be there, should you breach those walls. They won't stand a chance otherwise. And there are others. My sister by marriage. Her children."

"And your husband too, I suppose," Gaius growled, his face tensing.

"Since you mention it, I don't want to see him killed," Elena said. "Why would I? Any more than I imagine Helvia would want to see you slain."

"Hah! There's nothing she would like better."

"Well I wouldn't want my husband dead, even if I do dishonour him," she said, suddenly unsure just how she felt about Cethen. Her life had become a huge contradiction since Criff had told her that he still lived.

"Well, he's damned lucky then," Gaius said, ducking the low branches as they entered the woods and turned onto a small track that led along the riverbank. "When I was being cuckolded by my wife, I know for certain she'd have preferred me dead. It was only that prick Lucius pointing out she was a whore that softened her thoughts on the matter."

Elena found herself talking to his back as they padded along the trail, but she curbed her anger. She had been about to demand whether or not he thought she was a whore too, but realized that would only move her further from what she wanted. "Tell me then, Gaius Sabinius Trebonius," she said patiently, "if you were in my place, with Marcus and Aelia trapped inside a fortress about to be attacked by thousands and thousands of Venutius's warriors, where would you want to be?"

"I'm not in your place, though. *I* will be on the outside," Gaius said testily, as if her line of argument irritated him. "You are always doing that—asking me what I would do in your place. It isn't fair, because I'm never in your place. Nor do I want to be."

"Fine," Elena persisted, ignoring what she saw as his twisted logic, "then let's say Aelia and Marcus are on the outside. Then you would be there too, wouldn't you? And you would want to be. After all, you're their father. So why shouldn't I be there as well?"

"Because you're their mother and *their* father *is* already there. On the inside. So what's the problem?"

Elena wanted to run forward and pound on his back, but she could see that his last piece of logic had amused him, which might mean he was softening. It was infuriating dealing with the man, for he was much more difficult to manage than Cethen. Most times he would not be managed at all! She decided to play compliant. "That's easy to answer. The problem is: I should be there."

She received no response. Gaius had stepped into a small clearing almost roofed over by long, leafy branches of willow and yew. A mound, freshly seeded to grass, had been built up in the centre where a monument, about half the height of a man, had been erected on a sandstone base. Across from it a stone bench had been set in the shadow of the trees. He moved quietly across the parklike glade and sat down, beckoning her to join him.

"What do you think?" he asked, his mood seemingly buoyant again.

Elena studied the tall slab of stone. Angular Roman letters had been chiselled into its surface, and above them stood the figure of a soldier in full armour holding a sword and a shield. The writing she could not understand but the figure, she guessed, was supposed to be Gaius. It looked nothing like him. Even so, it was impressive and she said as much.

"As I said, the gift is long overdue and the gods have been kind," he said, and leaned forward to stare at the stone. "I have promised them many times, and now it is done. I can leave tomorrow with a clear conscience."

"What does it say?" Elena asked, for the moment letting go of her own problem; it could be addressed later, though not too much later, for there was little time.

Pleased at the question, Gaius moved forward and crouched by the stone. Pointing to the letters without touching the surface, he read the inscription.

TO THE GODDESS OF FORTUNE AND THE GENIUS OF THIS PLACE
GAIUS SABINIUS TREBONIUS, TRIBUNE OF THE VIIII LEGIO HISPANA
PAYS HIS VOW JOYFULLY, WILLINGLY, AND DESERVEDLY.
AND LET THE GIFT, THIS GIFT, BELONG: I MUST BEWARE OF TOUCHING IT

He looked back at her, smiling, and Elena was oddly reminded of Rhun showing off his first deer. In fact, if she remembered correctly, it was her son's only deer, and the memory injected more caution into her

GRAHAM CLEWS

reply. Sometimes it was difficult to see where the man began, and the boy left off.

"It is fitting," she said, carefully picking her words. "The gods will surely be satisfied with the gift. More than satisfied."

His reply startled her. "I think so too. If I die in the days to come, I owe them nothing."

Gaius returned to the bench and they both sat staring at the monument, lost in their own thoughts. Elena saw that he was glowing with a quiet pride, and realized that the stone was not so much a tribute as it was a memorial. Those who followed would remember Gaius Sabinius Trebonius, even though they would have no idea who he really was. Not like the gods. Hopefully they would simply welcome the gift and favour him accordingly.

But that was all for the future, and Elena shook her head. She had to deal with the present. She sat debating her next move, and decided it was best for Gaius himself to raise the matter of Stannick. If that did not occur, then she would not mention it again until they reached the eastern gate of the fortress. At the very earliest.

"Well," Gaius finally said, stretching his arms in front of him, "there is much to do. I should be getting back."

Elena made no move to rise. The ploy worked, for he sighed and turned to look at her. "It's impossible for you to go. Every precaution has been taken to keep this attack a surprise. As of this morning, nobody—you, Cartimandua's people, absolutely no one—will leave this fortress unescorted. The advance is secret, and it will remain that way."

"If I ride with you in the morning, then it will still remain a secret, won't it? Who could I possibly tell? If your army succeeds, then I can help save my children. If it doesn't succeed, then they will be safe. Either way, I will know where the boys are. I am their mother, dammit."

"I know where they are too. I was there, remember? I'll make sure they come to no harm," Gaius promised. "I'll detail a squad to protect them."

Elena's mind conjured a vision of Rhun and any others who might be nearby as a dozen Roman soldiers closed in on them. She shook her head. "That won't work. I have to be there," she said fiercely and added, "I will be there!"

Gaius stood and stared down at her. "No you won't," he said, his voice harsh. "Let me remind you of what you already know, should you grow headstrong, and take matters in hand. If a man's slave rebels against him, then every slave in his household is responsible. If death results, then they all die. That's not my law, that's the law of Rome. The matter would be out of my hands. Your daughter is my slave and so is Metellus. I would hate to lose him."

Gaius stalked to the edge of the clearing where he paused, as if suddenly hesitant, and turned. His voice had softened slightly when he spoke. "I would hate to lose Coira, too. Aelia has grown quite attached to her. Now come, there's still a lot to be done."

The night before the Ninth marched, Cartimandua invited the senior legion officers to dine at her quarters. Nearly all attended, for she kept a good table, and besides, none of them knew when they would sit down to their next decent meal. There was as much drink available as food, but for once everyone took nearly everything in moderation. The mood was brittle, as might be expected, and not lightened at all by the presence of Criff. The bard was as morose as the music he plucked from his harp, and when he sang, it was of lost battles and thwarted love. Gaius commented on the man's melancholy when he found Cartimandua standing beside him as he prepared to leave.

"I think it's because of what happened to his Tungri cavalryman," she said. "He was found dead, after you spoke on how well your own salacious life was faring."

"The surgeon told me those two men died the previous day."

"Really?" Cartimandua's eyes widened in the now familiar look of surprise that Gaius found far too innocent. "Then perhaps he's a fickle bard with more stamina than I credit him for. Perhaps he was not meeting the Tungri cavalryman."

"The governor tells me Criff's tastes lie in the other direction."

"Not true. He takes after me, in one way, I suppose. He's quite comfortable keeping one foot in either camp." She giggled. "Only with him, I suppose it's not his foot he keeps there."

"That's not what I meant," Gaius growled, sure she was being deliberately obtuse. "I meant if the Tungri died the day before, then Criff was probably seeing one of Venutius's people."

"One of Venutius's people?" Cartimandua said, and her eyes narrowed to two dark slits. "That's absurd. But let me pose a question to you, Roman. What if he had? What if he did pass information that day? All he could do was tell my first husband that you're not due to attack Stannick for another week or two. So who was doing who a service?"

"Are you implying …?" Gaius was suddenly perplexed, and his voice faded.

"A-hah, you see the question? Is he working for your people and passing on the word you want? Or is he being duped, and in turn duping Venutius?" She reached up and patted his cheek, tilting her head to one side with a coy smile. "Or is he working for anyone at all? I doubt whether even Cerialis knows all the answers. So perhaps that's the reason Criff is morose. He's been duped. Or perhaps he simply regrets his role. Or does he mope for a dead foreign trooper? Or does it even matter?"

Gaius grunted, sure that it did, but not sure why.

"Anyway, I didn't want to talk about that," Cartimandua said breezily. "I want to talk about your female slave."

"Elena?"

"How many do you have in camp?" She shook her head in exasperation. "Of course Elena. I'm curious. What are your plans for the woman?"

"Plans?" Gaius looked puzzled. "She's a slave. I have no plans for her."

"If that's all she is, then that's fine. I just wanted to know," she said and turned as if seeking someone else to speak to, adding as she did, "Try not to get killed this time …turd."

"Wait a moment." Gaius spoke louder than he'd intended, turning heads nearby; he lowered his voice. "What are you up to?"

Cartimandua turned back, her expression bland. "Why, nothing. I just wanted to make sure she was nothing more than a slave. Do you suppose you'll one day sell her?"

"Of course not. Why would I do that?"

"You said she was just a slave. They all have a price."

"Yes, but—"

"I assume you have no affection for her."

"Well …"

"Of course you don't. I understand. You're simply using *her*, instead of the five-fingered widow. I'm certain it's far more gratifying."

"Stop it, dammit," Gaius snapped. "Of course there's some—well, some sort of feeling, I suppose. But that doesn't change her status, does it?"

"No. That's up to you, I *suppose*." Cartimandua shook her head. "How does she feel about you?"

"Well, warmly I think," he said defensively.

"Good. Then if you want it to remain that way, I suggest you take her with you tomorrow."

"Aaaagh!" Gaius yelped, finally realizing the thrust of the conversation. "The woman's been here enlisting your help!"

"No, she hasn't," Cartimandua lied blatantly, "but I did notice she's been walking around with a face longer than Criff's. The woman's a warrior, dammit, a she-bear, and her cubs are in danger. Let me tell you, Roman, if those boys die and she isn't there, then you might as well ship her to the arenas. She'll be no good to you for anything after that—absolutely anything, ever! And you'll have the blame of it. And oh—I wouldn't sleep next to her either, that's for damned certain. Not if you want to wake up in the morning."

Gaius swung his legs over the side of the bed and quickly began dressing, taking care to be quiet so he wouldn't wake Elena. But when he stood to pull the long, leather tunic over his head, he glanced down and saw her watching him. She lay on her back with the covers pulled up to her chin, her hazel green eyes unblinking and expressionless.

"It looks like there'll be rain later," he said, and when she made no reply added, "I suggest you take the leather cloak that's been oiled.

And something for your head, too."

Elena's eyes widened and at first she said nothing, continuing to stare.

"I thought you wanted to go," he said gruffly, setting his breast armour in place and working to secure it. "Here, help me with this."

Elena got quickly out of bed and Gaius raised his arms, giving her room to fasten the leather ties.

"You won't carry any arms," he muttered, pulling at the chest pieces when she finished, testing the snugness of the fit, "and until we get there, you'll remain with the headquarters dispatch riders. Stay close, for they will kill you if you start to wander." Elena raised her eyebrows and Gaius shrugged. "Cerialis's orders," he said, stretching the truth. He had suggested the order himself when he saw doubt in the governor's eyes. "You can understand why."

The Ninth and the attached auxiliary units already at Ebor assembled on the drill field to the east of the fortress before the last shades of night disappeared. The lead elements were already on the rough-cut road leading to Derventio when daybreak tinted the horizon. The sun itself never appeared. It remained hidden behind rolling banks of scudding cloud as the vanguard of Cerialis's legion veered north, taking a crude trail hacked through the forest over the previous week. The artillery and supply wagons followed behind before the night dew had dried, leaving no trace of the army behind other than its tracks.

A steady drizzle started later that afternoon and grew heavier as evening wore on. The path north had been hacked out along high ground where possible, avoiding the gullies and the low flatlands that sucked up rain, and quickly turned the soft earth into marsh. The crude track continued for almost ten miles before striking a second, well-used trail that led northwest.

There, the long, ponderous column turned, falling in behind the faster-moving Derventio auxiliary cohorts that had arrived a few hours after dawn and stood waiting. By midafternoon, the reinforced column caught up with the auxiliaries from Isurium. Quintus had left the fort earlier that morning, leading the mixed force of infantry and cavalry directly east in order to cut the same path. He had then marched them several miles north before settling down to wait.

Cerialis was immensely relieved to see the three separate forces unite. The logistics had been difficult, but his half of the army was now complete. The column was making excellent time despite the onset of a drizzling rain, and there had been no sign of the enemy. This, in itself, was a worry to the governor, and he ordered a hasty staff meeting. Certainly the weather was turning miserable, and certainly the route was planned to gain a certain element of surprise, but he had expected to find the advance detected in its early stages.

"Has anyone, anywhere, seen sign of the damned barbarians?" he asked, searching the dripping faces of his cohort commanders.

"Not since about three days ago, sir," one called out.

Cerialis squinted through the drizzle at one of the senior troop commanders from Derventio. "What did you see, Lucinius?" he asked. "Or more important, what did the enemy see? And where are they now?"

"I believe they saw nothing, sir," the man replied, and grinned. "And even if they had, none lived to tell. There were about two dozen of them, on horse. My men gave chase. Ended up driving them straight into the soldiers clearing out the road to Ebor. I spoke to the centurios. They heard them coming a mile away. Crash, bang, boom!" The commander smacked his hands together for emphasis.

"Casualties?"

"Some, sir," Lucinius said, and shook his head regretfully. "In fact, quite a few. The leader was a great, black-headed bastard the size of a bull. He took several down himself. And strangely, his men fought with a certain skill that cost us. But I'm sure we got them all."

"Anyone else? Quintus? You're in the vanguard."

The praefectus shook his head. "Not a thing, sir. All day. Perhaps the weather?"

Doubtful, Cerialis turned away and stared to where the dark moors sat forbiddingly to the north-east, barely visible through the increasing drizzle. Which meant his own people were also barely visible if someone was up there, watching. Which was unlikely in this miserable weather. Was it possible he had actually stolen a march on Venutius? The governor paced back and forth, pounding his fist into the palm of his hand. It was all very good, but not necessarily part of the plan!

"We thought the Ninth would gain their attention first, while Agricola slips his force over the high country, and past their backsides," Cerialis muttered almost to himself. "*Someone* must have seen us?"

"It's three days before we meet up with him, isn't it, sir?" Quintus asked.

"Three, possibly four. We allowed some flexibility," Cerialis murmured, his brow puckered in thought. He again stared up at the moors. "Quintus, how far ahead have you marked us for camp?"

"About four or five miles, sir," the praefectus replied with a satisfied smirk. His scouts had reported back with a suitable area barely moments before the two columns had united.

"I want to do better than that," Cerialis said, still thoughtfully biting his lip, "much better. I don't want to make camp until night is well upon us. Find another place farther on that would match such a schedule. One way or another, deal with any barbarians you find who might let Venutius know we're coming. Gentlemen!" The governor raised his voice so that everyone would hear. "I do believe the enemy has no idea we're here. I want to take advantage of that!"

Conditions had deteriorated miserably by the following morning. The rain fell in sheets from a black sky, driven sideways by a wind that uprooted tents and threatened to pluck even the sharp wooden stakes from the mud ramparts of the marching camp. The huge enclosure flickered under the eerie glow of jagged lightning, and the sky cracked with long, rolling peals of thunder.

The troops, particularly the auxiliaries, were reluctant to move. Word spread that the gods were angry, and the attack was doomed. Cerialis went almost berserk. Part of his mind wondered if the men might not be correct; the other boiled with an anger he was more than willing to share. He moved among the cohorts with his senior officers, bullying and coaxing, forcing the unit commanders to their feet to start marching.

Gaius followed in his wake, shocked at the dumb, bovine resistance. It seemed as if all the effort so far would be wasted by troops that stood like cattle in a wallowing bog of mud. Then, almost unexpectedly, a century from one of the regular cohorts moved out, reluctantly shuffling off down the sodden trail leading north. Another soon followed, and finally, one by one, unit by unit, the sullen troops formed up in order of march. It was haphazard and disordered, individual kit was badly packed and sometimes abandoned, but Cerialis was everywhere. The moment a unit fell into some sort of order, he browbeat the commander until he got them moving. The previous day's slop-plodding pace gradually resumed, but it was almost mid morning.

The heavy baggage wagons quickly fell behind in a growing mire of mud. The huge column snaked its way north under a dark pall that seemed to double the load of every man. Around mid afternoon, conditions started to ease. The rain once more eased to a steady drizzle and, more important, the black clouds lightened, driving back the pervading sense of doom. As if a curse had been lifted, the men moved faster, even though the ground was, if anything, heavier than before.

The line of march continued under the sharp slopes of the endless moorland to the east, the feeling of exposure overpowering. Scouts rode ahead and on both flanks, even up onto the moors, vainly searching for sign of Venutius's people. As evening overtook the slow moving column, a horrible feeling began to plague Gaius's mind: the Ninth legion was marching into a trap. As if terrified by the same thought, Cerialis doubled, then tripled the patrols.

The army camped the second night amidst a steady stream of cursing—at the mud, at the rain, and the governor's decision to keep marching until nightfall. The weather had settled to a dull, heavy drizzle that lacked its earlier fury. The huge army threw itself into the routine of pitching tents, digging ramparts, and feeding itself. Cerialis increased the guard twofold even as the soaked earthworks were being dug; and when the cavalry patrols sent out earlier in the day began to trickle in, new ones promptly vanished into the darkness.

The third day dawned with no change. The rain continued, a steady drizzle that sapped the will, bogged the wagons and the artillery, and turned the line of march into a plodding, slogging progress made even more miserable by exhaustion. When the constant down-pour finally eased shortly after midday, the army still remained in sight of the brooding presence of the moorland almost ten miles to the east. More than a day and a half of sodden march had hardly gained them twenty miles.

The Ninth was to meet up with Agricola at a point south of Stannick, which Cerialis's scouts told him now lay due west of their position. With a sigh of resignation, the governor ordered Quintus to lead the vanguard in that direction. The delay probably meant Agricola would reach his objective first. Could the man be trusted to stay his hand?

Cursing, Cerialis pushed the exhausted column onward until nightfall under a canopy of dark, rolling clouds that threatened to erupt into yet another downpour. The terrain grew more firm as evening fell, and the flat plain between the moors and the central hills gave way to higher ground. The army trudged on, over land that now offered firmer footing. When they finally made camp in a place that Quintus assured him was the site where the two forces were to unite, Cerialis sighed in relief. Agricola was not yet there.

But if not, then where was the bastard? He was supposed to be there!

Again the patrols were sent out, double those of the night before. And again, Cerialis was surprised that no contact had been made with the barbarians. Unease knotted his belly to the point of paranoia; per-haps he was, after all, being led into a trap. The feeling was reinforced by the lack of word from Agricola, and no sign of the second army marching up from the west.

The berms for the marching camp had already been dug and stakes pounded in on top, when two dispatch riders from the Twentieth fi-nally rode into camp.

Elena stood against the leather wall of the command tent, talking with the two guards assigned to watch her. Gaius smiled as he moved her way. It was difficult to tell who was supposed to be watching who.

The tent was packed with the ever-present clerks and dispatch riders, plus a good many others with no excuse to be there, other than the warm brazier that glowed off in one corner. The coals threw off a surprising amount of heat, and the odour of sputtering oil lamps, wet clothing, and hard-used bodies soon ripened the air.

Gaius eased Elena away from her escort and ushered her into the central module, where a score of senior officers waited for Cerialis. The orderlies had placed a table to one side, and it seemed that everyone had one hand busy with food, and the other with a drink of some kind. A low, steady chatter filled the tent, most of it speculation on what the governor's next move would be. Gaius felt sure he knew.

"I suspect we'll be moving out before dawn, which is not as planned," he said to Elena as they stood by the table, deciding what to eat. "You will stay close to me. The same rules will apply."

"Rules?" she asked, absently eyeing the food. She was hungry. A platter of sliced cured ham, a wedge of cheese, and a large slab of bread had her attention. The wine was of little interest.

"Yes, rules. Don't play the innocent. If you break away, you become a target." Gaius eased a half-dozen shucked oysters down his throat one at a time, each followed by a morsel of bread dipped in *garum*. "Let me remind you, your position here is viewed twofold. Most think it's because of your knowledge of Stannick. There are others who believe your intention is to warn the enemy at the first opportunity. So stay close, or your life is forfeit."

"I intend to," Elena said, looking him straight in the eye as she bit first into a slice of ham, and then a chunk of bread. "It's the best way to ensure my children will survive."

Cerialis surprised them all by calling the officers over to his own tent, which was pitched alongside. Gaius found the governor and the legate Petronius in discussion with the cavalry praefectus, and Agricola's dispatch riders. Quintus's muddied clothing bore testimony to where he had been, as did those of Agricola's men.

"Quintus says the fortress is less than ten miles away." Cerialis's face still wore the frown that had been present all day. "Perhaps as little as eight. It's hard to tell at night. A short period of rest, followed by a forced march, will get us there before dawn. Any comments?"

One of the dispatch riders from Agricola, a young soldier who already held decanus rank, looked very keen to comment, but a glare from Cerialis held him to silence. Gaius decided the man was second-guessing the governor's train of thought, and didn't like it. Neither would the man's commander. Which proved his own thoughts, which he'd expressed earlier to Elena: Cerialis figured he had the edge on surprise, and if he could catch the enemy sleeping, he wasn't going to wait for the other half of his force. He couldn't help thinking about the lecture he'd received at Ebor on the politics of war, and hindsight versus foresight. Nor could he forget the governor's words to Agricola, not to attack until the two armies united.

Titus replied with a question of his own, "Any sign the enemy is on the move?"

Cerialis nodded to Quintus, who answered with a tired smile. "My men met one of their patrols, if you can call it that—three men, shortly after dark. At first they thought we were barbarians, and demanded to know who we were with. They were a quite surprised," the smile broadened as Quintus's index finger slashed across his throat, "but I think it shows that no one's expecting us."

"There's been no other sign," Petronius added. "It's incredible."

"Is there a good path from here to the fortress, Quintus?" Gaius asked.

"There's a well-used cart track we crossed about a mile farther north of here. It leads straight to the fortress. I've got riders out looking for others, but this one is good. We'll likely find no better. It should take infantry in column."

"Was there enough light to see how it met the fortress?"

"No, it was pitch black." Quintus held one arm out as if orienting himself. "The track comes upon it from the south east. The trail twisted as we got there, running across a rise of hills with trees on top. The fort was below us."

Gaius's eyes met those of Titus, and they both nodded. "That's probably as good as any place to attack," he suggested, recalling the wooded hilltop, exactly as Quintus had described.

"Why is that?" Cerialis asked.

"Two reasons, sir." Gaius forced his mind back to picture the site. "There's ample room to deploy the army, and the south walls are the more easily breached—a simple rampart with a palisade, some of it stone and some wood, not too high. It encloses a huge area crowded with people. The layout was designed by a headless chicken. No order at all. Once we breach the wall, we'll be through it like sand through a sieve."

"If we have the surprise of them, sir," Titus added, "we'll also have them divided. A major part of Venutius's force would be eliminated before it could gain the stronger walls of the older fortress."

"That would mean breaking from our original plans. We would be attacking with half our army." Cerialis spoke carefully, as if still considering the matter, and nodded to the two riders. "The earliest we expected Agricola was tomorrow, but these men say he'll be hard put to arrive the day after. Rivers are high on the way North, and there's been some flooding."

"He will be thoroughly pissed," Titus muttered under his breath.

Gaius absently nodded agreement, his mind on the weak ramparts that bordered the south enclosure. That part of the stronghold, at least, should be easy to subdue. "The lack of the second force will be evened somewhat, sir," he said. "They don't seem to know we're here. The element of surprise doubles our numbers."

"We do have total surprise!" another voice called eagerly.

Several others murmured agreement, and Cerialis seemed bemused. "I like that, young Trebo," he murmured. "Who first said that? Surprise doubles our numbers."

For a moment Gaius didn't understand, then he chuckled. "I'm sure it was you, sir."

Elena stood to one side of the headquarters tent, watching in awe as the orders flew thick and fast: forced rest for all troops until midnight; the tenth cohort is detailed to guard the camp and the baggage train;

senior cohort commanders will report to the third tent module for an immediate orders group; lead auxiliary elements will depart shortly after midnight; the order of march will remain as posted for the past two days, other than the tenth; the army will deploy in darkness, and be in position before dawn breaks; the attack will be concurrent with the first grey of dawn, as the objective is revealed; Governor Cerialis himself will verbally issue the command for the actual assault; there will be ...

It was all so very different from the haphazard manner in which Venutius's warriors had deployed for the attack on Isurium, that she was surprised the fight at Bran's Beck had even hung in the balance. One order, however, was received by the Roman troops with the same casual disregard as her own people received orders: the one regarding forced rest. It was virtually ignored. Elena could understand why. It was a rare soldier who found the balm of sleep in a damp, frigid tent, with a battle waiting at dawn.

Later in the night she watched as the vanguard of the column, more than a thousand auxiliaries cavalry, departed in apparent good order. She couldn't see much, but there seemed to be little confusion. When the Ninth legion finally started moving out, the troopers assigned as her guards ordered her to mount up. Moments later Gaius appeared quietly out of the darkness, and gestured for the two men to fall back. Much to her annoyance, he snapped a halter rope to her bridle and settled his own horse alongside.

The last troops marched into position above Stannick just before the first sliver of morning marked the horizon. Elena found herself in the front ranks of the First cohort, staring down on a shallow valley that was nothing more than a dark void. To both her amazement and anger, the Ninth legion was deployed to attack, and its enemy was sleeping. It seemed as if the gods were giving Rome their blessing.

As the dim glow of dawn appeared beyond the eastern hills, Cerialis sat comfortably on his horse at the centre of the army, flanked by his staff officers, a full troop of mounted dispatch riders, and the troopers of his personal guard. "Any moment," he muttered to Titus, staring into the night as the dark silhouette of the fortress took shape in the shadows of the valley below. "Take a final look at the place where …"

His voice faded as shouting drifted from somewhere off on the left flank. Hooves thundered across the slope and the sound of voices, hundreds of them, grew louder. The governor's features twisted both with anger and alarm, and he pushed himself up in the saddle, squinting off into the darkness. "What the fuck is going on?" he demanded.

Chapter XXV

When Cethen kicked Gadearg from the darkness of the forest, he was simply urging the chestnut forward. It was an instinctive act, with no thought given to its wisdom. There had been no thought, either, that the others might follow, and when they did, he silently cursed. He pulled on the reins and sat waiting for those behind to catch up. One of the twins led what was left of the tiny force, all of it now bunched up behind him.

Cethen whispered the obvious. "I must warn them."

"And how are you going to do that?"

"I don't know, dammit, but for certain it can't be done hiding in the forest," Cethen said. "Is that you, Borba?"

"Doesn't matter."

"It does. Borba can see like a cat. I want to know who's following us."

"We can both see like a cat," the voice said, followed by a chuckle.

Each of them squinted into the darkness. "Not much to see," Cethen muttered. "It's as black as a bear's arse."

"Speaking of arses, there's a troop of Roman cavalry pushing up ours. Keep moving."

"Shit," Cethen muttered, and kicked Gadearg forward into a walk.

"Don't worry, it'll be light soon." Luath actually sniggered. "You'll be able to see for yourself."

"That's when we do worry, idiot," Cethen said, but it was nerves speaking, for he knew Luath was baiting him. "How many are with us?"

There was a pause and some whispering. "There's nine following me," Luath said, then, since Cethen's way with figures was well known, he added, "That makes eleven altogether."

"I can do the sums," Cethen said testily, glaring into the darkness. "What's ahead of us?"

"Same thing as behind." Luath sniggered again. "More fucking Romans."

A few moments later the riders ahead of Cethen halted and he almost ran into them. But the dark mass of horsemen quickly started again, and this time he kept his distance, his mind grappling with what to do next. Perhaps it was wisest to sidle left again, and lose themselves in the shelter of the forest. Yet he couldn't. The children lay off to his right!

Once more the column halted, but this time the shadow of a single rider grew out of the darkness, his horse moving at a slow trot. The man repeated an order in a dialect that none of them could understand, and the troops ahead turned their mounts to form three ranks facing the fortress. Cethen muttered for his own people to do the same, and they all wheeled in a ragged turn that would have left Morallta in tears.

Cethen struggled to keep his distance, but the cavalry unit behind seemed to have closed up. Despite the cold and the sopping weight of his wet clothing, a prickle of sweat broke out on his back. "We've got to do something, Luath," Cethen muttered to the twin, now alongside.

"It's Borba."

"I don't give pig shit," Cethen snarled as he drew his sword. "We've got two choices. We either charge down to the fortress and warn them, or we turn and skulk back into the trees."

"There's only once choice, really."

"You're right. We have to warn them. It's a matter of honour."

"I suppose there are two, then," Borba said dryly, and chuckled. "The best way to do it would—" The twin broke off and whirled.

The soft, rhythmic thump of a thousand booted feet tramping over sodden earth, sounded farther up the slope. The relentless throb drew closer, slowly edging its way across the ground behind. It echoed like the dull beat of a thousand hearts all pounding together. It matched the throb of Cethen's own heart, and suddenly everything struck him as being so very unfair.

"Why is their lousy infantry moving in behind the cavalry?" he demanded in a hoarse whisper. "According to Vellocatus, they should be in the middle, with nobody in front of them."

"Give them time," Borba muttered as the infantry halted, and subdued voices haggled in the rear. "Someone's probably shitting in his own nest."

"We haven't time to give," Cethen said, nervously eyeing the sky to the east.

A few moments later, Borba's judgement proved correct. The same rider cantered back along the column, only this time his voice was a snarl as he repeated yet another order. Farther down the line, the Roman cavalry were turning their horses away from the fortress, and once more forming column. The man looked ready to pass by Cethen's small band of warriors, but darkness was fading, and their shadowy figures stood in stark contrast to the other riders; at the last moment, he reined in his horse.

The troop commander's voice was demanding, but he spoke in a Tungri dialect that no one could understand. Cethen licked his lips, his mind a blank. The man switched to the Brigante tongue. "Any barbarian scouts should be back with headquarters staff by now. What are you doing here?"

The words caught Cethen by surprise. "We got lost, sir," he mumbled.

The commander seemed ready to go but hesitated, frowning at the cluster of riders. Cethen decided the man was having second thoughts, wondering why barbarian scouts were there in the first place. As the Roman wavered, he grasped the boar by the tusks. Sweat prickled his back as he urged Gadearg forward, gesturing eastward to where he hoped the headquarters staff might be found.

"I think we should be over there, sir," he said, riding closer to the man. Behind him, Borba kicked his own animal forward.

"Yes …" the Roman responded uncertainly, then seemed to realize he was threatened, not by one, but by two barbarians. He jerked back on the reins, but Borba already had hold of the horse's bridle. The animal snickered and the Roman balked, struggling with the reins as he opened his mouth to shout. "There are—"

Cethen lunged forward with his sword and caught the man under the chin. The end of the blade bit deep, turning his cry to a gurgle. Borba rode up and caught him as he fell. For a moment they held their horses on either side of the Roman, each propping him in the saddle as he slumped forward.

"He's pointing the wrong way," Cethen hissed.

"I don't think it matters," Borba muttered, and Cethen shuddered as he realized it was getting light enough that he could see the twin's ghostlike grin.

"Then let's move. To the gate. Now," he hissed, and turned to call to the others, "We're going. We must try to give warning."

Cethen released the dead weight of the Roman trooper and thumped his heels into Gadearg's belly. Luath, Ligan, and the others followed, their tired animals gamely pounding toward the stronghold in a lathered, gasping gallop. Borba did the same, leaving the Roman's startled horse alone on the slope. Once free of the Roman lines, Cethen screamed a warning toward the dark fortress, a cry quickly taken up by the others.

The big chestnut started wheezing almost at once, drawing breath in deep gasps that were painful to hear. The other animals were in no better condition, their lungs labouring as they galloped down the slope.

Cethen glanced fearfully over his shoulder, and his heart dropped to his belly. The Romans were in pursuit! Led by the two troops of horse that had flanked them on either side, the entire line of auxiliary cavalry was moving forward, gradually breaking into a full charge. The yips and yells of a hundred voices echoed down the slope, growing louder and louder as more joined in, until the whole world seemed nothing but a dull, steady roar.

Again Cethen cursed the fickleness of the gods, and beat Gadearg's rump with the flat of his blade. The chestnut lurched forward, but barely gained a stride. He gripped the sword tighter and kicked, but to no avail; the poor animal seemed to have given its all. They were barely halfway to the fortress walls, and the Roman cavalry was breathing down his back. Another quick glance told him that not one, but a dozen riders were closing fast.

The chestnut, its heart pushed to the limit, began to falter. Cethen cursed. An attack from behind, especially with the sharp end of a spear, was almost impossible to defend. Their small, brave band had come so close! The desperate ride had been magnificent, one that might have become legend had it succeeded, yet it was all for nothing. And as for the promise of retaking Ebur itself, that would surely end here too. Damn the druids, and damn their "visions"!

He turned in the saddle, anger at the unfairness of it boiling up inside and drowning his fear. The first of the Romans was thundering up, closing in from the left, bearing down on Gadearg as if the chestnut was merely loping. Cethen braced the sword in his hand and made ready to parry the spear, but the tip of the man's weapon remained angled upward.

The Roman was intent on lunging from the side, Cethen decided, yet that was where his shield protected him. He was momentarily confused, and in the moment it took to ready the blow that, with luck, might knock the trooper from his horse, the man pounded past, rushing onward to the fortress. Within the space of a heartbeat, a dozen more thundered by on either side, then a hundred more, and a hundred after that. Every last one seemed intent on being first to reach the low, dark walls of Stannick.

The mad whirl of horses and howling riders seemed to gallop past forever. When it was finally over, Cethen found no need to pull in on Gadearg's reins. The tired animal slowed to a halt by itself, its head down and its sides heaving. The Roman cavalry thundered on, plunging headlong toward the stronghold. Only a few stragglers remained behind, scattered haphazardly across the empty slope: eleven, to be precise.

"Shit!" It was all that Cethen could manage.

"I think those inside now know the Romans are coming," Luath said dryly as he walked his horse up alongside.

"Maybe if you hadn't yelled," someone else suggested. Cethen could have killed him.

A dull, threatening rumble started behind them, and they each turned to look. For a moment no one moved as the noise continued to grow, echoing down the gentle slope like a distant roll of thunder. The Roman infantry was on the move.

"Cethen, we have to get away from here," Ligan said. "It's getting light. They'll know we don't belong."

Cethen said nothing. After a glance at the Roman infantry his gaze returned to the fortress, where the great mass of cavalry milled about the walls. Some seemed to have breached the gate. It had probably been open anyway, he thought angrily, and the guards half asleep. Not that it mattered. The Romans would have been over the walls as soon as their infantry got there, anyway. He pondered the idea of pushing Gadearg onward; to get inside, and try for the two boys. He'd have no chance, of course, but it would be a good death. And he would never have to face Elena again.

Ligan seemed to read his mind. "You have your people to think of," he said patiently, for the moment ignoring the roar of the closing infantry. "They need you to lead them."

"Hah! Why?" Cethen said miserably and looked up. Some of the others had already moved off toward the west, but he showed no inclination to follow. "I couldn't lead a hog to a wallow."

"Hey, what kind of talk is that?" Luath said almost cheerfully, and sniggered. "You just led the whole fucking Roman army into battle!"

"Bastard!"

The twin's gibe roused Cethen from his self-pity and he raised his fist to lash out, forgetting it still held the sword. Ligan misunderstood, and grasped his wrist.

"Luath didn't mean it," he said, then released his grip as Cethen relaxed.

"It's true. I did start if off," Cethen mumbled, and stared dumbly down at his sword, then at Luath. "I'm sorry. I meant no harm."

"We all did it." Borba glared at his twin. "Every last one of us was right behind, yelling our stupid heads off."

The roar of voices and the pounding of feet drew closer. Ligan glanced nervously up the slope. The infantry had broken into a slow jog.

"When I die, it won't be foolishly," Ligan said firmly, and swiped the flat of his blade hard on the chestnut's rear. "Let's get out of here."

Gadearg lurched forward, doggedly following the other riders as they moved toward the low ridge of forest that lay to the west. Cethen sat uncaring on the animal's back, escaping the closing ranks of infantry by the narrowest margin. When they found the shelter of the trees he turned the chestnut around and held it steady, peering through the foliage at what looked to be the death throes of the huge stronghold.

Roman infantry poured through the gates, as others scaled the low parapets. Resistance seemed almost nonexistent. Throughout the large enclosure his people were waking, certainly, but they swarmed about as aimlessly as bees forced from a toppled hive. Perhaps—he glanced north toward the long stone walls of the older fortress—perhaps Venutius might be able to hold them off up there.

"What are the idiots doing there?" Gaius growled.

The first cohort had marched into line to find the Batavi infantry deployed further down the slope, as they were supposed to be, but ahead of them were the Tungri cavalry.

"The horse humpers didn't trot far enough west," a senior centurion suggested. "It's what happens when you're riding and don't count your pacing."

The man stood on the soggy ground alongside Gaius, who had pushed himself up on the pommel of his saddle in an effort to see more of the dark mass of troops farther down the slope.

"Is something wrong?" Elena asked. She sat her horse on his other side. Gaius had given her a Tungri mail tunic to wear and a pair of woolen britches, but no helmet or weapons. She had refused the former. He had refused the latter.

"The cavalry's supposed to be on the flanks, and instead they're in front, damn them," Gaius muttered. He turned to the nearest dispatch rider, then changed his mind. "Come on. It probably needs someone with a bit of rank to straighten it out. Stay close."

The last order was a reflex, for it hardly mattered anymore if she did break away and try to warn Venutius's people. Her two guards apparently agreed. With a final questioning glance toward Gaius, both rode off to rejoin their units farther along the face of the hill.

Gaius galloped his horse around the flank of the first cohort and down past the auxiliary infantry, where he turned the animal in behind the offending Tungri cavalry. Elena followed, her eyes on the east, where the dawn glimmered grey over the trees. As they moved forward, shadowy ranks of soldiers emerged from the darkness like a silent phantom army.

"Shit!" Gaius cursed, as the thud of galloping hooves erupted farther along the slope. A small section of the cavalry column had pounded off toward the fortress, leaving only a single horse behind. Startled, he urged his own animal forward to where the errant troop had broken away, only to find that all around him other riders were following. Baffled, he looked for the praefectus who had have given the order, but no such man appeared to exist. Only the single, riderless horse…

As he closed in on the beast, Gaius saw a trooper slumped across its withers. He bent forward to catch the animal's bridle, but it pulled back, and the rider slid slowly to the ground. Gaius quickly dismounted and turned the man over. It was Lucinius.

He climbed to his feet, watching open-mouthed as the entire cavalry cohort charged down on the fortress. Soon all that remained was the fading echo of battle cries drifting back on the crisp morning air.

"Shit!" he muttered again.

"I would guess they weren't supposed to do that," Elena said, her face devoid of expression.

Gaius scowled and swung back onto his horse. An officer from the Batavi infantry cohort ran over clutching his sword, his eyes on the vanishing cavalry. Gaius recognized Marius.

"You order them off?" He asked the question almost as an accusation.

"Of course not; something is wrong," Gaius growled, and gestured toward Lucinius. "He's been killed by one of his own."

Marius looked down at the corpse. "Have they gone over to the barbarians?"

The question shook Gaius, and he stared hard down the slope. The cavalry were closing in on the Brigante defences, charging across the grassland in long, even lines, which was hardly the way to defect. They were also yelling and screaming as if trying to wake the dead, but that could have meant anything. "I don't think so," he muttered doubtfully. "I think they're attacking, not going over. Get your men ready to advance. I want to see what the governor thinks of this."

Without waiting for an answer he tossed Elena the end of her halter rope, then lashed at his horse, sending it racing across the slope in front of the bewildered ranks of auxiliary infantry. As far as he knew, the entire left flank was now wide open. The Tungri advance was either a deliberate, traitorous ploy, or an idiotic blunder. If it was a ploy, then it meant Venutius was in the field and could be expected to fall on the exposed flank at any moment. Which in turn meant that he, Gaius Sabinius Trebonius, should not have abandoned it. As the thought struck, he almost reined in and went back, but he could see the headquarters party not far ahead, and nearly all, including Cerialis, were staring his way. And besides, Marius was back there. If anyone could look after a flank, the Batavi commander could. He again lashed his horse's rump, desperately praying the Tungri charge was nothing more than a blunder.

Elena sat quietly in the saddle, anxiously watching the field below. Waves of auxiliary cavalry swept across the slope like dark ripples on a muddy pond. About halfway toward the walls a few stragglers dropped back, and remained scattered across the slope as if lost. Perhaps this was a defection after all, she mused, and these men had changed their minds? Or perhaps it was the other way about, and these few were the only ones who wanted rid of Rome's yoke.

Then she realized, in the dawn light, that the stragglers were not defecting Tungri, but Britons. Elena squinted hard at the small group, and decided that at least two, possibly three, were women. What were those people doing there? They belonged inside the fortress, surely, not outside. Even as she wondered, the answer came. They had been trying to get back inside! Probably to give warning. Elena leaned back in the saddle and smiled sadly to herself. Of the thousands gathered outside the great stronghold, only she could probably guess what had occurred.

Yet other, distracting events were taking place. An enormous roar drifted up the slope, and her eyes moved to Stannick's ramparts. The first onslaught of cavalry seemed to have taken the gate—there were riders on both sides of the entrance, and fighting on top of the wall. One hand went instinctively to her mouth and she gasped. Elena suddenly realized that she desperately wanted Venutius, old bastard that he might be, to throw every last one those riders back out again. But where was he? And how could his people have been so unprepared?

Even as the questions rose in her mind, another roar, much closer, rippled across the slope. She whirled around in the saddle. A dispatch rider stood close by the Batavi commander, his horse circling the man. A dozen centurions were shouting orders. The infantry was on the move!

Elena kicked her horse westward to get out of the way as the long ranks of auxiliary infantry marched forward. She turned to where Gaius's cohort stood waiting in readiness, but she saw no trace of him. Her gaze returned to the walls, where the cavalry had gained command of the gate, and were rushing through like water down a sluice. Their success had obviously prompted the order to commit the infantry.

Her heart sank as she looked beyond the parapets. The inside of the huge enclosure swarmed like an anthill, but the foot soldiers would reach the ramparts long before any real resistance could be organized. Elena dropped her eyes in despair, and they again fell on the stragglers, all seemingly oblivious to the cavalry bursting through the gate, and the solid wall of advancing infantry. What, in the name of Dagda, were they doing?

She watched, both curious and anxious. The group had clustered together and appeared to be arguing. One man raised his sword as if to strike, only to be restrained by another. Almost immediately, most of the riders began moving west, leaving only four at the centre of the slope, still arguing. Elena smiled sadly, recalling the temper of her people.

Three of the men seemed to be haranguing the fourth. One gestured angrily toward the approaching infantry with his sword. The fourth man glanced briefly upward, just as the warrior with the sword slammed the weapon down on the rump of his horse. The animal stumbled forward and finally, with less than a spear's throw to spare, the riders began leaving the field.

Elena found herself watching their retreat as if through a fog, for the man whose horse had been struck by the sword was Cethen!

Criff had told her he was alive when she returned from Rome. Typically, the bard had said far more than necessary. Even so, the shock of seeing him sent her mind reeling. Her first instinct was to gallop forward, but she had to see to the children first—she had to be there when the Romans found Rhun and Tuis at the lodge. But would they be found there? If Cethen was outside the walls, was that where the children were too?

Elena glanced over her shoulder. The massed might of the Ninth legion itself stood ready to march. The soldiers were now clearly visible, though dawn had still not fully broken. A centurion roared an order, his breath a cloud of morning mist, and a moment later, rank after rank of soldiers began thumping their way toward the fortress. She searched for Gaius, but still didn't see him. In the distance a rider galloped his horse across the front, but he was too far away to identify. *It has to be him. The helmet …*

Elena hesitated just long enough to curse, then lashed at her horse, sending it careening across the slope.

"Over here."

The voice came from within the forest, and Elena kneed the horse through the thick undergrowth. Her husband urged his own mount forward, distancing himself from several riders clustered farther back in the trees. The animal plodded forward and stopped; Cethen sat staring, his shoulders hunched. Both horse and rider were covered with a cracked coating of mud, and each had the exhausted eyes of a wounded stag.

For a moment neither spoke, each appraising the other as if strangers. Then Elena broke the silence after glancing quickly back to the fortress, reminded of the spur that had goaded her there. "The boys. They are well?"

Cethen frowned. "They were, last time I saw them."

"Where are they?"

He nodded toward the clamour around the stronghold.

"They're inside?"

"With Nuada."

"Then why aren't you there protecting them?" Elena cried angrily.

"I tried, dammit," Cethen barked, equally annoyed, "but your lousy, arse-sniffing friends got there ahead of me."

Elena cursed under her breath, and pulled back on the reins. "I have to go. I needed to know if they were inside. Are they at the lodge?"

"With Nuada and her brood." Cethen's tired face grew taut with his own anger and frustration, and as Elena made to go, he said, "So, is he ploughing you?"

She glared. "You dare to even ask. I hear from Criff that a Carvetii woman is pregnant," she snapped, then, as Cethen's words sank in that Nuada was at the lodge, she added, "are you humping Cian's wife, as well?"

Cethen avoided the question. "The boys belong with me."

"They belong with whoever has the balls to keep them alive," Elena said, and turned her horse to leave.

"Wait, please." The plea, it sounded like a plea, made her pause. "Shit, Elena, how did it come to this?"

"Because that's exactly what it is, Cethen. Shit!" Elena snapped, then sighed, staring hard at her husband's worn features. He had aged five years in less than one. Or did she now view him through different eyes? She relented, and inclined her head toward Stannick. "It was that old bastard down there. If he'd left us alone, everything would have been alright."

"Maybe if your Romans had left us alone."

"They're not my Romans, dammit," Elena cried. Just as quickly she softened her voice, as she saw how hopelessly tired he was. "Oh,

Cethen! 'Ifs' are nothing more than wishes. The gods made life an 'is,' not an 'if.'" She shook her head, vainly trying to sift a hundred whirling thoughts. One popped out, the ultimate irony of all. "It's strange, isn't it? The way they work their whims."

"The gods? How so?"

"You promised that one day I would get home again. I'd guess I'm back there now, aren't I?" Elena's lips tightened as she felt a lump well up in her throat, and she dug her heels violently into the horse's belly. It leapt from the trees and burst into a gallop, heading straight toward the beleaguered fortress. Cethen simply sat staring after her, as if unable to move.

Elena rode into the fortress, overwhelmed by fear she was too late. The few dead outside the gate were hardly worth a glance, but inside it was worse than the slaughter of cattle at Samhain. She reined in, stunned by the sight of the killing. Bodies littered the muddy ground like blood-soaked pebbles, and there was scarce a trace of Roman colour among them. In places it was as if the dead had been strewn like leaves, except nothing stirred but the windblown flutter of loose clothing. The Roman infantry had left no wounded behind.

The fighting had already moved a third of the way across the enclosure. The Roman line stretched from one side of the fortress to the other, a distance over a mile. Cerialis had gambled, committing most of his precious legion. But it was paying off. The battlefield behind the advance was a graveyard. Half the cavalry, no longer needed inside the ramparts, had been sent north to cut off any retreat. It was a gesture of sheer confidence.

Elena cursed and focussed on reaching the lodge, which lay half-way across the huge compound. It was still ahead of the Roman line. Thankful for at least that, she once more kicked the horse forward. The animal balked, eyes rolling and nostrils flaring at the scent of blood and smoke. She lashed angrily at its flanks with the loose end of the reins, and the terrified creature bolted. It raced on, tearing past a score of burning hovels, stumbling and kicking in growing panic, careless of the bodies beneath its flying hooves. Elena fought to regain control and almost crashed into the rear ranks of Roman infantry, but the animal stopped suddenly short, its legs as stiff as stilts. She hurtled forward over its neck.

"Noooo!"

The word was screamed by a harsh male voice. Elena stared upward through a star-riddled haze to see the decanus Octavius, wrestling with a wild-faced infantryman. The soldier glared red hate as his sword hung a hair's breadth from her throat. For a moment she thought the man would thrust anyway, but the glare focussed and the light of battle dimmed in his eyes. Without a word, he turned and ran, for the line had already moved a dozen paces ahead.

Octavius offered an arm and pulled her to her feet.

"Over there," he said curtly, answering her question before it was asked by pointing his stained sword vaguely along the ranks of infantry. Then he, too, ran forward, but not before burying his blade in the twitching body of a fallen Briton on the off chance the man was not yet dead.

For a moment Elena stood in dizzy confusion, then realized one hand still clutched the horse's reins. She swung shakily back into the saddle, both frightened and angry. Immediately she caught sight of Gaius. He was mounted, riding back and forth across the rear of the slow-moving Batavi battle line. A second line of regular legionary troops followed in close support. Elena prodded her animal forward, careful not to lash out with the reins.

"You decided to come back," he muttered, not sparing a glance from the fight raging ahead. Venutius's warriors, thousands of them, had finally roused themselves, and appeared to be gathering strength. The Roman line pushed inexorably forward, but not nearly as steadily or as rapidly as it had been.

Elena ignored the comment, her eyes searching out the lodge. Smoke swirled like a fog across the carnage, making the stronghold unfamiliar. "Have you seen anything of them?"

"The lodge is over there." Gaius pointed directly ahead with his sword. "A hundred, hundred and fifty paces. What did your husband have to say?"

Elena glanced sideways in surprise.

"My eyes are as good as yours," Gaius muttered.

"He said the children are still here," she replied, and was annoyed to find herself making excuses. "I had to go. I needed to know if they were inside Stannick or not."

"And if they were not, it would have saved the trouble of coming back."

Elena decided the comment was not worthy of reply, perhaps in part because she was unsure of its truth. Instead, she stared anxiously over the heads of the battling Batavi infantry and the fight-crazed hordes of Brigante warriors. Oddly enough, she felt almost detached from the battle itself. After nearly a year of missing them, her mind had no room for anything other than Rhun and Tuis—and the cruel whims of the gods. They, above all, were not to be trusted when hope dangled close enough to taste.

"There, see!" She grasped Gaius's arm and pointed, then just as quickly groaned.

Nuada stood outside the lodge, staring toward the line of advancing soldiers. The four children were gathered close behind her. She held a shield and a spear and appeared ready to fight; so did Rhun, only his weapon was a ridiculously large sword. The two were arguing. When Rhun started forward, Elena gasped; but Nuada grabbed his collar and pulled him back, almost jerking him from his feet. A few more words followed, then the two turned and she ushered the three younger children toward the stone walls of the older fortress.

"I was hoping she'd go back inside," Gaius muttered. "We might have been able to rush the hut and stop it being burned. As it is ..."

They both watched as Nuada pushed the children between a scattered jumble of huts and granaries, to where thousands of people, mostly women and children, were trying to cram through a single gate in the stone-walled fort. At first it was easy to follow her path, for she wore a bright dress of red and yellow squares that stood out, even among a host of other bright garments. But when she entered the crush around the gate, Elena lost sight of them all, and found herself again filled with despair.

"She's showing good sense," Gaius murmured, his attention divided between Nuada and the slow-moving ranks of infantry.

"What do you mean?"

"The small ones would be trampled in the crush about the gate. She's changed her mind and—" Gaius turned as a triumphant roar erupted from the centre of the line.

The stolid ranks of Batavi infantry bulged backward, faltered, then broke where a crazed horde of Venutius's warriors had forced a gap. Two troops of Tungri cavalry quickly spurred forward, smashing into the stream of frenzied Britons and shattering their triumph at the moment of its birth. As the riders stemmed the flow, the broken ranks of infantry surged in behind; but instead of halting, the Tungri charged on, swept up in their own success.

Cerialis, well back in the centre of the line, spoke quickly to Quintus. The praefectus thundered off, and moments later the Tungri cavalry reserve plunged forward to reinforce the two troops. It was a bold move. Several hundred riders poured through the gap even as it closed, scattering the Batavi infantry, who fled sideways to avoid the flailing hooves.

"That should do it." Gaius's face glowed with satisfaction as chaos erupted behind the barbarian line. The infantry quickened its pace. "A bold blow in the right place at the right time."

"Nuada. The children." Elena's voice cracked with fear.

Venutius's men fought viciously, but as the fighting spread, panic was setting in. Roman cavalry now wheeled in the cluttered space to their rear, running free across the huge compound as if it was their own. The crush of fellow Britons struggling through the gate to the stone fort were scattered like sheep, and on either flank, beaten warriors were fighting their way to the outer walls in the hope of escape.

"I see them," Gaius shouted, urging his horse forward to keep up with the quickening pace of the infantry.

The roar of battle rose as the Batavi cohorts smelled victory. All across the front, the barbarian line began to crumble as Venutius's warriors stumbled backward, falling in bloody piles or simply running, wounded or not. A dozen centurions screamed for order as their own men threatened to break rank and follow. The rigid lines quickly grew ragged as the infantry broke into a slow trot, ignoring the rage of their commanders.

"Where? What do you mean?" Elena screamed as she struggled to keep her horse alongside Gaius.

He turned to her, his face impassive. "As I said, the woman has sense." He pointed to a tall, rounded structure less than a hundred paces ahead. "I'd guess she knows we won't burn the granaries. I saw her take refuge inside."

The long ranks of infantry surged forward, cutting through any resistance as if scything grain. Elena glanced quickly over her shoulder, appalled at the destruction. Dense smoke blew southward across acres and acres of ruined buildings, most of it a withering mass of flames. Everywhere she looked, blood-soaked bodies covered the ground, and hardly a one moved. Cattle and horses ran terrified about the huge compound, and squabbling herds of swine, free of their pens, were already rooting at the dead.

She saw the Roman governor, Cerialis, sitting calm on his horse in the middle of it all. He was surrounded by riders and men in clean uniforms, while beyond, several large units of infantry had yet to bloody their blades. Elena shook her head. The man might have been directing a practice battle on the training field, and appeared no more excited.

She turned back to the fighting, startled to see how close they had struggled to the granary. Venutius's warriors were falling back now, defending themselves on the run, which only added to their slaughter. Panic, anger, and desperation etched every face. A wave of guilt swept over Elena, mixed with a shamed relief that none of those faces were familiar.

"We have to move. Now," Gaius called.

He turned and roared over his shoulder, pointed toward the round granary, then kneed his horse into the rear ranks of Batavi soldiers. A centurion loped forward, a score of men at his heels. It was so neatly done that Elena realized Gaius had arranged the order beforehand. She glanced his way, both surprised and grateful.

He caught the look and dismissed it with the flippant sort of remark that always infuriated her. "Have you any idea what a young, healthy slave brings in Rome?" he shouted as his horse lunged forward.

"Too damned well," she yelled back, and followed.

The Batavi foot soldiers, instead of giving way to allow Gaius and the small phalanx to pass through, charged ahead, spurred on by the pressure. With a roar, they crashed into the remaining wall of Britons, backing them hard against the granary. With no other choice, Venutius's men desperately tried to stand firm, slashing wildly at the Roman infantry, who methodically stabbed and thrust.

A large, blood-spattered warrior staggered heavily against the granary door, a Batavi blade deep in his belly. The man tumbled inside, his assailant following. A moment later the Batavi reappeared, his weapon gone, and one hand vainly trying to stem a stream of blood gushing from one eye. Elena saw a quick blur of red and yellow, and realized Nuada stood in the doorway, her spear striking again. This time it took the man in the throat.

"No!" Elena cried as she saw another soldier step forward and thrust with his sword.

Nuada caught the weapon neatly on her shield, but someone else wrenched the spear from her grip. She bent and plucked a sword from the ground, thrusting upward in the same motion. The blade slid under the soldier's mail tunic, slicing into his groin with a bone-crunching thud. For a moment her elfin face lit with triumph, then another blade slashed down from nowhere, leaving only a bloody stump halfway down her forearm.

Nuada pulled back in disbelief, waving the limb in vain defence, as if still wielding her weapon. Spouting blood arced across the face of yet another Batavi, who rushed forward to finish the kill. The roar of battle deafened Elena's ears as she saw the boss of the man's shield smash Nuada's face. His sword sliced back and forth, striking with the swiftness of an adder. Without a sound, she crumpled.

"Noooooo!" Elena screamed, not for Nuada, but for Rhun. Her son had burst from the granary, his small frame almost hidden behind a huge shield, and a warrior's sword clasped tight in his hand.

"Don't harm the boy!" Gaius roared and lashed at his horse, his heels digging sharply into its belly, heedless of those ahead. "Leave him be...."

Rhun ran blindly at the man who had felled Nuada, slashing wildly with the great sword. The Batavi deftly pushed the blade aside, thrusting back with his own weapon. Rhun caught the blow on his shield more by luck than by skill, and for the blink of an eye found himself staring death in the face: a panting, square-jawed, blood-spattered face, coated with three days of stubble and grime, and topped by a pair of hard, red-rimmed eyes that glinted wild below an iron helmet.

Elena never knew whether the soldier heard Gaius's repeated screams, or simply decided the pale-faced, half-grown boy who stood helpless in his path was either too young to die, or worth too much to kill. She almost fainted with relief as he swung his shield forward with practised ease and caught Rhun hard on the forehead with the boss. The Batavi stepped past the boy as he fell, and peered inside the granary. Then, seeing nothing inside that posed a threat, he turned and ran to catch up with his line, which had again closed ranks and pushed on.

Elena slid from the horse and caught Rhun's limp form in her arms, cradling his head as she ran her hand over his cold forehead. A wicked but healthy bruise was already forming and his breathing, while shallow, was steady. Not that she could see any of it through the tears streaming down her face.

"The boy alright?"

Elena looked up to see Gaius looming above, his face still expressionless. She nodded and wiped at her cheek. Gaius bowed his head and pulled the reins to one side, kneeing the horse on its way.

"T-thank you," she sobbed.

"Stay here. I'll be back."

Elena watched him disappear into a gust of rolling black smoke. The man could be so damned cold, and so hard to measure. And he never left anything to chance, she decided a few moments later, when a decanus from the Ninth came trotting around the granary with the seven soldiers of his squad following close on his heels. He seemed relieved to have found her.

"The tribune. Sent me. See you safe," he said, speaking brokenly in her own tongue before ordering his men into a small, defensive arc.

"From what?" Elena muttered in Latin.

The decanus grinned as he switched to the same language. "Probably from both sides."

She lay Rhun gently on the ground and struggled to her feet. The other children needed tending to, and she had to make sure of Tuis.

Tuis! Her heart lurched at the thought that he might not be inside the granary, but even as it leapt, she saw his face peer around the door, then quickly pop back inside. She started forward, but a low moan made her stop. She looked down at Nuada, surprised to find her alive. Her belly was torn open below the breastbone, and a glistening coil of gut had erupted, twisted in a dark river of red. Something else moved within the coiled innards, and Elena almost vomited when she realized what it was. She knelt and forced herself to look into Nuada's face instead. It was almost as bad. The small, upturned nose was bent hideously to one side, leaking blood that had already begun to congeal. The pert, lively mouth was split open, and black, liquid gaps showed where once her small white teeth had been.

"Nuada?" Elena said and reached out, but was afraid to touch her for fear of causing pain.

"Here. She's dying, but it might help," a voice said in Latin.

Elena looked up, surprised to find the decanus offering her his wineskin. She took it, unsure what to do. She gazed down at Nuada. The vinegary liquid might cause more pain than any relief was worth.

"The wine's long gone," the decanus said, reading her hesitation. "It's full of water. You might try some on her forehead."

Elena nodded and poured a trickle across Nuada's brow, gently rubbing the liquid with her fingers. She heard another low moan and she found herself staring into eyes that were now unfamiliar: a dark, spidery red and dazed with pain. "Nuada," she whispered.

The eyes focussed and narrowed, then recognition came and the mouth smiled grotesquely. "Elena. You—you're ...The children. Where are the children?"

"They're safe." She glanced uncertainly toward the granary. "They're all safe."

The decanus edged over and opened the door, sword ready. When he saw what was inside he stepped back, leaving it to swing wide on its leather hinges. He nodded confirmation.

"Tuis, it's Mam," Elena called out, unwilling to leave Nuada, but suddenly wanting more than anything to have her youngest safe in her arms.

She rose as Tuis's face again peered cautiously from the doorway.

He hesitated, his expression puzzled. Then recognition came, and he ran gleefully to his mother's side. Elena scooped him up and kissed him, clutching him hard against her side with one hand while gripping the Roman's wineskin in the other. She began sobbing, and stared blindly at the open granary door as two other small figures emerged from the gloom.

The decanus stepped forward. "Are these yours or hers?" he asked, his voice neutral.

"Hers," Elena replied, then, unsure of his intent, asked, "Why? They've done no harm."

"Perhaps it's best they don't see her." He gestured toward Nuada, who lay moaning with pain.

Elena hesitated, staring at Nuada, then shook her head. "She's their mam," she said firmly, and gently set Tuis to one side. "They must know that she died looking after them. More important, she'll travel to the other side with their faces painted firm on her mind, and knowing they're safe. Let them come." She beckoned them over.

The two youngsters came quietly and sat unbidden by their mother. They both gazed blankly at the gasping, bloody face, and the older child, Emla, started to cry. The other, a girl called Mergen, a year younger than Tuis, simply stared. Nuada's hand moved feebly, and Elena told the two children to clasp it.

"You—you must take care of them both," Nuada quavered, her sunken eyes on the two children.

"Of course. It would be done without asking."

"They must be with their own people." Nuada's body heaved with violent coughing, and she gasped at the pain. Her back arched and Elena thought she was gone, but the harsh, heavy breathing resumed. "Promise me that. They—they can't—can't stay with the bastards who—who would destroy them."

Elena sat numb, unable to make a promise she felt unable to keep. For Gaius held the key—both literally and otherwise. Coira remained with his household and Elena herself was bound to him, but what if that tie *was* undone? In fact, what would Coira herself do now, if that tie were undone?

"You don't answer!"

The voice was suddenly strong and accusing, and Elena looked down at Nuada's blood-reddened glare. "Nuada, the Roman has Coira," she said quietly, unsure if her words were merely an excuse. "Even if I could escape, *her* life could be forfeit."

"Then give them to Cethen," Nuada said fiercely, then fell into another fit of coughing; when it finally ended, she managed a hideous smile. "He's—he's been father to the two of them the p-past year—would have been da to a third, too. There's more—more dying here than just me. The bastards!"

Elena said nothing. She knew about Cethen's living arrangements, but he could have at least told her Nuada was carrying. Though why should he? Her own winter had not exactly been different. Not in so far as bed sharing, anyway. Oh, but the gods loved to mock! If only Cethen could have seen what she had seen, though. For a moment, the notion of showing him the wonders of the past winter filled her mind; then she laughed bitterly at the absurdity of such thought.

"Elena. Promise me," the frail voice pleaded.

"Nuada, I promise you. I will see they both get to Cethen."

Gaius returned just shy of midday. Nuada lay beneath a red cloak stripped from one of the few Roman corpses on the battlefield. The boy Rhun sat dismal and sullen, his back against the granary, his head cradled on his knees. The three younger children sat solemn and silent in a small circle. He suspected Elena had placed them so they could look at each other, rather than the carnage that lay elsewhere.

"Sir!"

Gaius reined in alongside the decanus, returning the salute as he swung down from the saddle. "Have your men eat, soldier, but stay close."

"Sir?" The man's eyes slid toward the smoke and the stone walls barely visible to the north.

"All over on this side. Gathering up the living." He turned to Elena as the decanus left, and found her placing Nuada's girls on the saddle of her horse. "What are you doing?"

She nodded toward the covered form on the ground. "I promised her I would see the two of them were taken back to their own."

"They're not yours to promise."

"Doesn't matter," Elena said stubbornly. "It was a death promise. It cannot be broken."

Gaius bit his lip as he thought that one over. A death promise! She had set herself a task he was certain she was willing to die trying to fulfill; and if he knew the woman, that was exactly what she would do. It wasn't so much the return of the two youngsters that angered him, though, it was more that she had promised without asking.

As if she read his thoughts—something she seemed to do all too often, which also bothered him—she said, "It's a damned pity she didn't stay alive until you got here. You could have talked to her yourself."

Gaius sighed. "Where are you taking them?"

Elena sighed in turn. "Cethen."

Gaius couldn't stop the question. "Are you coming back?"

She laughed, as if mocking him. "Over there are my two sons. And you have my daughter. Of course I'm coming back!"

Gaius was about to retort by demanding when, but something made him stop. He was suddenly tired—not physically, but tired on the inside: tired of the barbs and the bickering, tired of sharing with the woman what was really nothing more than an undeclared truce. He lifted his gaze to meet the calm yet defiant hazel green eyes, unconsciously moving one hand to his lips, and plucking at them thoughtfully. The words of Cartimandua echoed through his mind, and on impulse, he decided it was time to toss the spear and see where it fell.

"I'll send a pair of horses. You can take the boys with you, as well."

Elena's eyes narrowed in surprise, and her reply was cautious. "You still have Coira."

"Then how about this?" He swung back into his saddle. "I'll send her to you. That's a promise. Though only if she wants to go; I'll not send her if she doesn't. I would let you know that, too."

Gaius tugged on the reins, turning the horse to where the army had regrouped, readying itself to assault the older part of the fortress. With the slightest pressure of his knees, he urged the animal forward.

There was still a lot to be done, and he was needed. But he deliberately held the animal to a slow walk, holding his breath as it picked its way over the detritus of the battlefield. He smiled to himself, inordinately pleased, as her voice rang out.

"Gaius!"

He stopped the horse and, with one hand resting on its rump, turned in the saddle. He didn't say anything, simply looked.

"It sounds as if you want me to leave. Do you?"

Gaius pulled sideways on the reins, and the horse turned until it faced her. For a moment both stared at each other, then finally he shook his head. "Not particularly."

Elena stared back. She deliberately placed her hand to her mouth as he had done and pulled at her lips, but allowed a smile to play at the corners. "So you want me to stay, then?"

He shook his head as if in despair, then broke into a grin. "Of course I do, fool."

Elena nodded her satisfaction, but pushed it one step further, although she too grinned. "Why? Because I'm worth too much as a slave?"

"You, woman—" Gaius pointed with his index finger and held it there "—you have to decide where your value lies." He pulled hard and the horse spun around. His heels slammed into the animal's belly, jolting it forward in a gallop.

He wasn't totally sure if Elena would be there when he returned, but he was damned near certain. Damned near. Midafternoon, though, would perhaps be the earliest time to return and make sure, while still maintaining a degree of pride.

In the meantime, he might discreetly send someone to watch what the woman was doing. Perhaps Octavius ...

Epilogue

Veteria, Lower Germania, 79 A.D.

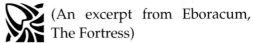 (An excerpt from Eboracum, The Fortress)

Rhun strode through the street entrance of the legate's residence, his mind dredging through past sins. In all honesty, they were few in number, and not a single one should have pressed hard against the man's shield. Even so, with the nagging guilt that haunts a man of clear conscience when authority calls, he turned left and headed for the reception room. A tall, hulking trooper stood outside, slouched against the wall as if holding it up. His face was lost under a mop of black, shaggy hair, and his features, but for the large nose and dark eyes, were all but hidden by a full beard. Were it not for the man's armour and weapons, which were, Rhun noted, clean and in good order, the creature might have been dragged from a cave. As he passed by, the brute nodded balefully, like a bleary eyed bear.

Rhun's features were drawn tighter than a bow string as he stepped inside the reception room. One foot slammed on the stone floor, and drawing himself to attention, he cried, "Sir!"

"Rhun." The legate of the Fifteenth Primigenia Legion, a man called Marius Flavius Rufus, acknowledged his presence without looking up from his reading, and casually motioned for him to sit down.

Rhun saw that a second man was already seated, an auxiliary cavalryman like himself. This one was also a decurio, but not, apparently, a particularly disciplined one. The trooper sat with his feet stretched

434

before him, ankles crossed, and one arm hooked languidly around the back of his chair. It appeared to be only thing stopping him from sliding off the seat.

"Sir!"

Rhun's reply was stiff as he took the only remaining chair, which left him sitting directly across from the ill disciplined stranger. The man was staring through half lidded eyes, a knowing, lopsided grin on his face. He appeared to be amused; very much so. Was there some sort of trouble? Or, and the thought left Rhun cold, was he being mocked?

The decurio was much older, perhaps the same age as Turren. He was the sort of man, Rhun decided, who would search out trouble, and not give a soldier's damn where he found it. His face was tanned to dark leather, except where a livid scar ran down one cheek. His brown hair was drawn back in a pony's tail, and his wispy, greying beard and long moustaches were in sore need of trimming. The nose was as battered as his face: large, and bent by more than one breaking. If he were to lay odds, Rhun would have placed brawling as the cause. Yet the man's mail corslet, which still retained the old shoulder pieces, was clean and well oiled; and the metal on his scabbard glittered, as did the hilt of his sword, though that might simply be from use.

"What do you know of the Ninth Hispana's legate?" The question came like an arrow from a dark forest, and Rhun turned to face the legion commander, lost for an answer.

"Where is the Ninth?" he asked, cautiously. "Last I heard it was in Brigantia."

"Still is."

Rhun shook his head, baffled by the query. "Then that's the only thing I know about it, sir. I certainly don't know who the commander is."

"Well, I do. Now!" The legate grunted his annoyance and gestured to a dispatch pouch that lay open on the table, then to the lounging trooper. "And I find this specimen does, too. And if *you* don't know who the legate is, then I'll tell you. He's the bugger who's been given leave to rob Lower Germania of its best cavalrymen. A full cohort is being commissioned from this area. I have to find fifteen troops, yours included."

"Mine?" Rhun was surprised. He'd been at Vetera a mere fifteen months, and expected to remain on the frontier for some time. Perhaps forever. Certainly for the foreseeable future, which was counted in years, not months. Then it struck him that the transfer was to the Ninth Hispana, which was stationed at.....

Rhun's body sagged as the full meaning of the words sank in. Was he actually being transferred home? Or at least, back to the Roman province where he had once lived? Where he had been born? But instead of pleasure welling up inside, only anger followed, his mind boiling as memories flooded back: torn from his family, treated as no more than a slave. And his father, along with his brother and his sister, all of them lost to him! And his mother.... Shit! There had been his mother! And Rome wanted him back there?

There was no longer hope to be had in such a return, for what did such a journey matter in the end? The Province of Britannia was no longer his home. As far as he was concerned, and the thought struck like a bolt of lightening, no such place as home existed anymore, both literally, or in his mind.

But why send him there? And why would a Brigante tribesman be transferred back to the land of his people at all? The army made it a hard and fast rule: native auxiliary troops do not serve in their own land.

Oh, it had been done, but only when dictated by necessity. Or, of course, by politics. And the rule, in all fairness, was not a bad one. Vetera itself bore proof to its wisdom. Less than a decade past, this same fort had been razed by the local Batavi auxiliaries. The village beyond the walls still bore the black scars of their rebellion. For their betrayal, a good many of those who had lived were sent to serve in Britannia; and in turn, yes, some Britons now served in Lower Germania.

Which made Rhun wonder. Were those same Britons going back too, or would they be spread among the other cohorts? No, they would surely stay. They would likely be culled, and held back. In fact, was *he* even going back? If his men were being sent somewhere, that didn't necessarily mean he was going with them!

What had the legate said? A full cohort was being formed? Fifteen troops? Rhun shook his head. That didn't make sense; had he heard correctly? He turned to ask, but the man was droning on about his own lack of troops, and wondering from what bog's bottom he was going to dredge up the replacements.

"It's Agricola, of course," Marius Flavius complained. "He wants his legions at full strength to ensure success in Britannia. He'll return to Rome piled high with glory, and…"

"Sir?"

"What?"

"Did you say fifteen troops?"

"Yes, most of them from my command. I'll have to rob cohorts scattered from….."

"You said a full cohort. There are sixteen troops in a cohort, so …."

"So? So, that's why this insult to Rome's discipline now disgraces my building!" The legate barked the words, and pointed to the strange decurio. The trooper's grin broadened, as if the slur was a compliment. "There, believe it or not, sits the leader of the sixteenth."

"Where did he come fro…"

"From the far side of the Rhine. And you saw that big oaf standing outside the door when you came in?"

Rhun thought for a moment. "Built like an ox? Looks about as bright?"

"That's the one. It's our man's second in command!" The legate leaned back in his chair with a sigh. "Mind you, if you think this piracy has *my* piss boiling, you should see what the commander of the Tenth Gemina wrote about giving them up."

The decurio stirred, and spoke for the first time. "The man's just superstitious."

"He is?"

"We saved his life once."

The legate gestured once more toward the dispatches. "And that of the previous commander, I gather. Plus a few other odds and ends in between that seem to have turned out well. Horseshit luck, no doubt."

"My men are considered lucky." The decurio managed to shrug his indifference without sliding off the chair. "It's not true, of course. You make your own luck. The fact is, we're good at what we do. We're from Brigantia."

Rhun's eyes widened, but he couldn't resist a retort. "I see you're also modest. How did you arrange an order to transfer back to…"

"He was asked for by name," the legate interrupted. "The same as you were. The requests…." he hesitated, and glanced down at the dispatches as if they were poison. "Dammit, I suppose they're really orders, not requests. The Ninth's legate may have phrased it that way, but everything's signed by Agricola in the name of Vespasian. Nonetheless, the dispatches, so far as they pertain to the pair of you, do offer the privilege of refusing the transfer. You might want to consider that if you…."

"I'm not going to do that," the decurio said emphatically. "I'm going."

"You never mentioned the commander's name, sir." Rhun leaned forward, his mind racing over the possibilities, all of them slowly ebbing until only one remained. His belly, suddenly, felt sour inside.

"No, I didn't, did I?" the legate agreed, and selected one of the dispatches which he studied at length, as if the name was not already scribed on his mind. "Yes, here it is. He's a Sabinius. Gaius Sabinius Trebonius. Do you know him?"

Rhun slumped against the back of the seat. Oh yes, he knew Gaius Sabinius Trebonius. Only too well! The legate Sabinius---how did the rotten bastard ever get that rank?---was the man who had destroyed his home, dishonoured his mother, and torn his sister and brother away from them both. He was the man who had ordered the killing of Nuada, his aunt, even as he, still half child, had tried to defend her. And there was more. Oh yes, he knew the man. And one day, he had promised himself, they would meet again. And when that happened….

"I said, do you know him?"

Rhun looked up to find the legate staring, as if puzzled. He coughed to clear his throat, surprised to find his voice cracking as he fought back his anger. "Y-yes, sir. I know him."

"And you're going to accept the transfer?"

"I…" Rhun was surprised to find he wasn't sure. The posting would almost certainly bring him face to face with the man. Was he ready for that? What would he do? The revenge he'd sworn would be visited on the Roman loomed suddenly real. And what, exactly, was it? Acceptance of the transfer would likely prove a death sentence for both….

"He'll go!"

The words came from the decurio and Rhun turned, his face red with annoyance. "I'll be the one that decides!" he snapped.

"No, you won't. I will. It's for your own good, you stupid bugger." The decurio's lopsided grin was almost a laugh, and his eyes danced with merriment. "I've more than once changed your nappies when you were a bairn, boy. You did as you were told then, and you'll do as you're told now. You'll take the transfer."

Rhun and the legate stared in amazement, but only Rhun found himself able to speak. Even then, the words faltered as the decurio's tanned and battered face suddenly grew vaguely familiar. "Y–you're…"

"Aye, lad, I'm your Uncle Cian. Now stop gawking, and start gathering your kit."

Appendix J

A Brief Description of The Roman Legions, Late First Century A.D.

A Roman legion did not march alone. It normally had auxiliary units attached, both infantry and cavalry, that might as much as double its numbers. To some extent they were organized on similar lines as the legion, especially the infantry, but there were differences. The following briefly outlines the strength and organization of a legion such as the Ninth Hispana, as well as an auxiliary cavalry regiment, and an auxiliary infantry cohort. In some instances, the modern equivalent names have been used for certain elements of a legion (such as squad instead of *contubernia*) rather than the lengthy, unfamiliar name, in order to make the reading flow.

The Legion

Each *legio(n)* was made up of 10 *cohort(e)s*, which were officially 480 strong, except for the most senior cohort—the first cohort—which had 800 men. There appears to be some debate about the reason for the extra large first cohort. Based on modern army needs, I have adopted the position that those extra numbers were likely support or specialist soldiers, much like a modern service battalion. In total, the basic legion strength was 5,120 men, though 4,000 seems to have been its normal garrison strength, perhaps dipping as low as 3,000 after some hard campaigning.

The legion was commanded by a *legatus legionis* (legate), who was of senatorial rank. He was assisted by mainly ex-rankers, the senior being the *primus pilus* (definition: the first spear, a rank that might be compared to a supercharged regimental sergeant major, and in some ways equivalent in power to that of the legate himself) and the *praefectus castrorum* (a senior ex-ranker who remained in charge of the base when the legion was in the field). Each cohort (except the senior cohort) consisted of 6 *centuriae* (companies) of 80 men. It was commanded by a *centurio(n)*, who was assisted by a second in command (*optio*). A regular cohort was normally commanded by a senior centurion, and the larger, first cohort by the primus pilus himself. The book, however, has Gaius commanding the first cohort, which was possible for a senior, career tribune.

Each company of 80 men was broken down into 10 8-man *contubernia* (squads). The leader, or "squaddie," was called a *decanus*.

The legion strength also included 6 *tribunes* of varying seniority and career paths; four thirty man cavalry *turmae* (troops) which were used primarily for general duties; there was also the artillery, which was dispersed amongst the cohorts; and a complement of musicians.

Auxiliary Cavalry

Cavalry cohorts (regiments) were called *alae*, and were normally of two sizes, though each regiment was made of a number of 30 man *turmae* (troops) A cohort of 16 troops was an *ala quingenariam*, and one of 24 troops was an *ala milliaria*. The cohorts were commanded by a *praefectus alae*, the position normally being the career peak of an officer of the equestrian order. The troops themselves were each commanded by a *decurio*, with an *optio* being second in command. There were musicians and other supernumeraries, all them fighting in the ranks.

Auxiliary Infantry

The auxiliary infantry was grouped by cohorts of two sizes: a *cohors quingenaria* of 6 companies (*centuriae*), totalling 480 men; and a *cohors milliaria* of 10 companies, totalling 800 men. The makeup of the companies, or centuriae, was the same as in a legion. The cohors quingenaria was usually commanded by a *praefectus cohortis*. However, if honoured with the designation *civium Romanorum*, which effectively gave it the status of a legion, the cohort might be commanded by a *tribunus*. The larger cohors milliaria were also, normally, commanded by a tribunus.

Imperial Rome kept a standing army, on average, of around 250,000 men. It was largely funded by the people it was either conquering, plundering, or protecting, the description likely determined by which side you were on. A small and easily understood softcover book, *The Armies and Enemies of Imperial Rome*, by Philip Barker (Wargames Research Group, ISBN: 0950029963), provides a very quick and readable reference for not only the Roman forces, but, as the title indicates, those of her enemies. Details include uniforms, shield patterns, weapons, etc.

Appendix II

Glossary

Aggripinna:

-the mother of Nero and a veteran political schemer. History records her as having poisoned Caudius (her uncle and third husband) in order to have her son Nero made emperor. (Nero subsequently had her murdered in turn).

ballistae:

-(singular: ballista) a war engine resembling a huge crossbow that hurled equally huge dart-like missiles.

Crodha:

-from the Celtic, meaning the valiant (man).

equestrian:

-also referred to as 'equites', or knights. It was an order of citizens that ranked below senatorial status (see below), often following a mixed career that involved the military, civil service, and trade and commerce. This was usually carried out (like those of senatorial rank) in an orderly, progressive career pattern. As to the military, command of an auxiliary cohort was probably the peak of an equestrian's career.

garum:

- this was a garnish, or thin sauce, that was probably applied as liberally as North Americans use ketchup. It was a strong, pungent fish seasoning and one of the more simple recipes is as follows:

Take the entrails of tunny fish and its gills, juice and blood, and add sufficient salt. Leave it in a vessel for two months at most, then pierce the side of the vessel and the garum, called Haimation (presumably the name of this particular recipe) will flow out.

Horrible as this recipe may sound, the general effect of the various types of garum was something resembling the taste of an anchovy paste.

honour price:

-a little difficult to describe in today's terms, but it was an assessment of a man's worth in terms of his dignity (face), or present weight in the community, and yet was also directly related to his material worth. In this way a prosperous man might ascend considerably in rank, but the honour-price fluctuated according to his fortunes. This was particularly important as to compensation for wrongs that were committed, and where redress was awarded.

intervallum:

-a cleared space around the inside perimeter of the fortress. It was useful in that it provided an open area to protect buildings from missile flying over the walls, and to provide ready movement of troops along the inside of the defences. It accommodated a street for this latter use called the *via sagularis.*

kin:

-the kin could, in some ways, be best described as a smaller, related unit within the actual tuath (see below). It was a very extended family, and an example in the book is the *Eburi,* led by the minor chieftain Cethen Lamh-fada. It would include anyone who is closely and even loosely related (second and third cousins, adoptees, etc).

lorica:

-Roman upper body armour made from leather or metal sections fastened together.

Porta Praetoria, et al:

- the main gate leading into the fortress. In the instance of Ebor, it was from the south. Using the same fortress as a bearing, the others were as follows: *North: porta pecumana; West: porta principalis dextra (the left); East: porta principalis sinistra (the right).* The use of 'principalis' was used because these gates opened onto the main street leading east and west, known as the *via principalis*

procurator:

-a powerful administrative position in a Roman Province held by a man of equestrian rank. He was responsible for the finances, taxation, control of imperial property and census. He also acted as a 'check' to the governor's authority, in that he reported independently to the emperor himself. An earlier example was the procurator Julius Classicianus, a man primarily responsible for the recalling of Seutonius due to his brutal reprisals following Boudicca's rebellion (which uprising was largely created by a former procurator's ruthlessness).

pteruges:

-on a legion soldier's uniform, the leather straps that dangle vertically over the lower portion, or skirt, of his tunic. At the time period of the book, the rank and file likely had a fairly narrow set that only protected the groin area.

puls (or pulmentus):

-a cereal gruel or porridge, prepared from barley or spelt wheat that was roasted, pounded, and cooked with water in a cauldron. (Possible ancestor of the word porridge?) The mix is similar to the modern Italian *polenta.*

senatorial rank:

-this rank essentially described the privileged few who belonged to the senate. The senate itself, and membership therein, changed throughout the Republic and into the times of Imperial Rome, and even a basic overview would require several pages. It might, however, be in some ways likened to a Roman House of Lords, with rankings that could determine whether the individual even had the right to speak.

stola:

-much like the men's long toga, a rectangular cloth draped around a woman's body to form a long, flowing garment.

tuath:

-a word that originally meant "people," but which acquired a territorial connotation. In population and extent it was fairly small, and normally conformed to an area with natural topographical boundaries. Depending on size, it could have its own aristocratic structure that might even extend to a king, nobles (chieftains), and common freemen. In the book, the word 'king' has been applied to Venutius only. The Brigante tribe itself, quite scattered, occupied Lancashire, most of Yorkshire, and, on the west coast, extended perhaps as far south as the Mersey.

tuba and cornu:

-two musical instruments that were essentially horns. The former was a long, straight instrument flared like a modern trumpet. The latter was also a long and thin horn, but shaped in a manner that made it almost a huge circle: it curved away from the mouth in a downward arc that turned under the elbow, then came back over the top of the head; it was braced across the centre by a decorated tube.

Via Praetoria:

-the road immediately inside the primary gate (*Praetoria*) that led directly up to, and stopped in front of, the headquarters building. This building, in turn, sat on the main street leading east and west, called the *Via Principalis*. The *Principalis* was also the site of the commander's residence, usually alongside the legion headquarters.

Appendix III

Place Names and Detail

Abus. The River:

-history appears to have left no Roman name for the river at York, which is now called the Ouse. The river runs all the way to the North Sea, however, where it becomes the River Humber, or then the Humber Estuary. It is known that the Romans called this section the Abus. Since the river actually flows uninterrupted all the way from York, I believe it is reasonable to speculate that the Romans may have referred to it as the Abus along its entire distance. Eboracum was, after all, still on the tidal reach; there is no "dramatic" site where the Ouse becomes the Humber; and, as to the derivatives—dare it be pointed out that the *-us* on the end of the Abus sounds very much like *Ouse*? As to the Fosse, the smaller river (which has seen service similar to a canal over the years), it is now called the Foss. An *e* has been added to conform to the spelling of the "Fosse Way," a reference to a main road leading north, which in A.D. 71 terminated on the south bank of the Humber, across from Petuaria.

Aqua Sulis:

-the resort town of Bath.

Calcaria:

-now Tadcaster, about nine miles south-southwest of York, on the river Wharfe. It was the source of much of the sandstone used in the building of York, both in Roman times and later. York's medieval walls were built of this stone and still stand; they are, for the most part, built on top of the old Roman foundations. Tadcaster is also the longtime home of the famous John Smith Brewery. A rule of thumb in England: the farther north, the better the beer.

Cataractonium:

-though not mentioned in the book, this was a Flavian fort twenty-three miles north of Isurium. It was built on the site of the village reconnoitred by Gaius and Titus, not long after the time of the story. The present-day town is Catterick, home to an RAF base which sits alongside the A1 North. (Many of the main arterial roads in England still follow the old Roman roads).

Camulodunum:

-now Slack, west Yorkshire, and a Celtic centre at the time of Rome's invasion. Some believe that the site was later the focus of the legendary kingdom of Camelot.

Derventio:

- now Malton, east Yorkshire. A base was established here not long before the fortress was built at Eboracum, likely during the initial incursions into Brigante territory before Cerialis began his full-scale subjugation. Derventio was situated either at the extreme southeast of Brigante territory, or the extreme northeast of Parisi territory (it is difficult to ascertain where the two actually overlapped). It would make strategic sense to first establish a sizeable base here in the hillier country above Eboracum, in order to secure the logistics of building there. Based on excavations, original construction was likely a thirty-acre camp that provided security in which the Ninth and its auxiliary units, totalling as many as ten thousand men in all, could shelter when the full-scale assault came.

Ebor(acum):

-the Roman name for the city of York. The origin is the subject of debate. Three theories appear to be the most popular. One is that the name was derived from a man called Eburos who, legend says, fled Troy; though doubtful, it's even more doubtful that he ever lived at Eboracum. The two others are both alluded to in the book. *Ebor* is apparently vaguely similar to, or has connotations with, a Roman word for boar. *Ebur* is a cognate found in the old Irish word *ibhar* or *iuhbar*, which means "yew." As such, its meaning could be extended to "place of the boar" or "place of the yews." This book also omits the suffix *(acum)* at this time, though it is brought in part way through the subsequent book, '*Eboracum, The Fortress*'. The suffix *ium* or *(a)cum* was normally attached to the end of a place name where a civilian settlement had been built up or was attached (Viroconium: Wroxeter). Since such settlement did not happen immediately, I have, for the moment, omitted this suffix

Gesoriacum:

-the French port of Calais.

Isurium:

-now the town of Aldborough, about seventeen miles north of York. It was already a substantial Celtic centre before the Romans invaded Brigantia.

Lindum:

-the present city of Lincoln.

Petuaria:

-the port of Brough, on the north side of the River Humber (Humber Estuary). It is one of two possible routes for Cerialis's advance north from Lindum, the other being via *Danum* (Doncaster). It is possible that both were used in a pincer movement. I have kept it simple, by keeping to Petuaria. However, the small detachment I used to establish Isurium would likely have come in through Doncaster. Petuaria, in some ways, seems the likelier route for the main advance, due to the establishment of Derventio prior to moving on Eboracum. As to the Humber itself (see comments on the River Abus, above), any crossing would likely have been by ferry, rather than using transport by sea.

Senaculum:

-referring to the ambassadorial reception hall in Rome.

Appendix IV

Commentary and Trivia

- The gap torn in the bridge over the River Nabalia was indeed an arrangement, demanded as part of the terms upon which negotiations could begin with the rebellious General Civilis.

- Real-life characters either seen or mentioned in the novel are Cartimandua, Vellocatus, Venutius, Cerialis, Caradoc, Boudicca, Agricola, and Civilis. Cartimandua's divorce from Venutius, and her marriage to Vellocatus, Venutius's shield bearer, is fact. Their behaviour in the book is, of course, sheer speculation.

- Cartimandua did turn Caradoc (Caractacus) over to the Romans, and history has very much maligned her for doing so. The premise used in the book (which I believe very likely for the reasons given) is that she made a deal before doing so. History seems to differ, primarily due to Tacitus's brief detail which (naturally) gives benign credit for such mercy to Claudius.

- There appears to be no conclusive evidence for a settlement at the two rivers where the Eburi (name invented, though see above under *Ebor*, place names) lived before the Romans arrived; nor is there any evidence that there was not.

- The use of the Roman numeral VIIII is not an error. Nowadays the number nine is expressed as IX. However, the "VIIII" usage was common with the Hispana Legio. It has been found stamped on their roofing tiles, and chiselled into their monuments and other relics.

- Chronology of names for the city of York:

Ebor(acum), see description above under place names.

Eoforwic was next. It was named by the Angles (sometime prior to A.D. 627), and may owe some ancestral origins to the Romans, as it was likely pronounced " Evrauc" or "Everwick."

Jorvik (pronounced "Yorewick") followed, and was in use under the Danish occupation (A.D. 867). It seems to be a slight shift in pronunciation and spelling from Eoforwic. By the end of "Danelaw," which came with the successful invasion of the Northumbrians in 954 A.D., the name appears to have been abbreviated to York.

- Gaius's words on his dedication to the gods is an actual transcription from an excavated monument—with, of course, his name substituted.

- The two battles that take place in the book are both, to some degree, conjecture. The one at Bran's Beck is simply plot convenience, and is nothing more than representative of the skirmishing and unrest prevalent at the time. The one at Stannick quite probably took place, either at the fortress or close by. Sir Mortimer Wheeler, a noted archaeologist who dug there in the fifties, surmised that there was such a battle at the stronghold, and the book has kept true to his conclusions. He paid particular attention to bones and weapons found by the south gate, where the wall seemed to be incomplete. The latest thought, however, casts doubt on an outright pitched battle that resulted in Stannick's destruction. It surmises that the fortress, in some form, may have survived for years after its supposed destruction. As to the timing of a battle, if indeed it did take place, there isn't any certainty of the year. If it did occur, it was between A. D. 71–74. The book places it in the spring of A.D. 72.

- There is no record of what happened to Venutius, Vellocatus, and Cartimandua after the battle at Stannick. In fact, I found no references to any of the three even just prior to the invasion by Cerialis. There also seems to be no record of their death.

ISBN 142511999-9